Post-Communist Nostalgia

Post-Communist Nostalgia

Edited by
Maria Todorova and Zsuzsa Gille

Berghahn Books
New York • Oxford

First published in 2010 by

Berghahn Books

www.berghahnbooks.com

©2010, 2012 Maria Todorova and Zsuzsa Gille

First paperback edition published in 2012.

All rights reserved. Except for the quotation of short passages for the purposes of criticism and review, no part of this book may be reproduced in any form or by any means, electronic or mechanical, including photocopying, recording, or any information storage and retrieval system now known or to be invented, without written permission of the publisher.

Library of Congress Cataloging-in-Publication Data

Post-communist nostalgia / edited by Maria Todorova and Zsuzsa Gille.
   p. cm. — (Vacant history, empty screens: post-communist german films of the 1990s 263 anke)
   Includes bibliographical references and index.
   ISBN 978-1-84545-671-9 (hbk.) -- ISBN 978-0-85745-643-4 (pbk.)
   1. Post-communism—Europe, Eastern. 2. Europe, Eastern—Politics and government—1989– I. Todorova, Maria Nikolaeva. II. Gille, Zsuzsa.

JN96.A58P663 2010
947.0009′049—dc22

2010007978

British Library Cataloguing in Publication Data

A catalogue record for this book is available from the British Library

Printed in the United States on acid-free paper.

ISBN: 978-0-85745-643-4 (paperback)   ISBN: 978-0-85745-644-1 (ebook)

In loving memory of Daphne Berdahl

Contents

List of Figures ... ix

Introduction   From Utopia to Propaganda and Back ... 1
Maria Todorova

Part I:
Rupture and the Economies of Nostalgia

1. From Algos to Autonomos: Nostalgic Eastern Europe as Postimperial Mania ... 17
   Dominic Boyer

2. Strange Bedfellows: Socialist Nostalgia and Neoliberalism in Bulgaria ... 29
   Gerald W. Creed

3. Today's Unseen Enthusiasm: Communist Nostalgia for Communism in the Socialist Humanist Brigadier Movement ... 46
   Cristofer Scarboro

4. Nostalgia for the JNA? Remembering the Army in the Former Yugoslavia ... 61
   Tanja Petrović

5. Dignity in Transition: History, Teachers, and the Nation-State in Post-1989 Bulgaria ... 82
   Tim Pilbrow

6. Invisible—Inaudible: Albanian Memories of Socialism after the War in Kosovo ... 96
   Stephanie Schwandner-Sievers

7. "Let's all freeze up until 2100 or so": Nostalgic Directions in Post-Communist Romania ... 113
   Oana Popescu-Sandu

Part II:
Nostalgic Realms in Word, Sound, and Screen

8. Sonic Nostalgia: Music, Memory, and Mythography in Bulgaria, 1990–2005 129
   Donna A. Buchanan

9. "Ceaușescu Hasn't Died": Irony as Countermemory in Post-Socialist Romania 155
   Diana Georgescu

10. *Good Bye, Lenin!* Aufwiedersehen GDR: On the Social Life of Socialism 177
    Daphne Berdahl

11. "But it's ours": Nostalgia and the Politics of Authenticity in Post-Socialist Hungary 190
    Maya Nadkarni

12. Looking Back to the Bright Future: Aleksandr Melikhov's *Red Zion* 215
    Harriet Murav

13. Dwelling on the Ruins of Socialist Yugoslavia: Being Bosnian by Remembering Tito 227
    Fedja Burić

14. The Velvet Prison in Hindsight: Artistic Discourse in Hungary in the 1990s 244
    Anna Szemere

15. Vacant History, Empty Screens: Post-Communist German Films of the 1990s 263
    Anke Pinkert

Postscript 278
  Zsuzsa Gille

Notes on Contributors 290

Index 295

Figures

Figure 2.1. Restaurant "Rio" in Sofia. 31

Figure 2.2. Advertisement for restaurant "Checkpoint Charlie" in Sofia. 40

Figure 8.1. Cassette cover for the Poduene Blues Band's *Komunizmŭt si otiva* (Communism Is on Its Way Out). RTM 1993. 131

Figure 8.2. Cassette cover for *Dobrudzhansko zlato: Folklor ot Dobrudzha i Severna Bŭlgariya. Glasove ot Bezkraya,* 5 (Dobrudzhan Gold: Folklore from Dobrudzha and Northern Bulgaria. Voices from Infinity, 5). Unison Stars, n.d. 135

Figure 13.1. The flag of the Socialist Republic of Bosnia-Herzegovina. 229

 **Introduction**

From Utopia to Propaganda and Back
Maria Todorova

In a recent issue of the *Balcanis Book Review* printed in Ljubljana, the Slovenian sociologist Mitja Velikonja opened his rubric with a spoof of Churchill's Cold War speech: "From Stettin in the Baltic to Trieste in the Adriatic, an iron curtain has descended across the Continent." In Velikonja's words, "Od Szczecina na Baltiku do Trsta na Jadranu," what has descended is ... nostalgia (Velikonja 2004: 37). The journal dedicated to the theme is in itself a monument to nostalgia. *Balcanis* is printed in Ljubljana by two publishers (the cultural society Balkanika in Slovenia and the Balkanis society in Belgrade, Serbia), with two co-publishers (the companies buybook in Sarajevo, and Attack in Zagreb). The publication's organization is already evoking the specter of the lost nostalgic space: Yugoslavia.

I personally happen to prefer Marx to Churchill, so my own post-spoof is based on the *Communist Manifesto*: "A specter is haunting the world of academia: the *study* of post-Communist nostalgia." From Berlin, Warsaw, and Sofia, through the Mormon corridors of Salt Lake City (which housed one of the recent conventions of the American Association for the Advancement of Slavic Studies in 2005), to Toronto, Philadelphia and Urbana,[1] (the last three at the same time), academics seem obsessed with this most elusive of concepts. But then, as Jürgen Kocka (2004) has perceptively observed, "The attractiveness of a concept rarely correlates with its precision."

This volume has been put together in part to deliberate whether we can apply some precision to the concept (quite apart from its attractiveness or repellence) that is being used to name a phenomenon observable in very different locales (truly from Central Europe to Central Asia). If nostalgia is, very loosely, about some form of remembrance, our task is to analyze all of this—in short, to put thoughts to memories. Of course, one might be allowed to be less sanguine about the result. I was nostalgically rereading *Hamlet* recently, and there is the wonderful scene (IV, 5) when the deranged Ophelia enters, muttering, "There's rosemary, that's for remembrance: pray, love, remember; and there is pansies, that's for thoughts." Her brother Laertes exclaims, "A document in madness, thoughts and remembrance fitted." This could be a fitting motto for this volume.

It may not be too bold to state that there is a broad consensus on the fact that the phenomenon exists (or at least something that is represented as a phenomenon under the designation "nostalgia"). It is certainly not confined to the former Communist world. While practically all studies of nostalgia start with brief accounts of its history and etymology (as a neologism diagnosing a medical condition in the eighteenth century— yearning for a lost home, and expanded to mean a desire to return to a lost place or time), it is clear that as a concept it has long ago surpassed the boundaries of the medical profession and has entered the terrain of writers and poets. More importantly, in the past two to three decades the term has been expanded, and it also has been heavily theorized (mostly critically and negatively for what has been seen as its inherent conservatism and distance from real history). It has been linked to memory, history, affect; it has been attached to political allegiances and models of consumerism; it has been variously approached as "a form of psychological whiplash, a cultural style, the abdication of memory, an aesthetic treatment, an ornament, a technique, a part of the narrative of history, or a part of the narrative of critical theory."[2]

More importantly, as Sean Scanlan reminds us (in the special 2004 issue of the *Iowa Journal of Cultural Studies* dedicated to nostalgia, and featuring pieces on rock music, history, film, African American, American Indian and émigré literature), nostalgia is no longer treated as the programmatic equivalent of bad memory, as a social disease (Susan Stewart), the abdication of memory (Christopher Lasch), or the symptom/cause of the rifts between historical signifiers and their signifieds (Frederic Jameson): "Now, nostalgia may be a style or design or narrative that serves to comment on how memory works. Rather than an end reaction to yearning, it is understood as a technique for provoking a secondary reaction." Linda Hutcheon (2000) proclaims nostalgia to be "transideological," something that "can be made to 'happen' by (and to) anyone of any political persuasion." For Kathleen Stewart, "nostalgia, like the economy, is everywhere. But it is a cultural practice, not a given content; its forms, meanings, and effects shift with the context—it depends on where the speaker stands in the landscape of the present" (1988: 227).

But how about the specific case of post-Communist nostalgia? Is it so different from "normal" free-world nostalgia? Media coverage would let us believe this is the case. It consistently treats the phenomenon as a malady. In the conceptual apparatus of journalism (but also in plenty of academic discourse) the comparative notions are communism and fascism, or communism and Nazism, not capitalism and communism, or liberalism (including neoliberalism) and communism. Roger Cohen (2005: 2) in the *International Herald Tribune* regrets that "years of debate have not resolved how the terrible twins of the 20th century, communism and fascism, should be viewed on a scale of evil." For him, communism was more murderous than Nazism, and the "dirty laundry of communism has not yet been hung in the sun." In such circumstances post-Communist nostalgia can be subsumed only (and appropriately) under the Marxist notion of false consciousness.

And it is not only journalists. The famous moral philosopher Tzvetan Todorov (2005) moralized in an interview on the occasion of the fiftieth anniversary of the end of World War II that in Russia, communism was less dead than anywhere else, and that "nationalism can keep an illusory hope, a nostalgia for communism." Chuckling, and unabashedly cutting off Russia from "the European world," he explained that in Europe "we don't have this problem" because there is not the conflation of imperial or state grandeur with communism: "In Eastern European countries, we were slaves. I think that today it is a much more important task to acquire a sense of lucidity about the communist ideology than about Nazism. Because apart from a few cranks in Germany and other countries, nobody extols the Nazi ideology anymore. Whereas the communist ideology continues to be extolled by significant minorities. In France, in the Third World. Therefore it is important to recall that this ideology, which at a certain level of generality can be seductive—it will bring us all fraternity, a glorious radiant future—, is a deadly one. It is important to call in mind that nothing good can come from this ideology." And he concluded that "the idea of communism, unfortunately, is not definitively compromised." Only a few pages earlier in his interview he had explained that the appeal of communism in France, when he arrived in the country in the 1960s, came from the Communists' premier role in the Resistance and also that "the Communists were the only ones who were ready to go from house to house, to do the shopping for an old lady who didn't have a car, to help an old handicapped man and so on. They did what Christians do, as a rule." This at the end is summarized as seductive but deadly. But then, Todorov is a moral philosopher, not an analytical one.

To this day there is a pervasive prescriptive or normative quality to much of the research on Eastern Europe, which may be defined with one word: the obsession over *Vergangenheitsbewältigung*. This German term—meaning reassessment, coming to terms with the past, coping, dealing with it, but also including redress, even retribution—is untranslatable, and the Hungarian writer Péter Esterházy in his acceptance speech for the peace prize of the Frankfurt book fair (2004: 7) maintains that "it is no wonder that there is no corresponding word for *Vergangenheitsbewältigung* in Hungarian," the reason being that the corresponding activity, which he calls "work, a European duty," is absent. He went on to criticize his compatriots and the rest of Eastern Europe for not dealing squarely with the recent past as the Germans had done after the Second World War.[3] Indeed, Timothy Garton Ash (2001/2002) posits the existence of a new norm of integrity, a DIN-standard (i.e., Deutsche Industrienorm) in history writing. On the other hand, James McAdams (2003) poses the question whether this is not yet another German *Sonderweg*. To counter the moralizing and mildly patronizing motif, it needs to be pointed out that it is not only the East Europeans who are not following this road. It took a whole generation in post-Franco Spain after 1975 to reach the climatic moment of opening mass graves in 2000 and putting the issue on the table. It is enough to evoke the lag of a generation and over two decades for the Germans to begin to come to terms with their legacy, a process that is still not complete.[4] Besides, it is not entirely true. Practically all capital cities of Eastern Europe have a monument to the victims of communism, and most have museums, not commemorating but condemning Communist rule: from the House of Terror in Budapest to the Occupation Museum in Riga and the Museum of Genocide Victims in Lithuania, the Stasi headquarters in Berlin, and so on.

The point is not to explain, admonish, or excuse why *Vergangenheitsbewältigung* is not a household item in Eastern Europe, but to question the mandatory character of this approach. First and foremost, it is premised on drawing a straight line between Nazism and the comparatively long East European experience, which went through different stages and displayed amazing geographical varieties. Even the straight parallel between the Nazi and the Stalinist episodes can be questioned, let alone the qualitatively different historical stages across and within national borders. What to me is amazing (probably because I am deeply steeped in the conventions of my own discipline) is that most of the early efforts at approaching "real socialism" (or however we would prefer to name it) started with theory and not with empirical research: first the challenges to democratic theory; then the whole transitology enterprise, which needed a dozen years before it was robustly critiqued; the dominant civil society paradigm, which is only now beginning to be cautiously questioned (Bunce 1999, 2003; Carothers 2002; King 2000).

Scholars who do on-the-ground research tend to refrain from big moralizing lectures (although their research contains big moral lessons). A lot of precious studies are already accumulated although not quite yet coordinated. What they have come up with is a serious symptomatology. Here is a kaleidoscopic and impressionistic overview:

A study, carried out by two Polish sociologists and presented at the American Sociological Association's 2003 meeting, discovered strong symptoms of nostalgia among middle-class, middle-aged Poles, "the social group which is commonly thought to have been the chief beneficiary of the process of market transition." All opinion surveys report vast majorities of respondents with positive attitudes toward socialism, but since these are scorned in the public discourse and the media, they are subject to self-censorship. The study concludes that the main source of nostalgic attitudes is the merging of economic and social status after the transition: "The ongoing fusion of social and economic status gives those less financially successful a feeling of being deprived of both social position and of economic well being." More ominous is the other conclusion of the authors that this "is likely to transform itself into a more militant opposition to the principles underlying the transition to market-based economy." (Wieliczko and Zuk, 2003)

Another study on Poland points out that "what people remember about socialism is a pride in production and in their labour and also a sense of being part of a project that was *modern* and directed towards the general good. When people speak angrily about Poland being turned into a 'Third World' country, their anger is both about economic decline, about what they see as a two-sided coin of dependency and exploitation, and about being transformed not into the (even more modern) capitalist future but back into a pre-socialist past." This "trauma of deindustrialization" has brought about alcoholism, drug abuse, homelessness, and the feminization of poverty. Frances Pine (2002: 111) is very cautious in her conclusion, however: "Rather than a case of collective amnesia or even nostalgia, I think this should be taken partly as an invocation of a past in order to contrast it with, and thereby criticize, the present. Social memory is selective and contextual. When people evoked the 'good' socialist past, they were not denying the corruption, the shortages, the queues and the endless intrusions and infringements of the state; rather, they were choosing to emphasize other aspects: economic security, full employment, universal healthcare and education."

I purposely start out with Poland because of its paradigmatic status as the A-grade transitioning country. Another unlikely, because unexpected, carrier of the affliction is Romania. David A. Kideckel, in his study on the unmaking of the Romanian working class, describes the alienation of workers who decry politicians of all stripes and "see the whole process as designed to keep workers down" (through unemployment, low salaries, deindustrialization, education toward business, foreign languages, etc. rather than engineering and others needed for the industrial workplace):

> Reacting against the increased class divisions and insecurities of neocapitalism, many workers long for a return to the security and predictability of socialism. Like miners and workers elsewhere in Russia and East-Central Europe, from the best case of the Czech Republic, through war-torn Serbia, to prostrate Russia and Ukraine, declining economic circumstances encourage a turn to socialist nostalgia, nationalist cant or frustrated inaction. In Romania some workers even display portraits of Ceauşescu on lathes, lockers and workbenches. When they are asked what is needed to put Romania right, they say "an iron hand," "a six-month military dictatorship," or "Hitler, Stalin, and Vlad the Impaler rolled into one." (2002: 124)

Ruth Mandel (2002: 280) has documented striking percentages of the population preferring the old system in Central Asia, and the "Barometer of the New Europe," a 2005 study by the Institute for Social Research in Budapest that polled Czechs, Slovaks, Slovenians, Estonians, Bulgarians, Hungarians, Romanians, Poles, Ukrainians, Russians, and Byelorussians, found smaller but still significant numbers in Eastern Europe.[5] In China, the nostalgia for Mao is not even post-socialist: the regime still claims to be Communist, and rural unrest accosts the state for not being faithful to this claim (Kahn 2006; Barmé 1999: 316–44).

In Bulgaria, the traditional response both before and after the fall of communism has been jokes. A popular one is about a woman who sits bolt upright in the middle of the night in panic. She jumps out of bed and rushes to the bathroom to look in the medicine cabinet. Then, she runs into the kitchen and opens the refrigerator. Finally, she dashes to the window and looks out into the street. Relieved, she returns to the bedroom. Her husband asks her, "What's wrong with you?" "I had a terrible nightmare," she says. "I dreamt we could still afford to buy medicine, that the refrigerator was absolutely full, and that the streets were safe and clean." "How is that a nightmare?" the husband asks. The woman shakes her head, "I thought the communists were back in power."

The joke nicely captures the ambivalence of attitudes toward the Communist past. It has been asserted that the nostalgic discourse is binary by definition, with the past always depicted as better (Velikonja 2004: 39). This is certainly not the case in Eastern Europe. Even the polls reflecting positive attitudes are most often responses to questions of the type: "What predominated: the good or bad parts of the system?" "Would you evaluate the past in extremely negative, moderate, or even positive terms?" Ivan Klima, the great Czech novelist, told United Press

International in an interview, "Nobody is nostalgic for the Stalinist era but many old people are nostalgic for their youth. They miss the security of Communist times when they knew they would get a pension they could live off, prices were stable and they couldn't lose their flats or their jobs" (Harding 2004). Klima shook off the phenomenon apologetically, by confining it exclusively to an aging and passive minority, but given the stereotypes expected in the Western press, this is understandable. What he could have said is that the longing for security and stability often leads people toward stupidity, but it is not a stupid longing.

And it is not only the longing for security, stability, and prosperity. There is also the feeling of loss for a very specific form of sociability, and of vulgarization of the cultural life. Above all, there is a desire among those who have lived through communism, even when they have opposed it or were indifferent to its ideology, to invest their lives with meaning and dignity, not to be thought of, remembered, or bemoaned as losers or "slaves." Lastly, there is a new phenomenon: the tentative but growing curiosity among the younger generation.

This brings us to the agents of nostalgia, and to the whole range of analytical questions we ought to ask about the issues we are dealing with:

1. Who is speaking or performing nostalgia? After all, none of the subjects of nostalgia, the ones who are producing its artifacts and who are identified as its agents, define it as nostalgia. *Nostalgia* or *"post-Communist" nostalgia* is an ascriptive term, and when it was first used, mostly in journalistic accounts, it had a strong tinge of censure. It continues to be avoided as a self-description. But the obvious analytical parameters should follow divisions such as rural-urban; different generation clusters, especially within the generations having the lived experience of the system; the pronounced gender differences; and political orientation. For example, Kristen Ghodsee has convincingly analyzed the gendered consequences of emerging capitalism. While women's experiences in any society are mixed, she shows that in Bulgaria as well as in other East European countries, women are more likely to be represented in leftist and centrist parties (Green, liberal, socialist, and Communist, rather than in right-wing ones (people's parties, Christian parties, etc.) (Ghodsee 2004: 33, 45–46).

2. What does nostalgia express? What is its content? It was already pointed out that there are the elements of disappointment, social exhaustion, economic recategorization, generational fatigue, and quest for dignity, but also an activist critique of the present using the past as a mirror and irony alongside a purely consumerist aesthetics not much different from the one that we see in the West (Gries 2004). Can

we offer a typology of post-Communist nostalgia, one that is also sufficiently discriminating between regional and national differences? After all, the Communist experience was diverse enough to produce different post-Communist responses despite the systemic similarities. There is the post-Communist nostalgia with a certain tinge of imperial or colonial nostalgia (the case of the USSR and even Yugoslavia); Svetlana Boym (2001: viii, 41–56) introduces the distinction between restorative and reflective nostalgia that she uses to differentiate between national and social memory. In her reading, restorative nostalgia is about truth and tradition, whereas reflective nostalgia, ironic and ambivalent, calls absolute truth into doubt. But one could distinguish between restorationist (in the sense of the desire to restore the past) and restorative or curative nostalgia.

3. What are the spheres of life and particular genres in which nostalgia is expressed? How much is it censured and self-censured? Here we have everything in the oral domain from casual conversations to scholarly interviews, and formal genres from song and literature to film. Monumentalization (the proliferation of theme parks, sculpture gardens, and museum exhibits) as well as celebrations belong to this domain. How we document nostalgia, how we analyze and represent it—with what kinds of analytical tools and within what kinds of narrative or other genres—also falls within this rubric.

It is questions such as these that the present volume addresses. In a gesture of love and appreciation for her wonderful research, it is dedicated to the memory of the social anthropologist Daphne Berdahl, who passed away in October 2007. This volume publishes her last scholarly piece that we heard performed, despite her advanced illness, in a room where Daphne nostalgically remembered her wedding ceremony years ago.

Acutely aware that we cannot cover the subject in a comprehensive way across the whole region, we are aiming, given logistical and financial constraints, at the widest possible geographical and disciplinarian coverage. What we are offering are the observations and analysis of scholars from the fields of anthropology, history, literature, musicology, and cultural studies covering case studies from (in alphabetical order) Bosnia, Bulgaria, Germany, Hungary, Kosovo, Romania, Russia, and the former Yugoslavia.

While rupture and continuity are dialectically interwoven and cannot nor should be dogmatically set apart, they serve as organizing principles of the two parts of the volume. In fact, practically all chapters deal with both sides of the issue. Dominic Boyer emphasizes not *Ostal-*

gie per se, but rather Western, liberal discourses about the alleged obsession of the East with its past. In a broad review of post-*Wende* films, Anke Pinkert shows that in most cases dealing with the complicated effects of historical loss, the socialist past never transpires in the narratives, and ironically, even the phenomenon of *Ostalgie* supports notions of Western success.

Continuing his decade-long field research in the Bulgarian countryside, Gerald Creed suggests, contrary to Boym, that nostalgia always involves the impossibility of return; its appearance is furthering the project of neoliberalism. Tanja Petrović's study of the discourses through which memories of performing military service in the former Yugoslavia are shaped reaffirms that nostalgia occurs because of the irreversibility of the process. Fedja Buric, in a similar vein, documents generational differences by showing how the centrality of the Tito image in different visions of Bosnian Muslim identity is expressed in the older generation's nostalgia for modern secularism against the younger generation's rejection of Tito's project as oppressive to Muslims.

Tim Pilbrow, on the other hand, examining the practices of remembering on the basis of how secondary-school history teachers in Bulgaria construct their professional identity—as cultural processes articulating social relationships—finds nostalgia inadequate as an explanatory model. Similarly parting with most other contributions, Maya Nadkarni argues for the existence of post-Communist nostalgia in Hungary as it manifests itself in cinema, books, and public discourse, but considers it a depoliticized commentary on the past and the present that has no political valence.

The chapters of Stephanie Schwandner-Sievers, Oana Popescu-Sandu, Cris Scarboro, and Harriet Murav explore the uses of nostalgia in four different contexts. In Kosovo, the commemorative silence as an effect of the war trauma conceals a private nostalgic discourse. In Romania, there is no place for nostalgia; instead, there is a metaphoric desire for cryogeny, with the past forced to oblivion, the painful present to sleep, until the bright future has emerged fully formed. Scarboro documents an interesting case of intra-Communist nostalgia in Bulgaria, where the early, heroic socialist ethos is nostalgically memorialized in late, reformed, and postcathartic socialism. In a similar vein, applying Boym's distinction between ironic and restorative nostalgia, Murav analyzes two post-Soviet works by Aleksandr Melikhov that can be described as both post-Jewish and post-Communist nostalgia for the world of the 1930s, to which there is no return.

How and if nostalgia is expressed in musical performance is dealt with in the chapters by Donna Buchanan, Diana Georgescu, and Anna

Szemere. In Bulgarian "popfolk," instead of nostalgia, communism is only invoked through comic and ironic images and remixes. However, there is an underlying continuity with the Communist era's instrumentalization of ethnic culture for ideological purposes. Likewise, in the Romanian case, the use of Ceaușescu as the subject of songs and musical performances in an ironic key is not a "survival" of communism but an active and strategic response to present-day challenges. In Hungary, on the other hand, there is an interesting blend of two kinds of nostalgia: the 1980s longing of the underground rock music scene suffused with experimentation and dissidence, and the postsocialist nostalgia of former underground artists for independence and noncommodified performance, free from the pressures of the new mass-produced consumption.

Finally, to come back to my opening, what is our stake as scholars, in this endeavor? Why would we pay such attention to something ephemeral (even if a real phenomenon) and something that is most often represented as reprehensible, something that is destined (according to the ones who believe in the "end of history" to "the dustbin of history"? This goes, it seems to me, beyond the usual motives to describe and analyze a significant social phenomenon. Communism had been at its outset—and there exists broad consensus on this—a powerful utopia. It continued to exert a forceful influence as a utopian project even after it was wedded to the state in 1917. It was only after 1956, and especially after 1968 that communism, in the words of one of its greatest analysts, the late Polish philosopher Lezsek Kołakowski, "seized to be an intellectual issue and was transformed into a power problem" (quoted in Baeva 2006).

Despite the fact that Tzvetan Todorov is my compatriot and namesake, I prefer another French philosopher, Alain Badiou, who wrote an essay on philosophy and the "death of communism" in 1998. He premised his reflections on a simple hypothesis that the political and subjective history of communisms is essentially divided from their state history. He admitted that "at the level of the order of the State (of things) there is the 'death of communism.' But for thought, it is no more than a second death." For Badiou, communism, which he saw as a philosophy of the community existing in political thought not only since 1917 but since 1793, had became obsolete at least since 1968. Yet, he argues, "Communist" is not reducible to "the finished sequence during which parties attributed the term to themselves, not to the sequence during which the idea of a politics of emancipation was being debated under this name," and he exclaims, "How could the 'death of communism' be the name of an event once we remark that every historical event is communist, inasmuch as 'communist' designates the trans-temporal subjectivity of emancipation?" (Badiou 2003: 96–97, 103).

Speaking specifically about the fall of state communism in 1989, he bemoans the fact that this was entirely a state affair. He is aggravated that East Europeans did not come up with something new, a real social alternative, a new utopia: "And how could it have been otherwise if it is true, as affirmed by all and sundry, that what they think and want, the people of Russia and Hungary and Bulgaria, is nothing other than what already exists, and has been for quite a while, in our sad countries called, who knows why, 'Western'?" This desire, he contended, could do nothing but "comfort the pre-eminence of the state and constitutional views of these processes. Elections and property owners, politicians and racketeers: is this all they want?" (Badiou 2003: 101).

Post-Communist nostalgia is a partial answer to this question.[6] As far as we as scholars are concerned, one can hear in Badiou's lament overtones of Benjamin's activist stance: "To articulate the past historically does not mean to recognize it 'the way it really was.' It means to seize hold of a memory as it flashes up at a moment of danger. ... The danger affects both the content of the tradition and its receivers. In every era the attempt must be made anew to wrest tradition away from a conformism that is about to overpower it. ... Only the historian that will have the gift to spark hope in the past is firmly convinced that *even the dead* will not be safe from the enemy if he wins" (Benjamin, Walter. 1968).

I am a great admirer of Benjamin, but lest this sounds too melodramatic, I will end by evoking a coregionalist, a Polish wit who commented on this—the sixth of Benjamin's theses "On the Concept of History"—that we don't know yet what our past is going to be (Singer 1999).

Notes

1. Only in 2005, there were two important meetings in Berlin alone: "Zwischen Nostalgie, Amnesie und Allergie: die Erinnerung an den Kommunismus in Südosteuropa," 1–4 December 2005, Freie Universität; and "Nostalgischer Blick auf der Zeit des Kommunismus: Ensteht in Osteuropa ein neues kollektives Gedächtnis?" 17–18 June 2005, Centre Marc Bloch-Berlin. See also "25 Years of Changes in the Post-Communist World," Warsaw, 5–7 July 2006; "Samizdat and Underground Culture in the Soviet Bloc Countries," Penn Humanities Forum, University of Pennsylvania, 6–7 April 2006; and "What Is Soviet Now? Identities, Legacies, Memories," University of Toronto, 6–8 April 2006.

2. Call for papers for the 2004 issue of the *Iowa Journal of Cultural Studies* dedicated to nostalgia, with guest editors Sean Scanlan and Tom Lutz.
3. A critical response is Alfred Gosser in *Frankfurter Allegemeine Zeitung*, N.248, 23 October 2004, 33.
4. It also bears mention that in the United States a law requiring the disclosure of classified records related to Nazi war criminals was passed only in 1998, but until today the CIA has subverted it by arguing that the law requires disclosure of records only for war crimes, not war criminals, thus effectively blocking information about the agency's postwar collaboration with former Nazis. In February 2005, the CIA finally agreed to reverse this legal stance and for the first time acknowledged the existence of such relationship (Douglas Jehl, "C.I.A. defers to Congress, Agreeing to Disclose Nazi Records," *New York Times*, 7 February 2005).
5. More than 60% in Kazakhstan, 27% in Uzbekistan; about 50% in Tajikistan and Kyrgyzstan. The results of the East European poll show about a quarter of the population preferring the old regime, with up to 38% for Bulgaria, 36% for Russia, and 31% for Slovakia. Czechs (52%) and Estonians (37%) seems to be the most satisfied with present arrangements (*Standart*, 10 March 2006. http://www.standartnews.com).
6. This volume was already in print when I came across the new book of Mitja Velikonja (2008), which brilliantly makes the case for nostalgia as utopia.

References

Ash, Timothy Garton. 2002. "Mesomnesie." *Transit. Europäische Revue* 22: 32–48.
Badiou, Alain. 2003. *Infinite Thought: Truth and the Return to Philosophy*, trans. Oliver Feltham and Justin Clemens. London, New York: Continuum.
Baeva, Iskra. 2006. "1956-a—nachaloto na dîlgiia zalez na sîvetskiia komunizîm." *Kultura* 7 (2402): 23 February.
Barmé, Geremie R. 1999. *On Contemporary Chinese Culture*. New York: Columbia University Press.
Benjamin, Walter. 1968. *Illuminations*, ed. Hannah Arendt, trans. Harry Zohn. New York: Shocken Books, 255.
Boym, Svetlana. 2001. *The Future of Nostalgia*. New York: Basic Books.
Bunce, Valerie. 1999. "The Political Economy of Postsocialism." *Slavic Review* 58, no. 4 (Special Issue: Ten Years after 1989: What Have We Learned?): 756–93.
———. 2003. "Rethinking Recent Democratization: Lessons from the Postcommunist Experience." *World Politics* 55, no. 2: 167–92.
Carothers, Thomas. 2002. "The End of the Transition Paradigm." *Journal of Democracy* 13: 5–21.
Cohen, Roger. 2005. "Unraveling the Truth from a Painful History." *International Herald Tribune*, 11 May.
Eszterházy, Péter. 2004. "Also: die Keule." *Frankfurter Allegemeine Zeitung*, N.237, 11 October.
Ghodsee, Kristen. 2004. "Red Nostalgia? Communism, Women's Emancipation, and Economic Transformation in Bulgaria." *L'Homme. Europäische Zeitschrift für Feministische Geschichtswissenschaft* 15, no. 1.

Gries, Rainer. 2004. "'Hurrah, I'm Still Alive!' East German Products Demonstrating East German Identities." In *Over the Wall/After the Fall: Post-Communist Cultures Through an East-West Gaze*, ed. Sibelan Forrester, Magdalena Zaborowska, and Elena Gapova, 181–99. Bloomington: Indiana University Press.

Harding, Gareth. 2004. "East Europe's Communist Nostalgia." *Washington Times*, 11 August.

Hutcheon, Linda. 2000. "Irony, Nostalgia, and the Postmodern." *Methods for the Study of Literature as Cultural Memory, Studies in Comparative Literature* 30: 189–207.

Kahn, Joseph. 2006. "A Sharp Debate Erupts in China over Ideologies." *New York Times*, 12 March.

Kideckel, David A. 2002. "The Unmaking of an East-Central European Working Class." In *Postsocialism: Ideals, Ideologies and Practices in Eurasia*, ed. C. M. Hann, 114–32. London: Routledge.

———. 2004. "The Undead: Nicolae Ceausescu and Paternalist Politics in Romanian Society and Culture." In *Death of the Father: An Anthropology of the End of Political Authority*, ed. John Borneman, 123–47. New York: Berghahn Books.

King, Charles. 2000. "Post-Postcommunism: Transition, Comparison, and the End of 'Eastern Europe.'" *World Politics* 53, no. 1: 143–72.

Kocka, Jürgen. 2004. "The Middle Classes in Europe." In *European Societies during the Nineteenth and Twentieth Century*, ed. Hartmut Kaelble, 15–43. New York: Berghahn Books.

Mandel, Ruth. 2002. "Seeding Civil Society." In *Postsocialism: Ideals, Ideologies and Practices in Eurasia*, ed. C. M. Hann, 279–96. London: Routledge.

McAdams, James. 2003. "Vergangenheitsaufarbeitung nach 1989: Ein deutscher Sonderweg." *Deutschland Archiv* 5: 851–60.

Pine, Frances. 2002. "Retreat to the Household? Gendered Domains in Postsocialist Poland." In *Postsocialism: Ideals, Ideologies and Practices in Eurasia*, ed. C. M. Hann, 95–113. London: Routledge.

Scanlan, Sean. 2004. "Introduction: Nostalgia." *Iowa Journal of Cultural Studies* 5.

Singer, Daniel. 1999. "Exploiting a Tragedy, or Le Rouge en Noire." *The Nation*, 25 November.

Stewart, Kathleen. 1988. "Nostalgia—A Polemic." *Cultural Anthropology* 3, no. 3: 227–41.

Todorov, Tzvetan. 2005. "Memory of Evil, Enticement to Good," *Eurozine* (http://www.eurozine.com), 19 August (first published in a Latvian version in *Rigas Laiks* 5 [2005]).

Velikonja, Mitja. 2004. "Tistega lepega dne: Značilnosti sodobnega nostalgičnega diskurza," *Balcanis* 12–16, Letnik 5, pomlad-zima.

Velikonja, Mitja. 2008. *Titostalgia. A Study of Nostalgia for Josip Broz*. Ljubljana: Mediawatch.

Wieliczko, Barbara and Zuk, Marcin. "Post-Communist Nostalgia Among the Middle-Aged Middle-Class Poles" *Paper presented at the annual meeting of the American Sociological Association, Atlanta Hilton Hotel, Atlanta, GA*, Aug 16, 2003. http://www.allacademic.com/meta/p_mla_apa_research_citation/1/0/6/7/0/p106706_index.html

PART I

RUPTURE AND THE ECONOMIES OF NOSTALGIA

# 1

FROM ALGOS TO AUTONOMOS
Nostalgic Eastern Europe as Postimperial Mania
Dominic Boyer

Grief or Obsession?

What distinguishes nostalgia in Eastern Europe today? For one thing, that so many people agree that it exists, not only in individuals, in individual countries, but rather also as a regional phenomenon. One finds a curious agreement between external observers and the internal afflicted. Eastern Europe is nostalgic; it yearns.

But, why and for what is Eastern Europe yearning? Popular and scholarly representations may diverge in their particulars but they usually sketch what amounts to a standard history of the cultural effects of post-Socialist transformation. Here is how the narrative unfolds: Eastern Europe suffered a mighty cultural displacement in the aftermath of the events of 1989–1990. On the one hand, its borders and horizons opened. Yet, its internal lifeworlds were shaken and in some cases shattered, its populations unsettled in all senses of the term. Then, in the ensuing fifteen years, forces of change stormed across the region, moving, as weather mostly does, from West to East. Although it is difficult to plot the vectors of a tempest, the dominant historical forces at play in post-Socialist Eastern Europe have nevertheless been assembled under rubrics like: (neo)liberalism, late capitalism, globalization, marketization, Europeanization, technocratic governmentality, even, in my colleague Jakob Rigi's arresting phrase, a "chaotic mode of domination" (Nazpary 2001). A certain market-centered modernity, a modernity that state socialism had been straining to resist for decades, hit Eastern Europe fast and hard in the 1990s. And this was only the half of it. The other, not unrelated blow was the precipitous expansion of Western European sociopolitical imaginations and institutions into Eastern Europe, largely for economic and security reasons, although proceeding always under the banner of civilizational union and redemption.

Staggered, reeling under this double confrontation, observers found Eastern Europeans reaching backward, seeking to balance themselves. In the words of West German media entrepreneur Hubert Burda, "Looking for some support and stability in politically, culturally, and economically new worlds, these people [East Germans] demand emotional bridges to their own past." Only in memory, then, could Eastern Europeans retrieve the senses of security and autonomy otherwise denied them as new market and governmental forms of sociality innocently filled the social and historical "vacuum" created by the collapse of totalitarian states. Thus, Eastern Europeans naturally tethered themselves to recalled, also always fantasied aspects of life before 1989 that seemed better—warmer, more human, safer, more moral—than the chaos and devolution of life today.

Enter the epidemiology of nostalgia. In his remarkable 1688 medical dissertation for the University of Basel, Johannes Hofer coined the term *nostalgia* by combining two Greek terms—*nostos* (the return home) and *algos* (grief)—to identify a pathological variant of the common condition known to his contemporaries simply as *Heimweh* (homesickness). To validate his neologism, Hofer explained that *Heimweh* itself was not lexically adequate to the task of medical diagnosis. But then, almost apologetically, Hofer offered the less-celebrated terms, *nostomania* and *philopatridomania,* obsession with the return home or with love of the fatherland, as equivalents for those dissatisfied with his first choice (1934: 380–81). Hofer's diagnosis, gathered under the term *nostalgia,* thus signals both grief and obsession with a return to the place of origin. Nostalgia concerns the autophagous desire to deny the truth of the present by returning to a source. For Hofer, this source was explicitly *Heimat* (home) and nation—his medical analysis of nostalgia was humoral and climatological and centered on the aggravation of mental spirits and fibers acclimated to a certain territory when the afflicted undertook extended travel (note that "extended" travel in Hofer's lifeworld could mean 50 km or even less). The afflicted, meanwhile, could only be cured by returning to their native climate.

In the postmedical era of nostalgia, however, we confront a less corporeal notion of grief and obsession. Also, a less territorialized one—today, nostalgia most often appears discursively not as a search for a place, a home or nation, but as a sociotemporal yearning for a different stage or quality of life (as Kant put it, for our youth). In this respect, post-Socialist nostalgia is most often interpreted not literally as a desire to return to state socialism per se. Instead, it is understood as a desire to recapture what life was at that time, whether innocent, euphoric, secure, intelligible. In other words, such nostalgia is understood as a psychological or emotional prop, a "coping behavior," what sympathetic West Germans in my experience described to me as a "completely understandable" defense mechanism for people who lived half their lives in a state-imposed stasis only to have all those certainties, true and false, swept away in the second half of their lives by the uncomfortable forces and, of course, "realities," of life in a market-centered society.

The standard history closes with the prosthesis of memory stabilizing the shaken Eastern European, a figure whose past trauma casts into doubt his/her capacity to function effectively as a historical actor in the future. The narrative has a decidedly liberalist tinge to it, but one must admit that it is not a bad description of the facts in some respects. Perhaps its chief virtue beyond descriptive accuracy is that it is so intuitively familiar, both because it has been well publicized as a mode of legitimating projects of external intervention into Eastern Europe and because it taps into long-standing narratives of Eastern European past-orientation and backwardness that have exercised powerful historical influence over social identities in Eastern Europe, particularly regarding their relationship to the West (Boyer 2006; Glaeser 2000). Let me offer a few necessary corrections to this story that could help us to sharpen our attention to the phenomenon in sentiment and discourse we have come to know as Eastern European nostalgia, or better yet, "nostomania," which, I think, better captures the obsessional essence of Hofer's initial diagnosis.

Five Theses on Eastern European Nostalgia (*Nostomania*)

Nostalgia Is Heteroglossic

To borrow Bakhtin's terms, upon close analysis it becomes clear that nostalgia is by no means the kind of "unitary language" or stable and internally consistent discourse that is often described, for example, in international news journalism (1981: 270–71). All of us who have lived or worked in post-Socialist Eastern Europe are familiar with talk of "how life once was" uttered in distinction to some judgment on the present. Here are just three brief examples selected from among countless similar dialogues during my research in the former GDR between 1996 and 2002. My friend Albert tells me, speaking of journalism, "You know, although there was enormous surveillance of our work back then, at least it had a purpose. In this system you have a formal freedom but nothing ever goes anywhere." On another occasion, a former GDR satirist tells me that you can judge a society by how it treats its most vulnerable members: "The strong will find their way in any society, but socialism did a much better job of caring for the weak than this *Leistungsgesellschaft* (performance-based society) does. One should judge a society by how it cares for its weakest members." Finally, my friend Karl, ruminating glumly upon the successes and failures of his professional life, says, "You know, some day, as this society gets harder and harder, the West Germans are going to realize that the values, the *Menschlichkeit* (humanity), we had the in the GDR was good."

So, no one can dispute that the discourse phenomenon exists. But I think it is mistaken to assume that such talk transparently signals a grief for, or obsession with, the past, even when speakers themselves gloss their talk as "nostalgic" in character. Beneath the surface of speech, we should work to recognize and represent the dialogical gossamer of idiosyncratic references, interests, and affects that are channeled through nostalgic discourse. There are speech situations, of course, when such talk may represent precisely a grief for a faded past. But there are other times when it is deployed, for example in political rhetoric, to mobilize a present- or future-oriented project of identification and belonging. And, still other cases when such talk is less about transacting meaning and more about coordinating or cultivating intimacy through shared expression, a part of speech used to signal and bind "us-ness," as in the case of two friends commiserating over the trials of life over coffee or beer. At the level of sign and discourse alone, one should be suspicious at talk of the ubiquity and uniformity of nostalgic expression in Eastern Europe without even raising the more vexing issue as to whether the "sentiments" of nostalgia such discourse is assumed to represent are uniform as well. Finally, we must understand the gesture to define nostalgia as a unitary language as an interested and therefore political speech act in its own right that seeks to dampen down nostalgia's actual heteroglossic character and to give it the appearance of a shared discourse and consciousness that typifies Eastern Europe as a cultural unity.

Nostalgia Is Indexical

It is common enough to consider nostalgia as a descriptive, evaluative or, even analytical practice; in other words, as a way of grappling with the presence of the (external) world through a past-oriented medium of expression. But nostalgia is also an indexical practice, a mode of inhabiting the lived world through defining oneself situationally and positionally in it. And, therefore, as a kind of discourse that is evoked to create and maintain social distinctions between groups and between persons, it can never be entirely separated from ongoing politics of identification and belonging both inside and outside Eastern Europe. In these politics, accusations and embraces of nostalgia are never value neutral. Consider, for example, the small castes of social elites across Eastern Europe who quite willingly identified themselves with the external business, professional, and political interests that moved into the region in the 1990s. These are also the eastern citizens—owing to their acceptance of a particular future orientation desired by the arriving powers—who are normally exempted from association with nostalgia. If anything, they are the ones who claim legitimacy as social elites based precisely on their ability and desire to extricate their fellow citizens from their endemic past-orientation and backwardness. In a place like Eastern Germany, many of the most vociferous publicists and critics of so-called East German nostalgia (*Ostalgie*) are not West Germans, but rather the liberal wing of the former GDR civil rights movement, who count among their membership the current Chancellor Angela Merkel. Parenthetically, I participated recently in a podium discussion for Berlin public radio on East German nostalgia where another speaker was Marianne Birthler, the current special representative of the German government charged with managing the enormous archive of Stasi files. Herself born and raised in the GDR, Birthler drew a sharp distinction between the East German citizen of the future and the nostalgic *Ossi*. She said that she had "no sympathy" for people who clung to the past so desperately that they were willing to glorify a "perverse" and "oppressive" regime. She offered instead a number of exemplary tales of East Germans who had rightly chosen to put that past behind them and to embrace the "new possibilities" of a democratic state. Such discourse on East German nostalgia from GDR-born elites, heavily seasoned as it is with the public Western liberalism of individual choice, rights, and accountabilities, both legitimates their position as spokespersons of a "more healthy" East German identity and performs work on behalf of the dominant interests in West German political culture to delegitimate as "nostalgic" those East German voices that seek greater discussion of inequalities and legacies of the unification process or that, once upon a time, even sought alternatives to the West German colonial status quo.

Nostalgia Is Allochronic

Anyone who has read Larry Wolff's (1994) wonderful history of the constitution of "Eastern Europe" as an object within the social imagination of the Enlightenment should realize that contemporary nostalgia talk participates in a civilizational discourse of the *longue durée* that offers the solid lump of Eastern European pastness as the base point from which Western Europe charts its lightness, its futurity, indeed its very "Europeanness." We should thus recognize that the facticity of Eastern European nostalgia is every bit as vital for Western European sociopolitical imagination as it might be for local or individual senses of belonging in Russia, Poland, or Romania. The idea that nostalgia "belongs" somehow exclusively or even especially to Eastern Europe is pernicious, an aspect of the persistent allochronization (that is, temporal displacement) of Eastern Europe into the imagined margins of the urban, industrial, and scientific centers of Western European modernity. According to these centers, how could Eastern Europe be anything else other than past-fixated? For one thing, its pastness is genetically constitutive of Western futures. For another, if the polities of Eastern Europe were capable of generating and governing their own futurity, what would that say about the legitimacy of the long historical project of Western Europe to colonize and civilize the territories and polities lying between it and its perpetual civilizational nemesis, China? Paraphrasing the anxiety at slavery and social domination simmering within the kettle of European Enlightenment, Montesquieu once mused, "It is impossible for us to assume that these people [Negroes] are men, because if we assumed they were men, one would begin to believe that we ourselves were not Christians" (1989[1748]: 250). Eastern Europe's humanity poses a similar problem for Western Europe's humanism. We must therefore recognize that a Western desire to identify nostalgia and kindred modes of past-fixation in the East is one of the conditions of possibility of, and motivation for, our analysis.

Nostalgia Is Symptomal

This point, in essence, encapsulates the three previous corrections. But what kind of symptom is it? Critics as diverse as Arjun Appadurai (1996), Svetlana Boym (2002), and Frederic Jameson (1989) have characterized nostalgia as a modern symptom. They helpfully diagnose the temporal and spatial displacements of modern social relations domesticated at the level of social consciousness in the subject yearning for past or future utopia. They thus reference the subject of modern *Entfremdung* (estrangement) that Hegel and Marx articulated with such dialectical vigor. Recall that Marx's estranged subject displaced his failed knowledge of present social relatedness into the institutional fantasies of transcendental salvation (religion), autonomous humans (liberalism), and socialized objects (fetishism). Yet, even historical materialism revealed a symptomal communitarian fantasy in its futurist imagination of "communism" as world-historical transcendence of alienation. Nostalgia is surely a symptom in these terms, but the limitation of the *Entfremdung* argument is that it lacks historical specificity. It can explain a basic epistemic disposition toward nostalgia, but not necessarily why nostalgia seems so pervasive in Eastern Europe today. I would argue, following upon the discussion of allochrony above, that we should regard Eastern European nostalgia always also as a *postimperial symptom*, a symptom of the increasingly manic need in Western Europe to fix Eastern Europe in the past. The key point here is that Western Europe has been aware since its phase of imperial dissolution and retraction in the 1950s and 1960s that it no longer governs its own futurity either. What is the post-1960s European fascination with "postmodernity" if not a recognized and repressed sign that modernity has become significantly plurinodal—that the remains of European empire, notably places like the United States, Japan, China, and India have pushed Europe significantly into their own margins of intellectual and material productivity? Personally, I am fond of the Deleuzian rhizome and the Foucauldian network of enablement (*pouvoir*), but they efface, as it is the enterprise of philosophy to do, their social conditions of origin, here in a destabilized Western European intellectual culture. These are cybernetic-semiological theories of power that sought (and continue to seek) to suppress the growing global dispersement and marginalization of Western European authority around them. In fact, Western Europe is not just becoming one node in a distributed network of power, but also *a significantly lesser* node—no longer the indisputable "surplus power" of Foucault's sovereign, but rather an evaporating center whose own futurity can now be questioned. In this postimperial environment, the need for Eastern Europe as a *still lesser* node, a space that Western Europe can still suppose itself to dominate, has been vital. Indeed, the post-1989 Western European obsession with Eastern Europe's obsession with the past must be understood as an anxious lateral signal that the pastness of Eastern Europe can no longer be taken for granted. It is routinely observed these days that politically, economically, and technologically, Eastern Europe (or at least parts thereof) are poised to leapfrog the West into the liberal global future. Such a fear of Eastern civilizational advancement has harried Western Europe at least since the Enlightenment. And, what could have been more unsettling for Western European states than when the proverbial village idiot of the West (Bush-era US diplomacy) looked to Europe and pronounced that it saw "newness" in the East?

If you are looking for a familiar example of what these anxious signals look like, think of the rather desperate embrace throughout the West of the film, *The Lives of Others*. On filmic grounds, personally I find it a rather mediocre effort, unlike, say, *Goodbye, Lenin!*, another West German film about the GDR, which offers a very well-crafted and -executed farce. When I interview friends and colleagues about what precisely they like about *The Lives of Others*, the answer is usually something concerning its "universal human message" (of the struggle between creativity and power, faith and disillusionment, trial and redemption, between spirit and system). I'm not disputing a universalist thematics in the film's narrative, of course. But I would suggest that the political fantasy of the film tells a rather more specific story. From the first moments of the film (black screen, the sound of boots marching with military precision down a hall) the East German party-state is depicted as rife with the despotism, corruption, and moral degeneracy that has been the semiopolitical burden of the East since the Enlightenment. True, signs of humanity and decency stir here and there in the East, even, as it turns out, within the state security apparatus itself. But the seedlings are stunted in the socialist gloom and only truly flourish after 1989. In this respect the last scenes in the film are particularly telling. Justice and the rule of law only appear to emerge in the context of the absorption of the former GDR into the Federal Republic. Even the good Stasi-man finally receives his due with the help of the investigative apparatus of the West German state. Please note that the West German presence in these West German films about the GDR is always minimized as a technical, enabling presence, a prosthesis for East Germans to do what they supposedly would have wanted to do anyway—that is, to release their long repressed yet "natural" liberal ambitions. This suppression of the mediating governmental agenda and interests of Western market liberalism is precisely what gifts the political fantasy of the film its symptomal universalism. But, to be clear, the fantasy falls short of a "universal human message" in that it does not communicate effectively outside Western liberalism, and, more to point, to many former GDR citizens, the very subjects of this history. My friend, Albert, who both was the target of a Stasi OPK proceeding and also a successful professional ravaged by doubt and despair about the GDR—in other words, more or less the protagonist position of the film—wrote to me that he watched the film as though he were watching a movie about a foreign country (later he said he identified with the film *The Queen* as much as with *The Lives of Others*). He summed up his review pithily: "Was da gezeigt wird hat es alles gegeben. Aber eben SO WAR ES NICHT. Es stimmen 1000 Details nicht." (Everything that was portrayed in the film happened. But it didn't happen LIKE THAT. 1000 details were off.)

Nostalgia Always Carries with It a Politics of the Future

The crucial problem with ceasing our analysis of the sentimental cultures of post-Socialist Eastern Europe at terms like *nostalgia* and *nostomania* is their analytic closure around a sign of pastness. To put it bluntly, these sentiments and discourses have, in the final analysis, no more to do with the past than with the future, no more to do with the desire to return to a remembered or idealized past than with the project of defining and claiming autonomy in the present.

Politics of the Future

Returning to the end of the seventeeth century, Johannes Hofer completed his dissertation on nostalgia with the following story: "Thus not long since it was told me by a Parisian that he himself had an Helvetian bound servant who was sad and melancholy at all times so that he began to work with lessened desire; finally, he came to him and sought dismissal with insistent entreaties, of which he could have no hope beyond him. When the merchant granted this immediately, the servant changed from sudden joy, excused from his mind these phantasma for several days, and after a while remained in Paris, broken up no longer by this disease" (1934: 390).

What Hofer located as a sort of anecdotal remainder to his thesis contains, as is often the case, the key to reimagining the entire diagnosis. The freed Helvetian longed not for a return to his place of origin—even though this is what both he and his master were convinced afflicted him—he longed instead for the right of future-determination. Having won this right, he surprised all parties, including doubtless the admirable Dr. Hofer, by remaining precisely where he was.

In my opinion, Eastern European nostalgia contains a similar secret. Perhaps it ultimately has less to do with the recovery of a past or past-phantom than, as in the case of the Helvetian servant, with the politics of the future. The moral here is not to doubt either *algos* or mania in post-Socialist Eastern Europe. Both, I think it is safe to say, abound. What we should doubt is that the primary object of reference for either of them is *nostos,* the return home (Berdahl 1999: 201–2). What I think we are witnessing instead in Eastern European nostalgia are tropes of idealized pastness that set out to accomplish two very contemporary projects in communication and knowledge: (1) to signal and voice estrangement from the fact that post-Socialist transformation in Eastern Europe has been a process steered by social and political interests largely lying outside Eastern Europe, and, (2) to make a claim upon a right of future self-determination. Given the social reality of contemporary Eastern Europe, it should be clear to us why both these projects are vitally important and so contingent as to give rise to a repetitive practice of signaling that is easily interpreted as either full of grief or obsessive. So, *algos* and mania, yes, but with the core referent of *autonomos* (self-rule) rather than *nostos*.

Am I not quibbling over semiotics? I don't think so. Circling back to points made above, the very real propensity of Eastern Europe to govern and to direct its own future is powerfully suppressed within a discourse environment where Eastern European citizens' estrangement from the external steering of their social transformation is labeled (also autolabeled) nostalgic, where "modernizing" Eastern European elites persistently apologize for the nostalgia of their fellow Eastern European citizens, where Western European elites accept such apologies as tokens of reassurance that Eastern Europe is still the way it always has been—that is, full of productive promise, slow to develop, prone to anticivilizational tendencies, and, always in need of developmental attention from the West. This discourse environment extends beyond Western Europe, of course. The funniest, also saddest, thing to me about the recent global Borat craze is not its exposition of the anticivilizational underbelly of the United States, but with the way that underbelly—and by extension many others who laughed in recognition—found it rather unexceptional that Eastern Europe would represent itself as a space of degenerated modern humanity rife with rape, incest, filth, murder, Jew-hunting, Gypsy-baiting, and so on and on. US theaters were filled with people who didn't entirely get the joke of what Yurchak (2006) might call the "overidentifying parody" of Borat, perhaps precisely because the caricature was already so thoroughly banal. Irony only works, after all, at a distance, when a gap between sign and subject can be recognized.

A good direction for our analytical work on Eastern European nostalgia is toward an impact with such caricatures. Like any schema in knowledge, it cannot be shattered through force of argument alone, since through institutions and the "spontaneous consent" of its targets it generates a sufficient evidentiary and interpretive basis to sustain its reasonableness. After all, can we not find many Eastern Europeans seemingly eager to announce their nostalgia? So why am I creating so much trouble over what seems like a nakedly empirical problem? Because it is also an *ideological* problem. What Žižek, for example, terms "everyday spontaneous ideology" is the repression of the historical contingencies of knowing in order to produce the sense of epistemic universality requisite for action (1994). The nostalgic Eastern European (as unitary subject of unitary language) is, in a very important way, an ideological necessity of postimperial Western Europe, a suppressed recognition of a constitutive practice of domination upon which the imagination of Western European (and also more generally Western) freedom, autonomy, and futurity is contingent.

So, chronicling the self-knowledge, even the critical knowledge, of Eastern Europe as channeled through nostalgic estrangement seems not quite the right scale of response. Put another way, it is a necessary but not a sufficient response. The ethnography of nostalgia is an important project, but it should also be a symmetrical ethnography that takes seriously the *mania* of past-fixation issuing from Western metropolitan centers of intellectual production and circulation. It also needs to be a critical ethnography that disengages this mania from *nostos* and grasps instead the hovering desire for *autonomos* both historical and contemporary, both in Eastern *and* Western Europe.

Let me emphasize this point. I am not arguing that Western Europe is solely responsible for generating the figure of the nostalgic Eastern European. I am suggesting instead that we view this figure as the faultline between two politics of the future, two projects of *autonomos*. As things stand, these projects are at cross-purposes and their conflict is epistemically generative in ways we do not yet fully grasp.

In the end, all I am really arguing is that we should listen to nostalgia discourse more carefully. That is, we should take seriously the fact that nostalgia talk in many contexts means something more or other than resignation to "westernization" and melancholy for how much better or easier or younger life once was. I interpret much nostalgia talk in Eastern Europe as precisely the opposite of this—nostalgia's obsessional method of past insistence can also serve as a way of drawing attention to an emergent politics of the future that is by no means settled.

References

Appadurai, Arjun. 1996. *Modernity at Large.* Minneapolis: University of Minnesota Press.
Bakhtin, M. M. 1981. *The Dialogic Imagination.* Austin: University of Texas Press.
Berdahl, Daphne. 1999. "(N)Ostalgie for the Present: Memory, Longing and East German Things." *Ethnos* 64 (2): 192–211.
Boyer, Dominic. 2006. "Ostalgie and the Politics of the Future in Eastern Germany." *Public Culture* 18 (2): 361–81.
Boym, Svetlana. 2002. *The Future of Nostalgia.* New York: Basic Books.

Fabian, Johannes. 1983. *Time and the Other.* New York: Columbia University Press.
Glaeser, Andreas. 2000. *Divided in Unity.* Chicago: University of Chicago Press.
Hofer, Johannes. 1934. "Medical Dissertation on Nostalgia." *Bulletin of the History of Medicine* 2: 376–91.
Jameson, Frederic. 1989. "Nostalgia for the Present." *South Atlantic Quarterly* 88 (2): 517–37.
Montesquieu. 1989[1748]. *The Spirit of the Laws.* Cambridge: Cambridge University Press.
Nazpary, Joma. 2001. *Post-Soviet Chaos.* London: Pluto Press.
Wolff, Larry. 1994. *Inventing Eastern Europe.* Stanford, CA: Stanford University Press.
Yurchak, Alexei. 2006. *Everything Was Forever Until It Was No More.* Princeton, NJ: Princeton University Press.
Žižek, Slavoj, ed. 1994. *Mapping Ideology.* London: Verso.

 2

Strange Bedfellows
Socialist Nostalgia and Neoliberalism in Bulgaria

Gerald W. Creed

In 2007 I marked twenty years of intermittent research in the village of Zamfirovo in northwest Bulgaria. This experience, spanning Socialist and post-Socialist contexts, provides a unique perspective on eruptions of Socialist nostalgia in the twenty-first century. However, it's not an unequivocal vantage point. Nearly two years of life under socialism provided a baseline experience from which to challenge romantic recollections of the period, but firsthand exposure to the subsequent difficulties of "transition" made me susceptible to my own reevaluations of that past. In short, I know the dynamics of nostalgia personally. In this context, my own analysis replicates the nostalgic narration of "informants" and the lines between analyst and subject become even more blurred than usual.

My research in Zamfirovo began in 1987 with the intent of documenting the impact of collectivization on village and household economies. I soon discovered that collectivization was only a segment in an ongoing process of agrarian reform that predated collectivization and continued unabated after the completion of that watershed event in 1956. Contrary to dominant models of socialism at the time, many of these "reforms" actually responded to popular village reactions to prior policy efforts. While many of the reforms attempted to circumvent rather than accommodate village recalcitrance, some policy changes reflected the latter, and even the former provided an avenue of local input into purportedly top-down Socialist planning in an arena (agriculture) at the heart of state planning. In this way, over decades, villagers helped domesticate state socialism.

It was from this context that they evaluated "the changes" beginning in 1989. My subsequent research followed the agrarian dimensions of these changes, mapping the process of land restitution in the village, which proved to be as difficult and devastating as collectivization. This time, however, village resistance and recalcitrance failed to have the same ameliorating impact and instead left villages outside of economic development altogether as Bulgarian capitalism progressed along the paths of least resistance. Life in the village continued to decline as agriculture stagnated, local enterprises shut down, and working-age residents migrated to cities, both in Bulgaria and abroad. By 2005 the village economy finally began to show signs of gradual recovery, not so much in agriculture, but in the development of successful local enterprises, including independent startups and subcontracting units for larger companies. Ironically, this improvement accompanied an increase in the expression of "Socialist nostalgia," a paradox I explore in this chapter.

In January 2006, spurred by my own growing sense of nostalgia as well as increasing scholarly attention to the phenomenon, I returned to Zamfirovo. When I told a friend upon my arrival that I was gathering information for an article on Socialist nostalgia, he quipped, "An article? We'll give you enough to write another book." I might have interpreted his comment as simply validation of my research topic and set about gathering the promised examples, but I was taken aback by how conversant he was with the notion. Further discussion revealed that Socialist nostalgia was not simply a shorthand term for a variety of pro-Socialist sentiments deployed primarily by the unafflicted, as I had imagined, but rather a phenomenon of Bulgarian popular culture.

The common components of this popular category replicated those documented in studies of nostalgia elsewhere in the post-Socialist world: a revalorization of Socialist-era consumer goods and products (Ghodsee 2004; Jung 2005),[1] a revitalization of some Socialist ideals, and the transvaluation of maligned Socialist material culture (especially that of more propagandistic character) into kitsch. Figure 2.1 gives an example of the latter from the restaurant "Rio," a casual, smoky joint near Sofia University where didactic signs and other Socialist paraphernalia cover the walls.[2] So in a sense there is not much new on this issue to report from Bulgaria, at least not in form. However, in the village, an earlier and continuing discontent with postsocialism has been mapped onto this increasingly popular term, making it now a useful tool for understanding an array of rural dynamics, which in turn raises questions about the timing of the term's appearance as a vehicle of discontent.

This chapter then is an interactive effort that uses the growth of Socialist nostalgia as a way to examine socioeconomic discontent in a Bulgarian village, and then uses the village case, attending to its timing and variant meanings, to interrogate the ideological consequences of labeling such disaffection "Socialist nostalgia." As the title betrays, it highlights the ways that notions of Socialist nostalgia facilitate neolib-

Figure 2.1 Restaurant "Rio" in Sofia.

eral programs, notably by trivializing capitalist discontent and commodifying Socialist contentment. However, the difficult circumstances in Bulgaria make these strategies a bit risky, producing nostalgic hybrids with a significant dose of negativity and precautionary counter-discourses that follow the forms of nostalgic expression but broach no Socialist affirmation.

Nostalgia, Modernity, and the Depoliticization of the Past

As is well known, the term *nostalgia* is from the Greek roots *nostos,* meaning return home, and *algia,* meaning longing. As Svetlana Boym (2001) points out, this meaning is connected to the word's first usage as a medical malady afflicting displaced people in the late seventeenth century. It is thus in its original meaning a synonym for the term *homesickness,* but as Dominic Boyer (2006) points out in a wonderful exegesis, the German medical student who coined it did so precisely to highlight a more visceral embodied impact than that commonly associated with homesickness (*Heimweh* in German). Interestingly it is this understanding of nostalgia as homesickness that I first encountered in Bulgaria in the 1980s. To my knowledge no one in the village suffered from nostalgia during that period, but I was constantly queried by villagers about whether or not I did. I denied my occasional bouts of homesickness for fear they might be misinterpreted as a lack of enthusiasm for my life in the village. The possibility that I didn't have such feeling, however, seemed so unlikely as to contribute to some people's sinister interpretations of my objectives. This meaning—that is, homesickness—is the only way I encountered the word *nostalgia* in Bulgaria in the 1980s. The perhaps more amorphous notion of a longing for or reverie of the past (a temporal rather than spatial home) was never invoked.

I can plot the advent of this meaning of nostalgia in Zamfirovo to the years since 2002. In numerous trips to the village between 1992 and 2002 I never heard the term invoked to describe either someone's personal validation of Socialist life or the pro-Socialist assessments of others, and there was plenty of such talk (see Creed 1995a, 1995b, 1999). In other words, I heard a lot of comments that I could have called "Socialist nostalgia," but the term was not used by the people making such statements. On my visit in 2006, as suggested above, I came across the term frequently in terms of this meaning and never in terms of homesickness. Following Boyer's (2006) insights, I suggest that some of the resonance of the term for Bulgarian villagers harkens to this notion of ailment. The ideas included in the term *nostalgia*, which are separated somewhat in the English and German usage, remained more integrated in Bulgarian (where there is only one word), so that we cannot make the same assumptions about the meaning of the term. In other words, where it exists, the alternative term *homesickness* operates to turn nostalgia into a term of uncertain longing for, or simply reveling in, a romanticized past, while its more visceral and embodied dimension—that is, as a psychological disturbance with possible somatic effect (as with depression)—is elided. Thus, ironically, a term that was introduced precisely to mark the seriousness of the condition has itself been stripped of that possibility. Why can't the notion of serious somatic consequences from spatiotemporal displacement be conceptually sustained? Part of the answer lies in the dynamics and ideologies of modernity within which nostalgia is interpreted.

The redefinition of nostalgia as simply homesickness for the past makes it possible to dismiss these intense feelings as ephemeral, an outcome that Daphne Berdahl (1999), drawing on Michael Herzfeld (1997), locates in the notion of "mere." A debilitating social and psychological condition is recast as "merely nostalgia" by those who are not experiencing it. This sentimentalization may not be the way it is experienced by villagers—different epistemic frames lead to different consequences—but any alternative meaning it has for villagers is refused by a Western cosmopolitan frame that redefines their nostalgia in its own terms, an outcome made easier (if not overdetermined) by the combination of definitions in the same word. The urban cosmopolitan frame evident not only in "the West" but among urban and urbane observers in Bulgaria casts distress over spatial displacement (homesickness) as an atavistic quality of a preglobalized, if not premodern, world, exhibited only by its noncosmopolitan remnants, and likewise, anxiety over temporal displacement (nostalgia) as a retrograde attachment to the past incompatible with the fast pace of change since the nineteenth century. This links the evisceration of the term *nostalgia* to the very processes of modernity that summoned it: the modern forces that provoked a psychological dynamic so pervasive as to merit medicalization quickly and inevitably rendered the same mundane. Trivialization may have been politically encouraged by the proponents of progress since the claim that modernity produced a pervasive pathology could certainly be read as a social critique of modern forces requiring some abatement or redress by political leaders. But there may have been no need for political manipulation, because without connection to a more extended program of resistance, the challenge probably took care of itself: since nostalgia was a product of modernity, the consolidation of modern processes made the effects commonplace and routine.

The story of nostalgia, then, is just another example of how modernity helped depoliticize the experiences of the past. Change can provoke reevaluations and reactions, but the unrelenting pace of change that accelerates with modernity quickly renders such responses quaint. By the time a broad or concerted resistance could organize around any particular loss, it was already too far removed from current practice to seem viable. The very processes that might be expected to produce resistance or criticism render such responses old fashioned or backward. Over time, this pace of change becomes naturalized and criticism is eviscerated by the seeming inevitability of progress. "Luddite" becomes an absurd, derisive appellation, the Amish a tourist curiosity, and everyone else who isn't up-to-date simply backward and undeveloped. Nostalgia is further hamstrung by generality and selectivity that make it vulnerable to the accusation of misrepresentation and romanticism.

In the case of nostalgia, this dynamic has only been furthered by the amplification of modern processes referred to as postmodernity. Concomitantly the time-space compression characteristic of postmodernity (Harvey 1990) rendered spatial and temporal displacements nearly synonymous. Sentimental attachments to a earlier time and different place become isomorphic and so generic as to seemingly disallow serious psychological consequences, at least among citizens of this new world order. There is a dialectic operative as well, as the seeming banality of both displacements makes the distinction between the two even less important. This is not the place to debate the significance of homesickness itself, but psychological research into the continuing significance of homesickness (van Tilburg, Vingerhoets, and van Heck 1996) does suggest that this dismissal is at least partially a political product.

Nostalgia as Trauma

Many of the villagers who my friend believed could help me write a book about nostalgia are in my perspective just now working their way out of (some more successfully than others) a psychosocial condition tantamount to a sickness. While the perceptive analysis of Allan Young (1997) might caution against facile parallels with posttraumatic stress disorder, the socioeconomic disruptions villagers lived through certainly qualify as "social trauma" (cf. Dudley 2000: 125–42; see also Butler 1997: 36–37). In the decade between 1992 and 2002 many areas of the Bulgarian countryside went through an experience that was as transformative and disorienting as collectivization (Creed 1995b). This is not hyperbole. Not only did villagers lose their professional occupations (as many workers throughout the Socialist world), but they were forced to return to subsistence production characteristic of the nineteenth century as a result of the ill-conceived "liquidation" of collective farms (see Creed 1995a, 1998). Their families (the foundation of village social structure) were disrupted by arguments over property restitution. Nonfamilial village relations were torn asunder by the same arguments as well as the new fractious political divisions. Traditions and rituals were threatened by economic privation (Creed 2002).

All these areas of village life were further diminished by massive out-migration. According to Mike Donkin of BBC News (2006), Bulgaria is losing population at a faster rate than any other European country "and the sense of abandonment is even greater in the countryside. … Scattered across the landscape now are dozens of deserted or almost deserted villages." Zamfirovo could soon be one of them. In 2006 the village had half the population it had when I left there in 1988. Of the remaining official residents, perhaps 100, mostly women, are away working in Greece, Italy, Spain, and Germany as housekeepers and caregivers for children and the elderly. Interestingly enough, the homesickness that so many villagers thought must surely accompany being away from home when few villagers left the country, is no longer discussed now that many people do. This is not just a result of their cosmopolitan exposure, but also because the home/village they have left behind is not a place one would want to be, so there is nothing to be homesick for. Instead I found depression and anxiety among villagers who had worked abroad in the past but were unable to do so again for either health reasons or difficulties securing employment. Should we say these villagers are nostalgic for foreign lands? More likely, the overwhelming sense of nostalgia for the past that they experience daily in Zamfirovo is making staying at home unbearable.

A quarter of the houses in the village are empty. What was a thriving school with eight full grades, now runs parallel classes combining two grades. In some cases there are barely enough students to sustain the combined classes, and an increasing number of those are Roma. The school may well have to close, forcing parents to send their kids to a neighboring town beginning with the first grade. In the meantime, parents are worried about a decline in the quality of education even as they recognize that education has become more important with the declining economic prospects for employment in the village. The desire of young people to get out of the village, which was strongly evident under socialism, has taken on even greater urgency as the alternative has become more sinister. The *chitalishte* (a pre-Socialist cultural institution in Bulgarian villages that was retooled in the Socialist period into a Soviet-style culture house) has limited activities as amateur singing ensembles, dance troops, theater groups, and film programs have gone the way of the collective farm. The village is a shell of its former self. The process resembles what Osha Gray Davidson (1990), describing the midwestern United States, calls the rise of the rural ghetto.

To listen to the descriptions of villagers who have witnessed this, most of whom were actually the workers and builders of the very institutions and constructions that were destroyed in the 1990s, is to be moved, not by the political motives usually assumed to underlie their stories, but by the events they relate and their associated emotional trauma. The ruins remain around in a haunting landscape that cannot help but evoke more distress. So as the notion of nostalgia is increasingly used to describe their disappointments, one must ask about its appropriateness. Is it nostalgia to see the ruined foundation of a sheep farm and wish that it were still standing and productive? Is it nostalgia to pass dried-up orchards or vineyards and wish that they were still bearing fruit? Is it nostalgia to see the empty hull of a former factory workshop and wish that it were still productive and employing villagers? The absurdity of such conceptualizations is perhaps more obvious when we think comparatively: Would we call the outrage and disappointment felt by General Motors workers in Flint, Michigan, when they see the abandoned businesses in their neighborhoods "nostalgia"? Would we call the rash of suicides that accompanied the flurry of farm foreclosures in the United States in the 1980s "nostalgia"?

The experience of the so-called transition was extremely variable across Bulgaria, and the part of the country where Zamfirovo is located was particularly hard hit. Still, the trauma I relate was common enough to describe it as a national syndrome. This is one reason why the post-Socialist insistence that villagers take entrepreneurial responsibility is ludicrous. Since 1989 a common refrain heard from economists, development experts, and politicians in the United States, Western Europe, and Bulgaria itself, is that villagers must learn that they are responsible for their own situation and take the initiative to change/improve it. In short, they must give up the expectations of Socialist paternalism and get with the capitalist program. Their apparent refusal or inability to do so is blamed on their conservatism, their age, their ignorance, and their character, but not the possibility of psychosocial trauma. Expecting people who have gone through the trauma of socioeconomic "liquidation" to take initiative and make things happen is like telling a person suffering from depression to just snap out of it. I suggest that the recent local resonance of the notion of nostalgia reflects in part its meaning as a psychological illness with physiological consequences.

This begs the question, why now? Why have villagers only recently taken up the term *nostalgia*? Certainly a syndrome is often only recognized as such after a period of reflection and analysis, and I do believe the same logic applies in this case. Villagers in Zamfirovo (and across the country, for that matter) only gradually came to recognize the similar collective impact of their very diverse discontents. Moreover, many had not been fans of the Socialist system, so it took some distance for them to conceptualize their emotional trauma in a way that might validate the Socialist past. The latter suggestion reveals another dimension to this timing that connects to nostalgia's meaning as a reverie for lost times. Interestingly, my trip to Bulgaria in 2006 was the first time that a broad array of people beyond villagers, including some politicians, urban intellectuals, and journalists, agreed with me about the stupidity of the liquidation campaign that had devastated the villages. It was also the first time I saw some improvement in the village economy. As mentioned at the beginning of this chapter, the turnaround was evident not so much in agriculture but rather in the establishment of small enterprises that had begun to offer a sizeable number of villagers decent work for reasonable salaries. Thus, my dismal description of the village was clearly starting to ameliorate. I began to suspect that these two developments—the increasing critique of the liquidation program and village economic improvements—were not coincidental to the apparent embrace of the notion of nostalgia.

I suggest that the term *nostalgia* only resonates when two criteria have been met: when there is no chance of going back and when improvement is evident. Now that no one expects or fears a return to socialism, nostalgia is apposite. This suggests nostalgia indexes a particular type of memory, one that is based on lived experience and thus not too old or too far back, yet one that despite being relatively recent is not reversible or restorable. Nostalgia signals a rupture between past and present; a separation. Thus the timing of nostalgia's appearance as a term in its romantic conceptualization is revealing. It suggests that villagers have given up on the possibility of domesticating the transition, which can be explained by both exhaustion after fifteen years of trying unsuccessfully and some evidence of improvement without any extensive amelioration. The increasing certainty of joining the European Union (EU) operated on both sides: making a return to "socialism" more inconceivable and increasing expectations of improvement. The new resonance of the concept of nostalgia indexes a tipping point, when there is still lived memory but little hope or even desire for return because of an exhaustion of options and some improving hope for the future. That's why nostalgia emerged quickest in the East German case, in the wake of reunification, and last perhaps in cases such as Bulgaria where a Socialist return seemed more possible due to strong Socialist heritage parties, declining economic circumstances, and equivocal timetables for joining the EU. The timing also confirms that nostalgia is experienced in relationship to the present: it is the disadvantaged who feel nostalgic, but their nostalgia is evoked by recognition of the possibilities or inevitabilities of the present.[3]

This shift is also evident in the urban context. In the mid-1990s an exhibition of Socialist Realism in a small Sofia museum produced vehement emotions. I attended the exhibit, spoke to people there about their impressions, eavesdropped on their conversations with others while they were viewing the exhibit, and read the comments they wrote in a book provided for that purpose. Artistic types derided the aesthetic failures of the genre, others were ambivalent and described their major motivation for viewing as curiosity about the exhibit, a few fans expressed shameless admiration, while others were upset that there would even be such an exhibition and came expressly to complain to the curator and record their disgust in the book. These results were so predictable that I didn't really think any more of the event until my trip in 2006, when I found similar items and emblems all over the place absent such negative commentary and clearly being received in a different vein, which I would call nostalgic. Such examples make it possible to see the rise of nostalgia as clear evidence of the end of transition. This profile is important, but I suggest the vestigial notion of sickness also makes nostalgia a viable representation of the continuing trauma from which many villagers are still suffering and others are only uneasily emerging.

If nostalgia references the posttraumatic consequences of liquidation, why didn't villagers suffer similarly after collectivization? Many elements of the collectivization campaign were as bad as or worse than those of liquidation, and some reports of it gave emotive impressions more traumatic than those I witnessed around liquidation. Similarly, collectivization triggered massive out-migration, resulting in a significant population loss and changing village life drastically in multiple ways (see Creed 1998). Yet older villagers in the 1980s never characterized their own or others' emotional attachments to, and images of, the past as nostalgic. There was no concept of "prewar nostalgia" or "capitalist nostalgia." Certainly, by the time I was talking to villagers in 1987, a lot of time had passed and much of the population lacked the personal experience with pre-Socialist life that I have suggested is elemental to nostalgia, but there are other reasons why nostalgia probably didn't fit this earlier trauma. First, because nostalgia implies a positive or romantic image of the past, it was certainly not encouraged by the newspeak vocabulary of communism—as Boym (2001: 59) puts it, nostalgia was "not merely a bad word but a counterrevolutionary provocation." Nostalgia would have been a dangerous political violation potentially marking anyone who expressed it as a class enemy. While this may have been the official logic, my argument suggests the opposite outcome: by discouraging a rhetoric of nostalgia, the state sustained people's memories of presocialism as viable options in the future, whereas the notion of nostalgia would have marked them as less probable if not impossible. The other reason nostalgia in its psychosomatic manifestation was not evident in the traumatized countryside of the 1950s and 1960s is that the state stepped in to cure it. There was a plan, indeed many plans (relentless plans, one might say), and while they were certainly not successful in relation to their aspirations, they did provide villagers a blueprint and a way to keep going. The Communist agricultural programs that followed collectivization were a treatment for the trauma. This is not to say they were at all desirable, so they did not really redress discontent, but they did provide a mechanism that literally forced villagers to work through their psychological and social trauma—"work" being the operative word as the treatment was basically hard labor. There was neither time nor political space for nostalgia.

Commercialization and Counternarratives

In emasculating the past of its potential for resistance nostalgia also makes it marketable. It is no coincidence that the rise of nostalgia is often signaled by the appearance of consumer items that evoke the past. Of course there is an interaction here: while the move to nostalgia makes the Socialist past marketable in a capitalist economy, the commercialization of these ideas and images further associates them with capitalism rather than an alternative. In other words, the commercialization of socialism depends upon the domestication of the past accomplished by nostalgia, but it also furthers the process. The ability of the capitalist system to commodify these particular representations of resistance is nothing more than it has done for years, as described well in Dick Hebdidge's (1979) trenchant analysis of style. I'm simply suggesting nostalgia plays a useful role in this scenario.[4] In this way nostalgia becomes a resource for the expansion of capitalism—perhaps the only one where local entrepreneurs have an advantage over the foreign investor.

It is not surprising then that Bulgaria's most famous example of Socialist nostalgia is also one of its poshest and most successful restaurants, a stylish place in the center of Sofia called "Checkpoint Charlie." Like its namesake, this chic eating establishment is divided into two sides—one representing capitalism and the other communism. While the same expensive food is served by an equally accommodating staff on both sides of the reimagined border, the decor is completely different. The capitalist side is white and embellished while the communist side is dark and minimalist. A large picture of a border guard dominates the communist half (see figure 2.2), where protected pages from the old Communist Party daily, *Robotnichesko Delo* (Worker's Action) replace tablecloths and place mats.[5]

What we see here, however, is not simply nostalgia, or rather we see that nostalgia is not so simple. Checkpoint Charlie represents a dual effort that attempts to capitalize on the current popularity of Socialist nostalgia, but also insists on a critical edge that simultaneously challenges the romanticism or sentimentality commonly associated with nostalgia, which might otherwise provide a challenge to capitalist success and future ambitions. The negative portrayal of communism is restrained by the commercial need to make both sides appealing to customers paying high prices (indeed a realistic recreation of a Socialist-era restaurant might not even have food to sell), but the lesson is discernible in the aesthetic codes of interior design (one might say, as clear as black and white), as well as the very theme and name of the restaurant (it is hard to romanticize Socialist border points). Still some Bul-

Figure 2.2 Advertisement for restaurant "Checkpoint Charlie" in Sofia.

garian acquaintances who had dined there did not recognize it as a particularly negative presentation of communism. This subtlety allows the restaurant owners to tap the commercial promise of nostalgia and thereby further commodify and co-opt it without running the risk of affirming socialism.[6] It will come as no surprise then that the owner of Checkpoint Charlie is from a family of established supporters of the right wing of Bulgarian politics.[7]

A similar duality is evident in the advertising campaign of a large Bulgarian gasoline company. The company's new service stations are attractive, full-service convenience stores with internet access. One of the promotions offered to customers at station openings in 2005 was free *etar,* a Socialist-era soft drink with the taste of roses, which is quite hard to find nowadays. This Socialist comfort, however, was countered by television commercials that began with images of a Spartan (read Socialist) gas station and quickly morphed into an elaborate consumer paradise while a voice-over reminded the viewer that "there was a time" when gas stations only provided gas. Here the warm feelings for a Socialist product are tapped to engender positive associations with this former state enterprise, but they are joined with a media campaign that makes the more significant differences of socialism central: socialism gave you *etar,* but not much else. Nostalgia is fun but don't be seduced or fooled by it.

What we see in these examples is a lingering concern by some of the beneficiaries of the transition about the popularity of Socialist nostalgia. My previous discussion suggests that this is a misreading of the dynamics of nostalgia, a misunderstanding they share ironically with old Communist Party leaders. They may not recognize the political effacement accomplished by nostalgia, which leaves it open to a more literal interpretation as a desire to return to the past. But this (mis)interpretation is also enabled by the fact that the interpreters are at least somewhat aware of the socioeconomic conditions under which the nostalgics live and work as well as the serious trauma they have gone through. If so, they no doubt recognize a material and psychological context in which elements of the past might be attractive. This concern underlies a common complaint among anti-Socialist Bulgarians over the lack of historical instruction in schools about the Socialist era and the fear that young people who have no experience and little knowledge of Communist horrors might find the current Socialist nostalgia politically appealing. This concern provoked an extended article in the *International Herald Tribune* in the fall of 2004 (Wood 2004). A short excerpt conveys this concern:

> Some youths take the view that the lessons of socialism have no relevance for people living in today's world. "They don't care about the past–they are living here and now," said Jasen Bosev, who was ten years old when the Berlin Wall came down. "They care about money and fashion. The past is not useful to them."
>
> This outlook has stirred concern at a time when socialism is seen in an increasingly positive light among the elder generation. While there was a backlash against communism in the 1990s, many older Bulgarians now wax nostalgic over a period they regard as having provided employment and security.
>
> In a study published in January, a team of experts from the Association Global Bulgaria Initiative, said: "It should be noted we live in a society in which the vast majority of people do not know what is good about democracy, and have forgotten what is bad about socialism."

Interestingly, no one in the United States ever expresses concern that the nostalgia for the past that most children grow up hearing from their parents will be attractive to American young people even though they are equally ignorant of the past. This fear has to do with the lack of a positive present in Bulgaria. The problematic economy that drives young people out of the country is a fecund context in which they might actually start to imagine the nostalgia of their grandparents as more attractive.

Consequently Bulgaria's neoliberal program requires a more explicit counternarrative. While many diverse efforts constitute this phenomenon, including the desire to introduce the negative experiences of socialism into primary and secondary school instruction, the most accessible example is the internet project "Az Zhivyah Sotsializma" ("I Lived Socialism"), which can be found at http://www.spomeniteni.org (our memories). While the site replicates a nostalgic form and invites people of all ages to send in their memories of socialism, both good and bad, postings are almost exclusively negative. Indeed, the website's founder, Diana Ivanova, said in the same *International Herald Tribune* article quoted above that she launched the site in reaction to the increasingly rosy view of the past promoted by some former politicians and the media. The fact that it is on the internet also clearly biases it against the older generation and the economically marginal who are the main reservoirs of such ideas. To close this circle, one could read on the website in 2006 that its new sponsor was none other than the restaurant Checkpoint Charlie.

Conclusions

As is clear by now, Socialist nostalgia is an amazingly complex construct (Yuchak 2005). I do not pretend to have fully explicated it here; rather, I have tried to highlight one element of its operation in Bulgaria: the way it actually furthers the consolidation of neoliberal capitalism. It does so through multiple deflections. It invalidates the complaints of the disenfranchised and traumatized by labeling their desires "nostalgic" (i.e., retrograde and romantic). It then encases them in marketable knickknacks and symbols, which accomplishes a further trivialization as well as a concomitant devaluation since most Socialist-era material culture seems patently inferior or naive by contemporary capitalist standards. Finally, it associates all these (mis)recognitions with the entire Socialist system. The Bulgarians I know who define their feelings about the past as nostalgia are not advocating a wholesale return to communism, or what Boym (2001) calls "restorative nostalgia." Socialist nostalgics are usually fairly particular in their veneration of the past (much as I [1999] have suggested in regard to their electoral support for Socialist parties), and different people have different things they are nostalgic about. Most are nostalgic for reliable and affordable healthcare, a living wage, and job security, but to lump such attachments into a generic desire for Communist restoration is to disallow these very legitimate political concerns. Moreover, it is contrary to the actual dynamics I have documented here. The recent embrace of the term *nostalgia* to characterize villagers' specific discontents is enabled by the fact that a return is now impossible; it is the lack of that threat that validates nostalgia, or simply put, the impossibility of restoration allows them to be nostalgic. The foreclosure of return authorizes a generic Socialist nostalgia while the very concept delegitimizes the discontent that inspires it. This is, of course, a moot issue for many villagers because they have given up hope anyway, which is another condition for embracing the notion of nostalgia. If nostalgia always implies the impossibility of return, its appearance is furthering the project of neoliberalism. Linking these particulars to socialism is what makes it possible to call it nostalgia, while calling it nostalgic is of course to assume a neoliberal model of the world and the future.

So the Communist refusal of nostalgia sustained the possibility of a return to pre-Communist models, whereas the post-Socialist embrace of nostalgia has helped foreclose any Socialist restorations. Thus nostalgia gained resonance for villagers only after a long effort to sustain Socialist elements failed and when some sign of improvement suggested that there may be an alternative solution (although the nostalgics themselves do not expect to benefit much from it). Throughout the 1990s there was no use of the term *Socialist nostalgia* in the village because villagers were still committed to sustaining or reviving elements of socialism via mechanisms like voting and even collective action. By 2002 this was no longer sustainable, and the idea of nostalgia became an appropriate idiom for their vain hopes now reduced to memories. But nostalgia also resonated in its other [original] meaning as a visceral sickness or syndrome that by 2002 villagers had come to recognize in themselves and each other. As one male villager in his sixties put it, "Of course we have nostalgia—look what we've been through, look what they've done to us." In the context of (post)modernity, however, the nostalgia discourse can recast this significance into one of mere romantic reverie. A middle-aged village school teacher who had nodded in agreement with this man's comment later in the same conversation insisted that I should return in May for the village fair because "that's not nostalgia, that's *reality*" (my emphasis). Nonetheless, the prior, more potent meaning in a locale with obvious and extreme economic difficulties makes the beneficiaries of the new system less confident in nostalgia's unqualified effectiveness as a neoliberal facilitator and anxious about where it might lead instead. This has provoked a nuance in the commodification of Socialist nostalgia that insists on including damning elements, and also produced a more explicit counterproject of Socialist memory that is overwhelmingly negative. Socialist nostalgia can serve neoliberal ends, but in the difficult context of Bulgaria those who deploy it seem to want some qualifications and backup in case it gets out of hand. Neither of these would be necessary if these sentiments were in fact mere nostalgia and if Bulgaria were in the place it should be for nostalgia to work its political magic effortlessly and predictably.

Notes

1. This is a variation of the well-discussed "ostalgia" in eastern Germany (Bach 2002; Berdahl 1999). See also Klumbyte (n.d.) on related dynamics in Lithuania.
2. Based on conversations overheard at the restaurant, the common reaction by the few patrons who commented was one of amusement.
3. This is confirmed by Sarah Green's (2005: 212–15) investigation into environmental opinions in different rural districts of Greece along the Albanian border. Nostalgia was less evident in the areas that had benefited more from economic changes.
4. Marilyn Ivy (1995) implies as much when she distinguishes a nostalgia of style from modernist nostalgia.
5. The contrast with the restaurant Rio mentioned at the beginning of this essay (figures 2.1 and 2.2) confirms that nostalgia is marketable across class divisions.
6. One friend and colleague who was not sympathetic to socialism confided to me that she felt more comfortable on the Communist side of the restaurant, a testament perhaps to the lasting importance of practice.
7. Thanks to Yuson Jung for this information.

References

Bach, Jonathan. 2002. "'The Taste Remains': Consumption, (N)ostalgia, and the Production of East Germany." *Public Culture* 14 (3): 545–56.
Berdahl, Daphne. 1999. "'(N)Ostalgie' for the Present: Memory, Longing, and East German Things." *Ethnos* 64 (2): 192–211.
Boyer, Dominic. 2006. "*Ostalgie* and the Politics of the Future in Eastern Germany." *Public Culture* 18 (2): 361–81.
Boym, Svetlana. 2001. *The Future of Nostalgia*. New York: Basic Books.
Butler, Judith. 1997. *Excitable Speech: A Politics of the Performative*. New York: Routledge.
Creed, Gerald W. 1995a. "The Politics of Agriculture: Identity and Socialist Sentiment in Bulgaria." *Slavic Review* 54 (4): 843–68.
———. 1995b. "'An Old Song in a New Voice': Decollectivization in Bulgaria." In *East European Communities: The Struggle for Balance in Turbulent Times*, ed. David Kideckel, 25–46. Boulder, CO: Westview Press.

———. 1998. *Domesticating Revolution: From Socialist Reform to Ambivalent Transition in a Bulgarian Village*. University Park, PA: Pennsylvania State University Press.

———. 1999. "Deconstructing Socialism in Bulgaria." In *Uncertain Transition: Ethnographies of Change in the Postsocialist World*, ed. Michael Burawoy and Katherine Verdery, 223–43. Lanham: MD: Roman and Littlefield.

———. 2002. "Economic Crisis and Ritual Decline in Eastern Europe." In *Postsocialism: Ideals, Ideologies and Practices in Eurasia*, ed. C. M. Hann, 57–73. London: Routledge.

Davidson, Osha Gray. 1990. *Broken Heartland: The Rise of America's Rural Ghetto*. New York: Free Press.

Donkin, Mike. 2006. "Bulgaria Hit by Population Slump." BBC News. http://newsvote.bbc.co.uk/mpapps/pagetools/print/news.bbc.co.uk/2/hi/europe/6148244.stm. Accessed on November 16, 2006.

Dudley, Kathryn Marie. 2000. *Debt and Dispossession: Farm Loss in American's Heartland*. Chicago: University of Chicago Press.

Ghodsee, Kristen. 2004. "Red Nostalgia: Reconstructing Memories of Communism in Bulgaria." Paper presented at the Annual Soyuz Symposium. 13–14 February, Portland, Oregon.

Green, Sarah F. 2005. *Notes from the Balkans: Locating Marginality and Ambiguity on the Greek-Albanian Border*. Princeton, NJ: Princeton University Press.

Harvey, David. 1990. *The Condition of Postmodernity: An Enquiry into the Origins of Cultural Change*. Cambridge, MA: Blackwell.

Hebdige, Dick. 1979. *Subculture: The Meaning of Style*. London: Methuen.

Herzfeld, Michael. 1997. *Cultural Intimacy: Social Poetics in the Nation-State*. New York: Routledge.

Ivy, Marilyn. 1995. *Discourses of the Vanishing: Modernity, Phantasm, Japan*. Chicago: University of Chicago Press.

Jung, Yuson. 2005. "Shifting Perceptions of Standardized Food in Postsocialist Urban Bulgaria." Paper presented at the 37th National Convention of the American Association for the Advancement of Slavic Studies, Salt Lake City, UT. 3–6 November.

Klumbyte, Neringa. n.d. "The Soviet Sausage Renaissance." Unpublished manuscript.

Van Tilburg, M. A., A. J. Vingerhoets, and G. L. Van Heck. 1996. "Homesickness: A Review of the Literature." *Psychological Medicine* 26 (5): 899–912.

Wood, Nicholas. 2004. "Bulgaria Struggles to Remember Its Past: Youths Know Little of Communist Era." *International Herald Tribune*, 10 November, 3.

Yurchak, Alexei. 2005. *Everything Was Forever Until It Was No More: The Last Soviet Generation*. Princeton, NJ: Princeton University Press.

 3

Today's Unseen Enthusiasm
Communist Nostalgia for Communism in the Socialist Humanist Brigadier Movement

Cristofer Scarboro

In the 1960s and 1970s in Bulgaria the brigadier movement—a mass movement in which young Bulgarians were encouraged to volunteer in socially useful, collective labor—was a central theater for both negotiations about the manner of Socialist work and nostalgic evocation of a Communist past. At its height, first in the late 1940s and later from the mid-1960s until the fall of the Socialist state in 1989, nearly 500,000 young Bulgarians per year spent some of their summer in fields, construction sites, and factories to "build for the homeland" (*stroim za rodinata*). Throughout the movement, the brigadiers understood that their time on brigade was intended to result in their internalizing properly Socialist notions of work discipline: "We are building the pass (or the railway line, or the dam) and it is building us!" was the oft-quoted ethos of the brigadier movement.[1] What was being built, however, and the values the brigadier movement was intended to instill, changed dramatically during the Socialist humanist period of the 1960s and 1970s.

Recent scholarship of socialism paints an ideology working in two primary tenses: an ever-receding utopian future and a perpetually frozen present—as such, socialism is presented as a fundamentally anti-nostalgic space. For Svetlana Boym (2001), socialism was intrinsically a future-oriented discourse: nostalgia for a past capitalism was an impossible apostasy and, within an ideological framework relentlessly focused on the future, people had no time for past (or even present). Boym speaks of the immediate period after the October Revolution framed by an "invisible nationalization of time," where nostalgia was "not merely a bad word but a counterrevolutionary provocation." (2001: 59) After 1968, the dynamic of "memory and forgetting," made famous by Milan Kundera, allowed nostalgia, albeit for a pre-Communist time, to function as a source of dissent within Socialist space. Memory of the abuses of socialism also served as a reservoir of discontent within the Socialist system. (1999: 61)

Alexei Yurchak writes of late socialism as a period marked by a general feeling of living in an eternal present tense—a space in which both the great deeds of the past and the utopian future of communism seemed divorced from the realities of the everyday (Yurchak 2006). For Yurchak, a sense of routinization and ritual replaced the motion of past-present-future in both language and deeds. Official life in the Soviet Union became "immutable—rituals were reproduced, reports were filed, plans were fulfilled, and parades attended." Past and future faded fully from the picture until they reappeared, completely unexpectedly, in the mid-1980s (Yurchak 2006: 290). Both Yurchak and Boym's visions of time under socialism fully silence the past as an officially acceptable rhetorical device for those living under socialism.

My own reading of late socialism in Bulgaria echoes that of Yurchak with the (frozen) present as the dominant tense of the era. A profound shift in the official notions of time and space occurred in Bulgaria during the Socialist humanist period. In official ideology, the September 1944 revolution had severed ties with a backward, exploitative, terrifying capitalist past; the epochal days of the first postrevolutionary years had created the possibilities for developing socialism; and thus, Socialist humanists found themselves living in "developed socialism" waiting, and waiting, like materialist premillenialists for the advent of the final transformation of communism. Ironically, this eternal present tense, the ritualization and increasingly bourgeois nature of Socialist humanist brigadiers and society, was met by some Bulgarians at the time not with a desire to move time forward toward the Communist future but rather, to reflect with nostalgia and ennui for that "unseen enthusiasm" of the past. Communist nostalgia for "communism" was a product of the Socialist humanist system.

This chapter investigates attempts by brigadier memoirists, writing and remembering under Socialist humanism, to re-create early Socialist understandings of tense by detailing their own transformation under the early brigadier movement. Socialist humanism was defined in large part by the transition from "building socialism" in the immediate post-revolutionary years to "living in developed socialism" in which Bulgarians were to begin enjoying the fruits of their labor. As a result, the promotion of a Socialist good life under Socialist humanism was often couched in notions of living standards, free time, and the measured consumption of consumer goods. This desire for Socialist consumption and leisure came both from the public at large and from party officials—legitimacy on the part of the Socialist system was in large part measured by its ability to "deliver the goods" in terms of ease and comfort. While early Socialist ideology was furiously focused on the future—working at breakneck speed to hurry its arrival—Socialist humanism seemed to lose both the future and the past in a pleasant present tense. The brigadier memoirists sought to reconnect with the past to move Socialist humanism from its lethargic present.

Rhetorically at least, every generation of brigadiers encountered a movement that was geared to the problems of tense. While the early brigadier movement was focused on the future. laying the foundations for communism, the brigadier movement of the Socialist humanist period was about the present—living in, and enjoying, the delights of advanced socialism. As work receded and pleasure became a more prominent part of "living as a Communist," the meaning and message of the brigadier movement changed. Ritual became more important than work and the movement itself became understood as something of a "Socialist summer camp."

In many quarters this was seen as a very good thing. During my several trips to Bulgaria from 1996 to the present, Bulgarians were almost universally excited to tell stories from their Socialist humanist brigadier past filled with romance, youthful bad behavior, and fun. Post-Socialist memories of the brigadier movement generally fulfilled the role traditionally accorded to nostalgia. Few of my interlocutors were pining for a return to collective volunteer work (though some did). For most, talking about their time in the brigadier movement was an opportunity to relive and recount their youth.

Official memoirs of an earlier brigadier movement collected during the Socialist humanist period, however, often took umbrage at the seemingly lax and comfortable nature of the brigadier movement of the period. These memoirs were fundamentally about reintegrating past and future into the contemporary Socialist landscape. Contrary to understandings of socialism as an antinostalgic space where the past was continuously overcome, or the present lived, without a backward glance, Socialist humanism was fully engaged with the Socialist past. For the brigadier memoirists, writing about the early days of the brigadier movement entailed a wistful longing for the days of youthful enthusiasm and but also importantly imagined and (re)invented a horizon that led to the future. The memoirists' evocation of the past brigadier movement, meant to be emulated in spirit by the Socialist humanist brigadiers, was a nostalgic critique of the Bulgarian socialism of the 1960s and 1970s—a call for the return of the future voiced by recalling the past.

The early brigade movement (1947–1951) in which several important "national objects" were erected, was a series of monumental events, enacted under terrible conditions, on the backs of youthful enthusiasm. The brigadier enthusiasm and their finished products, including the Hainboaz pass, cut through the Stara Planina mountains, the Pernik–Voluiak rail line, and the city of Dimitrovgrad, that first Socialist city in Bulgaria, provided one of the foundational myths of the Bulgarian Socialist state. This so-called Golden Age of the brigadier movement also provided models for correct understandings of work and subjectivity. During this period, from the perspective of the party, proper Socialists were to be unwavering in their commitment to work, willing to sacrifice and struggle for the collective good.

The Socialist humanist period in Bulgaria, the mid-1960s to the early 1980s, radically transformed the brigade movement and memories of its early past. As the economy of the new Socialist state industrialized, there was less need for the type of brigade work of the early years. The collective good came to include personal pleasure. Work continued to be a central plank in the process of socializing Bulgarians in the intricacies of correct Socialist subjectivity, but the labor itself lost much of its romance. Rather than building mountain passes or laying foundations for entire cities, later brigadiers more often found themselves working as cheap labor in canning factories or harvesting fruits and vegetables on collective farms.

As the brigadier movement retreated from its era of heroic, romantic suffering, it underwent two significant transformations. First, the connection between the earlier and later brigadiers became increasingly ritualized. The movement itself came to emphasize the importance of symbols and stories to make up for the connection in real between the contemporary (1960s and 1970s) brigadier movement and its antecedents. The movement became increasingly (from the perspective of those in power at least) about performance rather than results in any measurable sense. While the brigadier movement from the beginning was concerned with perfomativity, it was, at the very least, also couched in the language of transforming the landscape as well as the brigadier. Dimitrovgrad and Hainboaz stood as symbols and products of early brigadier labor. In contrast, the products of the Socialist humanist movement were almost exclusively the brigadiers themselves—canned peppers were nice and, brigadier writers maintained, important to the economy, but they could not stand up, and were not held up, as symbols of the movement. The product, so to speak, was a series of "frozen forms"—the acts of going on "brigadier summer," wearing the blue shirt of the brigadier and singing brigadier songs—which brigadiers were to replicate. Ritualized participation in the building of socialism became the goal in itself. (Yurchak 2006)

Second, the brigadier movement itself began to echo the general trend towards leisure and entitlement of the Socialist humanist society writ large. The early brigadier movement, at least in official writings, was about sacrifice and deprivation; young people working hard to dramatically alter the landscape and social order of Bulgaria. A collective ethos permeated the movement as individuals transformed themselves into model workers. This was particularly true in gender relations and questions of leisure and consumption. The early brigadiers were to be stripped of their "soft bourgeois" (often coded "urban") manners and become steeled through labor as exceptional workers. Masculine traits and habits were esteemed and promoted above all others—the female brigadiers were expected to be transformed more than most into workers that were always understood as male or at least highly masculine. Later as the country as a whole became more urban and "developed," female brigadiers saw themselves moved into more traditionally feminine work: childcare in brigadier nurseries, cooking in brigadier canteens, cleaning the brigadier quarters. The work as a whole became less physically tasking—the "scientific technical revolution" created opportunities for brigadiers to work in their specialties and manual labor became more attuned to agroindustrial labor.

Fears that Bulgarian youth were losing their connection to manual labor led to the reinvigoration of the brigadier movement in the mid-1960s. Youth, earlier the builders of the new Socialist era, were during the Socialist humanist period increasingly regarded by Communist Party planners as victims of Western cultural practices and as purveyors of an unhealthy relationship to a life of ease and comfort. (Taylor 2004)

The advancement of the Socialist state had in effect made the brigadier movement, as it was understood and modeled, irrelevant. The Socialist humanist brigadier handbook promised a new vision of the movement: "Today they don't teach brigadiers the pick and shovel. These are the tools of unqualified labor and belong today in museums" (Lizhev 1972). The growth of the capacities of the Bulgarian economy and the emergence of an entirely Socialist generation transformed the brigadier movement. By the 1960s and 1970s, it was clear, however, that the time of Hainboaz, the "central epoch in the brigadier movement, had passed" (Lizhev 1972).

Despite this passage of time, brigadiers were asked to be "no less Revolutionary" than their precursors, to be worthy as a generation to the "rich Revolutionary, fighting traditions of the early brigadiers." To bear in their "hearts and souls the flaming patriotism, burning Revolutionary zeal and willingness for self-sacrifice of the past generations, who made great sacrifices for the triumph of Communist ideas and the freedom and happiness of the people" (Dyulgerov 1967: 59). With the triumph of socialism, neither the younger generation nor those calling it to "great deeds" were sure what that meant.

Beginning in the early 1970s, in an attempt to answer this question, the National Museum of the Brigadier Movement in Dimitrovgrad (later the Museum of Socialist Construction) began collecting the memories of those early brigadiers in the *okrug* (provinces) with the intention of establishing a permanent exhibition on the lives of those during the early, heroic days of building socialism in Bulgaria. The museum opened in 1951 as the last of the Dimitrovgrad brigadiers were leaving the city or settling into its new apartment blocks. By the 1970s the museum was already a set piece for Communist nostalgia. Initially conceived as an exposition space dedicated to demonstrating the past, present, and future projects of the brigadier movement, it came into being as the last of the great early national projects were being finished and the brigadier movement moved to smaller, local projects. Workers and students visiting the museum were to view the relics of a bygone age and vicariously participate in the Golden Age of the brigadier movement. The museum itself was intended to look backwards towards the future and shake the current generation of brigadiers from their present torpor. Nostalgia was a means of reinstituting the movement of time.

Memoirs of the brigadier movement were to serve as a central link in this project of communing with the sacred, an evocation of past in order to conjure collective memories and proper understanding of Socialist work (even if this understanding was understood to be definitively "past.") These memories, commissioned by the museum, were to serve the dual purpose of creating a historical archive of the experiences of the "epochal days" of the brigadier movement and through their dissemination establish a series of models upon which the younger generation of workers and brigadiers could access to come to terms with idealized early notions of Socialist work.[2] As such they were a nostalgic, generally negative, commentary on the state of the Bulgarian Socialist humanist project.

From the perspective of the brigadier memoirists, the Socialist humanist brigadier movement, intended as an inoculation from these vices of uncultured consumption and selfish idleness, tended to reproduce them. As the great deeds of the earlier brigadiers were replaced by the mundane tasks of the brigadier of a developed Socialist economy, the movement as a whole became important primarily as ritual—reinforcing through mass participation the collective memory of the brigadier past—the evocation of the extraordinary in the face of the banal. The memoirist sought to invert (or at least critique) this dynamic by presenting older visions of the passage of time illustrated by the remembrance their own past.

The authors of the short collected memoirs saw the brigadier experience as formative in the development of the Socialist country, their own development as individuals and as Socialist subjects. Their own participation in the building of "national objects" was seen as instrumental in creating the understanding of Bulgaria as a country of the future (one that by the 1960s and 1970s had arrived). The memoirs spoke to the new, to the technological prowess of centrally planned socialism, and to the possibilities of youthful enthusiasm on both a personal and national scale, enthusiasm that was powerful and defining.

Many of these memoirists found themselves living in the past and present simultaneously. The frozen present precluded fantasizing about the future (for many it had already arrived) and the present itself lacked vitality. Nadka Slavova Hadzhieva, who worked in Dimitrovgrad as a brigadier in 1950, often found herself transfixed and returned to the brigadier past during the ubiquitous "hours of rest" she endured in the 1970s. She often "looked back over her memories, like a movie before my eyes." The movement, for her, encapsulated the goals, dreams, and personalities of her generation, friends, and acquaintances and rendered the city a developed ruin. Walking around Dimitrovgrad, which she helped build and came to make her home, at every turn she encountered "the faces of the young people of our brigade: Ginka Mazeneva from the village of Zvinitsa near Kurdzhali, Nikola Prodanov from the village of Mihalkovo near Devin and others, tens, uncountable."[3] Remembering, the brigadiers conjured a disappeared world peopled by ghosts and spirits. A tangible feeling of loss and dissatisfaction permeates the memoirs—loss of their own youth, to be sure, but also the loss of socialism's early vitality. Evocation of a glorious past ensured that the present paled by comparison.[4]

Writing the memories for the museum powerfully evoked all the senses of the early brigadiers—the smell of sweat and rubber shoes mixed with the sound of songs around the campfire, the trumpet summoning them from their barracks, and the taste of potatoes and sausages eaten as sleep overcame tired and sore muscles. The overriding motif of the memoirs is, unsurprisingly, the passage of time, the past's irretrievability and its irreconcilability with the present. Nostalgia and ennui frame the works:

> As I write these lines, my mind travels back to the strong, burning summons of the brigadier march: "Come you thousands of youth / To our country of hope. ..." This march remains in the heart of every brigadier of that time, that strong patriotic time, and now as a retired teacher when I hear it, something washes over me, the most tender feelings, like a wave of magic.[5]

Mixed with this nostalgia was a sense that something important had retreated into the past and something was rotten in the movement of today. The memoirs stood as a rebuke to the youth of the Bulgarian Socialist humanist period who were seen by the authors as self-centered, unwilling to work, and retreating into a bourgeois idleness.

While Socialist humanist would-be brigadiers huddled in smoky cafes, the memoirs proclaimed the importance of the early brigadier contribution to the development of socialism in Bulgaria. The introductory paragraph of Staiko Talev Vukov's submission was typical: "We the young generation (early brigadiers) have much to be proud of. With our young enthusiasm many national objects were built as a contribution of our generation. 'Hainboaz,' the 'Pernik-Voluiak line,' the reservoir 'Koprinka' and many others. The youth from my time did their part to bring about the flowering of our Socialist homeland, the People's Republic of Bulgaria."[6] Unanswered was the nature of the Socialist humanist brigadier contribution. Returning to their thoughts of their years spent in the struggle for a new and better Bulgaria brought about a feeling that the "youthful enthusiasm" and "sense of purpose and struggle" displayed by the brigadiers in their youth and in their "young, new Socialist state" was absent from the children that were to inherit the mantle.[7]

For these brigadiers their participation in the movement was a central generational saga resulting in the simultaneous birth of a new Bulgaria and themselves. The stories were narratives of growth and transformation, of a new form of subjectivity and relation to the state, of new notions of work, progress, and self. Past, present, and future (all seen and related from a Socialist humanist present) are on full display in the narratives, one heading inexorably and with increasing speed into the other. The brigadier journey in the memoirs always began with the summons of the state to great deeds.[8] Notices on school doors and village squares marked a definitive break from their previous life—they left home, often without their parent's permission and over their objections to participate in the grand experiment.[9] For many it was their first time outside of the immediate region of their village and a step into the unknown. A new world was being built upon the sweat and toil of their labor, which was exhilarating, empowering, while at the same time befuddling—the signs and geographies of the new world were not yet mapped. Exiting the newly built Dimitrovgrad station to report for duty as a new brigadier, Kosta Evlogiev remembered his anxiety at trying to find the city where he was to report (he worked there on brigade from 1946–1950): "No one who had been with me on the train seemed to know how to get there." At the station he asked to no avail for some time "which way I needed to walk to get to Dimitrovgrad. Finally, a person explained that Dimitrovgrad was being built on the site of three villages here on the banks of the Maritsa (the station was built where the village of Rakovski used to sit)." Pointing in the direction of the newly built factory, Vulkan, the man explained, "There, there is Dimitrovgrad."[10] The future was encroaching on the present with brisk clarity.

Remembering, the Golden Age brigadiers immediately understood that they were participating in something new, immense, and transformative. The young brigadiers traveled to work sites by special trains filled with young people. Atanas Aleksandrov Atev could not hide his excitement upon preparing to leave for the first of his work sites in the Lovetch region. He was one of the few early brigadiers who informed his parents of his intention to join the movement and they, "being poor people, were not opposed."[11] After walking for two days to reach the office of the RMS then in charge of organizing the brigades, Atev stood barefoot before the secretary with a request to join the youth brigade. His happiness increased when he saw that eight other boys from his village had likewise decided to join up. He explains his departure thus:

> The day came to leave. Close friends and family and others sent us off from the station—as a surprise the train from Lovetch was greatly overfilled with boys and girls. In one wagon were the students singing; in another you could hear young revolutionary songs. Everywhere flags were waving. There were bodies surrounding me, on top of me, my body was frozen (out of pleasure and surprise) and I couldn't move but I didn't complain. We were all of one feeling a readiness to do everything requested of us.[12]

The journey was from the routine to the extraordinary and was enough to bring about a temporary paralysis to those that made the trip.

A new era of order and hard work in order to speed the arrival of the future is written throughout the memoirs. Arriving at Levski station, Atev and the brigadiers walked to their camp. Atev had "no idea how many kilometers it was but it was enough." Bringing little from his earlier life, Atev walked to the brigadier camp with only one box on his shoulder carrying an ironed shirt. The troop moved on without a word: "We were exhausted but could think of nothing better. This is how it was in the camp 'Vasil Levski.' We never knew what time it was since none of us had a watch." After unpacking his shirt and a short break spent drinking a glass of water, a trumpet sounded announcing the arrival of the brigade commander. The commander—Fikish, a former partisan—"briefly informed the group of the order and discipline that we were absolutely expected to maintain and let us know that tomorrow we would be heading to the work site."[13]

The trumpet and commander welcomed the brigadiers to a new life of order and discipline, toil and triumph. The commanders were often presented as early citizens of a new age. They were often heroes of the partisan struggle or early Communist martyrs to the previous "monarcho-fascist regime" who in state/party mythology bore the initial birth pains of the new world. The commanders often took a parental role on the life of the new brigadiers and were seen in the memoirs as formative in the creation of their new selves. Subi Nastrov Kostov's commander "was famous to all: Asen Mihailov, who was on the frontlines of the fatherland war and injured when shrapnel entered his head. He had a phenomenal memory for names, which he attributed to his wounds. 'I am a miracle of modern medicine,' he would say," emblematic of the marvels of a new age.[14]

The leadership provided food, clothing, and shelter—which many of the brigadiers still remembered as singularly important. Atanas Atev recounted receiving shoes as one of the most important moment in his brigadier experience. After the "difficult war years, barefoot times, having shoes was a great luxury." Being awarded an apple and an undershirt (*potnik*) as a model shockworker (*udarnik*), he was moved to tears. He explained, "Today after thirty years of brigadiers' labor, when every citizen of our country is well pleased with absolutely everything, this might not seem much."[15]

The commander set the working plans, norms, and orders for the day. Asen Mihailov set his brigadiers off with work instructions to the music of Bach and Schumann—setting an early example of the well-rounded individual that would come to be the ideal in the later brigadier eras. Generally when it was "time for us to get up with the sun," he would wake the brigadiers up with a "waltz preformed by woodwinds." Then, once the trumpet sounded, the commander "would quickly and loudly gather us and take us outside for our morning gymnastics. He would give us our instructions for the day. After that we would head to work with our picks and shovels on our shoulders."[16]

The work site itself could prove strange and new. Workers used to farming small village landholdings were thrown into a massive communal work environment with military discipline. While the tasks themselves were generally straightforward—carrying sand from the bank of the river in wheelbarrows, hewing rock, laying concrete—the magnitude and "scientific rationalism" overwhelmed the brigadiers. Unknown and unheard-of engineers and managers peopled the site along with strange machines. Subi Kostov on the Mlada Gvardiia brigade in Dimitrovgrad in 1950 was impressed with his first and only conversation about the future with the brigade's lead engineer: "I don't remember the name of the engineer but I do remember that he told me that the machines for the future factory were to be imported from Italy and cost millions of eggs."[17] The brigadier commander and larger state would make the incomprehensible future possible and intelligible.

Suffering was a central ethos of the early brigadier movement—difficulties to be overcome with youthful enthusiasm for the victory of socialism. Aleksandra Georgieva Paleva, working at Hainboaz from 1946 to 1950, saw the struggle as a way to distinguish herself and her village from those less prepared for toil. She explained:

> The work was very hard. We were digging the ground with picks, shovels, and our fingers. I was used to it because I worked very hard in my own village like all the other girls. You could tell us because the girls from my village had switched out the light wheelbarrows that they gave us for the heavy ones. I don't remember what the norms were at Hainboaz. If I am not mistaken, however, they were at least twice as hard as the work we did in the village.[18]

Village workers were often contrasted favorably with those from the cities who were unschooled in urban labor. Much of the early brigadier process was engaged with countering *embourgeoisment* and the excesses of a urban, leisured lifestyle (this is rather ironic as Bulgaria was a very much a rural village society prior to 1944).[19]

Often the facilities were inadequate or missing. Arriving in Dimitrovgrad in 1947, Tsonka Hristova Ivanova's brigade's first task was to build themselves a quick shelter. "The brigade promised to quickly build barracks near the station on the right side of the Maritsa River in the direction of Haskovo."[20] While Kosta Evlogiev noted that in the barracks, "we were at home and felt at home," and tried hard to make the camp "spick and span, painting the barracks inside and out with lime" and making a "little garden with slogans written out with white pebbles," the conditions were deplorable:

> During the winter it was very cold. We only received our winter jackets, pants, and gloves at the end of winter. There was no bathroom anywhere. During the spring a sanitary train arrived and then we washed and bathed. During the winter the fountains froze and there was no

water for drinking and washing. I remember melting snow in the dining hall for drinking and shaving. This only worked, of course, when it snowed. The brigade was "paid" but the money was very little because we had to purchase food, heating, lighting, and other things.[21]

The food was generally remembered as "very bad," and those brigadiers who were able supplemented their meals with deliveries from their families. The work was taxing, and the brigadiers were hungry enough that they "devoured everything they brought us" despite its taste.[22] The clothing that the brigadiers received was often late in arriving (easier borne in the summer than winter) and of very poor quality. Tsonka Hristova remembered waiting for two weeks before receiving her brigadier uniform and rubber boots, a moment she remembered with great pride—she still had her emblematic blue brigadier shirt decades later. The rubber boots, however, were something of a disaster. "Nearly every brigadier only wore these shoes for one or two days before they became oily on the feet and we threw them away. A small part of the group received new, better shoes from their parents, but for the rest of us during the entire forty-five days that we were on this brigade we went barefoot. I well remember how after returning to my village after the brigade, for many weeks I could not wear any shoes because my feet were ruined."[23] Aleksandra Paleva dryly summed up her material circumstances while on brigade: "Our facilities were very bad, but it is important to note that there were no accidents in our group."[24]

Suffering and deprivations, the dislocations and excitement of creating a new world, were central motifs of the Golden Age memoirs—they were rhetorically absent understandings of the new Socialist humanist world. Sacrifice for the building of a glorious future had been replaced by the enjoyment of its arrival—the meaning of the brigadier movement, its purpose, replaced by more mundane ritual and reading of earlier exploits. The excitement of bringing the future into the present was replaced by the simple pleasures of a Socialist bourgeois life.

Kosta Evlogiev summarized the purpose of the exercise of writing memoirs for the benefit of brigadiers to come. The motivation of the brigadiers—their desire to work, to participate in something larger than themselves—was central to the early brigadiers' memories of their past:

> I have often wondered this question: Why did the youth come here? What drove them to come? What kind of people were they? Enthusiasts or maniacs? Idealists or fools? Patriots or opportunists? Some came because they understood that it was a place to find work. Others were drawn by the feeling of optimism. Still others came to escape from the police hoping that being an outstanding brigadier would grant them a new life, though they were the exception. The largest part of the people were workers and

villagers who had heard that something big was going on here. To come here and to be a part of it was a point of honor.[25]

It was that desire, that participation in the heroic, that point of honor and enthusiasm—today unseen—that was the general leitmotif of early brigadier memories. Ironically, these memoirs themselves became part of the ritualization of the brigadier movement that they so often bemoaned. Socialist humanist brigadiers and school children came to the museum and read the memoirs as evidence of a past divorced from the present developed socialism. The heroic act of transformation had made toil and struggle irrelevant in a transformed world—rendering the memoirs a nostalgic genre.

Notes

1. Informatsiia na muzeia na sotsialisticheskoto stroitelstvo ot 1.I.1968 g. do 31.VII.1968 god., Haskovo State Archive, f. 1101, i.o. 1, a.e. 3, pp. 30.
2. The brigadier memories were intended for publication. For some reason, the project never got beyond their use as documents in the museum's archive and as a source in the creating of exhibits (often extended quotations from the memories were included in the exhibitions).
3. Kolektsiia "Dokumenti, snimki i spomeni za brigadirskoto dvizhenie 1946–1950," "Spomeni ot Nadka Slavova Hadzhieva—brigadirka v Dimitrovgrad prez 1950 g.," Haskovo State Archive, f. 1325, op. 2, a.e. 32.
4. "Now I understand that the rail line is regularly used and we the former brigadiers go out to meet it in our memories—an unconscious happiness brings me back to the brigade. We have given our contribution to creating this line." Kolektsiia "Dokumenti, snimki i spomeni za brigadirskoto dvizhenie 1946–1950," "Spomeni ot Bano Petkov Banov ot Dimitrovgrad na uchastieto mu v brigadirskoto dvizhenie prez iuli 1948–49 g. na obekt 'zh. P. liniia Samuil Silitra," Dimitrovgrad Museum, f. 1325, op. 1, a.e. 62
5. Kolektsiia "Dokumenti, snimki i spomeni za brigadirskoto dvizhenie 1946–1950," "Spomeni ot Nadka Slavova Hadzhieva—brigadirka v Dimitrovgrad prez 1950 g.," Haskovo State Archive, f. 1325, op. 2, a.e. 32.
6. Kolektsiia "Dokumenti, snimki i spomeni za brigadirskoto dvizhenie 1946–1950," "Spomeni ot Staiko Talev Vukov ot selo Stambolovo za uchastieto mu v brigadirskoto dvizhenie prez 1946 g. na 'Hain Boaz,' 'Mlada gvardiia'—Dimitrovgrad prez 1950 g.," Haskovo State Archive, f. 1325, op. 1, a.e. 65.
7. Kolektsiia "Dokumenti, snimki i spomeni za brigadirskoto dvizhenie 1946–1950," "Spomeni ot Nadka Slavova Hadzhieva—brigadirka v Dimitrovgrad prez 1950 g.," Haskovo State Archive, f. 1325, op. 2, a.e. 32. These feeling permeated most of the memoirs. In particular see those of Kosta Evlogiev (Haskovo State Archive, f. 1325, op. 1, a.e. 57); Raino Delchev Vukov (Haskovo State Archive, f. 1325, op. 1, a.e. 60); and Aleksandra Georgieva Paleva, (Dimitrovgrad Museum f. 5269).

8. Kolektsiia "Dokumenti, snimki i spomeni za brigadirskoto dvizhenie 1946–1950," "Spomeni na Todor Bancheev Todev ot selo Trakiets za uchastieto mu v brigadirskoto dvizhenie prez 1947 g. na obekt 'Zh. P. liniia Lovetch-Troian'," Haskovo State Archive, f. 1325, op. 2, a.e. 66.
9. Typical is the example of Tsonka Ivanova Hristova from Liubimetz, who left home much to the chagrin of her parents who were counting on her help in the fields during the summer: "When the call went out to join the national brigade in building Dimitrovgrad, I signed up without my parents knowing; they were waiting for me to join them during the summer vacation to help them with their work in the fields, particularly the harvesting of tobacco." Kolektsiia "Dokumenti, snimki i spomeni za brigadirskoto dvizhenie 1946–1950," "Spomeni ot Tsonka Ivanova Hristova—brigadirka v Dimitrovgrad prez 1947 g.," Haskovo State Archive, f. 1325, op. 2, a.e. 31.
10. Kolektsiia "Dokumenti, snimki i spomeni za brigadirskoto dvizhenie 1946–1950," "Spomeni ot Kosta Evlogiev ot Dimitrovgrad na uchastieto mu v brigadirskoto dvizhenie prez 1948–49 g. v brigade 'Al. Matrosov,' 'Mlada gvardiia'—Dimitrovgrad prez 1950 g.," Haskovo State Archive, f. 1325, op. 1, a.e. 57.
11. Poverty and wealth was often used as a metaphor for the entire brigadier project and the transformation of Bulgaria that their work was bringing about. The brigadiers contrasted their own poor condition and status prior (and Bulgaria's) to becoming brigadiers with their current status (retired engineers, teachers, and doctors).
12. "Dokumenti, snimki i spomeni za brigadirskoto dvizhenie 1946–1950," "Spomeni ot Atanas Aleksandrov Atev," Dimitrovgrad Museum f. 5269, Kolektsiia "Dokumenti, snimki i spomeni za brigadirskoto dvizhenie 1946–1950," "Spomeni ot Tsonka Ivanova Hristova—brigadirka v Dimitrovgrad prez 1947 g.," Haskovo State Archive, f. 1325, op. 2, a.e. 31.
13. "Dokumenti, snimki i spomeni za brigadirskoto dvizhenie 1946–1950," "Spomeni ot Atanas Aleksandrov Atev," Dimitrovgrad Museum f. 5269.
14. Ibid.
15. Ibid.
16. Kolektsiia "Dokumenti, snimki i spomeni za brigadirskoto dvizhenie 1946–1950," "Spomeni ot Cubi Nastrov Kostov za uchastieto mu v maldezhkata stroitelna brigada 'Mlada gvardiia'—Dimitrovgrad prez 1950 g.," Haskovo State Archive, f. 1325, op. 1, a.e. 56; Kolektsiia "Dokumenti, snimki i spomeni za brigadirskoto dvizhenie 1946–1950," "Spomeni ot Staiko Talev Vukov ot selo Stambolovo za uchastieto mu v brigadirskoto dvizhenie prez 1946 g. na 'Hain Boaz,' 'Mlada gvardiia'—Dimitrovgrad prez 1950 g.," Haskovo State Archive, f. 1325, op. 1, a.e. 65.
17. Kolektsiia "Dokumenti, snimki i spomeni za brigadirskoto dvizhenie 1946–1950," "Spomeni ot Subi Nastrov Kostov za uchastieto mu v maldezhkata stroitelna brigada 'Mlada gvardiia'—Dimitrovgrad prez 1950 g.," Haskovo State Archive, f. 1325, op. 1, a.e. 56.
18. Kolektsiia "Dokumenti, snimki i spomeni za brigadirskoto dvizhenie 1946–1950," "Spomeni ot Aleksandra Georgieva Paleva," Dimitrovgrad Museum f. 5269.

19. 24.7% of the population was urban in 1946. Robert N. Taaffe, "Population Structure."
20. Kolektsiia "Dokumenti, snimki i spomeni za brigadirskoto dvizhenie 1946–1950," "Spomeni ot Tsonka Ivanova Hristova—brigadirka v Dimitrovgrad prez 1947 g.," Haskovo State Archive, f. 1325, op. 2, a.e. 31.
21. Despite his assurance that "no one however complained about the conditions asked about the pay because they were not the important things. More important was where we were situated in the brigade, who were deemed the best workers and other things—to win emulation, to win an award was why we worked." During the cold months the brigade dropped from 200 members to 77. Kolektsiia "Dokumenti, snimki i spomeni za brigadirskoto dvizhenie 1946–1950," "Spomeni ot Kosta Evlogiev ot Dimitrovgrad na uchastieto mu v brigadirskoto dvizhenie prez 1948–49 g. v brigade 'Al. Matrosov,' 'Mlada gvardiia'—Dimitrovgrad prez 1950 g.," Haskovo State Archive, f. 1325, op. 1, a.e. 57.
22. Kolektsiia "Dokumenti, snimki i spomeni za brigadirskoto dvizhenie 1946–1950," "Spomeni ot Aleksandra Georgieva Paleva," Dimitrovgrad Museum f. 5269.
23. Kolektsiia "Dokumenti, snimki i spomeni za brigadirskoto dvizhenie 1946–1950," "Spomeni ot Tsonka Ivanova Hristova—brigadirka v Dimitrovgrad prez 1947 g.," Haskovo State Archive, f. 1325, op. 2, a.e. 31.
24. Kolektsiia "Dokumenti, snimki i spomeni za brigadirskoto dvizhenie 1946–1950," "Spomeni ot Aleksandra Georgieva Paleva," Dimitrovgrad Museum f. 5269.
25. Kolektsiia "Dokumenti, snimki i spomeni za brigadirskoto dvizhenie 1946–1950," "Spomeni ot Kosta Evlogiev ot Dimitrovgrad na uchastieto mu v brigadirskoto dvizhenie prez 1948–49 g. v brigade 'Al. Matrosov' 'Mlada gvardiia'—Dimitrovgrad prez 1950 g.," Haskovo State Archive, f. 1325, op. 1, a.e. 57.

References

Boym, Svetlana. 2001. *The Future of Nostalgia*. New York: Basic Books.
Dyulgerov, Nikolai. 1967. *The Dimitrov Young Communist League in Bulgaria*. Sofia: Foreign Languages Press.
Kundera, Milan. 1999. *The Book of Laughter and Forgetting*. New York: Harper Perennial Modern Classics.
Lizhev, Tosho. 1972. "Na brigade prez liato." *Narodna mladezh*, br. 299, 16 December, 3.
Taffe, Robert N. 1990. "Population Structure," in *Südosteuropa-handbuch, Bulgarien*, vol. VI, Ed. By Klaus-Detlev Grothusen, Vandenhaoeck & Ruprecht in Gottingen.
Taylor, Karin. 2004. *Lennon Not Lenin: Youth Between Socialist Discourse and Realities in Bulgaria of the 1960s and 70s*. PhD dissertation, Geisteswissenschaftliche Fakultät, Karl-Franzens-Universität Graz.
Yurchak, Alexei. 2005. *Everything Was Forever Until It Was No More: The Last Soviet Generation*. Princeton, NJ: Princeton University Press.

 4

Nostalgia for the JNA?
Remembering the Army in the Former Yugoslavia

Tanja Petrović

At the end of the 1980s and the beginning of the 1990s, it was not only socialism that was dying out in the former Yugoslavia: in a process that has been considered "in many ways the most tragic transition to post-communism" (Holmes 1997: 291), the country itself disintegrated through violent ethnic conflicts. Almost two decades after the disintegration of the federation, all six former Yugoslav republics are independent national states, but their citizens still share memories of the common past: experiences dating from the Yugoslav period, which are for the middle generation simultaneously experiences of socialism, connect people who are nowadays divided by national borders and who even fought against each other during the 1990s.

Most men from the former Yugoslavia presently older than thirty-five years share the experience of having served in the Yugoslav People's Army (*Jugoslovenska narodna armija,* JNA). Many of these men may be recognized by a visible souvenir from their army days—a tattooed heart on their arms with the inscription "JNA," and dates denoting the start and end of their service. Dragan, a Macedonian who presently lives in Slovenia and works there as a software engineer, served in the JNA in the late 1980s in the Croatian town of Pula; he also has such a tattoo on his right arm. In summer he frequently travels from Ljubljana to the nearby Croatian coast, to the same area where he did his military service. Each time he goes to the beach he covers the JNA tattoo with an adhesive bandage, afraid that some Croats might express a negative reaction to the symbol of the once common army that was widely identified as an instrument of Serbian aggression in Croatia in the 1990s.

Tattoos are visual markers that indicate belonging to a group of people who performed service in the JNA; less explicit signs of membership in this group reveal themselves through cultural practices of narrating memories from the army in the form of "army stories." Many of these stories seem to fit a familiar mold concerning their contents and structure of narration, regardless of their narrators' social and educational backgrounds, and their authors—similarly to soldiers all around the world—like telling them despite the fact their audience usually finds them boring. The Croatian writer Miljenko Jergović describes this storytelling habit in the following way:

> Sooner or later, every Croatian male feels the need to tell of his experience in the Yugoslav National Army. We mostly do that in the most inappropriate social situations. Then the ladies scold us and roll their eyes and those nice boys, who were released or have served their time recently by cleaning windows in dorms or bringing kindergarten teachers snacks from the shop, think that our stories are completely outdated. Fuck, perhaps they are right, those who object because of their conscience, but we cannot give up a year of our lives just like that, just because it is not trendy anymore. (Jergović n.d.)

"Army stories" of the former JNA soldiers are an example of a gendered narrative practice: they are essentially "male stories" because they are told only by men[1] and—more importantly—they serve a narrative function of performing masculinity.[2] According to Brickell (2005: 37), "those performing masculinity are ... constructs and constructors of symbolic orders; simultaneously productive and produced, loci of action and participants of interaction, they may perpetuate and/or resist hegemonic social arrangements." Masculinity is therefore "performed within a restricting order of symbolic meaning, constantly negotiating, producing and reproducing what it entails to 'do masculinity' in relation to the surrounding culture and social structures" (Andersson 2008: 140). This may also explain pervasiveness of the "JNA stories" in the post-Yugoslav reality: they are still around despite their outdatedness and impossibility to fit into current dominant narratives, because for their authors they are means to prove, emphasize, negotiate—all in all to *perform*—their masculinity.

What is common to both the visible signs of belonging to the group of JNA soldiers, such as tattoos, and the narrated memories of the army days, is a discomfort felt by those who possess them, who feel that their memories are outdated, problematic, and inadequate in the new post-Yugoslav circumstances. The JNA was an institution organized and ideologically shaped both as a central embodiment and main agent of the unity of all people living in Socialist Yugoslavia. It was considered as one of the most important pillars of Yugoslav unity, and often referred to as "the forge of Yugoslavism" (*kovačnica jugoslovenstva*) and a "school of brotherhood and unity" (Bjelajac 1999: 13). To strengthen the idea of unity among all Yugoslav peoples, the JNA had a policy of sending recruits as far as possible from their homes, always to another Socialist republic. Warren Zimmermann, who witnessed the disintegration of the country as the last US ambassador to the Socialist Yugoslavia, stresses in his memoirs the fact that the JNA was the most Yugoslav of all institutions, since "people from all parts of Yugoslavia were meeting there" (Zimmermann 1996: 64). In the post-Yugoslav states and societies, where the pluralistic ideology of Yugoslavism[3] was replaced by national(ist) ones, official discourses, through which criteria of acceptability and normativity are set and which are supposed to simultaneously reflect and create attitudes of the majority of society members, were highly unfavorable toward any positive attitude regarding the legacy of the Yugoslav state and society, as well as any manifestations of an inherited supranational identity. In academic and intellectual discourses dealing with these societies, it is often stressed that this replacement was followed by processes such as the suppression of positive memories of the common Yugoslav past or their erasure, "collective amnesia" (Jansen 2005: 220) or "confiscation of memory" (Ugrešić 2002: 275). Any positive stance toward the Yugoslav past is seen as a lack of patriotism and is pejoratively marked as "Yugo-nostalgia."

Closely associated with the ideology of "brotherhood and unity" of the former multinational state, the JNA is seen as one of the most salient symbols of Yugoslav socialism; it was, in addition, symbolically opposed to the newly established national armies that, as Miroslav Hadžić stresses, had an essential role in the formation of national states (Hadžić 2001: 173). Under the pressure of prevailing views and ideologies in the Yugoslav successor states, a positive identification with a JNA soldier is perceived as problematic even by the former soldiers themselves. On the other hand, this identification is persistent despite its conflict with the other identities an individual may bear in the former Yugoslav lands, and with national identity above all. The contested nature of the memories of JNA service is a consequence of the end of socialism, which in the former Yugoslav lands coincided with the end of the common state and was followed by outbreak of ethnic violence. If socialism had never disappeared and the former Yugoslavia still existed, these memories of the JNA would be just another kind of story about an exceptional male experience from the past—quite universal, rather boring for everyone except other men who shared the same experience, and not widely recognized as a manifestation of nostalgia. In the new circumstances, however, those who consider the fact that they were JNA soldiers to be an important part of their past and of their identity, just like all others who are not ready to give up their personal memories from the Yugoslav and Socialist period, are readily marked as Yugo-nostalgics. This post-Yugoslav and post-Socialist context makes it possible for a positive attitude toward the JNA to be labeled as nostalgia, despite the fact that it does not imply any desire to restore the previous state of affairs. The former JNA soldiers would by no means want to return to military service; on the contrary, in serving in the army, soldiers could hardly wait for it to be over (and probably a significant number of them would not have gone into the army at all had they had a choice). The mandatory "requisite" of every soldier was a pocket calendar for counting down the days left until the end of the service. The internal hierarchy among the soldiers was also based on the quantity of days left until the end of the service: "freshmen" were in the worst position, while those close to the end enjoyed numerous privileges. What makes possible a kind of nostalgia toward the army days to occur is exactly awareness of irreversibility of that experience: as Creed persuasively argues in this volume, "the term *nostalgia* only resonates ... when there is no chance of going back." Because of this condition, even the remembering of traumatic experiences is not void of nostalgia: so Albanian writer Fatos Lubonja (2002) speaks on the nostalgia he feels for the seventeen years he spent in Communist prisons, which was doubtlessly the most difficult time of his life.

Another paradox related to the marking of memories of the JNA experience as "Yugo-nostalgia" lies in the fact that, in discourses on post-Socialist nostalgia, those marked as nostalgics are generally accused of weakness and an incapability to adapt to the new circumstances and to find their way around in a rapidly changing world, while on the contrary there is a widespread attitude among former Yugoslavs that JNA service was longer lasting, tougher, and more serious and demanding than contemporary service in the armies of the Yugoslav successor states. The latter are usually seen as "too soft," "not hard enough to make real men from immature boys," and "a kindergarten in comparison to the real army." In everyday communication in Slovenia, one can frequently hear the question, "Have you served in the real army [meaning JNA] or in the Slovenian army?" A similar attitude may be noticed in the other former Yugoslav republics, even in Croatia, where the Croatian national army got a heroic aura of defender and liberator of the nation (from the Serbs who were equated with the JNA) during the war in the 1990s.

This narrative of the JNA as "the only real army"—as opposed to today's existing national armies in the former Yugoslav lands—may be interpreted in manifold ways. It is certainly a part of nostalgia toward the past, universal and found in all domains of life; in such a discourse of nostalgia, which Michael Herzfeld labels "structural nostalgia" (Herzfeld 2004), the selectively remembered past is seen as better and laden with real qualities and values that do not exist in the present. In the post-Yugoslav context, similarly to other expressions of remembering life in the Socialist period, this nostalgic narrative of the JNA experience obtains additional quality and weight: it becomes contested and engages in a dialogue with dominant discourses that emphasize the importance of national armies for the "national projects" in each of the former republics, aiming to constitute them ideologically as the main factors of protection of the nation and its stability. The opposition between the JNA and the "new armies" may also be interpreted in the more general context of "changing masculinity" in the modern world: an initiation into manhood through the successful accomplishment of "tasks of endurance, infliction of pain and suffering" (Segal 1990: 32) is found in "primitive societies," but was also a characteristic of many mandatory military services in the world.[4] In the post-Yugoslav societies, the shortening of the duration of mandatory military service, its abolition, the performance of the service near one's home, as well as the possibility of civil service all resulted in the disappearance of the last collective initiation rite, which the army was perceived as being. According to the opinion of one of my Slovenian interviewees, it was not a good decision to abolish the mandatory army service in Slovenia for, as he stresses, "people still used to say in the countryside: 'If one is not good enough for the army, one cannot be good enough for a wife either'."

Narrating Memories of the Yugoslav Army

The stigma of the JNA in the former Yugoslav lands did not prevent former JNA soldiers from remembering and telling their army memories. They are a frequent ingredient of all-men casual conversations and may be triggered by a plethora of geographical and personal names, objects, smells, and tastes (*You live in Ljubljana? I served the army there in 1977; I heard about Hanka Paldum for the first time while serving the army in Kolašin; You are from Belgrade? My best friend from the army was from there; This food reminds me of days I spent serving the JNA; Each time I hear this song I recall my JNA service.* …), while characteristic army jargon and events constituting army life are still recognizable in the former Yugoslav space and are subject to narrative reproduction and an inexhaustible source of humor.

In 2005 I started a project[5] that aimed to show the ways in which the memories of former JNA soldiers of their army service are shaped, what the convergences and divergences between them are with regard to various ethnic and social backgrounds, and to what extent these memories are reshaped by developments from 1990 on and influenced by dominant discourses and ideologies. I made a number of interviews with former JNA soldiers from all the former Yugoslav republics and thus obtained narratives on their JNA experiences. In the open interviews, after showing my interest for their experiences in the army, I gave my interviewees freedom to shape their stories in ways that they found appropriate and to choose parts of their experience that they considered relevant to emphasize.[6] The obtained narratives are very uniform according to their structure and contents. The former JNA soldiers usually build their "army stories" along the following three storylines:[7] narratives of male friendship, "school of life" narratives, and narratives of subversive strategies undertaken by soldiers during the army service in order to make it easier or simply to confront the authorities. In the most widespread narrative about the institution of the army in the former Yugoslavia, the JNA is seen as a school of life that makes mature and responsible men capable of facing the challenges of adulthood. By the former soldiers, JNA service is perceived as an initiation necessary for boys to become men: the harder the experience of military service, the more one can demonstrate his masculinity. Such an image of the JNA was also a part of the official narrative, and was reproduced in Socialist popular culture as well: the film *Vojnikova ljubav* (Soldier's Love, 1976) is about a young Belgrade playboy, a spoiled child of a rich family, who changes for the better after performing service in the JNA.[8]

New means of communication enabled by the Internet have made possible an exchange of the JNA memories among a broad group of former JNA soldiers across the current national borders. A number of Internet forums in all parts of the former Yugoslavia contain discussions on memories and experiences from the JNA; these discussions may be found in Croatia (http://www.forum.hr in January 2006), Bosnia and Herzegovina (http://www.forum.bljesak.info in April 2005), Serbia (http://www.forum.b92.net in September 2004), Slovenia (http://yugokronika.mojforum.si/yugokronika-forum-15.html, topics regarding the JNA discussed in 2007 in 2008, accessed 24 November 2008). Thematic nuclei of forum posts are the same as those in narrated army stories. Members of these forums post information about where and when they performed their JNA service; they try to make contact with their army mates or at least with those who served in the army at the same place or time; they tell anecdotes from their army days, ridicule characteristic army jargon, and compete with each other in measuring "the extent" of their manhood by comparing the toughness of their service and thus reproducing the widespread narrative on the JNA service as a school of life that made "men of boys."

One of the most salient features of both the Internet forum posts on the JNA service and the orally transmitted memories of personal experience in the JNA is their precise temporal and spatial definition. Temporal distance notwithstanding, most former JNA soldiers start their army story with the exact dates of the start and the end of their army service, as well as the place where they performed it (name of city, name of barracks). They are also able to name most of their army mates and officers. Analyzing male talk, Jennifer Coates detected orientation toward details as a common characteristic of male stories and how "the language of these stories accomplishes masculinity" (Coates 2003: 45). The attention to detail, she stresses, "constitutes an important strategy in men's conversation: it enables men to avoid talk of a more personal nature."[9]

While attention to details certainly helps men to avoid emotional expressions in their narratives, it seems that in the case of the former Yugoslav soldiers' stories, this insistence on details and factuality has the primary function of stressing the extraordinariness of the army experience for their own personal lives (both in a positive or negative manner). The factuality also enables—when circumstances allow it—the establishment of solidarity among those who shared the same experience and provides evidence of closeness and the limits of the "army world": many years after performing military service, it seems very important for the former soldiers to identify their army mates, or at least to detect others who served in the same barracks, who knew the same officers, etc.—and the Internet is a means of communication that enables (re)establishing these connections.

Membership in the group of former JNA soldiers is revealed as a dominant aspect of the identity of people participating in the forum, while their national identity does not play an essential role, making it possible for Serbs, Croats, and others from the former Yugoslav nations to exchange their army experiences despite the fact that some of them fought against each other in the wars in the 1990s. While they remember both good and bad things from the army, their ethnicity does not play a significant role in the way that this memory is shaped. They sporadically stress (or reject) the usual stereotypes that various Yugoslav nations had about each other: that Slovenes are rather reserved, Albanians stick exclusively to each other and are uneducated/illiterate, etc.[10] The former soldiers' comments about the behavior and characteristics of their army mates from various parts of the former Yugoslavia vary highly depending on the place of the army service and personal experience. Here are some examples found on http://www.forum.hr:

> There were really good guys among the soldiers. The Macedonians especially were OK. On the other hand, my God. ... There was a great compe-

> tition for jerk of the day. Overbearing and stupid fellows from Belgrade, Sarajevo, Montenegrins. ... If I would have to chose the most stupid ones, it would definitely be Serbs from Bosnia. [11]
>
> Macedonians ... horror ... Bosnian Serbs were the most stupid. ... Guys from Belgrade were not bad ... as well as Slovenians. Bosnian Muslims were the most disciplined. Their corporal was great ... the best was a guy from Split who threatened an Albanian that he would kill him. Albanians were the worst ... complete isolation ... with a couple of exceptions.[12]
>
> Skopje, "Marshal Tito barracks," artillery, army post V.P. 3218/5. Belgrade fellows were overbearing, Serbs were relaxed, those from Zagreb were introverted, those from Zagorje dedicated, Dalmatians were reckless, Macedonians were full of themselves (because they were on their own territory!), Albanians were loners, Slovenians tried to avoid hard work, Muslims were hardworking, Montenegrins—there were none in my unit, Hungarians were cheerful, Roma guys were joyful, while those coming from abroad to perform the army service in the homeland were all confused.[13]

Although a great degree of ethnic awareness is displayed in these quoted excerpts, stressing ethnic differences was not the only—and not even predominant—expression of belonging and differentiation. In their narratives, former JNA soldiers also emphasize other aspects of immediate encounter with people from all parts of the former Yugoslavia. They point out the huge cultural, social, and educational differences among soldiers:

> The most shocking for me was an encounter for the June draft. Most of them were Serbs and Albanians from Kosovo. Only a handful out of two hundred had completed primary education. Most were illiterate and dumb. The army service helped me to realize that I was born in a nice and progressive area.[14]
>
> I have learned a lesson about IQ and education level of "average" people. Believe it or not, but then (in years 1989–90) we were not divided among ourselves into Serbs, Croat, Bosnians etc.—we were divided into those who had finished a secondary school (or higher) education, and those who had not (and they were a majority).[15]

Solidarity among recruits and tension between them and officers typical for mandatory army services are also frequently stressed in the former soldiers' recollections of their army days. The dividing line between two groups seems more important than divisions among the soldiers along the ethnic lines.

Taken as a whole, quoted forum messages are characterized by an independence from the present-day perspective—they could have also been articulated when Yugoslavia still existed. There are only a few references to the 1990s wars and the role these men had in them. The contested role of the JNA in these wars, widely identified as an instrument of Serbian hegemony, is mentioned only a few times. These messages are primarily a means of social construction of masculinity and are void of political contextualization both in reference to the present and the past.

Of course, similarly to other forms of remembering the Socialist past, JNA narratives may also be included into the broader narrative of the Yugoslav past, characterized by nostalgia and myths about prosperity, success, and importance, which are presented in opposition to the current state of affairs. This function of the JNA-related narratives does not even require membership in the group of former JNA soldiers. Moreover, it makes it possible even for those who are too young to posses the JNA experience and those who experienced violence in 1990s to have a positive attitude toward the JNA and to transmit its mythical image. A youngster from Bosnia, whose knowledge of the JNA is based on his father's stories, posted the following message on the internet forum http://www.forum.bljesak.info:

> There is no sense in claiming that the JNA did bad things to us here. Weapons that used to belong to the JNA did, but not the JNA itself. The army that attacked Croatia and Bosnia-Herzegovina was not the JNA — we all know whose army it was. The JNA ceased to exist with the first bullet shot in Slovenia at the very beginning of the wars. Besides, do you really believe that poorly armed Croatia and even more poorly armed Bosnia-Herzegovina would be able to make any resistance against the fourth largest army force in Europe?[16]

Such a discourse reflects what Svetlana Boym calls "popular nostalgia" to label the longing for past glory as opposed to the current state of affairs (Boym 2001: 66). In this function, the discourse of nostalgia "in positioning 'once was' in relation to a 'now,' creates a frame of meaning" (Stewart 1988: 227) and is about the production of the present rather than about the reproduction of the past (Berdahl 1999: 202).

Despite the fact that the army stories of the former Yugoslav soldiers are void of political contextualization and stress the personal aspects of remembering one's experience in the army in Socialist Yugoslavia, the former JNA soldiers nevertheless feel a need to justify their memories, thus showing an awareness of their inappropriateness in the new circumstances. For example, after sharing his JNA memories with the others, one of the http://www.forum.hr forum members writes the following: "However service in the JNA looked like, it took up one of the best years of our lives, and we must not let our memories from that time be thrown away."[17] Expectations that the memories of socialism should be "thrown away," and the unreadiness of individuals to do so, is a consequence of the discrepancy between prevailing "official" attitudes toward the Socialist past and the experience of *really lived communism*.[18] While the former are characterized by prescriptivism and assess socialism as a totalitarian system and an illusion and Yugoslavia as a "wrong" country and a false project, the perceptions of people who lived in socialism and participated in the "Yugoslav project" provide different accounts and make a different hierarchy of values. Quite often, the personal memories of socialism do not correspond with dominant narratives that have an "official" character and tend to be normative and totalizing. When such discrepancy occurs, the term *nostalgia* almost always enters the discourse. The same is true in the remembering of the JNA experience: while in totalizing, impersonal discourses coming "from above" the JNA is seen as a mirror of the totalitarianism of the Yugoslav Socialist system, the people who "lived the army" attach different meanings to their own experiences in the JNA: for example, they remember the good friends that they made while performing their military service, they like to talk about the sabotage strategies that they used to make their army days easier and to avoid torture from the officers, and they construe and maintain manhood through the army narratives. And, as Miljensko Jergović's comment and the quoted Internet post show, they feel that they have the right to keep their memories and not let them be "thrown away," thus giving sense to their personal past and justifying the role they had in that past. And that is exactly what the great deal of individually expressed nostalgia for socialism—and Yugo-nostalgia as its particular manifestation—is about: as the Belgrade journalist Teofil Pančić has written, whether we call it nostalgia or not, we have the right to keep our memories of socialism, since they are proof that "everything from our past that we remember so well was not a dream or an imagination, a proof that we were and remained somewhere and someone" (Pančić 2004).

Remembering the JNA in Post-Yugoslav Art: Neglected but Omnipresent Nostalgia

By acts of explicit justification of their memories and the demand for the right to keep them, individuals enter into dialogue with dominant discourses that are nationally oriented and unfavorable toward any form of a Yugoslav legacy that is supranational in nature. The JNA experience, although personal, is at the same time collective, since it is shared by whole generations, and almost all members of these generations will recognize a particular JNA narrative as their own, regardless of who the actual author is. This potential of the army narratives to be collective and individual at the same time makes them suitable as objects of artistic articulation in literature and film. Such pieces of art are not numerous in the post-Yugoslav period—this fact being easily explicable given the dominance of nationalist discourses in the former Yugoslav societies—but enjoy enormous popularity in the whole area of the former Yugoslavia.[19] In the remainder of this chapter, I will deal with a novel describing the JNA experience and the film based on that novel that appeared in the post-Yugoslav cultural space in recent years. I will focus on the question of how these pieces of art "communicate" with their audience on the one hand, given the fact that in the narrative that they present most of the former Yugoslavs will find a part of their own past, and on the other hand with dominant public discourses that tend to attach totalizing and negative values to that past.

The JNA jargon and expressions typical of communication inside this institution are still recognizable, not only to the former JNA soldiers, but generally to those who share the experience of Yugoslav socialism. From today's viewpoint, these expressions are a source of joy and humor that simultaneously trigger memories and images of the past in a very lively and effective way. This capability of particular words, expressions, and ways of speaking to reactivate images, senses, and memories of parts of our experience make these discursive elements self-sufficient: they are immediately recognized and understood and do not need any additional message or explanation; furthermore, they also invoke a whole set of memories from the past—similarly to artifacts from Socialist times that remind the former Yugoslavs of the past in the common country, such as pioneer blue caps and red kerchiefs, partisan movies and songs, the Yugoslav flag, Tito's portrait, etc. Again, the nostalgia that these artifacts emanate usually does not imply a wish to restore the previous state of affairs; on the contrary, for most of those who express this kind of nostalgia, it can be a warm feeling for one's own past from a safe distance exactly because of the awareness of its irreversibility.

Ništa nas ne smije iznenaditi (Nothing Should Surprise Us) is one of the easily recognizable phrases from the dictionary of JNA jargon that was used for the title of a novel written by Croatian writer Ante Tomić in 2003. The novel, set in 1983, shows the rather banal, everyday life at a small border post on the Yugoslav-Albanian frontier. Yet another generation of soldiers awaits the end of their service, tortured by Lieutenant Imre Nadj and making their army days shorter in all possible ways. Lieutenant Nadj seeks help from the only doctor among the soldiers, Siniša Siriščević, a Croat from Split, who finds out, very discreetly, that the lieutenant has syphilis. Not wanting his wife to know about it and trying to find excuses not to go home, Nadj declares a state of emergency, claiming that the Albanian army is preparing an attack against Yugoslavia. The only person who is allowed to leave the border post is Siniša, who goes to the nearby town to get medicine for the lieutenant and inform his wife that he will not come home for the next three weeks. The young man from Split has a love affair with Lieutenant Nadj's wife, while his best friend Ljuba Paunović, an urban man from Belgrade, announces that he wants to go on foot to *Kuća cveća* (the House of Flowers, the memorial center in Belgrade where Tito was buried) to honor the great memory of Tito on the anniversary of the late president's birthday—although he is in fact searching for a way to escape from the army, a project that he eventually succeeds in. Siniša goes back to Split when his service is over, and his first step back into the normal life that he left a year ago ends the novel.

Void of dramatic turns and tragic denouements, this novel would not be expected to attract and keep the attention of a broad segment of the public with the action, complexity of characters, or depth of the story being told. But it nevertheless attracted great attention from readers all over the former Yugoslavia and achieved unusual popularity: it was translated into Slovene and Macedonian (the weekly *Vreme* published the novel in installments), while in Serbia it was published in Cyrillic script. The Kerempuh theater in Zagreb also put on a production of *Ništa nas ne smije iznenaditi* based on Tomić's novel.

What made this novel so appealing to the former Yugoslavs were the authentic ways in which it presented everyday life during JNA service: every former JNA soldier could find chunks of his own experience in these lines. The humor and recollections of the atmosphere in Socialist Yugoslavia made this novel interesting also for those former Yugoslavs who did not share the army experience. Without dramatics, without heroes, this novel presents the JNA atmosphere, the language used within the institution, its rituals and jokes, and this simple but authentic picture is the main quality of this reading.

In March 2006 a film titled *Karaula* (Border Post) appeared in cinemas all over the former Yugoslavia. The novel *Ništa nas ne smije iznenaditi* was the basis for its scenario (coauthored by Ante Tomić and Croatian film director Rajko Grlić, who also directed the film).[20] In the film, the narrative is moved closer toward the breakup of Yugoslavia—to 1987. It seems that all the differences between the novel and the film screenplay were made in order to concretize the story and relate it to the tragic breakdown of Yugoslavia that followed. The film is supposed to be an allegory of Yugoslavia's tragedy; as the film's director Grlić stated:

On the eve of any natural disaster, be it a summer storm or a total cataclysm, there is always a moment of total silence. It's that fine moment when everything stops, but also the moment when no one wants to talk about it. It happens to nature, to societies, and to entire civilizations. *Border Post* is a comedy taking place at one such moment. The film enquires about those people who were to transform in a matter of months into soldiers, refugees, victims and criminals. How did they live? What did they really want? What was the everyday life that engendered war and who were the ones who had war implanted into their minds so quickly and so easily?[21]

The main difference between the film narrative and the novel is in the film's tragic ending: the fight between the soldier from Belgrade and the lieutenant (in the film this character is a Bosnian, not a Hungarian), which in the novel ends with no serious consequences, turns into a massacre in the film. The Bosnian lieutenant is killed by the Serbian soldier, while many other people also die, including the lieutenant's wife. Such a close connection to the violent end of the country for which the main characters in the film serve as soldiers should automatically prevent any association with nostalgia—as stressed by one of its critics, the film had to be an allegory, because otherwise it would be nostalgic, which is by no means good (Luketić n.d.). The director of *Border Post* was also very eager to stress the fact that the movie is not about (Yugo-)nostalgia: according to him, "Yugo-nostalgia is a political phrase, used by politicians to test if people are more in favor of the previous or the current regime" (Milek 2006: 24). On the official Web presentation of the movie, it was stated that "speaking about the not so distant past with no nostalgia and no hatred, *Border Post* is a comedy about people on the verge of tragedy."[22] However, the issue of nostalgia was a central point and omnipresent subject in the discourse on this film.

It can be said that the film itself was a post-Yugoslav (Yugo-nostalgic?) project: directed by Croat Rajko Grlić, the movie gathered actors from all ex-Yugoslav republics, including Bosnian actor Emir Hadžihafizbegović, Macedonian actress Verica Nedeska-Trajkova, Serbian actor Sergej Trifunović, Croatian actor Toni Gojanović, as well as Slovenian actor Tadej Troha. It managed to receive financial support from the Ministry of Culture in each of the former republics—something that no other movie in the former Yugoslav lands has succeeded in doing in the last twenty years.

In spite of the director's rejection of the idea of nostalgia as a basic feeling of the movie and a main motive behind its production, in the first two weeks of the movie's screening he had to answer journalists' questions about nostalgia more than fifty times (Milek 2006: 24). The metadiscourse on *Border Post* can therefore be roughly defined as a self-defense by the authors that the movie has nothing to do with Yugo-nostalgia. Negative criticisms that were heard in some of the Yugoslav republics show that the movie was nevertheless interpreted with regard to the common past of the Yugoslav peoples and seen as Yugo-nostalgic in the official discourse, where Yugo-nostalgia was understood as an intention to restore the destroyed Yugoslav state in its political aspects. What was said in these criticisms resembles the dominant official narratives on the eve of Yugoslavia's disintegration: in Slovenia, there were complaints that Slovenes were underrepresented in the film; in Serbia, criticism was directed toward the way in which "representatives" of various nations were presented, and the film was perceived as anti-Serbian in that respect, since the Serbian soldier was depicted as a cheater, provocateur, and troublemaker, the Bosnian soldier as a victim, while the Croatian soldier was presented in a positive light as an intellectual and seducer waiting for a bright future once his military service finished. In Croatia, on the other hand, the film was seen by some as anti-Croatian, having a tendency "to bring Croatia back to its own (dark, Yugoslav, TP) past" (Milek 2006: 24).

In spite of the negative responses of the defenders of "national interests," the film was met with great interest among the former Yugoslavs and enjoyed exceptional popularity: during the first two weeks of its showing it topped the box office in all former Yugoslav republics simultaneously (another record in the post-Yugoslav era set by this film). The first showing in Sarajevo was screened at Zetra Hall and gathered 7,500 spectators.

What attracted such outstanding interest for *Border Post* among people all over the former Yugoslavia? It seems that it was, as in the case of the novel *Ništa nas ne smije iznenaditi*, an expectation to see on screen everyday life in the Yugoslav People's Army, to hear its language, to laugh at the humor typical of it and all that which makes the telling of army stories so important and necessary. It also seems that the film's authors and producers were well aware of that: although they insisted that the film was an allegory of the violent destruction of the country, this allegory is present only in the film's last fifteen minutes (Luketić n.d.), while the rest of the film is, in fact, a humorous story about everyday life in the JNA, in which most former Yugoslavs will recognize pieces of their own past. Just the opposite to *Goodbye, Lenin*, a film about East German socialism that portrays everyday Socialist objects and practices recognizable and understandable for Eastern Germans and by that excludes Western Germans, emphasizing the East-West gap (although the film was hailed for "uniting easterners and westerners in laughter"—cf. Berdahl, this volume), *Border Post* produces the feeling of solidarity among the former Yugoslavs by showing recognizable details from their common past much more than dividing them by insisting on tragic end of the common history. The allegoric and tragic denouement of the film seems to be somewhat of an inappropriate and unnatural end to this cheerful and unburdening story: Slovenian journalist Andrej Gustinčič wrote that "the film's end with the spilling of blood, which is meant to be a symbol of the bloody destruction of Yugoslavia, is in discrepancy with the rest of it—it is like a prolonged joke to which a tragic end is attached" (Gustinčič 2006: 28).

Despite the fact that the authors of *Border Post* denied any presence of Yugo-nostalgia in the film, the way it was advertised and presented to the public indicates that they counted exactly on this feeling among its potential spectators. Other symbols of the Yugoslav Socialist past were used for the promotion of the film: the main press conference was conducted in the Blue Train traveling from Novi Sad to Belgrade (the original idea was to make a journey from Ljubljana to Skopje, but it was not realized due to organizational problems). The Blue Train was a luxury train used for Tito's travels and is most famous for Tito's last journey from Ljubljana to Belgrade after his death.[23] In Novi Sad the train and the film crew were greeted by children dressed as pioneers who waved the flag of Socialist Yugoslavia. Asked by a Belgrade journalist about the symbols of the Yugoslav system and ideology, such as Tito's portrait and the Yugoslav flag, used in the marketing for *Border Post*, director Rajko Grlić said that it was distributors who decided about that, again rejecting any personal responsibility for the nostalgia expressed or implied in and around the film (Kostić 2006: 51–52).

Remembering the JNA and the Reproduction of Masculinity

In this chapter, I have tried to outline the main characteristics of discourses through which memories of performing military service in the former Yugoslavia are shaped, transmitted, and employed in the reassessment of the Socialist past.

Todorova (2002: 16) emphasizes the importance of studying "the relationship between individual memory and the production of official normative assessments designated as public memory" in dealing with the remembering of socialism. Individual memories of the JNA experience are simultaneously shared by millions of former Yugoslavs. In this way individual memories become collective and cannot be ignored or overwritten by normative public memory, which provides a different version of the past and different image of the Yugoslav military institution. The official assessments and personal discourses of remembering the JNA are aware of each other; they are in constant dialogue and shape one another. The *Border Post* film should be understood as "part of the (collective) cultural act of remembrance," but also as "product of the memory industry" (Van Dijck 2007: 13). Its authors, who received financial support from state institutions of the Yugoslav successor states, and who at the same time made the film for former Yugoslavs who in large numbers possess an experience of socialism, faced a difficult task in considering both "official" and personal memories of the JNA in the film.

Military service in the JNA was an exclusively male experience, and the primary function of narrating army stories remains in the realm of (re)producing masculinity, through expressions of male solidarity and competitiveness. In this sense, army stories of the former Yugoslavs do not differ from any other stories from the army that are being told by generations of men all around the world. However, in the context of (post)Yugoslav postsocialism, characterized by the restoration and reinvention of national identities of the former Yugoslav nations, remembering the JNA becomes a problematic cultural practice and is perceived as an expression of the "dangerous" and "decadent" feeling of Yugo-nostalgia. Despite such a characterization and a generally suppressive attitude toward the positive accounts of the Yugoslav past prevailing in post-Yugoslav societies, remembering the army and narration of the army memories have proved to be surprisingly resistant. Although classified as Yugo-nostalgia, the term that usually marks attitudes and practices that express disagreement with the dominant ideology and is a kind of counterdiscourse to dominant discourses, the practice of remembering the JNA is usually not a political act that is opposed to prevailing nationalist ideologies. The reproduction of masculinity through the narration of JNA memories coexists with nationalist-masculine narratives of fighting in the recent wars, not only in the societies in the former Yugoslav area, but also in biographies of single persons living in these societies. However, initiation into manhood through performing the JNA service remains too important for individuals to be "thrown away" as a problematic remnant of socialism, and because of deep personal investments in the previous order, it persists even across ethnic lines, gathering men from all parts of Yugoslavia in the virtual space when they share their army memories, exchange anecdotes, and try to identify their army mates. In the context of the post-Yugoslav societies, it seems that masculine subjectivity, which was successfully employed in the construction of prevailing nationalist and patriotic ideologies,[24] simultaneously proves to be an unexpected point of ideological instability.

Notes

I thank Maple Razsa and Dean Vuletic who carefully and patiently read earlier versions of this chapter. Their insightful suggestions and comments made the text significantly better.
 1. There was a short-lived attempt to introduce army service for women between 1983 and 1985. It was voluntary and lasted two months and twenty-two days for female soldiers and six months for officers. The practice of including women in the JNA, justified with a need "to improve status of women in the Yugoslav society," was eventually abandoned in 1985 since it faced numerous difficulties, and interest for service among women declined significantly. Thus the idea to transform voluntary service for women into a mandatory one has never been realized in Socialist Yugoslavia (Gombač forthcoming).
 2. Judith Butler (1990) sees gender as performative and a culturally and discursively produced social category. Within Butlerian tradition, gender is regarded as "an emergent feature of social situations" (West and Zimmerman 1987; Andersson 2008: 140).
 3. On the idea of Yugoslavism, its birth, evolution, and fall, see Djokić 2003.
 4. Segal (1990: 132–33) discusses the case of the British National Service in the same vein.
 5. The individual project on remembering the Yugoslav People's Army was a part of the Centre for Advanced Studies in Sofia project "Roles, Identities and Hybrids," conducted from October 2005 to June 2006 and supported by Volkswagen Stiftung.
 6. I am well aware of the fact that performance of masculinity in this case—as always—is shaped by the relationship between me and my collocutors: the JNA stories would probably differ to some extent if the interviews were made by a man; furthermore, a man who had served in the JNA would receive different stories than the one who served some other army or did not perform army service at all. The narratives I collected while interviewing former JNA soldiers are nevertheless a reflection of JNA soldier identity that is worth of consideration, because of the fact that they are widely shared and easily recognizable (thus their similarity to other discourses of remembering the JNA such as Internet forum posts and articulations of the JNA experience in literature and film), and because they reflect my interviewees' ideas of what is an "appropriate" image of the JNA soldier (since they were aware of my purpose to use their stories for research).
 7. Drawing on Davies (1989), Søndergaard defines storylines as "collective and culturally dependent narratives that make up the pillars upon which individuals build their own personal stories" (Søndergaard 2002, quoted after Andersson 2008: 145).

8. This narrative is not specific for the Socialist Yugoslav context only, for it is exploited also in post-Yugoslav societies, but with different ideological references: instead of the Yugoslav ideology of defense based on World War Two (*people's liberation war*), national post-Yugoslav armies are ideologically based on the legacies of the establishment of post-Yugoslav states. In his speech on the occasion of the Day of the Army of Bosnia and Herzegovina, a member of the presidency of Bosnia and Herzegovina, Sulejman Tihić, addressed the soldiers who made an oath with the following words: "Dear soldiers! I wish you good health and success in the army training. I have no doubt that you will be able to meet the challenges of new times, like your fathers, brothers, and sisters did. Performing army service is not only a debt to the homeland, but also a school of life! I urge you to preserve and keep the legacy and moral values of the defense-liberation war!" (Tihić 2003).
9. Coates (2003: 45) provided an excerpt from David Jackson's "critical autobiography" showing that the focusing on details, characteristic of men, is often a deliberate strategy: "I often turn to the sports page in the daily newspaper, concerning myself with the raw material for endless non-emotional non-conversations with other men" (Jackson 1990: 221).
10. These stereotypes also circulated in numerous jokes about Yugoslav nations; on the other hand, stereotypes about different ethnic groups are a universal consequence of their encounters in multiethnic armies: cf. Strigl 2006 for this kind of stereotyping in the Austro-Hungarian army.
11. http://www.forum.hr/showthread.php?t=127325&page=2, posted 8 January 2006, accessed 24 November 2008.
12. Ibid.
13. http://www.forum.hr/showthread.php?t=127325&page=6, posted 15 January 2006, accessed 24 November 2008.
14. http://www.forum.hr/showthread.php?t=127325&page=5, posted 11 January 2006, accessed 24 November 2008.
15. http://www.forum.hr/showthread.php?t=127325&page=7, posted 19 January 2006, accessed 24 November 2008.
16. http://forum.bljesak.info/lofiversion/index.php/t7396.html, posted 15 April 2005, accessed 14 September 2007. In his history of the JNA, officer of the Slovenian army Zvezdan Marković (2007) pays significant attention to "the myth of the JNA as the third, the fourth or at least the fifth military force in Europe." In Marković's interpretation, those who reproduce this mythical image of the JNA are leading politicians of Slovenia, Croatia, and Bosnia-Herzegovina in 1990s, who in this way wanted to extol victories of respective national armies over the JNA. He does not even mention the fact that the positive image of the JNA as one of the leading military forces in Europe was widespread and is still narratively maintained among "ordinary people" all over the former Yugoslavia.
17. http://www.forum.hr/showthread.php?t=127325&page=6, posted 16 January 2006, accessed 24 November 2008.
18. Maria Todorova uses this term in order to "distinguish it from … communism as an intellectual/ideological endeavor" (Todorova 2002: 15).
19. On some Yugo-nostalgic post-Yugoslav films, see Daković 2008.

20. Cf. http://www.borderpostmovie.com/synopsis.php, accessed 24 November 2008.
21. http://www.borderpostmovie.com/directors_statement.php, accessed 24 November 2008.
22. http://www.borderpostmovie.com/synopsis.php, accessed 24 November 2008.
23. Plavi voz (Blue Train) is also the name of a nostalgic internet forum that "gathers all real Yugoslavs" (www.plavivoz.com, last accessed 14 September 2007).
24. There is extensive literature about the relationship between masculinity and nationalism in 1990s conflicts in the former Yugoslavia; cf. among others Milićević 2006, Papić 1999, Thomas and Ralph 1999, Žarkov 2007, and Živković 2006.

References

Andersson, Kjerstin 2008. "Constructing Young Masculinity: A Case Study of Heroic Discourse on Violence." *Discourse & Society* 19 (2): 139–61.
Berdahl, Daphne. 1999. "'(N)Ostalgie' for the Present: Memory, Longing and East German Things." *Ethnos* 64 (2): 192–211.
Bjelajac, Mile. 1999. *Jugoslovensko iskustvo sa multietničkom armijom 1918–1991* [Yugoslav Experience with Multiethnic Army 1918–1991]. Belgrade: Udruženje za društvenu istoriju.
Boym, Svetlana. 2001. *The Future of Nostalgia.* New York: Basic Books.
Brickell. Chris. 2005. "Masculinities, Performativity and Subversion; A Sociological Reappraisal." *Men and Masculinities* 8: 24–43.
Butler, Judith. 1990. *Gender Trouble: Feminism and the Subversion of Identity.* New York: Routledge.
Coates, Jennifer. 2003. *Men Talk: Stories in the Making of Masculinities.* Malden, MA: Blackwell Publishing.
Daković, Nevena. 2008. "Out of the Past: Memories and Nostalgia in (Post-)Yugoslav Cinema." In *Past for the Eyes: East European Representations of Communism in Cinema and Museums after 1989,* ed. Oksana Sarkisova and Péter Apor, 117–41. Budapest: CEU Press.
Davies, Bronwyn. 1989. *Frogs and Snails and Feminist Tales: Preschool Children and Gender.* Sidney: Allen and Unwin.
Djokić, Dejan. 2003. *Yugoslavism: Histories of a Failed Idea 1918–1992.* London: Hurst & Company.
Gombač, Jure. Forthcoming. "Slovenci v JLA" [Slovenians in the JNA]. In *Slovenska vojska: kratka zgodovina, dolga tradicija.* Ljubljana: Založba ZRC.
Gustinčič, Andrej. 2006. "Brez nostalgije in ljubezni" [Without Nostalgia and Love]. *Delo, Sobotna priloga* (23 April): 28.
Hadžić, Miroslav. 2001. *Sudbina partijske vojske* [Destiny of Party Army]. Belgrade: Samizdat B92.
Herzfeld, Michael [Hercfeld, Majkl]. 2004. *Kulturna intimnost* [Cultural Intimacy]. Belgrade: XX vek.

Holmes, Leslie. 1997. *Post Communism: An Introduction*. Cambridge: Polity Press.
Jackson, David. 1990. *Unmasking Masculinity*. London: Unwin Hyman.
Jansen, Stef. 2005. *Antinacionalizam* [Antinationalism]. Belgrade: XX vek.
Jergović, Miljenko. N. d. "O romanu" [On the Novel *Ništa nas ne smije iznenaditi* by Ante Tomić, Zagreb 2003]. http://www.fraktura.hr/tekstovi%20za%20stranicu/stranci/tomic/tomicbio.htm, accessed 24 November 2008.
Karaula [Border Post]. 2006. Rajko Grlić, dir., 94 min. UK / Serbia and Montenegro / Croatia / Slovenia / Republic of Macedonia / Bosnia-Herzegovina.
Kostić, Aleksandar. 2006. "Arheologija bivših života" [Archaeology of Former Lives: An Interview with Rajko Grlić, Director]. *Vreme* 794 (23 March): 50–52.
Lubonja, Fatos. 2002. Nostalgia i ból [Nostalgia and Pain]. In *Nostalgia. Eseje o tęsknocie za komunizmem*, ed. Filip Modrzejewski and Monika Sznajderman, 7–12. Wołowiec, Poland: Wydawnictwo czarne.
Luketić, Željko. N.d. "Rajko Grlić: Karaula" [Rajko Grlić: Border Post]. Electronic document. http://www.mikrokino.net/osvrt_arh.asp?counter=15#100, accessed 24 November 2008.
Marković, Zvezdan. 2007. *Jugoslovanska narodna armada 1945–1991* [Yugoslav People's Army 1991–1945]. Ljubljana: Defensor.
Milek, Vesna. 2006. "Kodak je prefin trak za politiko" [Kodak Is Too Subtle for Politics, an Interview with Rajko Grlić]. *Delo, Sobotna priloga* (15 April): 24.
Milićević, Aleksandra. 2006. "Joining the War: Masculinity, Nationalism and War Participation in the Balkans War of Seccession 1991–1995." *Nationalities Papers* 34 (3): 265–87.
Pančić, Teofil. 2004. "Leksikon YU mitologije—knjiga smeha i pamćenja" [Lexicon of YU Mythology—A Book of Laughter and Remembering]. *Vreme* 699 (27 May), http://www.vreme.com/cms/view.php?id=379992, accessed 24 November, 2008.
Papić, Žarana. 1999. "Women in Serbia: Post-Communism, War and Nationalist Mutations." In *Gender Politics in the Western Balkans*, ed. Sabina P. Ramet, 153–69. University Park, PA: University of Pennsylvania Press.
Segal, Lynne. 1990. *Slow Motion: Changing Masculinities, Changing Men*. New Brunswick, NJ: Rutgers University Press.
Søndergaard, Dorte Marie. 2002. "Poststructuralist Approaches to Empirical Analysis." *International Journal of Qualitative Studies in Education* 15: 187–204.
Stewart, Kathleen. 1988. "Nostalgia: A Polemic." *Cultural Anthropology* 3 (3): 227–41.
Strigl, Daniela. 2006. "Schneidige Husaren, brave Bosniaken, feige Tschechen. Nationale Mythen und Stereotypen in der k.u.k. Armee." In *Zentren, Peripherien un kollektive Identitäten in Österreich-Ungarn*, ed. Endre Hárs, Wolfgang Müller-Funk, Ursula Reber, and Clemens Ruthner, 129–44. Tübingen: A. Francke Verlag.
Thomas, Dorothy, and Regan E. Ralph. 1999. "Rape in War: The Case of Bosnia." In *Gender Politics in the Western Balkans*, ed. Sabina P. Ramet, 203–18. University Park, PA: University of Pennsylvania Press.
Tihić, Sulejman. 2003. "Prvi put u novijoj historiji imali smo bosansku vojsku koja se borila samo za svoju državu" [For the First Time in Our History We

Had an Army That Fought for Its Own Country]. http://www.tihic.ba/Tekst/Govori/Dan%20armije%202003.htm, accessed 14 September 2007.

Todorova, Maria. 2002. "Remembering Communism." *Centre for Advanced Study in Sofia Newsletter* 2 (autumn): 15–17.

Ugrešić, Dubravka. 2002. *Kultura laži: Antipolitički eseji* [The Culture of Lies: Antipolitical Essays]. Belgrade: Samizdat B92–Konzor.

Van Dijck, José. 2007. *Mediated Memories: Personal Cultural Memory in the Digital Age.* Stanford, CA: Stanford University Press.

Vojnikova ljubav [Soldier's Love]. 1976. Svetislav Pavlović, dir. 103 min. Yugoslavia.

West, Candace, and Don H. Zimmerman. 1987. "Doing Gender," *Discourse and Society* 1: 125–51.

Zimmermann, Warren. 1996. *Origins of a Catastrophe: Yugoslavia and Its Destroyers—America's Last Ambassador Tells What Happened and Why.* New York: Times Books.

Žarkov, Dubravka. 2007. *The Body of War: Media, Ethnicity and Gender in the Break-up of Yugoslavia.* Durham, NC: Duke University Press.

Živković, Marko. 2006. "Ex-Yugoslav Masculinities under Female Gaze, or Why Men Skin Cats, Beat up Gays and Go to War." *Nationalities Papers* 34 (3): 257–63.

5

DIGNITY IN TRANSITION
History, Teachers, and the Nation-State in Post-1989 Bulgaria
Tim Pilbrow

Immediately after the fall of communism (10 November 1989), when he would have been in the fifth grade, Mladen[1] had been an ardent anti-Communist. However, he had later come across his grandfather's Stalinist-era history textbook from the early 1950s, and as an eleventh-grade student in 1995 he now often carried this with him to his history class, where he assumed the role of a devil's advocate, countering the then-current conventional wisdom with the wisdom that had—at least officially—ordered his grandfather's world. His teacher, Mariia Nikolova, explained this to me after class on the first day I had visited her classroom at an elite state secondary school in Sofia in the autumn of 1995. She seemed to be unperturbed by Mladen's stance, and in fact welcomed the opportunities it presented for class discussions. Teaching in a specialized public school with competitive entry and a clientele of talented (and mostly socially privileged) children, Mariia encouraged her pupils to read beyond the set textbook. If not all the pupils were motivated to engage with questions of historical interpretation—or to engage with them with as much self-conscious irony and personal engagement as did Mladen—the concerns that motivated Mladen nevertheless derived from their common experience of having had to unlearn and relearn history over the course of the first five years of the post–state-Socialist era.[2]

This story—and its telling—encapsulate one of the central issues in the post–state-Socialist transition in Bulgaria and more generally in Eastern Europe: maintaining dignity in the face of rapid and disorienting social, political, and economic change. Moreover, it draws attention to ways in which the past is harnessed to present concerns in ways that defy simple reduction to such paradigms as nostalgia, legacy, or inertia. My concern, as I have alluded, is less with Mladen and his grandfather than with Mariia and her recounting of the story. Mladen's approach to the predicament that many experienced may appear to some as merely trite, amusing, perhaps creatively rebellious, perhaps mere youthful bloody-mindedness. My own sense from Mariia's version of events is that Mladen displayed a spirit of ingenuous inquiry. He was, after all, asking important questions, demanding (albeit tongue-in-cheek) that someone articulate no less than an embarrassing apologia for decades of what, paraphrasing Gail Kligman (1998), we might term the "duplicitous complicity" that sustained the state-Socialist project. Bloody-mindedness can, after all, be a vehicle for instructive irony through insistently marking a paradox and demanding that it be confronted. Like the boy in the story of the emperor's new clothes, Mladen was asking questions about truths that were at once patently obvious yet too embarrassing for most to confront: Both versions of history could not be right—assuming the regnant positivist bias in Bulgarian historiography and history teaching—but surely the past forty years count for something? Upon what grounds is current conventional wisdom to be accepted? Is the present official historical narrative any less fragilely grounded than that which it purports to supplant? If the history of years gone by was a fabricated sham, then who was responsible for this? How much responsibility do the parents' and grandparents' generations bear for their complicity, willing or unwilling, in sustaining the ever-changing fictions of Socialist self-presentation? Or, on the other hand, can the current conventional wisdom be taken at face value? These are questions that could be taken for granted as lurking in the backs of many minds, yet seemed sufficiently embarrassing as to remain largely unremarked (or strategically forgotten).

As with socialization into any cultural system, Mladen and his peers faced jarring moments as they learned to master the dilemmas and contradictions germane to their cultural milieu. If schooling is seen as part of a larger socialization process, an elongated rite of passage through which childish sureties are slowly displaced by adult conceptual and symbolic capabilities, then Mladen's attempt to signify these dilemmas makes sense as a liminal moment in a longer process of acquiring adult competence.[3]

Narrated Selves and Ethnographic Subjects

However, my concern here is less with Mladen and his possible motivations for drawing attention to the cultural dilemmas he was being socialized into than with his teacher Mariia's recounting of this story within her own broader narrative construction of self. Mariia, like many of the teachers I interacted with in Bulgaria, was quite at pains to present herself as an enlightened and conscientious teacher. It was through such stories as this one about Mladen that she sought to establish herself as having been and still being an innovative and sincere professional. As a teacher with about twenty years of professional experience, Mariia spoke nonchalantly of having taught model lessons when necessary during the state-Socialist period,[4] but having otherwise had the foremost aim of teaching her students to think logically and critically: "We knew when we had to perform, and the students knew what to make of that. The rest of the time, my aim was to teach them logical [critical] thinking skills, the ability to weigh factual evidence. In that, I have not changed." Other teachers also sought to couch their narrative framing of professional identification in similar terms, as bound up in a set of practices that had not been fundamentally altered by the end of state socialism. If I was impressed by their integrity in the classroom in the 1990s, I was regularly made to understand this as resulting from a continuity of practice. Mariia's enlightened indulgence in the classroom, through which Mladen's self-expression was enabled, was, she would have me believe, no sudden embracing of openness, but evidence of a more essential professional identity and integrity that enabled her to capitalize on the available opportunities for imparting knowledge and skills.

Mladen's story, thus, as an element in Mariia's self-presentation, indexes multiple and multifaceted concerns for dignity. As an outsider-anthropologist, my presence clearly shaped the context for the specific articulation of these concerns. However, the conversations I had with Mariia and other teachers were framed largely by their assumptions about what I needed to know about their work. I therefore regard these conversations as providing valuable insights into culturally salient practices of self-construction in Bulgaria several years into the post–state-Socialist transition. As with any ethnographic project, my claim turns on the assumption that any person or persons will utilize cultural frames of reference in meaningful and patterned ways. The centrality of the concern for dignity, as well as the particular ways in which claims to dignity were articulated, emerged from multiple conversations with about a dozen teachers over the course of a year. I focus here on Mladen's story not as an archetype for contemporary Bulgarian self-presentation (which it definitively is not), but as a poignant story that provides a window into the motivations for and practices of identification[5] of contemporary Bulgarians.

Locating Dignity as a Cultural Good

Mladen's story illustrates, thus, on a number of levels an engagement with dignity and dignifying practices: Mladen's own concern to define a historically informed identification for himself—and one, at that, that might salvage some dignity for his grandfather and wider family; the concerns of teachers, curriculum writers, academic historians, and students alike to define and present a reasonable legitimating story for the national present (and, by extension, their personal identifications); and the concerns of teachers and others involved in the formal educational process with professional integrity and dignity. These concerns coalesced in specific ways for teachers during the mid-1990s—and my analysis is limited to this moment—as they struggled to reclaim a public image that had been tarnished by the taint of having been functionaries of a now discredited state system, and to come to terms with their relative loss of economic status and social prestige in the initial transition period.

This story also illustrates clearly the scope of the complexities and contradictions involved in the reworking of history and the articulation of national ideology. Historical revision is far from being simply a matter for elite historians at the national universities to settle. Different currents of historical interpretation course through academic corridors and as these reach the broader public sphere, they enter into encounters with the private worlds of ordinary people. The history classroom is one particular and important site in the public sphere where such encounters take place, albeit not always as explicitly as in Mladen's case.

My interest was piqued immediately as Mariia related this story. I had set out to examine how history is received and used in the production of national ideologies broadly in society—hence my decision to investigate how history was being taught in schools. I had anticipated finding that, given the rapid pace of societal and ideological change, there would be jarring moments at which the mechanisms of symbolic transfer involved would be readily apparent. The incident of this story presented me with a way to engage with how history gets used in framing identities. The revisions of historical fact and interpretation and the selective process of defining a historical narrative (of the nation, or of world history), while of fundamental importance in this, represent but one aspect of the process of remaking history. I began to see Mladen's concern as a concern for emerging from the classroom as a whole self. If the text for the course (Bakalov et al. 1993) was written to provide a cohesive narrative of the Bulgarian past that would serve as an anchor for national identification, the reader engaging it has to reconcile this narrative with his or her own personal narrative of identification as a member of the nation. If not all pupils in the class experienced this as a jarring process to the extent that Mladen did (or chose not to articulate publicly in this setting their own coming-to-terms with their present experience), there were many other moments of jarring realization that teachers and pupils shared with me over the course of the year I was engaged in this research.

But why did Mariia tell the story? Was it purely, as I first understood it, to inform me of aspects of the classroom dynamic that I might otherwise not have picked up? Was it to indulge my senses in the delight of recognizing this subversive act? Was it to guide my attention to this more intimate aspect of the identification process? Or was this story part of her own self-presentation?

The story unfolded within a larger conversation that transpired between classes on the days that I visited her school. Mariia demonstrated a keen desire that I understand her position as a teacher who encouraged and welcomed debate and contention in the classroom. Situated in one of the few schools I visited with something akin to a functioning library, Mariia was able to set assignments that required library research. She had also managed to hold on to copies of old textbooks, anthologies of historical documents, and other teaching materials, unlike teachers in some other schools, who lamented to me how their principals—in their heady rush to be good post–state-Socialist entrepreneurs (and out of desperation as they assumed more of the real costs of running a school)—had sold such items off to raise cash, not recognizing, or not caring about, their continuing educational value.[6] What struck me most, however, was that Mariia was intent on presenting herself as someone who, despite all the rapid change around her, had not fundamentally changed her approach to teaching. Similar assertions of continuity in their practices of identification as professionals between the state-Socialist past and the post–state-Socialist present were central to the way other teachers sought to present themselves. Such narratives of continuity—Mladen's, Mariia's, and those of other teachers—do not evince merely individual attempts to transcend disjuncture. Rather, they exhibit commonalities in form and content, the kind of patterning that signals the presence of culturally and socially meaningful action. Indeed, Mariia's recounting of Mladen's story provokes us to examine the various ways in which an intensely personal engagement with history can also be an intensely cultural and social process—not only in regard to Mladen's self-positioning through textual reference, but also in regard to Mariia's purpose in narrating this to me.

Disjuncture and Narratives of Continuity

The relationship to the past that predominated in Mladen's and Mariia's narrative appropriations of the past was one of continuity, of transcending disjuncture. Creed has already drawn attention to the inadequacies of "legacy" models for explaining seeming continuities with the past, arguing rather that present (and pragmatic) concerns rather than inertia or nostalgia often underlay the political support for Socialist candidates in 1990s Bulgaria (Creed 1999: 224). In the narrative appropriations of the past that I consider here, as well, it is present concerns—for dignity—that appear to be primary. Moreover, if the hallmark of nostalgia is its reference to and articulation of a past that is irretrievable (Boym 2001), a "nostalgia" model is inadequate for illuminating the narrative strategies I consider here.

My concern here is to theorize and thereby illuminate the ways in which narratives of continuity are constructed and used as vehicles for transcending the kinds of disjuncture that the fall of state socialism represented to Bulgarians (and other Eastern and Central Europeans). This is not to deny the significance of nostalgia or inertia, but rather to suggest their limitations as means to comprehending the complex and multiple processes of reorientation that people in Eastern Europe are engaged in. Far from lamenting the passing of an age, Mladen, Mariia, and others, in choosing to dignify the past, were transacting important work towards their self-identification in the present. Far from evincing a nostalgic or backward-looking past-dependence, narratives of continuity, I argue, are a strategic resource in the management of present identifications and the memories through which present identifications are sustained.

Not just in relation to Mladen's and Mariia's narrative appropriations of the past, but more broadly in my conversations with Bulgarian teachers in the mid-1990s, I was struck by the care taken by my interlocutors to present themselves as having a dignity that transcended the disjuncture represented by the fall of state socialism. Alongside concerns for personal dignity, representations of the nation and national identity were also heavily imbued with notions of dignity, and, I will argue, there are correlations among these arenas of dignity: the personal, the national, and the professional. For history teachers this was perhaps more clearly marked than among those in other walks of life: articulating a dignified narrative history of the nation was for them a professionally apposite means to projecting a dignified sense of self; concerns for personal, national, and professional dignity were intimately connected with their performance as teachers.

My assertion is that the narrative affirmation of dignity is a commonly used symbolic device through which people seek to transcend the disjunctures of post–state-Socialist life, and to reconcile their past and present identities. That past and present identifications are measured in markedly distinct ways is beyond question: the Soviet bloc is no more, and identification—national, personal, professional—has to be organized in terms of, or at least in response to, a different set of values, namely, free-market capitalism, pluralist democracy, and a re-centered sense of Europeanness. Nevertheless, the legitimation of one's identification in the present necessitates the construction of a perspective on the past that sustains this present.

Teachers and Historians and the Maintenance of Professional Dignity

Two other teachers' stories are suggestive of how dignity is articulated through claims to continuity. Desislava Antonova is the head history teacher at a school in a residential neighborhood with a predominantly skilled-worker profile close to the northeastern edge of central Sofia. I spent several months observing her teach a tenth-grade world history class and an eleventh-grade Bulgarian history class. In her late forties or early fifties, Desislava had taught at this school for eighteen years, and was also pursuing graduate studies in history at Sofia University. Her lessons were always well-planned, clear, and interesting. She commanded authority in the classroom, while inviting and getting a high level of pupil participation. She was adept at provoking the pupils to think through the issues at hand, and challenged them continually to move beyond simplistic answers. When I asked her to contrast her present teaching with the way she taught in the state-Socialist period, she responded: "I don't think I teach differently now. I always saw my role as being to challenge the pupils … to teach them to understand cause-and-effect relations." This followed a class on the Post-Revolutionary Civil War in Russia, in which she had been dissatisfied with pupils' understanding of the transfer of power that this represented, chiding them: "The 'old power' didn't lose to the 'new power' just because it was 'illegitimate' [a superficial Marxist explanation proffered by one pupil], but because of bloody conflict—people don't just give up power, rights, privileges … anything." She had then guided the pupils through the task of weighing up the various factors that led to the ultimate victory of the Soviets, seeking to portray the war as much more than an ideological conflict, but rather as one of competing economic interests, and differential access to strategic resources, wherein the Soviets had little on their side but superior organization. She periodically asked pupils to personalize their understanding through imagining themselves into the situation.

Desislava's claim to continuity in her approach to teaching is clearly more than just that. It is also an affirmation of the positive social role of the history teacher and of the historian's profession. She is not denying the ideological and propagandistic role history was obliged to play under state socialism. Rather, she is asserting that, regardless of the ideological role of history, to teach history well is to teach the historical method of analysis, and this has not changed. Ideological baggage has been removed—but this was, from such a perspective, superfluous anyway.

This assertion of the dignity of the historian's role depends on a positivist understanding of history as the objective science of gathering data about the past with its presupposition that explanation is subservient to the facts: as Bulgarian historians and teachers continually reminded me, history is about getting the facts right, and if two competing explanations are plausible, what you have is in fact an insufficiency of facts. Positivism among Bulgarian historians was entrenched yet further both by the methodological doctrine of historical materialism and again more recently by reaction against the "ideological distortions" of state socialism, which could be challenged by factual research.

The very explicitness of the historical materialist paradigm within which historians were earlier obliged to write, moreover, seemingly absolves them of ideological complicity; it is seen as having been mere convention and as not having affected the factual analysis proper. This led to a variety of pragmatic responses on the part of historians, as indicated in a statement by the then head of the Institute of History of the Bulgarian Academy of Sciences, Mito Isusov, in 1991: "A significant number of historians found scholarly immunity against [the ideologization of history] in the documental-factual approach to historical processes, tendencies, phenomena and events, or in flight from the problems of modern, and especially recent, history" (1991: 5).[7] Nevertheless, Isusov continued, what counted first and foremost for academic advancement and publication remained the quality of the historical research (1991: 6). Scholarship could not be entirely compromised in the pursuit of an ideological agenda if it were to retain some credibility both at home and abroad.[8]

However, asserting dignity for the profession and for the self as practitioner through establishing continuity in practice between the present and the Socialist past is not the only approach taken. Indeed, this is largely only the approach of those who had no particular squabbles with socialism. On the other hand, there were teachers like Nina Dobreva for whom the fall of state socialism was marked by a significant break rather than a continuity. Some friends put me in contact with Nina, who was a history teacher at an outer suburban school in Sofia that operated under particularly adverse conditions: crumbling infrastructure, no resources apart from chalk (not even always a usable blackboard), highly disinterested pupils, senior classes in which Nina alone had a copy of the textbook;[9] she resorted to dictation as a presentation method in such settings, with limited success. Her classes with lower-grade pupils—for whom the Ministry of Education provides textbooks free of charge—were a more positive experience, though pupil disinterest was nonetheless high. I met with Nina several times but she was seemingly unable to arrange for me to visit her school.

Nina had been introduced to me as an exemplary teacher, one critically engaged with the curriculum and thoroughly dedicated to her teaching. During my first conversation with Nina, it became clear that she based her identification as a professional squarely in terms of approaching the curriculum and textbooks critically and through demonstrating her opposition to what she and some others perceived as overly patriotic, nationalist, and xenophobic subtexts in the curriculum and textbooks. Nina was at great pains to present herself as not being a nationalist. Rather, she outlined her efforts to address the perceived subtexts of the curriculum in the classroom, and to downplay and contextualize them. That she regarded this as central to her professional identification is clear from statements she made about the majority of her colleagues, who either wittingly or unwittingly are complicit in the transmission of these subtexts: such colleagues, in her words, "are not good professionals." That is, they do not approach the teaching of history as professional historians should, through critical evaluation of the factual basis for the views presented. The main example she cited had to do with the representation of the Ottoman period in Bulgarian history (fourteenth—nineteenth centuries), a particular bone of contention for teachers and historians concerned to present a balanced, nonnationalist, nonxenophobic national history. She explained how she took pains to draw her pupils into questioning the folk perceptions of the Ottoman period as nothing but five hundred years of persecution of (Christian) Bulgarians. Such folk perceptions are easily grafted onto or displace the textbook presentation. Her approach was to explain:

> For the system to have survived five hundred years and for the Bulgarians to have maintained a national self-consciousness, things cannot have been all bad. Moreover, the Ottomans cannot have been preoccupied with doing nasty things to Bulgarians, given that Bulgarians were such an important source of tax revenue.

The recent textbooks, indeed, do attempt to redress this unbalanced picture of the Ottoman period—detailing lifeways and charting the progress of economic advancement over the period—in stark contrast to those of the state-Socialist period, which dealt with the whole period in a matter of a sentence or two as a period in which nothing much happened, a black hole in national history, or those from the period before World War II, which focused primarily on the harsh treatment of the Bulgarian people.

This concern for critical reading of the texts and confronting folk beliefs is clearly part of a longer dialogue on professional identification. Under state socialism, such questioning of curricular materials was not possible openly, and thus the fall of state socialism represents for Nina and those with similar concerns a sharp break in the way professional identification and dignity are conceived.

The importance of professional dignity to history teachers derives not only from a psychological need to transcend the discontinuities that the fall of state socialism represents. Professional dignity has become an issue in large part as a response to the diminishing social prestige and economic well-being that teachers are experiencing. This diminishment of prestige and economic fortunes is the result of several intersecting processes. First, the Socialist state's administration of education did partially succeed in turning the teacher into a mere state functionary. Indeed, teachers I spoke to largely supported this view in reference to *unnamed other teachers* but usually presented themselves as having managed to hold on to their professional integrity as historians. Second, the Socialist state discriminated against the intellectual professions as regards remuneration. With the fall of state socialism and the consequent economic collapse, teachers, though not alone in this, have fared particularly badly. Indeed, hand in hand with assertions of the dignity of the profession goes a sense that this dignity is not reflected at the level of social prestige or economic recompense.

Desislava's and Mariia's representations of their professional integrity and dignity exemplify one route to the affirmation of professional dignity: dignity as deriving from a continuity with the past. Nina's representation of her professional integrity and dignity exemplifies a somewhat different route: dignity as deriving from a break with the past, whereby formerly clandestine and resistive identifications are affirmed and given dignity. In the first case, dignity is premised on a continuity between past and present, wherein the past validates the present; in the second, dignity established and acknowledged in the present is conferred upon the past, establishing and validating a continuity. In both cases, the teachers are concerned to present themselves as having an integrity in the way they identified themselves through the transition from state socialism, and to defend themselves as practitioners—whether exemplary or oppositional—during the state-Socialist period. Their remarks can also be taken as a defense of the history teaching profession, although this is clearer in the case of Desislava and Mariia, whose views are representative of many of the older teachers I got to know. Their investment in the past is greater than that of younger teachers like Nina, who are at times scathingly critical of some of their colleagues, yet nonetheless concerned to defend the profession, while suggesting that not all teachers live up to their calling.

The assertion of personal and professional integrity across the transition can also be read as an affirmation of Bulgarianness: possessing dignity and integrity in their identification in the present as both teachers and citizens—demonstrably holding one's head high—is an affirmation of Bulgaria's and Bulgarians' rightful place in the European and global community of nations, itself a central concern of the history curriculum.

Conclusions

The transition from state socialism to market capitalism and pluralist democracy in Bulgaria, as in much of the rest of Eastern Europe, has engendered new problems, not least among which is the mismatch between the aspirations of the people for inclusion in an expansive, unified Europe of economic plenty and the realities of an unequally prosperous, divided Europe. Bulgarians are no newcomers to such disenchantment: a series of "national humiliations," i.e., injustices suffered in the terms of peace treaties following major wars, forms a major theme in Bulgarian history, representing dignity denied. However, the reality of a still divided Europe in the mid-1990s was experienced as a heavy blow precisely because Bulgarians felt that this time they were finally getting things right—dismantling the Socialist state and returning to the democratic capitalist fold. For school history teachers, the experience of the transition has meant teaching a curriculum that in some ways jars with present experience. While the curriculum is clear in its presentation of a historical trajectory that places Bulgaria squarely in Europe, both present experience and the recent past attest to a dilemma of identification in which Bulgaria has not been accorded either the place or the dignity Bulgarians see as their due, a dilemma well recognized in the ironical humor of the broader public sphere (see Pilbrow 2005).

Teachers, for their part, are involved in presenting the official narrative of history and representing the state in its bid to recast itself as an integral part of Europe—and in promoting a positive sense of national belonging among youth. Being able to constitute their own professional activity—and the nation itself—in terms of a continuity between the past and the present is an important means to reclaiming dignity for themselves—as professionals, as nationals, as citizens—during a period of considerable instability and disjuncture. Through being good teachers—in promoting the search for truth and humanitarian values—they are also engaging in reclaiming dignity for the nation itself as they teach successive generations how to question and reexamine the past. Moreover, they are, in doing so, setting an example for their pupils of how one can reclaim dignity for oneself through troubled times. These aspects of what transpires in the classroom—the "subtexts" and "hidden" discourses that both explicitly and implicitly accompany the learning of the subject matter—are by no means merely incidental to the classroom process or to the broader processes of social reproduction within which formal educational practices fall (Bourdieu and Passeron 1977; Willis 1977).[10] Indeed, negotiating dignity is (particularly in the case of history[11]) intimately tied to the subject matter at hand. In outlining key issues and stakes in Bulgarian history teachers' perceptions of their professional commitment, I have sought to illuminate part of the broader context that must be considered in examining formal educational practices as processes of social and cultural reproduction.

I find the concept of nostalgia of little utility in explaining the attempts by these teachers, and by Mladen, the student, to reference the past in meaningful ways in their present constitution of self. Through focusing, at least in the case of the teachers, on the issue of dignity and dignifying practices, I have sought to orient my analysis towards the motivations and social contexts within which the past gets called up at such "moments of danger" (Benjamin 1968: 267). They and Mladen alike were attempting to thread together cohesive narratives for their present, not through fetishizing an irretrievable past or utopian longing, but through refusing to ignore or let go of the personal pasts and practices that had provided them a sense of ontological security, and, particularly in Mladen's case, that provided a framework for engaging searching questions about both past and present.

Notes

1. A pseudonym. All informants' names and identifying characteristics have been changed.
2. Field research supported by the Wenner-Gren Foundation for Anthropological Research (grant #5859) and the Open Society Foundation. Versions of this chapter have been presented at the Sixth Annual World Convention of the Association for the Study of Nationalities, Columbia University, New

York, 5–7 April 2001, and the Annual Meeting of the American Anthropological Association, Washington, DC, 28 November–2 December 2001.
3. I draw here from a long anthropological tradition in the study of ritual processes, particularly referencing the work of Victor Turner (1967), whose discussion of the liminal phase in rites of passage and the ritual juxtapositions of meaning has shaped my understanding of formal education as a drawn-out rite of passage.
4. This suggests a mode of self-presentation that was, for want of a more neutral term, dissembling; our reigning language ideologies in the West do not allow us to articulate such practices of multiple, situated identity negotiation except with a degree of censure; notable exceptions are Creed (1998) in his discussion of domestication and "conflicting complementarity" in Bulgaria, and Yurchak (2006) in his discussion of how Communist Youth leaders in the Soviet Union appropriated and subverted official discourse.
5. I follow here Brubaker and Cooper's eschewal of the term *identity* in favor of more processual terms such as *identification* (Brubaker and Cooper 2000).
6. Indeed, many teachers were quite bitter about having lost wall maps that they could have taught with, regardless of the fact that they were out of date. The cash raised from the sale of such items was not used to replace them with up-to-date materials. Textbooks had been rewritten, but other teaching aids either were no longer available or prohibitively expensive.
7. Medieval Bulgarian history, a period of Bulgarian prowess on the world stage, was—and remains—popular, especially in regard to tracing the origins of the Bulgarian nation.
8. The same is generally true across the board for academic scholarship in Bulgaria under state socialism, as two further observations will show. First, a scholar from one of the institutes explained that, due to her bourgeois/intellectual background and lack of party credentials, she was unable to gain a position in a university. However, a research position in an institute was not so problematic, since no teaching (and potential "contamination" of students) was involved. Second, a member of a university literature department also explained how it had initially been difficult for him as a non–party member to publish, but that once he had received his doctorate, thereby establishing his credentials as a scholar, this barrier to publishing was surmountable.
9. Pupils were, in the mid-1990s, provided with free textbooks up until eighth grade, after which they had to purchase their own. Textbooks, especially those written for senior classes, are extremely expensive in relation to average family income.
10. I develop my understanding of the processes of social and cultural reproduction through the lens of Giddens' (1984: 7) distinction between discursive and practical consciousness, and Bourdieu's (1977: 82) "habitus," suggesting that only part of what is learned in any given educational transaction is available to discursive consideration, and that much of what is learned is acquired as practical consciousness—cultural competence of which the native is not entirely aware or capable of discursively describing (see Pilbrow 2001).

11. This is explicitly stated in the curriculum for history (MONT 1995). The case would, I imagine, be similar also for geography, literature, and social studies.

References

Bakalov, Georgi, Petŭr Angelov, Tsvetana Georgieva, Dimitŭr Tsanev, Bobi Bobev, and Stoicho Grŭncharov. 1993. *Istoriya na Bŭlgariya. Za gimnazialnata stepen na obshtoobrazovatelnite i profesionalnite uchilishta.* Sofia: Bulvest.
Benjamin, Walter. 1968. "Theses on the Philosophy of History. In *Illuminations.* London: Fontana/Collins.
Bourdieu, Pierre. 1977. *Outline of a Theory of Practice.* Cambridge: Cambridge University Press.
Bourdieu, Pierre, and Jean-Claude Passeron. 1977. *Reproduction in Education, Society and Culture,* trans. R. Nice. London: Sage.
Boym, Svetlana. 2001. *The Future of Nostalgia.* New York: Basic Books.
Brubaker, Rogers, and Frederick Cooper. 2000. "Beyond 'Identity.'" *Theory and Society* 29: 1–47.
Creed, Gerald W. 1998. *Domesticating Revolution: From Socialist Reform to Ambivalent Transition in a Bulgarian Village.* University Park: Pennsylvania State University Press.
———. 1999. "Deconstructing Socialism in Bulgaria." In *Uncertain Transition: Ethnographies of Change in the Postsocialist World,* ed. Michael Burawoy and Katherine Verdery, 223–43. Lanham, MD: Rowman and Littlefield.
Giddens, Anthony. 1984. *The Constitution of Society: Outline of the Theory of Structuration.* Berkeley: University of California Press.
Isusov, Mito. 1991. "Istoricheskata nauka i nashata sŭvremennost." *Istoricheski pregled* 47 (1): 3–12.
Kligman, Gail. 1998. *The Politics of Duplicity: Controlling Reproduction in Ceausescu's Romania.* Berkeley: University of California Press.
MONT (Ministerstvo na obrazovanieto, naukata i tehnologiite [Ministry of Education, Science and Technology]). 1995. *Ukazanie za organizirane na obuchenieto po istoriia v srednite obshtoobrazovatelni i profesionalni uchilishta prez uchebnata 1995/96 godina.* Sofia: MONT.
Pilbrow, Tim. 2001. *Negotiating the Past for a Present in Transition: Secondary-School History and the Production of National Identity in Bulgaria.* PhD dissertation. Department of Anthropology, New York University.
———. 2005. "'Europe' in Bulgarian Conceptions of Nationhood." In *The Nation, Europe, the World: Textbooks and Curricula in Transition,* ed. Hanna Schissler and Yasemin Soysal, 122–37. New York: Berghahn.
Turner, Victor. 1967. *The Forest of Symbols: Aspects of Ndembu Ritual.* Ithaca, NY: Cornell University Press.
Willis, Paul E. 1977. *Learning to Labor: How Working-Class Kids Get Working-Class Jobs.* New York: Columbia University Press.
Yurchak, Alexei. 2006. *Everything Was Forever, Until It Was No More: The Last Soviet Generation.* Princeton, NJ: Princeton University Press.

 6

Invisible—Inaudible
Albanian Memories of Socialism after the War in Kosovo
Stephanie Schwandner-Sievers

Kosovo's postwar culture of commemoration was marked by a notable absence of any visible or audible signs of the memory of Yugoslav socialism. Most Yugoslav partisan monuments were destroyed and statues beheaded, suggesting not just a visual annihilation of these former heroes but possibly, following political anthropologist John Borneman, the symbolic "killing of the father" after the end of his patricentric form of leadership (Borneman 2004), here of Marshall Broz Tito. Indeed, no ironic, playful, and romantic expressions of reflexive "Tito-nostalgia", such as found in the cafés or art houses of Ljubljana (Boym 2001: 51–55; Velikonja 2008), openly existed in Pristina until the time of writing (in early 2008). For example, when the former Kosovar rock star of the 1980s and contemporary publicist Migjen Kelmendi and his friends indulged in reminiscences of their youth in the 1970s and 1980s under Tito through singing old Yugoslav pop hits, the café house owner turned on the vacuum cleaner loud so that no one outside the café could hear.[1] This chapter questions why the memory of Yugoslav socialism has been so notably absent from public space in postwar Kosovo; whether any alternative spaces can be identified, and if so which they still occupy; and what has replaced this memory, and in what ways.

A Notable Absence

In neighboring Macedonia's capital, Skopje, Marshall Tito Street still exists. But today Pristina's central boulevard is named after Mother Teresa, an ethnic Albanian and a national icon for Albanians transterritorially. Yet Pristina's former Tito Boulevard had already previously been renamed when the Serbs exclusively held municipal power. In the early 1990s it was called "Vidovdan" after the Serb Orthodox saint, St. Vitus, who holds a strong symbolic reference for nationalist Serbs. St. Vitus's day on 15 June (or 28 June, according to the Gregorian calendar) marks the day of the Battle on the Field of the Blackbirds of Kosovo against the Ottomans in 1389, an event that is at the core of nationalist Serbs' Kosovo salvation myth. As Howard Clark (2002: 6) noticed during the 1990s, a period of Serb-Albanian ethnic segregation and parallelism in Kosovo, "throughout the territory Serbian symbols proliferated—from road signs and place names to statues and buildings, especially newly constructed churches—each one claiming Kosovo for Serbia and communicating to Albanians 'this is not your place'." "They are provoking [the] local Albanian population by naming streets after Albanians traitors, Serb collaborators ... as well as names like Serbian Warriors, Serbian Upriser which are also very revolting for Albanians" [sic], thus the parallel Albanian news provider, Kosova Information Centre, informed the outside world in 1996 (KIC 1996). It appears that it is not so much established names from Yugoslav times under Tito but rather those that were installed as a sign of Serb hegemony under Milosević from the late 1980s and during the 1990s that prompted the Albanian post–1999 war renaming actions.

After a violent war, in gratitude to the US-led NATO intervention of 1999 that ended Serb hegemony in Kosovo, the main entrance road to the city was named *Bil Klinton* boulevard and a giant poster of the former US president saluted the visitor arriving there from the airport. Kosovo may be the most US-friendly, majority Muslim country in the world because of the recent history of domination that inverted the ethnic prefixes of power. Apart from the main roads and boulevards, most small roads have also been renamed since the end of the war in 1999. Fallen guerrilla fighters of the Kosovo Liberation Army (KLA) and important political and cultural figures of Albanian history and society have lent their names since then. Furthermore, the villages, towns, and hamlets across the province nowadays inhabit the official map with their previous, mostly unofficial, Albanian designations (and independent of yet another map existing in parallel: the map of international military street and place names). The most prominent ones, but not all, of these renaming effects have easily entered into popular usage. Forty-one-year-old ethnic Albanian Gani Bajrami says the renaming of streets has always been a kind of revenge of the victor: "After the 1999 war they replaced a Serbian hero with an Albanian hero, a Serbian town with an Albanian town," explains Bajrami. "Yugoslav People's Army Street became UCK Street, Belgrade Street became Tirana Street. I have three addresses today and I really don't know which one is valid." (Beardsley 2002)

In postwar Kosovo, as I have explored elsewhere and in greater ethnographic detail jointly with my colleague Anna Di Lellio, an Albanian messianic master narrative of militant resistance and sacrifice for the nation—perceived to have prompted NATO intervention and centered around the figure of the Legendary Commander of the early KLA, Adem Jashari, and his and his family's deaths under three days of Serb shell fire in March 1998—has hegemonized Albanian public discourse and public spaces in Kosovo. This powerful postwar icon of the Albanian nation has been ubiquitously visible in Kosovo's public spaces: on the one hand, through visual representations such as monuments, posters, media dissemination, and various material, ritual, and other symbolic reproductions emanating from this traditional Albanian family's destroyed houses, which since the deaths have become a popular pilgrimage shrine to the nation, and, on the other, evoked in all Albanian political references such as speeches and formal annual commemoration ceremonies (Di Lellio and Schwandner-Sievers 2006a, 2006b).

In this previous work we pointed to the strong psychosocial function that this master narrative fulfilled for many war-traumatized Albanians in postwar Kosovo, since "it has shifted the focus from 'shameful' experiences of victimization/humiliation to imparting pride" (2006a: 527). Albanian nationalism in postwar Kosovo, as social psychologist Blerina Kellezi (2006) found, from her interview respondents, allowed expressing and sharing private grief over losses within the sociocultural norms of Albanian postwar society, while shameful experiences (such as, for example, war rape) violated the shared norms to such an extent that these events became "unspeakable" and thus subject to "consensual silence" within the affected families and wider society (cf. Schwandner-Sievers 2006: 213). The Jashari myths, rituals, and monuments appear as a public expression of "the speakable," the brave and honorable, of this collective desire to distinguish pride from shame, the speakable from the unspeakable (Kellezi 2006) in shared memory. They also emerge as a strong example of the ways in which the political and psychological, the public and the private, can be entangled in and hegemonize the "commemorative arena" of war events (Ashplant, Dawson, and Roper 2000)—a phenomenon that, for example, was also observed in postwar Bosnia (Duijzings 2007). It is this concurrence of the private and the public realm that made this nationalist narrative so powerful. It was also a shared desire for personal and collective security through achieving national independence, which explains why across all the Albanians' divides, the master narrative underpinned a visual "territorialization of memory" in symbolic and ritual juxtaposition to Serb claims on the same, respectively sacred, Kosovar lands (Smith 2003; Di Lellio and Schwandner-Sievers 2006b: 37–38).

The speakable was also expressed through visual means, while the unspeakable remained invisible and inaudible in public war commemoration in Kosovo—even in cases when it was expressed in private. For example, Di Lellio and I sought to identify some discordant and critical voices to the Jashari master narrative in private encounters with cosmopolitan, urban elites including female activists, journalists, and artists during the postwar period of our ethnographic research visits between 2000 and 2005. However, these appeared too unstructured to form an effective counternarrative (Di Lellio and Schwandner-Sievers 2006a: 520–24). Even the death of former president Ibrahim Rugova in January 2006, who was long known for his anti-KLA stance—a fact that produced ambivalent attitudes towards him even amongst his closest followers after the KLA won its Albanian Liberation War—did not challenge the Jashari master narrative. In November 2004 Rugova had even awarded the Golden Order "Hero of Kosovo" to Adem Jashari, posthumously. The cult following Rugova's own death reproduced the martial style of commemoration evident in the Jashari cult, evidently in a bid to gain ground in the ongoing (and for the wider region, typical post-Socialist) *Gedächtniskämpfe* (Niedermüller 2004: 7): the struggles for political dominance through aiming to control the commemorative discourse and populate it with one's own faction's "war heroes" and "martyrs" rather than the others' (Schwandner-Sievers and Ströhle 2007). The *Gedächtniskämpfe* of the political elites were reflected on the ground, where since the end of the 1999 war the hamlets, villages, and cities across Kosovo competed in the production of statues for local KLA martyrs that were intended to demonstrate a place's particular aptitude in fighting and to claim its contribution to Kosovo's liberation.

There further existed groups in society that abhorred the style and heroicizing aesthetics of such commemoration cults as patriot kitsch or "megalomania."[2] Yet this did not necessarily imply disagreeing with the content and message of independence and resistance integral to the Jashari narrative. For example, a noteworthy group of artists affiliated with the so-called Missing Identity project of the Contemporary Art Institute, EXIT, Peja, in cooperation with the Laboratory for Visual Arts and the Center for Humanistic Studies Gani Bobi, Kosovo, explicitly challenged the Albanian proverb "What Is Missing Does Not Hurt,"[3] in particular reference to the lacking mainstream acknowledgement of Kosovo's multiethnic heritage and vision of a future identity (Project Missing Identity 2006). Possibly, this group attracted more outside and international than internal interest (they were long subsidized by the German Federal Cultural Foundation and associated artists have been invited to many international art events). In accordance with collectively shared concerns within postwar Kosovo society, their art event was directed self-ironically against the political stalemate in Kosovo and celebrated any breaking free from artificial shackles, whether imposed by monolithic, ethnic ideologies of any prefix, or the exclusionary international visa regimes, or the years of deadlock over the question of Kosovo's independence (Ptáček 2004). Even more, consistent with the messages disseminated by the most notoriously "radical" labeled groups (in following routine UN designation for activist groups such as the youth organization *Vetëvendosje*, "Self-Determination," or the major KLA veterans' organizations), one of this artist group's main protagonists, Sokol Beqiri, situated the international UN administration on a par with the former repressive Serb-Yugoslav apparatus: "UNMIK is a part of the former Yugoslav system, a bureaucratic, autocratic, ineffective and expensive administration" (Boynik 2003). In conversation in February 2005, the artist, who during the war had stayed in his home city, the horrendously affected city of Peja, explained to me that for him Adem Jashari's "suicide with all his loved ones makes your mind freeze. Yet it was extra-ordinary, crazy, a great victimization, in other circumstances unacceptable but in that moment [fighting back regardless of Serb armed superpower and scrupulousness] it was just grand performance."[4]

This artist may be the only one who attempted to visualize the absence of public remembrance of the pre-Milosević Yugoslav era in Kosovo through his art. As he told me in the same conversation, he believed that Kosovo's entire recent history should be part of public memory in order to make better sense of the difficult present. In particular, he ironically highlighted what now seems to him was a ridiculous ideology of fraternization and unification under Tito (Zeqiri 2005). In this he made use of war-damaged statues that represented the core icons of Tito's doctrine of "brotherhood and unity" in Kosovo: the Serb-Albanian couple of Second World War partisan fighters, Ramiz Sadiku, an Albanian, and Boro Vukmirović, his Serb friend. In a photo-documented triptych called "New Heroes," for example, Sokoli placed German KFOR soldiers aside the weathered statues of this partisan couple. On the pillars of beheaded statues, on which only the typical Yugoslav-Socialist "Hero of the People" can still be deciphered, he placed inflatable cartoon figures. It is noteworthy that already during the 1980s (Tito died in 1980) Albanian youth would subvert the dominant ideology in reference to this idealized, multiethnic partisan couple. The "youth center" in Pristina, then called the "Boro and Ramiz Center," was used in word plays on "snow" — in Albanian (determinate form) *bora* — because of its steep roof. Question: Why does the Boro and Ramiz center have such a steep roof? Answer: So that *bora* slips down while Ramiz remains.⁵ Also to many other Albanians, "brotherhood and unity" had never materialized even at the best of Yugoslav times, such as in cases where the family still suffered the long-term effects of previous political persecution during the so-called Ranković era (until 1966), through, for example, the mental health problems of a family member who had experienced prison and torture.⁶ Since the end of the 1999 war the Boro and Ramiz youth center was decorated at its prominent front with a giant poster of the iconic commander, Adem Jashari, overlooking the city in defiance of any need for formal permissions and asserting the Albanian militant statuary hegemony over Kosovo. Since Kosovo's independence declaration on 17 February 2008, a supersized sculpture forming the letters "New Born" was erected in front of the center and signed by thousands of citizens; a 3.5 meter and 900 kilogram statue of former president Bill Clinton, sprayed in gold, placed on the boulevard named after him; and Jashari's stylized face has spoken back to his monumental presence from posters and T-shirts across the city proclaiming "It is done," i.e., your testament of sacrifice for the nation has been fulfilled.

It can be preliminarily summarized that public memory of Yugoslav socialism was neither visible nor spoken about in public in postwar Kosovo until the independence declaration. Even the exceptions identified, artists and members of the cosmopolitan elite, employed a bitter tone when reminding the viewer of this period of Kosovo's past (e.g., Kelmendi 2001; Zeqiri 2005). The type of public memory of Yugoslav socialism thus encountered could be classified as *überlagerte Erinnerung*,⁷ a stratum of memory effectively supplanted by socially and politically more significant memories in the present, which until the independence declaration in February 2008 almost exclusively related to the recent war. The hegemonic war memories appeared as nearly concordant expressions of public and private concerns during the first years after the 1999 war in Kosovo. For example, the International Organization of Migration's (IOM) Archives of Memory project, which included conducting more than 120 in-depth personal interviews in Kosovo shortly after the war, found that despite their attempts to widen "the conversation to include a wide range of topics [i]n most of the interviews held within the Kosovar-Albanian community ... the interviewees made the war the center of their conversation, and, in some cases, the researchers were unable to address other issues" (Salvatici 2001: 21–22).

The commemorative silence and *Überlagerung* could thus be an effect of the trauma of war, the postwar national identity construction process itself (and thus a result of both privately and publicly shared political aspirations), or the ways in which the Tito period in Kosovo was experienced and thus transformed into "blocked" or "hurt" memory (cf. Ricoeur 2004: 78–80 and 444–48). Even though there may exist an implicit legacy of Tito's Yugoslavia in commemorative and political style and practice in Kosovo still,[8] political reference, which suddenly re-emerged on the day of the independence declaration, was aggressively anti-Yugoslav. On 17 February, 2008, the daily newspaper, *Express*, regarded as close to the government, visually equated Tito with Milosević as well as with the Prime Minister of the First Yugoslavia, Nicola Pašić, in a front page triptych of iconic photographs. The caption read, 'Fuck YU (1913 – 2008)'. Not surprisingly, playfully longing Tito-nostalgia could not yet be found openly displayed in postwar Kosovar society. It thus may come as a possibly unexpected revelation that in trusted, private encounters Tito-nostalgia can very well be traced amongst many Albanians in Kosovo.

Pride and Pain in Memory of Socialism under Tito[9]

When seeking evidence of "Yugo-nostalgia" amongst a small sample of my Albanian friends and acquaintances in and from Kosovo in preparation for a conference devoted to this topic in December 2005,[10] one close friend from Pristina explained to me: "Yugo-nostalgia? You would not be able to hear anyone speaking of Tito; and if so, then only in very private, when people are amongst themselves, within the family, or they would have to know you very well and trust you. Otherwise they would be afraid that this could be politically exploited." It is for this reason that my selected sample included no more than twenty people and remained confined to friends and acquaintances known for some time, whose identity I am keeping anonymous. I complement the findings from this restricted, qualitatively oriented survey with information collected during previous research periods in various villages and cities of postwar Kosovo since 2000, with a Balkan Crisis Report (Tanner et al. 2004) devoted to the same topic and memories assembled by the previously mentioned Migjen Kelmendi (2001).

Methodologically further relevant was the fact that only certain age cohorts can be expected to have any living memory of life during Yugoslav socialism before the period of the so-called parallel system in Kosovo of the 1990s, and this excluded anyone younger than twenty from my sample. Those of my respondents, who were aged approximately twenty to thirty, turned out to be hardly interested in Tito and his time at all, but some faint childhood memories could be evoked.

The following section is a summary of responses received mainly from interlocutors then in their late thirties up to fifty and older, thus a cohort of which the majority experienced "Tito's time" as adolescents or young adults in the 1970s or early 1980s when they went to school, began families, or experienced early employment.

The narrated memories refer to "Tito's time" as the period after the Ranković era, named after the Serb partisan and "hero of the people," serving first as minister of the interior and then as chief of political police and military intelligence in Yugoslavia until 1966, a period infamously remembered among the Albanians in Kosovo for its brutal persecutions of the ethnic Albanians. Strictly speaking, Tito's time lasted until the death of Josip Broz Tito in 1980. However, in some narratives the first years after Tito's death until the mid-1980s, with the very latest ending with Milosević's infamous speech in Kosovo in 1987 that effectively alienated the Albanians from local Serbs,[11] still appear as a prolongation of the blissful Tito time and are thus significant. Generally, amongst the post-Ranković generation, I encountered private Tito-nostalgia to be not much different from that of other national or ethnic groups in the former Yugoslavia; Tone Bringa found a decade after Tito's death that "the reverence and positive memory of Tito was perhaps strongest among the peoples who thought they owed him most: the Macedonians, Bosnians (and particularly 'ethnic' Muslims), and Albanians. All three peoples had been exposed to strong assimilation pressure in pre-Tito Yugoslavia" (Bringa 2004: 172). With the constitutional reforms of 1974 under Tito, Kosovo had been acknowledged as an "autonomous province" with extensive rights of self-governance. Even though cultural and elite continuities evident in the "Albanian socialism" of Rugova's political factions to the present day originated in this period and soon consolidated during Rugova's rule of the Albanian parallel system under Slobodan Milosević's Serb-nationalist regime of the 1990s (Schwandner-Sievers and Ströhle 2007), memories of the latter period appeared uneasy in my conversations and were hardly evoked. In comparison, private reminiscing for the period of the 1970s and most of the 1980s, including after Tito's death, was clearly nostalgic.

Without exception, memories of socialism in the post-Socialist countries of the wider region appear to be typically underpinned by notions of loss: loss of "security," formerly higher living standards, and relative "wealth" still in the late 1980s (Czismady 2003: 5). The Balkan Crisis Report, based on a survey in early 2004, confirms this finding for the Albanians in Kosovo: "For them it was a time when food and jobs were plentiful, crime was low, ethnic differences were downplayed and difficult political decisions were left to the uniformed Marshal, whose stern features stared down from thousands of portraits in offices, railway stations, shops and homes" (Tanner et al. 2004). An eighty-four-year-old Albanian man from Pristina, in the same report, remembers, "I was rich in Tito's time, there were factories and handicraft businesses—we had jobs, we had everything," and a sixty-two-year-old man recalls that "the standard of life was far better. ... With a low salary you could build a house—you can't do that now." My interlocutors made similar remarks, yet additional recollections included that this was the time when the family acquired its first car, went on holidays for the first time, and when one "could buy shoes." Kelmendi reports how easily available loans helped develop a new consumer society particularly in the cities, with people furnishing their houses, and buying modern kitchen appliances as well as foreign cars "like Renault, Peugeot, Volkswagen, and Fiat"; the "car needed to shine because it was a reflection of the family" (2001: 47, 50). These observations are consistent with the fact that "consumer culture appears to have been one of the relatively rare factors which worked to reinforce a pan-Yugoslav identity" across the ethnic divides in Tito's Yugoslavia (Hyder Patterson 2003: 5). During the same period, many villagers transformed into *gastarbeiters*, "making the German Mark the most acceptable currency in Kosova" and supplying the families at home with a British Ferguson tractor (Kelmendi 2001: 50), which soon became such an emblematic image carrying Albanian refugees across the borders at the peak of the war in 1998 and 1999. Generally, all respondents expressed that there was a general feeling of security in particular during the late 1970s.

Memories of childhood times at school were specifically marked. During focus group research and fieldwork in various villages for a World Bank project on postwar perceptions on conflict and security in Kosovo in 2000 (La Cava et al. 2000), I already encountered women in their forties who, with a sense of gratitude, emphasized that under Tito they were the first girls in their families, in contrast to their mothers, allowed to go to school (see also Luci and Krasniqi 2006). They further explained that times had become more difficult for young women since then (the times of parallelism forced a withdrawal into reliance on extended family cohesion and are thus, in the literature; associated with repatriarchalization processes; see Reineck 1993). Generally, a significant memory of school days included the experience of advancing through the hierarchies of the "young pioneers." A forty-eight-year-old respondent remembered how proud he was when first allowed to wear the red scarf in third or fourth grade of primary school and how he pledged in the ceremony that he would be a good student for love of communism, his fatherland (then Yugoslavia), and Tito. These findings appear similar to the recollection of a young Albanian politician cited in the above-mentioned Balkan Crisis Report, who fondly remembered the day when "she was selected for the honor of carrying a baton containing a message from the nation's youth to the president in a relay from Slovenia in the north to Kosovo and Macedonia in the south. The culmination was the handing of the baton to the president in the army stadium in Belgrade amid cheering crowds on his birthday on May 25" (Tanner et al. 2004). Every one of my respondents seemed to remember national celebrations and related school events, where the students happily and proudly waved their red flags. One respondent, in his late thirties, recalled the drama that arose when a blackboard eraser hit Tito's portrait in the class room and how the Albanian teacher secretly helped him to avoid punishment.

As with the other Tito-nostalgias (Bringa 2004), Tito, in the private memories of my Albanian interlocutors, often appears as a father figure: "He cared for us"; "He was a good father for all of us"; "He was our security guarantee." There were also memories of watching "this film of how Little Joža became Great Tito" (in Albanian: *Jozha i vogël— Tito i madh*) and how the students loved and identified with little Joža. Yet another respondent evoked how "in school you learned that Tito brought together the nations, and that he met all the African political leaders. ... he was Nasser's and Neru's friend, and you cannot even believe how many Albanians called their children Nasser and Neru at the time!" Slogans became ingrained in children's minds. For example, one remembered the giant wall slogan, *Prej Fjalëve në Vepra—Tito* (Tito: From Words to Deeds) fixed on a high building at Marshal Tito Boulevard (near where the statue of the early KLA fighter, Zahir Pajaziti, is placed today on Mother Teresa Boulevard) as a familiar sight of childhood long gone. There were further memories of Tito revered for his modern, powerful, and god-like, even supernatural, qualities: "Tito was that great that he even could grant refuge from racism to Josephine Baker"; "Elizabeth Taylor and Richard Burton spent their honeymoon on his holiday island"; "You could hardly ever see him in person, but there was this myth and magic of his omnipotence in our imagination"; "He had women, cars, an impressive entourage, international attention"; "Once I spotted his father behind the dark glass of his Mercedes when he was driven by"; "My granddad had a watch that was given to him by Tito, because he was a high Communist officer. When Tito died, his watch stopped." 1980s Kosovar rock star Kelmendi similarly remembers: "On May 4, 1980, Tito died. It was terrible. A disaster. Unbelievable. Television showed citizens sobbing, afraid of this death and what would happen—it wasn't possible, he couldn't die. Crying and mourning, they seemed more afraid than emotionally touched. ... As a sign of respect, all of Yugoslavia came to a halt at one moment, stopping life, stopping time" (Kelmendi 2001: 50).

Most of my interlocutors implicitly agreed that the remembered period under Tito and beyond, until the mid-1980s, the period of their childhood, adolescence, or young adulthood, was a formative time, which shaped their dreams, aspirations for the future, and hopes. It is in this context that the depths of the violation of personal memory must be understood when interpreting recollections of the experience of the situation changing, dreams falling apart, and previous self-evidences suddenly being called into question. It is such "hurt memory" of traumatic experiences that makes inter-ethnic reconciliation such a difficult task to achieve anywhere (Ricoeur 2004: 78, 457–506). Amongst my interlocutors these experiences are seen as the first of years of collective humiliation to follow. This "wounded" character of memory is likely to have contributed to today's public silence and avoidance of publicly discussing any memories of Yugoslavia amongst the Albanians in Kosovo, and this would be a different cause than mere political calculations.

Respondents of forty or fifty years of age emotionally reported how hurt they felt when their Serb colleagues, for example, as teachers in school or amongst employees in a bank or a factory, suddenly stopped responding to their greetings, and how old inter-ethnic friendships broke apart. There are plenty of stories of losing one's job and position, but these did not appear as prominently as the recollections of the sudden termination of small social gestures. A thirty-two-year-old respondent from Pristina remembers how, as a youth, he had laughed at his grandfather when the old man said, "Be careful, you cannot trust the Serbs. Think of history!" while the grandchild played in a mixed Serb-Albanian basketball team. Team identity and sportsmanship appeared much more important to him than ethnic origin at the time. However, one day when the police suddenly appeared and escorted the Albanian players out of the school, and the Serb teammates just stood by and laughed, he suddenly understood that "grandfather had been right all along: don't trust the Serbs." A number of other respondents told similar "lessons of experience," summarized by one: "Tito's death was the beginning of the end for us Albanians."

Yet this was not just the end of Tito's specific "brotherhood and unity" utopia affecting real relationships between Serbs and Albanians that had been possible previously. This was, for the time being, also the end for any nonnationalist utopias amongst the Albanians. Kelmendi remembers how he—as a cosmopolitan, Western-inspired rock singer—and other friends, all critical journalists and artists, felt silenced "as a family would silence an epileptic at home" (Kelmendi 2001: 141), while Enver Hoxha's neighboring Albania became the leading utopian leitmotiv for the Albanians of Kosovo until its demise into chaos and mass migration in the early 1990s (Kelmendi 2001: 145–47).

Also before the early 1990s, when the first pockets of militant Albanian resistance began to form in villages such as in the Drenica region in central Kosovo—from where the now revered legendary commander of the KLA originated—Tito's imagery in schools, on house walls, and on placards even during the Albanian strikes and demonstrations of 1989, served as a political symbol of resistance, sometimes in inverted ways. Rifat Jashari, the surviving brother of postwar Kosovo's most prominent family of KLA "martyrs", remembers in the family's memoirs: "The reason why we took down Tito's portraits during the demonstrations of 1989 was not that we did not want or love Tito anymore, but that the demonstrations were aimed at achieving the greatest internationalization possible" (Hamzaj and Hoti 2003: 32–33). The effect was lost on outsiders, who did not share the devotion for Tito of most former Yugoslavs, and they hardly took any notice. Ultimately, and regardless of long years of mainstream passive, civil, or nonviolent resistance of the parallel system under Rugova, who continued this quest for internationalizing the Albanian's cause, it was only the KLA-led violent, militant resistance that eventually succeeded in internationalization. It was "Adem Jashari's 'determination to fight until the final liberation of Kosova' ... [which] 'imposed upon the North Atlantic forces the need to take action' (Abdyli 2000: 25)" (Di Lellio and Schwandner-Sievers 2006b: 42).

In retrospect it appears as if the initially posited symbolic "killing of the father" (Borneman 2004), by eradicating the visual signs of his memory, was the first step to pave the way for a new messiah to arrive and, through even more spectacular sacrifice and martyrdom, lead the chosen people to their ethnonational redemption. Borneman (2004) has suggested that "the death of the father" in patricentric regimes, i.e., regimes in which authority legitimates itself through enchantment based on centralist leadership cults, can mark both the loss and liberation as the end of the political regime. These regimes, including the former Communist People's Republic of Albania under dictator Enver Hoxha or Yugoslavia under Marshal Tito, were patricentric since "they attempted to unify their subjects and create a modern subjectivity through identification with a leader who becomes the general equivalent of his subjects, the standard of all value, but who himself operates outside measurement (Borneman 2004: 3).

The Albanians lost many charismatic political leaders in recent decades. Tito died in 1980. Dictator Enver Hoxha in neighboring Albania—who to ethnonationalistically minded Albanians across the region had figured as the symbolic "father" of the entire Albanian nation and who styled himself as the successor of the Albanian national hero, Skanderbeg—died in 1985. After 1989, when Kosovo lost autonomy, Rugova eventually replaced Tito in the symbolic role as father of the nation, until he was increasingly challenged in this role by the victorious KLA leaders of the late 1990s. Today, Adem Jashari, who died in 1998, is situated in line with Skanderbeg and his death is perceived as testimony to the existence of the Albanian nation. Popular ways to address him, which can be found in the visitors' book at his shrine, refer to him as *bac* (paternal uncle)—a traditional form of respectful address to familial elders that is consistent with the patriarchally structured iconography of the revered extended Jashari family and underlines this new nationalist myth's collective identification potential. Since Ibrahim Rugova's death in January 2006, those followers, who, regardless of this leader's earlier misfortune in bringing about internationalization and liberation by nonviolent means, have always hailed him as "father of the nation," regained ground in the ongoing struggles for power in the commemorative arena of contemporary politics in Kosovo. Shortly before Rugova's death some of the respondents of my brief survey had still laughed at the suggestion that he could possibly be compared with Tito or that he may be regarded as the father of the nation, but after his death many Albanians in Kosovo mourned him as such. Since then an enormous full-body picture, the caption reading "Presidenti Ibrahim Rugova—Simbol i Pavarësisë së Kosovës" (Symbol of Kosovo's Independence) competed with Clinton, Jashari, and numerous other KLA memorials on its own wall of a high-rise block in the capital's center. Rugova's giant street poster replaced a former one of the KLA leader and short-term postwar prime minister, Ramush Haradinaj, reading "Our Prime Minister Has a Job to Do Here," affixed to the wall when he had just been transferred to the Den Hague International Crimes Tribunal in March 2005, and similar posters welcomed him back after his acquittal in April 2008. In summary, there seem to exist many fathers of the nation today in Kosovo—but Tito, with his nation gone, is not visibly among them.

As Katherine Verdery (1999: 26–7) previously highlighted, the enchantment of politics that emanates from the death cults surrounding deceased paternalist leaders may be particularly powerful. In this light, killing memory through consensual silence and the eradication of all visual representation in public space amounts to a death after death, which in the case of Tito for the Albanians, is a powerful sign in respect to Yugoslavia's utopia of brotherhood and unity. Within the generational cohorts discussed there exist many private memories of inter-ethnic friendship and cooperation during Tito's times, but, more significantly, there are also the "hurt memories" of when these ended, which have supplanted the former. In Kosovo today there is no visible and audible, positive-playful nostalgia, and memories of Tito are missing from public space, because it did, literally, hurt.

Notes

I am most grateful to the anonymous reviewer for his thoughtful comments and suggestions; Migjen Kelmendi, Gëzim Krasniqi and Isabel Ströhle for sharing their invaluable insights; to the numerous research respondents whose time and patience I can never sufficiently acknowledge; and to Garry Marvin for all his support.

 1. Story told by Migjen Kelmendi at the international conference Dealing with the Past: Memory and Reconciliation, Vienna, 10–11 November 2008, in response to my testing of some of the ideas presented here in my presentation; see also the podcast of Kelmendi's talk available at http://www.osservatoriobalcani.org/vienna2008, last accessed 24 November 2008.
 2. Conversation with Shkëlzen Maliqi, 5 February 2005.
 3. *Ç'mungon, s'të vret*, Project Missing Identity, http://www.projekt-relations.de/en/explore/missing_identity/index.php, last accessed 12 November 2008.
 4. My translation from the Albanian. Author's conversation with Sokol Beqiri in Peja, 5 February 2005. Some material relating to this artist has already previously been published in German in Schwandner-Sievers 2007.
 5. Thanks to Albert Prestreshi for sharing this joke with me in 2001.
 6. I am grateful to Edita Tahiri for alerting me to such events, conversation in Vienna, 10–11 November 2008.
 7. "Supplanted memory" is a common metaphor often used in German memory research in relation to memories of the Second World War and the supplanting of perpetration and responsibility for crime through memories of victimization.
 8. See, regarding the Yugoslav style of private death notice and other cultural continuities as such a legacy previously discussed, Schwandner-Sievers 2007; cf. Roth and Roth 1988; and for a discussion of the legacy of Albanian socialism since Yugoslav times, see Schwandner-Sievers and Ströhle 2007.
 9. This section is a translated and significantly revised and expanded version of a subchapter in Schwandner-Sievers 2007, previously also used in an abridged form in Schwandner-Sievers and Ströhle 2007 (both German publications). Interviews were conducted in Albanian, German, and English. All translations are my own.
10. Zwischen Nostalgie, Amnesie und Allergie: Erinnerungen an den Kommunismus in Südosteuropa, Berlin Free University, 1–3 December 2005.
11. In this speech Milosević told local Serbs, who were severely dissatisfied with Albanian dominance in the province, "No-one shall dare beat you" —

an event commonly regarded as axiomatic in having set his nationalist Serb platform.

References

Ashplant, Timothy, Graham Dawson, and Michael Roper. 2000. "The Politics of War Memory and Commemoration: Contexts, Structures and Dynamics." In *Commemorating War: The Politics of Memory (Memory and Narrative)*, ed. T. Ashplant, G. Dawson, and M. Roper. London: Transaction.

Beardsley, Eleanor. 2002. "Excuse me, but where do I live?" *UNMIK, Focus Kosovo, Municipal Affairs*. http://www.unmikonline.org/pub/focuskos/dec02/focuskmunaffair3.htm.

Borneman, John. 2004. "Introduction: Theorizing Regime Ends." In *Death of the Father: An Anthropology of the End in Political Authority*, ed. John Borneman. Oxford: Berghahn.

Boym, Svetlana. 2001. *The Future of Nostalgia*. New York: Basic Books.

Boynik, Sezgin. 2003. "Questions for Artist Sokol Beqiri." *Umelec: Contemporary Art and Culture International* 3. http://www.divus.cz/umelec/en/pages/umelec.php?id=1004&roc=2003&cis=3#clanek.

Bringa, Tone. 2004. "The Peaceful Death of Tito and the Violent End of Yugoslavia." In *Death of the Father: An Anthropology of the End in Political Authority*, ed. John Borneman. Oxford: Berghahn.

Clark, Howard. 2002. *Kosovo: Closing the Circle of Violence*. Working paper. Coventry, UK: Centre for the Study of Forgiveness and Reconciliation.

Czismady, Adrienne. 2003. "Poverty and Ethnicity in Six Post-Socialist Counties." *Berliner Osteuropa-Info* 19: 3–10.

Di Lellio, Anna, and Stephanie Schwandner-Sievers. 2006a. "The Legendary Commander: The Construction of an Albanian Master Narrative in Post-war Kosovo." *Nations and Nationalism* 12 (3): 513–29.

———. 2006b. "Sacred Journey to a Nation: The Construction of a Shrine in Postwar Kosovo." *Journeys: The International Journal of Travel and Travel Writing* 7 (1): 27–49.

Duijzings, Ger. 2007. "Commemorating Srebrenica: Histories of Violence and the Politics of Memory in Eastern Bosnia." In *The New Bosnian Mosaic: Identities, Memories, and Moral Claims in a Postwar Society*, ed. Xavier Bougarel, Elissa Helms, and Ger Duijzings, Aldershot, UK: Ashgate.

Hamzaj, Bardh, and Faik Hoti. 2003. *Jasharët (Histori e rrëfyer nga Rifat, Besarta, Bashkim, Murat dhe Lulzim Jashari)*. Pristina: Zëri.

Hyder Patterson, Patrick. 2003. "An Everyday for Everyman (and Everywoman, Too): Consumer Culture, the New 'New Class' and the Making of the Yugoslav Dream, 1950–1965." Paper presented at the conference *Everyday Socialism: State and Social Transformation in Eastern Europe 1945–1965*, London: The Open University, 24–26 April.

Kellezi, Blerina. 2006. "Social Identity and Trauma: The Case of the Kosovo Albanians." Unpublished PhD dissertation, University of St. Andrews.

Kelmendi, Migjen. 2001. *GjurmëtLP: To Change the World: A History of the Traces*. Pristina: Java Multimedia Productions.

KIC. 1996. "Serbisation of street names in Prishtina." *Bulletin of the Ministry of Information of the Republic of Kosova: Kosova Communication #265*, 20 May, Kosova Information Centre. http://www.hri.org/news/balkans/koscom/1996/96-05-20.koscom.html.
La Cava, Gloria et al. 2000. *Conflict and Change in Kosovo, The Impact on Institutions and Society*, Washington DC: Worldbank. http://web.worldbank.org/WBSITE/EXTERNAL/COUNTRIES/ECAEXT/EXTECAREGTOPSOCDEV/EXTSDISEE/0,,contentMDK:20442340~menuPK:983732~pagePK:64168445~piPK:64168309~theSitePK:629967,00.html.
Luci, Nita, and Vjollca Krasniqi. 2006. *Politics of Remembrance and Belonging: Life Histories of Albanian Women in Kosova*. Pristina: Center for Research and Gender Policy.
Niedermüller, Peter. 2004. "Der Mythos der Gemeinschaft: Geschichte, Gedächtnis und Politik im heutigen Osteuropa." In *Umbruch im östlichen Europa. Die nationale Wende und das kollektive Gedächtnis* (Gedächtnis–Erinnerung–Identität 5), ed. Andrei Corbea-Hoisie, Rudolf Jaworski, and Monika Sommer. Innsbruck: Studienverlag.
Project Missing Identity. 2006 Project Missing Identity with their Gallery in Peja, Kosovo. E-cart: Contemporary Art Magazine 7. http://www.e-cart.ro/7/erzen/uk/g/erzen-shkololli_uk.html.
Ptáček, Jiří. 2004. Report from a Country That Doesn't Exist. *Umelec: International Artist* 4. http://www.divus.cz/umelec/en/pages/umelec.php?id=394&roc=2004&cis=4#clanek.
Reineck, Janet. 1993. "Seizing the Past, Forging the Present: Changing Visions of Self and Nation Amongst the Kosovo Albanians." *Anthropology of East Europe Review* 11 (1–2) (Special Issue: War Among the Yugoslavs), http://condor.depaul.edu/~rrotenbe/aeer/aeer11_1/reineck.html.
Ricoeur, Paul. 2004. *Memory, History, Forgetting*. Chicago: University of Chicago Press.
Roth, Klaus, and Juliana Roth. 1988. "Öffentliche Todesanzeigen (Flugblatt-Nekrologe) in Südosteuropa: Ein Beitrag zum Verhältnis von Tod und Trauer." *Österreichische Zeitschrift für Volkskunde* 91: 253–67.
Salvatici, Silvia. 2001. "Memory Telling: Individual and Collective Identities in Post-War Kosovo: The Archives of Memory." In *Archives of Memory: Supporting Traumatized Communities Through Narration and Remembrance* (Psychosocial Notebook 2). Geneva: IOM.
Schwandner-Sievers, Stephanie. 2006. "'Culture' in Court: Albanian Migrants and the Anthropologist as Expert Witness." In *Applications of Anthropology: Professional Anthropology in the Twenty-first Century*, ed. Sarah Pink. Oxford: Berghahn.
———. 2007. "Stolz und Schmerz: Albanische Sinnstiftungen durch Erinnerung an Krieg und Sozialismus im Kosovo vor dem endgültigen Status." In *Schnittstellen: Gesellschaft, Nation, Konflikt und Erinnerung in Südosteuropa. Festschrift für Holm Sundhaussen zum 65. Geburtstag*, ed. Ulf Brunnbauer, Andreas Helmedach, and Stefan Troebst. Munich: Oldenbourg.
Schwandner-Sievers, Stephanie, and Isabel Ströhle. 2007. "Der Nachhall des Sozialismus in der albanischen Erinnerungskultur im Nachkriegskosovo."

In *Zwischen Amnesie und Nostalgie: Die Erinnerung an den Kommunismus in Südosteuropa*, ed. Ulf Brunnbauer and Stefan Troebst. Cologne: Böhlau.
Smith, Anthony. 2003. *Chosen Peoples: Sacred Sources of National Identity*. Oxford: Oxford University Press.
Tanner, Marcus et al. 2004. "Nostalgia Grows for Tito's Lost World," *Balkan Crisis Report* 500, 27 May.
Velikonja, Mitja. 2008. "*Red Shades:* Nostalgia for Socialism as an Element of Cultural Pluralism in Slovenian Transition." *Journal for Slovene Studies* 30 (2): 171–84.
Verdery, Katherine. 1999. *Political Lives of Dead Bodies: Reburial and Postsocialist Change*. New York: Columbia University Press.
Zeqiri, Lulzim. 2005. "Kosovarian Artists: A Selection by Erzen Shkololli. Art Guide Osteuropa: Kosovo, Serbia (2005)/Art-Guide Kosovo." *Spike: Art Quarterly (Kunstmagazin)* 3. http://spikeart.at.

 7

"Let's all freeze up until 2100 or so"
Nostalgic Directions in Post-Communist Romania
Oana Popescu-Sandu

> Let's all cram ourselves
> In some big refrigerators
> Let us freeze ourselves
> For about a hundred years
> And wait, calmly,
> For the Americans.
> —Taxi, 1999

In 1999, the song by the Romanian pop-rock band Taxi[1] ironically, but using an ominous-sounding hard-rock sound, suggested a solution for the troubles of the present: a long-term national cryogenic freeze.

Cryogeny
Saves Romania

Let us all freeze up
Until 2100 or so.[2] [Taxi 1999]

1999 was a year of lost hope. A good year had been 1996, when the democratic opposition, headed by Emil Constantinescu, finally won the elections, and brought the hope that everything would improve in Romania: the economy would develop rapidly, a just and impartial legal system would put a stop to the pervasive corruption, and the past would finally be truthfully and completely told by survivors, historians, and by the opened archives. However, in 1997, Romania was left out of the European Union accession process, having been described as the country with the worst economic results among the twelve candidate countries. Infighting in the government and the ruling alliance further aggravated the existing problems of the already weak ruling elite. In 1999, the fifth miners' march on Bucharest and on the government ended in an uneasy truce.[3] By the time the negotiations with the miners were over, the government lost what was left of its trustworthiness, and there was little hope for substantive social and political change that lingered. Therefore, a wish, even poetic, to exit the present with the hope to wake up in a better future might not have sounded that absurd.

By looking at several symptomatic popular culture productions, this essay explores possible reasons for choosing a self-imposed exit of the present and suggests an alternative entry into post-Communist nostalgia. Even more, here cryogeny can easily be read as another word for inertia, resistance to and fear of change. But I also think of it as the desire to protect oneself at all costs from the present, and, maybe more importantly, as the desire to obliterate the present with its social, economic, and cultural relationships while at the same time preserving one's self intact, by opting out of another "sacrificial generation" and not escaping into the past. There is no one past anyway because several versions of the past exist in contention, giving the past a multidirectional quality that further complicates the present.

One of the main questions I am asking is: why is it that some post-Communist subjects are not equipped for and cannot sustain their own transition through the present? The inability to connect with the vanishing multidirectional past and a structural fear of change cause the post-Communist subject to give in to the death instinct[4] rather than undergo the structural and substantive transformations necessary to succeed in the future. The self is ready to give up all pleasures, from the national panacea of beer to the satisfaction of basic needs and living itself, in order to avoid the responsibilities, risks, and uncertainties of the present. The inertia and fear of change characterizing the post-Communist citizen is here taken to a different level:

> We don't need food anymore
> We don't even need beer
> We'll lie quietly on our backs—
> A real pleasure.
> And if there's enough freon
> It's all gonna be great.[5] [Taxi 1999]

The post-Communist subject shares this denial of bodily pleasures with its predecessor, the Communist "New Man," but in a hollowed-out form. Discussing the "New Man," Slavoj Žižek writes that

> in the Stalinist vision, the Communists are "men of iron will," somehow excluded from the everyday cycle of ordinary human passions and weakness. It is as if they are in a way "the living dead," still alive but already excluded from the ordinary cycle of natural forces—as if, that is, they possess another body, the sublime body beyond their ordinary physical body. (1989: 145)

This persistence of Communist forms in postcommunism, in both its mental and institutional forms, has been often discussed by scholars.[6] In our cryogenic scenario, the post-Communist self wants to be excluded from the everyday and become suspended in time, physically become a "living dead," not because one wants to contribute to the present in some extraordinary way but because of the fear and the inability both to face the present and to turn nostalgically to the past. The past, as I will discuss later, is often unavailable.

This paralysis is also caused by the fact that, as Žižek points out, for most citizens of Eastern Europe, the freedom of post-1989 does not come accompanied by "truly free choice":

> The catch of the "transition" from Really Existing Socialism to capitalism was that people never had the chance to choose the *ad quem* of this transition—all of a sudden, they were (almost literally) "thrown" into a new situation in which they were presented with a new set of given choices (pure liberalism, national conservatism …)." (2001: 121)

This wave of new choices comes to a group of people who are not accustomed to choose a path for themselves, especially in political and social terms, and who experience a certain loss with the collapse of the Communist structure.[7] Svetlana Boym points out that "Communist teleology was extremely powerful and intoxicating; its loss is greatly missed in the post-Communist world" (2001: 59). Therefore, changing the given set of choices, what for Žižek is to "choose the impossible," is, truly, even less likely. This new sense of helplessness is also accentuated by the fact that, often, the choices that one had made until 1989 are now questioned and even invalidated by the emergent order of things.

Furthermore, the self actually desires to wake up in a ready-made future, the Golden Age of capitalism that bears some similarities with the Golden Age of communism. This attitude of awaiting a bright future is not new and has been prepared by the decades-long practice of communism. Somehow, out of the inertia and grayness of the Communist everyday, a new era was supposed to arise that would make all sacrifice worth it. Boym also talks about this redefinition of the old topos saying that "it was as if that lost revolutionary teleology that provided purpose and meaning to the surrounding chaos of transition was found again, only this time it was not Marxist-Leninist but capitalist" (2001: 64). However, few post-Communist citizens had the knowledge, the energy, and the courage to adapt to capitalism and succeed. In the 1990s especially, quite a number of new entrepreneurs were actually using assets accumulated, more or less illegally, during communism. The large mass of the population had to make do with increasingly sparse resources.

In postcommunism, this topos was superimposed with an even older, yet unfulfilled, expectation: the arrival of the Americans. These are the Americans of the late 1940s that were supposed to come and save a whole nation from the Soviet occupation and from communism. This is what Ion Ioanid, one of the foremost Romanian gulag memorialists, writes, talking about one of his fellow prisoners:

> As he was convinced that the Americans will save us soon, our duty was to try to resist, to spare ourselves, to skip work as much as we can in order to save our strength and to remain as informed as possible about the international situation. Being well informed, we will be able to save our life at the most critical moment, when the allies invade and when the Securitate might shoot us all. (1999: 78)[8]

The incarcerated self prepares for the future when the saviors will come. Until then one has to "spare/save oneself"—an attitude similar to the post-Communist cryogenic attempt. However, these Americans did not arrive. Now, the myth is being resurrected, casting the Americans and other equally capable nations in the role of carrying out the economic reforms and all required societal changes, as if by magic, smoothly and swiftly.[9]

> The Japanese can come
> The Germans can come, too
> To perform the reform.
> We'll have no complaints, see
> All we ask is that
> They don't forget us in the refrigerators.[10]

Yet, after the Communist take over in 1944, the imprisoned Romanians were forgotten in the carceral "refrigerators" by their own countrymen because they were "the enemy" of the present, superfluous for the future and for history. They were not isolated in order to separate and "conserve" the best and the brightest of several generations but in order to eliminate the cause of further tension in the new society the Communists were trying to mold.

Besides, the post-Communist present is not the static life of the Communist present, which some people have described as frozen in time. The Golden Capitalist Age will not materialize itself at a sign from "the Americans"—for both internal and external reasons. Among the internal reasons, one of the strongest is fear of change. This particular fear is even stronger in Romania where the transformations of the thaw and of perestroika did not have any effect and did not prepare the ground for the post-1989 period. As Vladimir Tismaneanu writes, at a time when other Soviet-style regimes had embarked on more or less radical reforms, when the politics of glasnost proclaimed by Mikhail Gorbachev threatened to contaminate and destabilize the long-slumbering East-European elites, the Romanian regime eccentrically stuck with a strange, baroque, vision of socialism that blended Stalinist tenets with ethnocentric, romantic nativist nostalgia for a fantasized past. (2003: 22)

The stronger the fantasy about the past, the more difficult it is to unravel or replace it. Lucian Pintilie forcefully illustrates this in his film *Niki and Flo* (Romanian title: *Niki Ardelean, colonel în rezervă*, 1993). In the film, Niki Ardelean, a retired colonel, sees his family torn apart by the accidental death of his son and then by his daughter's marriage and departure to the United States. He has to suffer the ridicule of his in-laws, especially Flo, who tries to be in step with the times, moves from one New Age belief to another, and who wants to convince Niki that his past, and everything he believes in, has no value. Until one day, the National Army Day, when Niki puts on his uniform, crosses the street to Flo's apartment and kills Flo. Lucian Pintilie himself gives an interpretation of the film:

> The story of the film is a story unraveling a complete dispossession, which one carries out on another. From the beginning to the end of the film, Flo takes away from Niki absolutely all values, physical, moral, and spiritual, which constitute his system of reference—his self-image, or the consciousness of his own dignity, as Dostoevsky calls it. (2005: 481)[11]

The values that Flo takes away from Niki are, in Pintilie's words, the theft of the son's funeral, of the daughter's presence, of her angelic image and of her exclusive love for the father, of the future grandchild, of his property, of Niki's dignity as a soldier and patriot, of his entire self-image including his cultural and historical beliefs. That is about everything that makes up Niki. Niki is unable to adjust to his new situation, unable to envision an exit from this situation. He has nobody to rely on, no value, idea, or attachment to fall back on in the past, the present, or the future. Even more, his wife—the only possible ally—has left the reach of memory, suffering from Alzheimer's disease. Niki is left hanging in the present but, unlike his wife, he cannot survive without grounding. Flo disables even the nostalgic sentimental address to Niki's family memories by editing the tape of the children's wedding into a grotesque spectacle. Pintilie's film ends with the gruesome murder of Flo. We know by now that Niki is already dead.

In Taxi's song and in the film, the past is not a solution to the issues of the present, not even as a refuge from the present. This is because the past is increasingly unstable—it is vanishing, it is almost absent, leading to an increased sense of insecurity and self-dissolution. Tismaneanu pointed out, as early as 1994, that memory survived in the marginal circles of intellectuals but the common person is "completely confused" (1994: 121). There is nothing stable enough in the past to hang on to. The past is continuously redefined; it is in flux and cannot offer grounding for the present.[12] The interwar period, a favorite post-Communist nostalgic destination, is often devalued, especially by mentioning the association of several prominent figures of the time with the right-wing nationalist fascist group the Iron Guard. Furthermore, official Communist history is largely rejected, but its replacement is late in taking shape because events are contested and obscured, especially those dealing with dissent and repression. Personal past, of people like Niki Ardelean, is made obsolete by the above-mentioned devaluation or rejection.

Although the events of the past, have, of course, been registered in the memory and in the narratives of their survivors and, for example, in the archives of the former Secret Service, their existence has not been widely known and has not been inscribed into the discourse of the public sphere. The consensus necessary for the coagulation of collective memory is not there. The importance of collective memory for the stability of the self has been underlined by Boym, who writes that "according to Maurice Halbwachs, collective memory offers a zone of stability and normativity in the current of change that characterizes modern life. The collective frameworks of memory appear as safeguards in the stream of modernity and mediate between the present and the past" (2001: 53). This also highlights the gap between generations, especially when it involves those who have no memory of communism at all and no understanding of its mechanisms. For most, the past of dissidents and prison memoirs did not happen. Following Slavoj Žižek we might say that this past exists "between the two deaths":

> Lacan conceives this difference between two deaths as the difference between real (biological) death and its symbolization, the "settling of accounts," the accomplishment of symbolic destiny. ... This gap can be filled in various ways; it can contain either sublime beauty or fearsome monsters. (1989: 135)

Therefore, the mission of numberless memoirs, public debates, non-profit organizations, etc. is to give existence to the events of the past and to create an image of the past for those that had been temporally or ideologically distanced from it. It should also give the ghostly past its symbolic meaning and release it from its "curse," prepare it for its second death, for possible reconciliation. However, the versions of history arising in the 1990s contest or devalue each other.

The process of memory is further slowed down by what Lucian Boia, in his book *History and Myth in Romanian Consciousness* (2001), calls a state of mythological blockage characterizing Romanian society since 1989. He uses Raoul Girardet's four fundamental political myths—the myths of Conspiracy, the Savior, the Golden Age, and Unity—to explain that Romanian political life has been organized by obsolete ideas of history and its events. For example, the 1989 events are explained through different conspiracy theories, different historical figures are seen as Saviors, and different historical periods as the ideals that should be followed. In order to preserve their historical coherence, institutions like the army, the church, the former Secret Service, and even historians refer back to periods before communism to maintain respectability, ignoring the formative effects of communism on individuals and institutions. Discussion of communism as a shaping agent is avoided, skipped over, effaced. Nevertheless, its effects remain deeply ingrained in the way memory works. Through repetition, the past as reference becomes obsolete, overly used, and soon loses its mystique.

In one sense the past is being *invented*. Versions of the past have been redeemed from the realm of the *(un)created,* a realm of events that have an in-between, ghostly existence as their truth is denied and twice veiled: after communism denied its dark past, now it denies/obscures itself, therefore doubly negating the past. The solid unity of the past has been broken. However, no version of the past is strong enough to create a common ground.

Moreover, the effacement or concealment of communism occurs on an additional level as well. Writers who want their past to become part of history refer to and describe a past that does not exist anymore in collective memory. This past is doubly removed, once by the Communists and the second time by the attempt to forget communism. Memory and its writers have no landmarks to which to attach themselves in order to legitimize their story. For most readers, this past did not happen; they have no landmarks to remember it, but they do have landmarks, provided by history books, politicians, the media, that impose a different story. Even if efforts are made to inscribe the unknown past into memory, this absence of landmarks makes it almost impossible, especially as this new memory content intends to occupy a place already filled by the ready-made stereotypical signposts of mythical blockage. Halbwachs, in his work *The Collective Memory,* warns of the fact that groups will not be able to communicate and create common collective memory if one sees the other's past as "totally alien"[13] (1980: 26).

Moreover, the continuity in political elite between the Communist and post-Communist periods, the overwhelming fear of change pervading both the political sphere and society at large, the lack of experience with the democratic process, and the hesitancy of civil society organizations to actively pursue their role as apolitical agents of education and reform, have delayed the reevaluation of the Communist past. For the governments under President Ion Iliescu the reasons were more or less clear: such an evaluation would have exposed the ruling elite's skeletons in the closets. They had already refashioned themselves as democratic leaders and capitalist businessmen, taking control of the temporarily ownerless assets of the Communist Party following its sudden collapse in 1989. More surprising was the failure of the opposition[14] to fulfill its own promises, when they finally did come to power in 1996. The opposition alliance itself could not come to a consensus of how this evaluation of the Communist past was to be performed. The revived historical parties, those that had been powerful between the two World Wars and the 1940s and then exterminated by the Communists, were unable to come up with a modern platform that would attract the population and bring forth a new vision. They themselves suffered from mythological blockage, insisting on reviving the political and national values and aspirations of the pre-Communist period. During the Iliescu regime, the media controlled by the government did its best to paint the elderly members of the political parties and the people associated with them as former members of the extreme right group the Iron Guard or as agents and spies of the West, to mention only the less offensive accusations.[15]

This process and mythical blockage further weakened the post-Communist self. Not wanting to suffer any longer, it wants to emerge unscathed into an already transformed future. Sleeping through it all would require no effort and, more importantly, no change at all.

> The whole country frozen
> Nobody's gonna work
> Not in Moldova, not in Ardeal
> Not even in Walachia.
> Ahead the future lies:
> Romania on ice.[16] [Taxi 1999]

This fantasy of waking up in a better future is reversed nostalgia, oriented towards what is to come instead of the past. The *nostos* is in the future, the capitalist economy, the European Union, the uncontested, and the solid. However, this future-oriented nostalgia has the tinges of a nightmare because the self is not willing to transform itself in order to survive that future.

In time, this nightmare seems to take more visible contours. The concern with this state of apathy was expressed in 2004, an election year, reflected in the song by the hip-hop group Morometzii entitled "Romania, Wake Up," a song that acquired anthem-like qualities[17]:

> Romania wake up!
> There're so many things to do and you lost your way!
> Romania, wake up!
> Nobody does anything and we're so poor nowadays.
> . . .
> The change should come, it'll come, when'll it come??
> . . .
> Your brothers who died in '89
> died so you can have it better
> but, say, where is the promised prosperity
> you'd think all Romanians are part of the Matrix,
> it's clear we're all sleeping and dreaming our hopes,
> while others take our money and give us receipts …
> if I see all this, you should see it too
> what are you waiting for, life after death?[18] (2004)

The song also brings to the fore concerns with the ideas of a different reality, of a phantasmal escape from the present, of the "living dead." This need to "wake up," to leave one's state of inertia, is felt more than ever. The urgency of this call was heard in 2004, when, after another Iliescu mandate, the vote went to the coalition led by Traian Băsescu.

In conclusion, the present of the 1990s had more fluidity than expected. The self was losing its grounding, and the only seemingly stable reference point became the imagined better future. The contestation of the past and of memory continued until at least late 2006, when the "Tismaneanu Report" on the Communist period and its abuses meant to give added intellectual, moral, and official weight to historical events and to stop the sliding of history. The report was heavily contested by members of the extreme right wing and by other political figures. Will this official act of condemning the Communist abuses stop the disappearance of the past and provide more grounding for the present by recuperating lost memory? That remains to be seen.

Notes

1. All translations from Romanian are mine. In the case of song lyrics, I sacrificed rhyme for the sake of meaning.
    Hai să ne băgăm cu toții
    În niște frigidere mari

>   Să ne congelăm
>   Pentru vreo sută de ani
>   Şi să-i aşteptăm
>   Liniştiţi p-americani.
2. Criogenia
>   Salvează România
>   Hai să ne congelăm cu toţii
>   Până-n 2100 şi ceva.
3. The fifth "mineriada" started on 18 January 1999 following a strike of the miners in the Jiu Valley. A large police force was directed to wait for the miners at Costeşti, in order to avoid another violent raid on Bucharest (like the previous four in 1990 and 1991). The unprepared troops were overwhelmed by the miners, partly because they did not see them as enemies and partly because of confusing, indecisive orders from their superiors. On 22 January, after talks mediated by the Orthodox Church, the miners agreed to return home.
4. Freud's opposition between the pleasure principle and the death instinct (Eros and Thanatos) is useful here in differentiating between the elements pulling apart the post-Communist self. According to Herbert Marcuse, "the death instinct is destructiveness not for its own sake, but for the relief of a tension. The descent toward death is an unconscious flight from pain and want" (1974: 29).
5. Nu ne mai trebuie mâncare,
>   Nu ne trebuie nici bere
>   O să stăm cuminţi pe spate—
>   O reală plăcere
>   Şi dac-avem destul freon
>   O să fie beton.
6. Of interest for the Romanian case is the study by Septimiu Chelcea 2000. See also Lavinia Betea 2005 and Alina Mungiu 1995.
7. This inability is also a Communist inheritance. Tony Judt points out that "by concentrating power, information, initiative, and responsibility into the hands of the party-state, Communism had given rise to a society of individuals ... with no experience of individual or collective initiative and lacking a basis on which to make informed public choices. ... It was older people who were least equipped to negotiate the transition to an open society" (2005: 692).
8. "Cum însă era tot aşa de convins că americanii ne vor elibera în curînd, datoria noastră e să încercăm să rezistăm, să ne menajăm forţele, să chiulim cît putem de la muncă pentru a ne economisi puterile şi să ne ţinem cît mai bine informaţi despre situaţia internaţională. Fiind bine informaţi, vom putea scăpa cu viaţă în momentul cel mai critic, atunci cînd vor intra trupele aliate şi cînd s-ar putea ca Securitatea să ne împuşte pe toţi."
9. Incidentally, Tom Gallagher thus concludes after pointing out the risk of the extreme right take over in January 1999: "All the evidence suggests that NATO would have been as reluctant to intervene militarily in Romania in January 1999 as it had been in December 1989" (2005: 211) and, may I add, in the late 1940s.

10. Poa' să vină japonezii,
    Poa' să vină și nemții
    Să ne facă reformă
    Ca noi nu avem pretenții
    Doar atât le vom cere,
    Să nu ne uite-n frigidere.
11. "Istoria filmului este istoria desfășurării unei deposedări integrale, pe care un om o execută asupra altui om. De la începutul pînă la sfîrșitul filmului, Flo îl deposedează pe Niki de absolut toate valorile fizice, morale și spirituale, care constituie sistemul său de referință—imaginea despre sine, sau conștiința propriei demnități, cum o numește Dostoievski."
12. It might be of interest to mention that, in 2006, a contest to establish the "greatest Romanian" ended by choosing, through popular vote, the medieval ruler Stephan the Great (Ștefan cel Mare, 1433–1504). Although several nineteenth- and twentieth-century personalities were in the top ten, the public felt the need to go that far back to find a relatively uncontested figure. Lucian Boia mentions a 1999 survey that chose Alexandru Ioan Cuza, who reigned 1859–1866, as "the most important historical personality." In that poll Stephen the Great was the third in line followed by Nicolae Ceaușescu (1997: 27–28). Boia comments that "the classification says a lot, not about the past, but about how Romanians relate to past, in other words, about the way in which they think nowadays. ... It is the choice made by a society oriented predominantly oriented towards the left, which feels closer to communist mythology and its representations than to what was before communism" (1999: 17–18).
13. One good example of this distance is present in the memoirs by former members of the armed resistance. Romania did not have an organized anti-Communist partisan armed movement. However, small groups of people have retreated into the mountains and avoided capture for years with the help of local villagers. Reports say that the last partisans were captured in the 1970s; however, many of the people captured were executed. Only a few partisans survived prison and even fewer were able to write their story. One of the best known narratives in this group is the story of Elizabeta Rizea, told to a reporter (Rizea 1993). Rizea was a peasant woman who was repeatedly arrested and tortured by the regime in order to reveal the location and methods of the other partisans.
14. In 1996, the opposition coalition was the Romanian Democratic Convention (CDR) led by members of the PNȚCD, one of the traditional historical parties revived after 1989 who now provided the moral legitimacy to the new government especially through the figure of Corneliu Coposu. In its "Contract with Romania" the CDR promised national reconciliation, to promote educated people in key posts in order to revive the economy and move away from the former members of the *nomenklatura* and to fight widespread corruption.
15. Ruxandra Ceseareanu, in her 2003 book *Imaginarul violent al românilor* (*The Violent Imaginary of the Romanians*), pointed out some of these strategies used in post-Communist Romanian media to discredit actions, ideas, and public figures.

16. Toată țara congelată,
    Nimeni n-o să muncească
    Nici Moldova, nici Ardealul
    Și nici Țara Românească
    Viitorul e in față:
    România la gheață.
17. The song was used during the 2004 election by the winning alliance led by now President Traian Băsescu.
18. schimbare tre' să vină, o sa vină, cân' să vină??
    . . .
    câți dintre voi simt la fel viața?
    și la câți dintre voi a murit speranța?
    frații voștrii care au murit in '89,
    au murit ca să vă fie bine tot vouă!!
    dar spune-ne acum unde-i binele promis??
    zici că toți românii fac parte din matrix,
    se vede că dormim cu toții și visăm speranțe,
    în timp ce alții ne i-au banii și ne dau chitanțe ...
    daca toate astea le văd eu, le vedeți și voi!!
    de ce mai așteptați acum viața de apoi??

References

Betea, Lavinia. 2005. *Mentalități și remanențe comuniste*. Bucuresti: Editura Nemira.
Boia, Lucian. 1997. *Istorie si mit în constiinta românească*. Bucuresti: Humanitas.
———. 1999. *Mitologia stiintifica a comunismului*. Bucuresti: Humanitas.
———. 2001. *History and Myth in Romanian Consciousness*. Trans. J. C. Brown. Budapest: Central European University Press.
Boym, Svetlana. 2001. *The Future of Nostalgia*. New York: Basic Books.
Cesereanu, Ruxandra. 2003. *Imaginarul violent al românilor*. Bucharest: Humanitas.
Chelcea, Septimiu. 2000. "Socialist Social Justice and Residual Communism in Romania After a Decade of Transition, A Secondary Analysis." *Sociologie Românească / Romanian Sociology*. Annual English Electronic Edition, Issue 2: 46–64. http://www.sociologieromaneasca.ro/eng/aeee-pdf/sr-rs.aeee.2000.3.pdf
Gallagher, Tom. 2005. *Modern Romania: The End of Communism, the Failure of Democratic Reform, and the Theft of a Nation*. New York: New York University Press.
Halbwachs, Maurice. 1980. *The Collective Memory*. New York: Harper & Row.
Ioanid, Ion. 1999. *Închisoarea noastra cea de toate zilele*. Bucuresti: Humanitas
Alina Mungiu. 1995. *Românii după 1989. Istoria unei neînțelegeri*. Bucuresti: Humanitas.
Judt, Tony. 2005. *Postwar: A History of Europe Since 1945*. New York: The Penguin Press.

Marcuse, Herbert. 1974. *Eros and Civilization: A Philosophical Inquiry into Freud.* New York: Beacon Press.
Morometzii. 2004. "România trezeşte-te." In *România trezeşte-te.* Bucharest: Roton.
Pintilie, Lucian. 2003. *Niki and Flo.*
———. 2005. *Bricabrac.* Bucharest: Humanitas.
Rizea, Elisabeta. 1993. *Povestea Elisabetei Rizea din Nucşoara.* Bucharest: Humanitas.
Taxi. 1999. "Criogenia salvează România." Bucharest: Intercont Music.
Tismaneanu, Vladimir. 2003. *Stalinism for all seasons: a political history of Romanian communism.* Societies and culture in East-Central Europe, 11. Berkeley: University of California Press.
———. 1994. *Irepetabilul trecut.* Bucuresti: Editura Albatros.
Žižek, Slavoj. 1989. *The Sublime Object of Ideology.* London: Verso.
———. 2001. *On Belief.* London: Routledge.

PART II

Nostalgic Realms in Word, Sound, and Screen

 8

SONIC NOSTALGIA
Music, Memory, and Mythography in Bulgaria, 1990–2005
Donna A. Buchanan

Introduction

What does postsocialism sound like? And how and to what extent are various repositories of memory being mined or manipulated, strategically and creatively, in its construction? In a recent study concerning the powerful play of reminiscence in post-1989 Eastern Europe, Svetlana Boym proposes a twofold typology of nostalgia to illuminate how individual and collective remembrances interact to construct senses of the past, community, home, and self (2001: 41). Boym anchors her typology in what she terms nostalgia's "reflective" and "restorative" properties or functions, which she locates in the cityscapes, material culture, artistic expression, sensibilities, and aesthetic dispositions embraced by the region's citizens. "Reflective nostalgia" fetishizes distance, whether temporal or geographic. It seeks not to reestablish the past, but reflects emotionally and sometimes playfully on its irretrievability, through sentimental dreams of and yearning for seductive, but ever unrealizable, alternative historical trajectories (2001: 49–50). By contrast, "restorative nostalgia" can be understood as a politicized transformation of its reflective cousin, one whose agenda of historical revision and identity formation is couched or disguised in an ahistorical discourse of origins, authenticity, truth, tradition, and ethnic or cultural purity (2001: 41, 45). Where reflective nostalgia comments on the past in the present, setting up any number of "What if?" scenarios, restorative nostalgia seeks to reinvent the past as a platform for potential future action, whether in relation to state building or identity formation.

Boym finds both phenomena at work among contemporary Eastern Europeans, who have employed them to restore a sense of normative social reality largely shattered by the disorientation and dispossession wrought by political transition. This "post-Communist nostalgia" valorizes an experiential grasp of history that provides an important, but no less ideological, corrective to official memory. It signifies not just a "new pastoral vision" of or longing for a romanticized Socialist past, invoked to cushion "the accelerated rhythms of change" prompted by "economic shock therapy" (2001: 64), but an attempt to retrieve that history which resides in people's memories rather than in official records or textbooks, whose contents frequently document political fiat more than the realities of personal experience (2001: 58, 61–62).

Boym identifies sound, including music, as one possible nostalgic trigger, although she does not examine this in any depth (2001: 4). This essay, then, represents a preliminary attempt to engage in a musical dialogue with her hypotheses. Based on ethnomusicological field research conducted in Sofia between 1988 and 2005, and through a more or less chronologically presented analysis of recent Bulgarian music recordings and videos, I wish to test the effectiveness of Boym's ideas for interpreting how postsocialism is being rendered through sound and what these musical commentaries might tell us about the Socialist condition and its aftermath. Here I do not aim to present a sonic corollary to Boym's more literature- and art-oriented exegesis, but to consider how music, as a complex sign vehicle operating in tandem and in resonance with textual and videographic imagery, may encode a spectrum of nostalgic sentiment that indexically and mimetically solicits imagined, potential, future-bound realities that seek to mitigate the sense of exilic-like displacement characterizing the post-Socialist predicament.

Remembering Socialism Musically

Rebellious Revelry

My analysis begins by comparing several musical remembrances of socialism that emerged in various spheres of Bulgarian popular culture in the early and mid-1990s. One such commentary comes from the Poduene Blues Band. Named for an outlying borough of Sofia, this band represents one of several new rock and blues groups that arose at the very moment of transition, and whose songs remark on the politics of the day. The paper insert accompanying their hit album *Komunizmŭt si otiva* (Communism Is on Its Way Out) bears a dedication (dated 1991) calling for the expulsion of the Bulgarian Communist Party (BKP) and toasting all those who sacrificed to help create a "non-Communist Europe."[1] Its cover imagery depicts the band's guitarist playing to a massive political demonstration as a helicopter detaches the ubiquitous Communist star from a statue of Lenin in the background (Fig. 8.1).[2]

Figure 8.1 Cassette cover for the Poduene Blues Band's *Komunizmŭt si otiva* (Communism Is on Its Way Out). RTM 1993.

Indeed, the lyrics of the album's title song (see below), set to a rousing blues progression, are indicative of the anger and heady euphoria that gripped the democratic opposition's rallies in 1990–1991, when the full extent of Party privilege, crime, and corruption became apparent. The lyrics refer specifically to practices that impinged upon personal liberty. As a Bulgarian friend explained to me, in verse 1, the reference to short hair and shaven beards relates to the Socialist regime's censure of the rebellious, straggly looks of American hippies and rock stars. "Stamps on legs" pertains to a police crackdown on short skirts. In the 1980s, women were forbidden to wear mini skirts. If caught wearing one by the police, a girl's legs were stamped with an ink that would not wash off for months, so that during that time, her skirt had to reach below the stamp. From a musical standpoint, that blues songs widely symbolize the struggle of black Americans for civil rights creates a significant link between the history of social protest in the US and the civil disobedience then occurring in Bulgaria. The fact that the guitarist wears a sleeveless denim vest decorated with a prominently displayed 1960s peace symbol patch, and that the album's other songs include "Born in Poduene" (a reference to Bruce Springsteen's 1984 antiestablishment "Born in the U.S.A.") and remakes of the much-recorded blues standard "Sweet Home Chicago" and Eric Clapton's 1977 "Cocaine," further support this interpretation.

Dŭrzhavna e zemyata,	The land is state-owned,
otroveni polyata,	the fields, poisoned,
zamŭrsena e vodata	the water is polluted
i podtisnata dushata.	and the soul, depressed.
Ostrigana kosata,	Hair cut short,
obrŭsnata bradata,	the beard shaved off,
pechati po krakata,	stamps on legs,
no smenyat se vremenata.	but the times are changing.
Refrain:	Refrain:
Komunizmŭt si otiva (4x)	Communism is on its way out (4x),
Spete spokoino detsa!	Sleep calmly, children!
Ot sveta ni zagradikha,	They barred us from the world,
v diversiya obvinikha,	they accused us of sabotage,
v "Militsiyata" ni bikha,	in the Militia bureau they beat us,
i medali si zakachikha,	while they hung up their medals,
v rezidentsii se skrika,	they hid themselves in "residences,"
lageri postroikha,	they built [labor] camps,
istoriyata izkrivikha,	they twisted history,
no neshtata se promenikha.	but things have changed.
Refrain	Refrain
Diktatori smenyavat,	The dictators have switched,
otnovo upravlyavat,	once again they are ruling,
lŭzhata si ostavat,	their lies remain,
zaborchava taz dŭrzhava,	this state is running into debt,
arkhivi unishtozhavat,	they destroy archives,
horata otchuzhdavat,	the people are alienated,
v chuzhbina zaminavat,	they leave for other countries,
no borbata prodŭlzhava.	but the struggle continues.
Refrain	Refrain

"Komunizmŭt si otiva." From the Poduene Blues Band's *Komunizmŭt si otiva*, RTM, 1993.[3]

There is little nostalgia evident in the text or musical setting of "Komunizmŭt"—certainly none for the Socialist period. The song's attitude is sharply critical and celebratory rather than yearningly reflective; Bulgaria's children may sleep safely and soundly, for the Communist bogeyman who haunted their dreams has been conquered. To be sure, the song cries out for political abuses of the past to be corrected, for moral order to be restored, for those responsible to be held accountable, and for the struggle against the recently elected Bulgarian Socialist Party (formerly the BKP) to continue—all salient features of postsocialism—and in musical style and imagery, the whole album alludes to the longing for a future democratic lifestyle—one that, I daresay, it was hoped relations with the United States would help facilitate.

However, as my previous work has demonstrated (2002, 2006), at this point in the transition many Bulgarians fervently believed that such a lifestyle was readily attainable; they were not so much nostalgic for it as eager to create it, if they only knew how. As my Bulgarian-born research assistant Mariya Radeva, now a doctoral student in anthropology at the City University of New York's Graduate Center, explained to me, "I have selectively forgotten socialism, but have nostalgic memories of the free and limitless 1990s when anything and everything was possible and public protests secured space for all sorts of uncensored creativity." To underscore the exhilarating quality of this moment, she quoted a slogan that emerged a few years later, during the 1997 protests when demonstrators stormed and burned the parliament: "Jump! Jump! Jump! Koi ne skacha e cherven! [Whoever doesn't jump is red!]."[4] A graffiti slogan scrawled in blue, the color of the democratic alliance, on either side of the entrance to Georgi Dimitrov's mausoleum in the early 1990s lends further significance to this quip. It reads: "All frogs are green, only ours is red."[5] Thus, to embrace the conservative, red platform of the Socialist leadership was to remain in the past. Red frogs don't jump. To jump suggests forward movement, progressive action, and the thrilling leaps of faith that characterized youthful sentiments and the public mood at this time.

Cosmic Antiquity

By the mid-1990s, as the euphoria waned, disillusionment and impatience with continued hardship set in. My field notes from the summers of 1994 and 1996 teem with remarks from musicians employed by major national folk orchestras in which they describe the breakdown in the moral fabric of their interpersonal lives as directly attributable to the post-Socialist climate. With massive cuts in state support for these organizations, relations between the directorship and orchestra as well as among musicians themselves became strained over issues of salary, professionalism (dignity, protocol, etiquette), leadership, and opportunity. Mutual courtesy, respect, and trust evaporated amid accusations of corruption and dishonesty in the distribution of tour invitations and remuneration. My associates described their work environment as "nervna rabota" (a stressful, anxious business), citing a litany of incidents beneath "human dignity" whose ramifications "tore their nerves" and "hurt their hearts."

While similar narratives of despair and moral decay are well documented in the scholarly literature on postsocialism (e.g., Ries 1997; Verdery 1999: 35, 38), an exacerbating factor here is the public's rejection of professional folk ensembles as Socialist-era dinosaurs engaged in a highly politicized restorative nostalgia that posited a romanticized, unsullied wellspring (*izvor*) of tradition as the foundation of an ethnically homogeneous nation-state that denied the existence and influence of Turkish, Muslim, Romani, Armenian, Vlach, and other minorities. Although major ensembles have greatly modified their performative approach in recent years,[6] the ideological legacy of their Socialist-era productions persists. LP recordings of ensemble arrangements cut by Balkanton and Bulgarian Radio prior to 1989 have been rereleased as CD compilations whose marketing imagery, directed largely at unsuspecting international consumers, continues to envelop these late twentieth-century compositions in a rhetoric of ancient and enduring cultural treasures. A selected panorama includes "The Eternal Songs of Bulgaria," a double-CD set of instrumental music and patriotic, religious, urban, and folk song arrangements from the Socialist-era "Golden Fund of Bulgarian Music," whose cover image is the Bulgarian flag; "Zebrovitsa: Treasures of Bulgarian Music," in actuality an album of contemporary pieces by composer and *gŭdulka*-player Angel Dobrev; and "Bulgarian Folk Heritage," featuring standard works for folk ensemble by composer Stefan Kŭnev.

Other compilations continue to portray the same ahistorically represented tradition in association with the marketing campaign of mysticism and exoticism that so pervasively accompanied "The Mystery of the Bulgarian Voices" choral recordings and tours of the late 1980s and early 1990s. Illustrations include albums by prominent professional folk choir soloists such as *World Famous Voices: Nadka Karadzhova, Kremena Stancheva: One Voice from the Mystery, Yanka Rupkina: The Voice of Bulgaria: "Keranka,"* and *Valya Balkanska: Voice from Eternity.* A post-1989 cassette series called "Voices from Infinity," produced by the short-lived

Figure 8.2 Cassette cover for *Dobrudzhansko zlato: Folklor ot Dobrudzha i Severna Bŭlgariya. Glasove ot Bezkraya,* 5 (Dobrudzhan Gold: Folklore from Dobrudzha and Northern Bulgaria. Voices from Infinity, 5). Unison Stars, n.d.

Unison Stars recording firm, showcases each of the country's many ethnographic regions under the encompassing canopy of the Bulgarian flag; the volume shown here, *Dobrudzhan Gold: Folklore from Dobrudzha and Northern Bulgaria,* features the singing of vocalist Galina Durmushliiska and Dobra Savova (Fig. 8.2). In each case, the Bulgarian female voice is presented as an instrument iconic of the post-Socialist state but steeped in cosmic antiquity.

An alternative but no less "restorative" take on the nation's origins can be found on post-Socialist "roots records" enshrining unarranged musical practices performed by village amateurs. One example is the multivolume "Magic Water" recording series developed by the publishing firm Rod (meaning kin, clan, stock, or tribe), whose packaging combines the emphasis on establishing an authentic past with the mysticism motif.[7] A more bizarre illustration is the 1997 CD *Bukya yabukya rodila* or, "A Bride Gave Birth to an Apple," whose songs, collected in 1994 in Draginovo, a Pomak village in the western Rhodopes, are presented as the true legacy of the *Veda Slovena,* or Slavic Veda, a controversial, probably fictitious compilation of epic and mythological songs—including several about Orpheus—allegedly collected in the mountains of Macedonia and western Bulgaria in the mid-1800s.

This collection, whose title makes clear reference to the *Ṛġ Veda* of India, with similar implications, was published in two volumes by Stefan Verkovich (1821–1893), a Bosnian-born archaeologist and antiquarian, in 1874 and 1881. If accepted as genuine, the Slavic Veda would provide Bulgarians and by extension, all south Slavs, with an epos that perhaps surpassed that of Homer in its mythological significance, one that situated the history of the south Slavic lands and languages in relation to two magnificent ancient mother civilizations—Greece and India. Additionally, it would lend further credence to the belief that the Rhodopes and greater Thrace are the homeland of Orpheus, as suggested by Ovid in his *The Metamorphoses*. Although the CD's connection with the *Veda Slovena* is construed, the tendency to market Bulgarian musicians as descended from Orpheus was well established before 1989 and continues today. One additional recent example: Stoyan Varnaliev's *The Songs of Orpheus: Thracian Songs from the Repertory of Vŭlkana Stoyanova*, published by Gega New in 2000.

While each of these trends uses formerly Socialist musical practices to forge a timeless sonic history dominated by Bulgarian Slavs of the pre-Socialist past, the post-Socialist public has emphatically dismissed them in favor of more cosmopolitan ethnopop genres whose stylistic inclusivity acknowledges and even cultivates the influence of minorities, border populations, and Western popular culture, thus situating Bulgaria more broadly in the Balkans and the world at large, and providing an important countercommentary on how the Bulgarian nation should be defined.

The Kinder, Gentler Past

The genre known as "Pirin songs," which arose in Bulgaria's Pirin-Macedonia region in the mid-1990s in conjunction with two festivals called Pirin Folk and Pirin Fest, displays many qualities of reflective nostalgia in sound, lyrical content, visual imagery, and aesthetic intent. Popularized by vocalists whose amateur status defied the music professionalism mandated by the former Socialist administration, the texts of these contemporary table songs, imbued with an aura of wistful domesticity, address unrequited love, family life, and emigration. Place names, topical references, and musical features situate the songs in a culturally unified Macedonia and signify a new, transbordered sense of belonging to that region. Some features, such as the use of local meters and diaphonic textures, are generally acknowledged as Macedonian. Others reflect both Macedonia and the former Ottoman presence there—a time when the Macedonian territory was not divided between three states.⁸ The melodies' lyricism and harmonization, which is rendered in parallel thirds and sixths, results in sweet consonances that are a sonic icon of sentimentality. Importantly, these characteristics also recall the old urban songs popular in Bulgarian towns during the early 1900s, a genre denied legitimacy after 1944, and, in fact, many Pirin songs make use of the ballroom-dance meters of that period. In addition to indigenous instruments, accompaniments feature symphonic, urban instruments such as clarinet and violin, as well as the electronic instruments of pop music, thus evoking the pre- and post-Socialist eras simultaneously. The following excerpt from "Makedonska svatba" (Macedonian Wedding), the title track from a recent CD by Sevdalina and Valentin Spasovi, illustrates several of the characteristics I have mentioned. Musical signifiers of Macedonia include the occasional presence of a melody-drone diaphonic texture, as well as the use of synthesized double-reed *zurnas* together with the vase-shaped *tarambuka* drum or bass-drum-like *tŭpan* (in Turkish, *davul*), all part of an Ottoman Turkish legacy shared broadly across the Balkan region.

Chuva se pesen ot Pirin planina	A song is heard from the Pirin mountains,
Svatba se vdiga, svatba golyama	a wedding is launched, a large wedding,
Sviryat zurnite, tŭpani biyat	the *zurnas* play, the *tŭpans* beat,
Tsyaloto selo horo izviva	the whole village joins hands in a *horo*,
Svatbari peyat, vino se lee.	wedding guests sing, wine is poured.
Refrain:	Refrain:
Svatba, svatba hubava	A wedding, beautiful wedding,
Makedonska svatba golyama	a big Macedonian wedding,
Svatba, svatba vesela	a wedding, a joyful wedding,
Nazdrave svatbari.	to your health, wedding guests.
Svatba, svatba hubava	A wedding, a beautiful wedding,
Makedonska svatba golyama	a big Macedonian wedding,
Ekh, che svatba vesela	Oh, what a joyful wedding,
Makedonska svatba hubava.	a beautiful Macedonian wedding.

"Makedonska svatba" (excerpt). Text and music by Sevdalina Spasova, arr. by Valentin Spasov.⁹

The sonic nostalgia of Pirin songs is reinforced by the titling and visual imagery of the original Pirin Fest cassette wrappers. As I have written elsewhere (2006: 452), *Wine and Violins* portrays a snifter of red wine on a table set with a white cloth amidst a bouquet of pink roses, conveying an aura of commensality and romantic charm; *The Heart Loves Another* shows a beautiful woman in a broad-brimmed hat and elegant gown of yesteryear, gazing away from the camera, lost in reverie; while *Borrowed Love* pictures a young woman similarly clothed in sophisticated evening attire, the tulle layers of her skirt adding a dreamy, filmy quality to her pensive pose.

Each of these wrappers draws upon the imagery of celebration, of the balls and social gatherings where the old urban songs, waltzes, and romances that are this genre's heritage were enjoyed by Bulgarian townspeople in the era between the World Wars. Importantly, Boym observes that during the mid-1990s in Russia, "old" took on new import; goods marketed as "old" sold successfully because they denoted, in her words, "an ahistorical image of the good old days, when everyone was young some time before the big change" (2001: 65). In the musical sphere, a similar phenomenon occurred in southeastern Europe, where the transition witnessed the establishment of new annual festivals of old urban songs in both Bulgaria and Macedonia and the release of related recordings. One illustration is the Adzhovi Sisters' 2003 CD of old urban songs, whose cover design evokes a scene from turn-of-the-century Sofia.

As manifestations of post-Communist nostalgia, contemporary Pirin songs do not advocate the restoration of a unified Macedonian state, but aim to recapture the carefree, stable, and romantic mood of conviviality and social intimacy, unmarred by trauma, interpersonal conflict, or economic privation, that the old urban songs aesthetically encode. Pirin songs comment most loudly on socialism by enacting the gestalt of an era and genre that immediately predate it. In this respect they contain elements of the predicament that Michael Herzfeld calls "structural nostalgia," or "the longing for a [more appealing] age before the state," an age whose properties are acknowledged and even advertised as part of one's national birthright, but which can also be invoked to "turn against the authority of the state itself" when rhetoric and reality collide (1997: 22). One could argue that this collision was fundamental in prompting the constant turnover in political parties that characterized Bulgaria's elections throughout the 1990s and that Pirin songs are a musical expression of the public's plea for a return to a more stable normality during this era.[10]

Post-Socialist Mythological Tales

While the popularity of Pirin songs continues today, since about 1997 the Bulgarian music scene has been dominated by a second type of ethnopop called *popfolk* or *chalga* that perhaps even more strikingly illustrates what Boym would call a "glocal" phenomenon—that is, a genre that "uses a global language to express local color" (2001: 67). Since its inception in 1993, *popfolk* has experienced an increasingly sophisticated technological evolution ranging from a grassroots cassette culture to mass CD production, to elaborately staged live shows, to an industry of MTV-style music videos broadcast on their own cable and satellite television stations. Both music and videos are internationally available through the Internet in the form of streaming audio or video, MP3 downloads, cell phone ringtones, or DVDs and VCDs exported by a variety of firms. The genre looks broadly across Eurasia for inspiration, amalgamating various regional traditions, but especially those of Bulgaria, Serbia, Greece, Turkey, and their Romani populations with pop, rock, and hip hop. Song lyrics are frequently multilingual, usually in Bulgarian, Romani, Turkish, or English, and musical devices and performance personnel are of diverse ethnic origin. Significantly, *popfolk* videos, as diasporas of the imagination whose terrain is in part a consequence of expanded freedom of movement, whether virtual or in reality, deploy a host of nostalgic devices to create what I perceive, following Caroline Humphrey (2002: 30), as "mythicized enactments" of Bulgarian modernity. To borrow from Arjun Appadurai (1996: 6), such videos allude to "new mythographies" representing "charters for new social projects," new ways of being in the contemporary world. Like these scholars, I do not use the term *myth* lightly to connote false consciousness or a fictitious story lost in the hoary mists of time, but rather in the sense of a discontinuous, "synchronic constellation of symbolic features" from whose syntagmatic interplay a discourse—here about postsocialism—can arise, one whose narrative potential and significance emerge "in the doing," or in other words, in performance (Humphrey 2002: 32).

Parodies of Power

Some *popfolk* productions are obvious spoofs on socialism—post-Communist reflective nostalgia par excellence. They represent a playful counterpart to more sober and contemplative reminiscences of Socialist-era Bulgaria, such as the sixty-minute 1994 recording on which former premier Todor Zhivkov narrates his memoirs, released by Unison Stars in an initial production run of 100,000 cassettes (World Press Review 1994), or the wistful *estrada* ballad "Nostalgiya" (Nostalgia), by *popfolk* star Gloriya, released by Payner Studio in 1997 on her album of the same name.[11] In the accompanying music video, the song's lyrics, a poignant plea for the country's many recent emigrants to return to their native land, are set against a bouquet of nationalistic images sure to pull at the heartstrings of—or, in Boym's terms, to invoke a sense of "diasporic intimacy" among—any red-blooded Bulgarian expatriates experiencing "shared longing without belonging" (2001: 252). Like a touristic slideshow, the video's imagery oscillates between shots of roses (for which the country is famous), the cathedral and monument at Shipka Pass (site of a terrible and definitive battle in the late-nineteenth-century struggle for independence from the Ottoman Empire), the Stara Planina mountain range, sunflowers (a source of cooking oil and major commodity), the fortress at Veliko Tŭrnovo (the original capital of the medieval Bulgarian empire), a well-known monastery that is also a cultural monument, the Black Sea coastline, several Orthodox icons, and finally, an elderly couple seated on the steps of an early-twentieth-century village house—a metaphorical mother and father forlornly awaiting the return of their (perhaps prodigal) children. The "parents" fade in and out of the frame like ghosts, suggesting their imminent demise and injecting the song's entreaty with a sense of haunting urgency.

Rodna Bŭlgariya, moya rodino,
Tuk sme rodeni pod sin'o nebe,
Bŭlgari mnogo ima po sveta
Nyama po skŭpa ot nashata zemya!

Refrain:
Elate v Bŭlgariya! Vŭrnete se bŭlgari!
Tuk vi chakat maiki i bashti,
Ne zabravyaite kletvata pred Bog,
che shte se vŭrnete pri bŭlgarskiya rod.

V imeto bŭlgarsko,
vŭrnete se priyateli,
tuk ste porasnali na rodna zemya,
bratya i sestri s trepet ochakvat vi,

znayat shte doide den, shte si spomnite za tyakh.

Refrain

Native Bulgaria, my homeland,
here we were born under a blue sky,
Bulgarians have much in the world,
there's nothing more dear than our native land!

Refrain:
Come to Bulgaria! Come back, Bulgarians!
Here mothers and fathers wait for you.
Don't forget to swear to God,
that you will return among the Bulgarian people.

In the name of Bulgaria,
come back, friends,
here you grew up in your native land,
brothers and sisters with excitement await you,
they know that a day will come, when you will reminisce about them.

Refrain

"Nostalgiya" (excerpt). Music by Iliya Zagorov.[12]

By contrast, the music video "Kalinka," performed by a quartet of adolescent girls called Malkite Panteri (Little Panthers) on their album

Sha lya lya (Planeta Payner), presents a catalog of obvious references that poke fun at Russia, the Soviet Union, and communism, while also exemplifying a recent trend to market *popfolk* videos to children. "Kalinka" is a well-known Russian male dance song of the *naigrish* or *pliaska* genre, which customarily becomes faster and more energetic as the basic melody repeats again and again. It was a staple crowd pleaser in performances by the Red Army chorus during the Soviet period, when it was often accompanied by a folk orchestra of reconstructed *balalaikas*, *domras*, *gusli*, and other Russian instruments. The Bulgarian video opens with an animation of the Kremlin under a smiling sun, as a mixed choir of Red Army vintage is heard in the background. A bullhorn attached to a lamppost authoritatively rumbles a "Govorit Moskva!" (Moscow speaks!) radio bulletin signal, which is saluted by one of the Little Panthers as she and the other three group members begin to sing a Bulgarian-language version of "Kalinka" in earnest, joined in unison by male "Red Army choristers" on the refrain. Mariya Radeva indicated that the song was very popular with Bulgarian youths, who learned it, as she did, in school or at Pioneer meetings, and continued to sing it for fun at social gatherings throughout their teenage years.

Loudspeaker: Govorit Moskva!	Loudspeaker: Moscow speaks!
Kalinka, Kalinka, Kalinka moya, Kato yagoda v gradinka, Kalinka moya.	Kalinka, Kalinka, my Kalinka, Like a strawberry in the garden, my Kalinka.
Koga s Kalinka nii zaedno letim Tseli nosht nii ne spim V sŭrtsata ni ima krila Vinagi peyem pesenta	When we fly off together with Kalinka We don't sleep the whole night In our hearts there our wings We're always singing the song:
Kalinka, Kalinka, Kalinka moya, Kato yagodi v gradinka, Kalinka moya!	Kalinka, Kalinka, my Kalinka, Like a strawberry in the garden, my Kalinka!
Loudspeaker: V Moskve, vodka, nyet!	Loudspeaker: In Moscow there is no vodka! (hiccup)

"Kalinka." As performed by Malkite Panteri (Little Panthers) on *Sha lya lya*.[13]

Shod in knee-high black boots, throughout the skit the girls engage in mock Russian military marching and dance moves characteristic of the *naigrish*, such as squatting with one leg extended in front and arms squarely crossed, against a predominantly red-on-red set studded with stars of various sizes and shades. The girls' cheerful frolicking and the cabaret-like, electronically synthesized *estrada* accompaniment to their song resonates with the blithe optimism of Soviet Socialist realist pop, while their outfits (short, full, red or gold mini-skirts decorated with white fringe at the hem, paired with matching halter tops with similar fringe at the neck), hairstyles (ponytails and braids secured with white ribbons), and stylized choreography are reminiscent of the Young Pioneers' uniforms and Socialist gymnastics displays. As the song draws to its fevered conclusion, the Kremlin cartoon reappears, but this time the sun is clearly inebriated. A tipsy young man, bottle in hand, staggers onto the scene, announcing somewhat shakily, "V Moskve, vodka nyet!" (In Moscow there is no vodka!). Whether a humorous reference to the public alcoholic woes of Boris Yeltsin or the escalating rate of male liquor consumption that has characterized Russia during the last two decades, the message of this parody is clear: the sun setting over the Russian empire (and Bulgaria's ersatz guiding light) is drunk.

Importantly, the video's overt political symbolism masks a more subtle but no less significant intertextual commentary of sorts. The Little Panthers are probably modeled on an older girl band, Panterkite (Panther Girls), whose 2004 CD *Katyusha* presents similar arrangements of other well-known Russian songs with new Bulgarian texts. In fact, all six selections on this recording are provided both with and without Panterkite's singing, so that aspiring young vocalists like the members of the Little Panthers can polish their skills at home, karaoke style. At the level of costuming, the short skirts and bared midriffs displayed by the Little Panthers, together with some aspects of their dancing, are in dialogue with the highly sexualized mode of self-presentation adopted by many adult female ethnopop stars, which in itself represents a marked shift away from the stamped legs of official Socialist fashion aesthetics.

MTV Meets Mobster Baroque

The styling of *popfolk* videos has been the source of intense, ongoing public debates (media discussions in newspapers, radio and television broadcasts, and academic conferences) concerning taste, class, gender norms, urban-rural relations, and morality. Although wildly popular with almost every segment of the population, *popfolk*'s detractors criticize the genre's lyrics and imagery as lubricious, insipid, or simply low class; its performers as amateurish; and its regionally omnivorous musical and choreographic content as problematically associated with Romani and Turkish culture (see Buchanan 2007; Dimov 2001; Kurkela 2007; Rice 2002; Statelova 2005). They point especially to the prevalent incorporation of rhythmic and choreographic patterns associated with oriental dance—what Bulgarians call *kyuchek*—in *popfolk* productions, an influence exerted by Serbian, Bosnian, and Turkish ethnopop in the Bulgarian music sphere since the 1970s.

Popfolk songs are usually solo romantic ballads of unrequited or unattainable love, sometimes with a post-Socialist twist. In Magapasa's video "Momicheto" (The Girl),[14] for instance, a male vocalist recalls passionate scenes with his ravishing blonde lover as he sits forlornly on his bed and walks dejectedly through a wooded park whose dying autumnal leaves mirror his mood, a mournful Balkan clarinet wailing his misery in the background. We soon see why: his sweetheart has rejected him for another. But this is not just any "other." Seated alone on a bench, the blonde beauty awaits her new beau by the side of the road. He swoops up momentarily in an expensive, silver-hued Western European sports car. Smartly dressed in an elegant, full-length black dress coat, this gentleman's older, slightly rounded, and fair-complected good looks mark him as a businessman of considerable means, perhaps even one of the many new northern European (German? Austrian? Belgian?) private investors in Bulgarian real estate or other profitable ventures. As they drive away, she pensively raises the car's electronic window, literally shutting out the Bulgarian love of her past in pursuit of the Cinderella dream that a future of wealth might afford.

The most melancholy *popfolk* videos, set in a minor key or Turkish *makam* (modal scale-type), incorporate antiquated curios, mirrors, ticking clocks, mythological symbols, dreamy camera techniques, and other nostalgia-triggering devices to good effect. In my next example, "Bezumna lyubov" (Reckless Love),[15] the vocalist Emiliya, garbed alternately in a stunning red evening gown and black silk pantsuit with hooded cape, performs in duet with the Arab vocalist Nidal Kaisar. The scene is palace-like: high ceilings, soaring arches and domes, chandeliers, albescent marble floors, and mythological frescoes connote opulence and refinement. A tormented Kaisar, handsomely suited in a dark brown leather sports coat and open-collared white dress shirt, unsuccessfully attempts to convey his feelings in the words and fluid script of his native Arabic. He serenades Emiliya while standing before a parched fountain, exclaiming that she is in his eyes and heart, and relaxes alone in the hotel's elegant lounge, sipping cognac and staring aimlessly into space as he crumples page after page of unsent love letters. The mournful vocal arabesques, together with the song's underlying Turko-Arabic rhythmic mode (a slow-moving variant of *baladi-maqsum*), suggest a Mediterranean ambiance that here underscores the song's melancholic quality. This is indeed a reckless love, these signifiers seem to imply, one destined for failure but made all the more poignant by insurmountable differences of language and culture.[16]

As each of the previous two videos illustrates, the *popfolk* debates have unfolded in a mediascape where democracy has signified, as part of the transition's mythology, a lifestyle of luxuriant wealth, leisure, and pleasure whose script plays out onscreen through an array of flashy objects and fashionable spaces that epitomize one definition of post-Socialist success. Such scripts draw their power in part from "imagined nostalgia," a phenomenon described by Appadurai as a longing for something one has never had and thus has never lost (1996: 77). Some *popfolk* videos are simply concert productions filmed live or in a studio against an abstract or futuristic set. Many others, however, spin their tales in posh hotels, beachside resorts, palatial Mediterranean villas, fancy clubs, amid old town architecture, or oneiric, ancient Greco-Roman ruins.

While these settings are certainly the stuff of fantasy, they are also overt signifiers of the new mafia whose members frequent the nightclubs, discos, and café/cocktail bars for which *popfolk* provides the soundtrack. Shortly after 1989, mafia figures gobbled up many of the resorts mushrooming along the Black Sea coastline; in the hills surrounding Sofia they also erected huge, expensive, gated villas whose ostentatious, bedizened architecture anthropologist Kristen Ghodsee terms "mobster Baroque." "They built houses like medieval castles and Roman temples," she writes, "with pillars, columns, and towers" being the "preferred architectural features" (2005: 135, 139). Throughout the 1990s, mafiosi were easily recognizable by their gold chains, Rolex watches, BMWs or Mercedeses, "mobi" phones, and other conspicuous symbols of wealth; not surprisingly, cell phones, whiskey, motorcycles, and expensive European automobile imports figure prominently as props in many *popfolk* videos.

Most *popfolk* vocalists are women and the majority in the late 1990s and early 2000s were contracted by Payner Music, which puts out compilations such as "The Hits of Planet Payner, " "Hot Hits," and "Payner Hit Bikini" several times a year. The Payner divas cleave to an almost identical marketing image: with few exceptions, all possess only a first name, highlighted hair worn long and loose, dramatic make-up, and slender, fashion-model physiques whose often considerable assets are usually displayed to provocative advantage. The absence of surnames is significant because, in this patriarchal society, it effectively strips the vocalists of their social identity, whether familial, marital, or ethnic. Like the similarly packaged women of "girlie" calendars and pornographic magazine centerfolds, they become "playmates," instantly and perennially available to anyone interested in consuming the commercially packaged fantasy (cf. Waxer 2001: 239).[17]

Whether posing as a denim- or leather-clad femme fatale, Black Sea bikini babe, or urban sophisticate in evening dress, the typical female *popfolk* protagonist projects a siren-like aura of seductive beauty heightened by the pervasive presence of oriental dance and attire. These range from conventional renderings of belly dance costuming and choreography to modified outfits and pseudo-oriental gestures merely suggestive of this tradition. In the video "Imam nuzhda ot teb" (I Need You), the promising nineteen-year-old Romani singer Reihan, who was killed tragically in a car accident during summer 2006, performs a bilingual duet with a Slavic Bulgarian male hip hop artist.[18] Reihan's text, sung in Turkish with Turkish styling, is subtitled in Bulgarian, and the rapper's Bulgarian lyrics, in Turkish. The song's narrative suggests that she is quite literally his dream girl; using Turkish words, he exclaims that she is his soul, his life, his "little Turkish lady." She is something exclusive, romantic, a "little different," exotic—a description that he punctuates with occasional sinuous hand motions. Reihan, clad in a two-piece black leather outfit that leaves her tatooed midriff bare, crawls provocatively toward her lover through a futuristic dream tunnel. Toward the video's close we catch a glimpse of Reihan's artful skill as an oriental dancer, which she plies at length in her other video productions. Meanwhile, three back-up dancers, identically dressed in black bikini tops and white pants, execute a homoerotic dance routine whose most sensual movements, set to Reihan's melismatic rendering of the word *aman* at the end of the clip, conjure up orientalist fantasies of the harem.[19] Throughout, a security camera that overlooks all seems to function as the voyeuristic Other.

Reihan:
A-a-a ...
Aşam Sallah.

Man:
V ochite ti potŭvam
shtom si do men v noshta.
Reihan:
Gözlerini özlüyorum.
Neredesin sevgilim?

Refrain (2x):
Man:
Ela, ela,
Imam nuzhda ot teb sega.
Reihan:
Gel, gel, gel. Ihtiyacım var sana.

Reihan:
A-a-a ...
Aşam Sallah.

Man:
I sink in your eyes
so long as you're near me at night.
Reihan:
I was homesick for your eyes.
Where are you, my loved one?

Refrain (2x):
Man:
Come here, come here,
I need you now.
Reihan:
Come here, come here, come here,
   I need you.

Rap (Man):	*Rap (Man):*
Canım, canım,	My soul, my life,
moya malka hanŭmka,	my little Turkish lady,
kak obicham da idvash	How I love for you to come into
vsyaka nosht v moya sŭn.	my dream every night.
Sladka si i v miga,	You're sweet and in the instant
v koito te vidyah, poludyah,	in which I saw you, I went crazy,
chak togava osŭznah,	I realized right then
che ti si neshto po-razlichno,	that you're something a little different,
neshto lichno, romantichno,	something exclusive, romantic,
bih kazal dosta ekzotichno.	I'd even say very exotic.
A sega iskam samo neshto da ti kazha: Ela!	And now I want only to tell you something: Come here!
Imam nuzhda ot teb sega.	I need you now!
Ho, ho, ho, ho ...	Ho, ho, ho ho ...
Reihan:	*Reihan:*
Aman, aman ...	Aman, aman ...

"Imam nuzhda ot teb" (I Need You; excerpt).[20]

The model of Bulgarian femininity emerging in these clips is at once regional and international, both empowered and on display, situated on a continuum of objectification and self-promotion ranging from beauty queens to pin-up girls, whose darker side is shadowed by the trafficking and prostitution of women that has plagued Eastern Europe over the last decade (cf. Silverman 2004: 227). The connection I am drawing here between criminality and popular culture is neither capricious nor frivolous. Several *popfolk* productions make direct reference to mafia activity or violence against women;[21] two recent pop artists, ethnopop vocalist Kond'o and rapper Vanko-1, have been arrested on charges of trafficking or forced prostitution (Sazonova 2005; Terzieff 2004); and the link between organized crime and CD/video piracy is well established.[22] Feminist scholars such as Catherine MacKinnon have argued that sexual objectification is perhaps the primary process through which women are subjugated, in part because it unites myth—here of the pliant seductress playmate with beguiling oriental charms—with reality (see Scott 1988: 34). To a certain extent, the manner in which *popfolk* singers are packaged portrays them as the musical analogue of the glamorously coifed *mutressa* (mobster girlfriend) paraded on the arm of the stereotypical mafioso. Here I do not mean to imply that all (or even any) *popfolk* vocalists have romantic liaisons with Bulgaria's mobster elite. The relationship is more subtle: as patriarchal attitudes have resurfaced and strengthened in post-Socialist Eastern Europe, aspiring fashion plates, *popfolk* vocalists, and *mutressi* all seem to be embracing a similar model of remarkably eroticized feminine beauty. As Kristin Ghodsee (2000: 10) observes,

> The ideological vacuum which followed the collapse of Communism also meant an implosion of the old Socialist role models. The rampant criminality that has characterized music of the post-Socialist world has promoted a Mafia aesthetic which glorifies the short-skirted, gold-digging *mutressa* as the ultimate expression of successful (if not predatory) femininity. Moreover, the popular pop-folk music called *chalga* has helped to elevate the "ambitious bimbo" icon to new heights in the national imagination. Young people see the life of easy money and kept women as a radical and therefore rebellious departure from the Socialist past where men and women were supposedly equal and equally shared an ever-declining standard of living.

My last illustration, Malina's "Leden svyat" (Ice World),[23] both plays into and reveals through self-commentary several of the stylistic conventions discussed above. The narrative opens in a club where an anonymous male customer sits down to read about Malina's latest video in a fanzine published by Planet Payner. He sips his whiskey, fingering the metal hood adornment from a Mercedes, cell phone and car keys on the table before him. Malina leaps out of the magazine's pages as he flips them, coming alive in his imagination. Headlines and photo captions in English blare information about Malina's character and accomplishments, while also suggesting that her admirer may be a member of the international jet set or a nouveau riche mafioso or *biznesmen*. Malina asserts that she will shatter his ice world, in which there is no place for love. Her song is accompanied by strident synthesized *zurnas*, melodic material inflected with Turkish gestures, and in the *kyuchek*-related dance scenes that follow, electronic Middle Eastern percussion. The beaded, skirted wrap over her pants, paired with a relatively modest halter, accentuates the seductive movements of her hips and bared torso; later these give way to a skimpier skirt and bikini bra, but both can be understood, in the context of the accompanying music and choreography, if not the longtime and central role of *kyuchek* in the *popfolk* genre, as extensions of belly dance styling.

At the 2006 conference at which I read an initial draft of this article, some of my younger colleagues took issue with this interpretation, submitting that they saw more of Britney Spears or Shakira[24] in Malina's choreography and dress than allusions to updated oriental dance. My reaction to this is, "And why not?!" I would argue, in fact, that this is the whole point. As expressive media, these videos incorporate both local and international trends; indeed, any resemblance to the work of Britney Spears or other major international artists only underscores the glocal quality of their production aesthetics. Importantly, the influences exhibited by *popfolk* videos are categorically not the result of a simplistic West–East trajectory; rather, they are much more tangled and multidirectional, with Bulgarian wedding music, Serbian *turbo-folk*, and Turkish *arabesk*, among other trends, all figuring in the resulting mix.[25] Indeed, I would suggest that Turkish songstress Sertab Erener's 2003 Eurovision Song Contest hit, "Every Way that I Can," as well as other contemporary Turkish pop song videos that similarly incorporate a direct or modified oriental dance motif, may be exerting as much influence on Bulgarian artists as the doyennes of American pop culture.

Summary

In his marvelous account of Tuvan sound artistry and its profound relationship to local ecology and cosmology, ethnomusicologist Ted Levin (2006) relates how he traveled in vain to the Tsengel district of Mongolia in search of the legendary River Eev, thought to be the original fount of throat-singing practices. "In the end," he writes, "I understood that whether or not the Eev really existed mattered little. What mattered was the power of music to bring it to life and evoke nostalgia for a place that perhaps no living person had seen, but that in the mimetic world of the imagination, was no less real for its lack of material existence" (2006: 124).

For me, the videos explored above function in a similar manner: through the performative interplay of sonic fabric, textual suggestion, and videoscripted images, they mimetically bring to life and invite emotional identification with place-eras no one has really experienced, but that allude to lifestyle options at once mockingly reflective (such as the Little Panthers' comic-strip presentation of a Soviet political manifestation) and alluring (such as the extravagant wealth displayed in "Ice World" and "Reckless Love") whose narratives, regardless, are always caught on the horns of a mythologized democracy. As such they are portals on the exilic nature of the post-Socialist predicament, where many feel neither at home in the Socialist past nor amid the radical challenges and obstacles of the post-Socialist present, for which democratic politics and capitalist economics, as they have played out in Bulgaria thus far, have offered inadequate solutions. Thus while it would be easy to interpret the unprecedented bilingual duets and abundant Middle Eastern references in these videos as simple cultural influence born of geographic proximity, or as reflective nostalgia reaching into an Ottoman past whose legacy was repressed from 1944–1989, I hesitate to cast every glance backward in these terms because, frankly, I am not convinced that nostalgia is either the chief motivating factor behind, or that it fully accounts for the complicated confluence of social, political, and economic forces that converge in the *popfolk* phenomenon. As Catherine Wanner remarks, "Although memory is a fundamental component of an individual's sense of self, history cannot be reduced to memory, nor can identity be specified in terms of history alone" (1998: 197). The act of memory, like fantasy, mythologizing, and historicizing, is always a *presentist* phenomenon, one inextricably entangled with contemporary consciousness (see Diehl 2002: 97, after de Certeau 1980: 211 and Naficy 1993: 172). The fantastical elements, irony, and hedonistic aspirations of *popfolk* productions represent one means of grappling with the ongoing stress of posttransition displacement, dispossession, and disorientation. But for me these creative, but also strategically marketed productions are more persuasively understood as mythicized, glocal enactments of repossession, reemplacement, and reorientation, in the context of a highly emergent Bulgarian modernity that resonates with the rest of the Balkans and world beyond.

Notes

I thank Zsuzsa Gille, Eran Livni, Mariya Radeva, and Maria Todorova for their helpful comments on this essay.
1. The dedication reads: "Na Vas, nemili-nedragi hora ot ulitsi i ploshtadi, nadzhiveli strakha, zaryazali vsichko i gotovi na vsichko v imeto na smelata mechta za bezkomunisticheska Evropa, na Vas studenti, ekstremisti, yastrebi, leshoyadi ... I izobshto—dolu BKP!!!" (To you, unkind-undear people of the streets and squares, who have lived their fill of fears, who have given up everything and who are ready for anything in the name of the courageous dream of a non-Communist Europe, to you—students, extremists, hawks, vultures ... And in general—down with BKP!!!)
2. The star serves as the letter "o" in the word "Komunizmŭt" in the cassette's title, while the Bulgarian letter "ŭ" in the same word is represented by a swastika. The statue being dismantled is probably that which once headed "the Largo" on the west side of central Sofia's Lenin Square and Georgi Dimitrov Boulevard (now Mariya Luisa Boulevard), a key site for political manifestations and parades during the Socialist era. It has since been replaced by a new statue christened the "Spirit of Sofia," which captures the Greek goddess of wisdom and patron saint of the capital in bronze and gold leaf.
3. Used by permission of Vasil Georgiev and the Poduene Blues Band.
4. I wish to express my sincere gratitude to Ms. Radeva for her many helpful comments on and invaluable assistance with this project.

5. A photograph of the mausoleum and this graffiti is available on the CD-ROM accompanying Buchanan 2006.
6. This topic is the subject of a separate study with which I am currently engaged. Briefly, groups such as the Philip Kutev Ensemble have broadened their repertories and approaches strikingly to be more inclusive of Bulgaria's many different ethnic populations, thereby situating local expressive culture in the larger context of the Balkans.
7. See, for example, the 1995 cassette *Dve bŭlgarski tamburi: Kyustendil & Shopsko* (Two Bulgarian *Tamburi*: From Kyustendil and the Shop District)/*Authentic Folk Instrumental Pieces Played on "Tambura" of Central West Bulgaria*.
8. For additional information on this genre and its relationship to Macedonian culture see Buchanan 2006 and Peters 2000.
9. *Makedonska Svatba: Lyubimi Pesni*. Orpheus Music, Ltd., 2001.
10. In her *Burden of Dreams: History and Identity in Post-Soviet Ukraine*, anthropologist Catherine Wanner documents a similar phenomenon among women who experienced spiraling impoverishment and disempowerment under the new regime. She notes: "They blame their incomprehensible woes and the elusiveness of a solution on the breakdown of the Soviet state. They recognize that recreating the Soviet Union and the economic and political systems that characterized it is an option that exists only in their dreams. But it is one that exerts tremendous nostalgic appeal. If they can't have the Soviet Union back, as a consolation, at least they want Russia back" (1998: 70).
11. At the time of writing, most of the videos described in this section could be viewed on the Internet site http://www.youtube.com.
12. As performed by Gloriya on *Nostalgiya*, Payner Studio, 1997.
13. Re-released on the compilation *Hitovete na Planeta Payner, Vol. 2*, DVD CD 2:10.
14. *Hitovete na Planeta Payner, Vol. 2*, DVD CD 1:8.
15. *Hitovete na Planeta Payner, Vol. 2*, DVD CD 1:5.
16. This video is but one production of several juxtaposing a Bulgarian-speaking vocalist with others of Romani, Turkish, Arab, or Albanian heritage. As such it is indicative of an innovative trend in Bulgarian popular culture whereby local artists are reaching out to and engaging and experimenting with contemporaries from the larger Mediterranean region.
17. I owe this observation to the work of Lise Waxer who, in her study of the first all-female salsa bands in Cali, Colombia, encountered a comparable phenomenon (2001: 239). Waxer found that in the early 1990s—the same time frame in which *popfolk*'s popularity was skyrocketing—recording companies purposefully accentuated the already eroticized image of these groups by placing only the first names of their members on their album covers, thereby infantilizing them as "cute, child-like playmates" in a manner analogous to that in which calendar girls and *Playboy* centerfolds are promoted. Although this packaging scheme dwindled by the mid-1990s in Colombia, the same cannot be said of Bulgaria.
18. This male singer is unidentified in the song's credits. The artist Lyusi, who is credited as Reihan's co-star, dances in the video.

19. *Aman* is a Turkish expression of deep emotion, whether of pain, sorrow, spirituality, or passion. The word is often interpolated as a refrain in Balkan folk songs (such as those in the Greek *smyrnaica* genre) and ethnopop songs, where it also frequently serves as the basis for vocal improvisation.
20. As performed by Lyusi & Reihan, *Hitovete na Planeta Payner, Vol. 2*, DVD CD 2: 9, 2004.
21. See, for example, Gloriya's 2004 video *"Krepost"* (Fortress) (*Hitovete na Planeta Payner, Vol. 2*, DVD CD 2:16). Interestingly, the security camera in Reihan's "I Need You" may also be understood as a veiled reference to the Mafia, as in the early 1990s, many mobsters—particularly former bodybuilding athletes and former police or secret service members—created security or insurance rackets. I explore the relationship between music videos and organized crime in more detail in a forthcoming article.
22. See Clark-Meads 1998 and Kaplan 1998, among many others.
23. *Hitovete na Planeta Payner, Vol. 2*, DVD CD 1:16.
24. See especially Shakira's music video "Hips Don't Lie," in which her dance moves resemble those of Malina in "Ice World" to some extent.
25. On the contemporary interplay of popular music and dance in the Balkans see the articles in Buchanan 2007. For more on Malina's dance routines and costuming, see the ten-minute compilation of *kyuchetsi* (culled from several of her videos), posted on youtube.com and entitled "Malina—Belly Dancing Mix" (http://www.youtube.com/ watch?v=ukS5LMlhepI). Other exemplary videos, with representative excerpts included in the preceding mix, include her "Strast" (Passion; http://www.youtube.com/watch?v=UUFYNxCUKE8) and (with Azis) "Iskam, iskam" (I Want, I Want; http://www.youtube.com/watch?v=9eIKwHJPnHo).

References

Appadurai, Arjun. 1996. *Modernity at Large: Cultural Dimensions of Globalization*. Minneapolis: University of Minnesota Press.

Boym, Svetlana. 2001. *The Future of Nostalgia*. New York: Basic Books.

Buchanan, Donna A. 2002. "Soccer, Ethno-Pop, and National Consciousness in Post-State-Socialist Bulgaria, 1994–1996." *British Journal of Ethnomusicology* 11(2):1–27.

———. 2006. *Performing Democracy: Bulgarian Music and Musicians in Transition*. Chicago: University of Chicago Press.

———. 2007. "Bulgarian Ethnopop along the Old *Via Militaris*: Ottomanism, Orientalism, or Balkan Cosmopolitanism?" In *Balkan Popular Culture and the Ottoman Ecumene: Music, Image, and Regional Political Discourse*, ed. Donna A. Buchanan, 225–67. Lanham, MD: Scarecrow Press.

Clark-Meads, Jeff. 1998. "Bulgarian Pirates Set Sites on the EU." *Billboard*, August 15: 54, 60, 65.

de Certau, Michel. 1980. "On the Oppositional Practices of Everyday Life." *Social Text* 3: 3–43.

Diehl, Keila. 2002. *Echoes from Dharamsala: Music in the Life of a Tibetan Refugee Community.* Berkeley: University of California Press.

Dimov, Ventsislav. 2001. *Etnopopbumŭt.* Sofia: Bŭlgarsko Muzikoznanie Izsledvaniya.

Ghodsee, Kristen. 2000. "Women and Economic Transition: Mobsters and Mail-Order Brides in Bulgaria." *CSEES Newsletter* 17 (3): 5–8, 10–13.

———. 2005. *The Red Riviera: Gender, Tourism, and Postsocialism on the Black Sea.* Durham, NC: Duke University Press.

Herzfeld, Michael. 1997. *Cultural Intimacy: Social Poetics in the Nation-State.* New York: Routledge.

Humphrey, Caroline. 2002. *The Unmaking of Soviet Life: Every Economies after Socialism.* Ithaca, NY: Cornell University Press.

Kaplan, Robert D. 1998. "Hoods against Democrats." *Atlantic Monthly* 282 (6): 32–36.

Kurkela, Vesa. 2007. "Bulgarian *Chalga* on Video: Oriental Stereotypes, Mafia Exoticism, and Politics." In *Balkan Popular Culture and the Ottoman Ecumene: Music, Image, and Regional Political Discourse,* ed. Donna A. Buchanan, 143–73. Lanham, MD: Scarecrow Press.

Levin, Theodore, with Valentina Süzükei. 2006. *Where Rivers and Mountains Sing: Sound, Music, and Nomadism in Tuva and Beyond.* Bloomington: Indiana University Press.

Naficy, Hamid. 1993. *The Making of Exile Cultures: Iranian Television in Los Angeles.* Minneapolis: University of Minnesota Press.

Ovid. 1958. *The Metamorphoses,* trans. Horace Gregory. New York: The Viking Press, Inc.

Peters, Karen. 2000. "Representations of Macedonia in Contemporary Ethnopop Songs from Southwest Bulgaria." *Balkanistica* 13: 131–63.

Rice, Timothy. 2002. "Bulgaria or Chalgaria: The Attenuation of Bulgarian Nationalism in a Mass-Mediated Popular Music." *Yearbook for Traditional Music* 34: 25–46.

Ries, Nancy. 1997. *Russian Talk: Culture of Conversation during Perestroika.* Ithaca, NY: Cornell University Press.

Sazonova, Liliya. 2005. "A Second Case against Kondyo in Sliven." *Stop Violence Against Women.* Electronic document, http://www.stopvaw.org/printview/ A_second_ case_against_Kondyo_in_ Sliven.html. Compiled from Darik Radio: http://www.darik.net/ index.php?p+article&tid=1&id= 30939, accessed 22 February 2006.

Scott, Joan Wallach. 1988. "Gender: A Useful Category of Historical Analysis." In *Gender and the Politics of History,* 28–50. New York: Columbia University Press.

Silverman, Carol. 2004. "'Move Over Madonna': Gender, Representation, and the 'Mystery' of Bulgarian Voices." In *Over the Wall/After the Fall: Post-Communist Cultures through an East-West Gaze,* ed. Sibelan Forrester, Magdalena J. Zaborowska, and Elena Gapova, 212–37. Bloomington: Indiana University Press.

Statelova, Rosmary. 2005. *The Seven Sins of Chalga: Toward an Anthropology of Ethnopop Music.* Sofia: Prosveta.

Terzieff, Juliette. 2004. "Bulgarian Trafficking Victims Face Hard Homecoming." *Women's eNews*, 26 September. Electronic document, http://www.womensenews.org.
Verdery, Katherine. 1999. *The Political Lives of Dead Bodies: Reburial and Postsocialist Change*. New York: Columbia University Press.
———. 2002 "Introduction: Whither Postsocialism?" In *Postsocialism: Ideals, Ideologies and Practices in Eurasia*, ed. C. M. Hann, 15–28. London: Routledge.
Verkovich, Stefan I. 1874. *Veda Slovena. Bŭlgarski narodni pesni ot predistorichno i predhristiyansko doba. Otkril v Trakiya i Makedoniya. Kniga 1*. Beograd: Drzhavna Shtampariya.
Wanner, Catherine. 1998. *Burden of Dreams: History and Identity in Post-Soviet Ukraine*. University Park, PA: Pennsylvania State University Press.
Waxer, Lise. 2001. "Las Caleñas Son Como Las Flores: The Rise of All-Women Salsa Bands in Cali, Colombia." *Ethnomusicology* 45(2): 228–59.
World Press Review. 1994. "Uncle Tosho's Greatest Hits." *World Press Review*, April:4.

Discography and Videography

Clapton, Eric. 1977. *Slowhand*. Polydor.
Dobrev, Angel. 2005. *Zebrovitza: Angel Dobrev: Treasures of Bulgarian Folk Music*. Riva Sound, RSCD 3129.
Gloriya. 1997. *Nostalgiya*. Payner.
Karadzhova, Nadka. n.d. *Nadka Karadzhova: World Famous Voices*. Serial # 060148. N.p.
Kŭnev, Stefan. 2005. *Bŭlgarsko narodno nasledstvo: Stefan Kŭnev: "Oi, devoiche"* (Bulgarian folk heritage: Stefan Kŭnev: "Oh, little girl"). Gega New, GD 298.
N.a. 1995. *Dve bŭlgarski tamburi: Kyustendil & Shopsko* (Two Bulgarian *tamburi*: from Kyustendil and the Shop district)/*Authentic Folk Inststrumental Pieces Played on "Tambura" of Central West Bulgaria*. Magic Water 16. ROD.
———. 1997. *Bukya yabukya rodila: Stari pesni ot selo Draginovo* (A bride gave birth to an apple: Old songs from the village of Draginovo). Gega New, GD 113.
———. 2004. *Hitovete na Planeta Payner, Volume 2* (The hits of Planet Payner, Volume 2). PaynerMusic MK15698/PDVD 401–402.
———. 2005. *Vechnite pesni na Bŭlgariya: Zlatniya fond na bŭlgarskata muzika* (The eternal songs of Bulgaria: The golden fund of Bulgarian music). Ministerstvo na Kulturata N 14404.
———. n.d. *Dobrudzhansko zlato: Folklor ot Dobrudzha i Severna Bŭlgariya* (Dobrudzhan gold: Folklore from Dobrudzha and northern Bulgaria). Glasove ot bezkraya, 5 (Voices from Infinity, 5). Unison Stars.
Panterkite. 2004 *Katyusha*. Ministerstvo na Kulturata N 17938.
Poduene Blues Band. 1993. *Komunizmŭt si otiva* (Communism is on its way out). RTM.
Rupkina, Yanka. 2005. *Yanka Rupkina: The Voice of Bulgaria: Keranka*. Ministerstvo na Kulturata N 9838.

Sestri Adzhovi. 2003. *Sestri Adzhovi, nai-dobroto: Stari gradski pesni* (The best of the Adzhovi Sisters: Old urban songs). Atanas Yankulov, producer. Stars Records.

Spasovi, Sevdalina and Valentin. 2001. *Makedonska svatba: Lyubimi pesni*. Orpheus Music, Ltd.

Springsteen, Bruce. 1984. *Born in the U.S.A.* Performed by the E Street Band. Bruce Springsteen, Jon Landau, Chuck Plotkin, and Steve Van Zandt, producers. Columbia Records, QC 38653.

Stancheva, Kremena. n.d. *Kremena Stancheva: Glas ot misteriyata/One Voice from the Mystery*. N.p.

Varnaliev, Stoyan. 2000. *The Songs of Orpheus: Thracian Songs from the Repertory of Vŭlkana Stoyanova*. Gega New, GR 70.

 9

"CEAUŞESCU HASN'T DIED"
Irony as Countermemory in Post-Socialist Romania
Diana Georgescu

Almost two decades after the fall of the Communist regime in Romania, Nicolae Ceauşescu's name and image populate the public sphere in the most unexpected ways. He has become the subject of songs and musical performances flaunting such titles as "Ceauşescu Hasn't Died," theater shows that tour the country with comic performances of "A Day in the Life of Nicolae Ceauşescu," and advertising campaigns featuring Ceauşescu delivering speeches or walking his dogs as efficient strategies to sell products or get messages of social relevance across. Ceauşescu's all-too-familiar portrait is carried during street demonstrations in support of demands for raises in student stipends or post office workers' salaries in Jassy and Bucharest, while the national and international press publish concerned reports about the yearly "pilgrimages" to Ceauşescu's grave to celebrate the former leader's birthday.

Despite their significant differences, these various invocations of Ceauşescu's name and image have often been dubbed in the press as "survivals" and "revivals" of communism or as unhealthy manifestations of "nostalgia" for Communist times and strong leaders. There are essays deploring the "Nostalgia for Terror in Advertising" (Cercelescu 2005) and the revival of Ceauşescu's "ghost" (Stanciu 2005), both of which are perceived to indicate popular preference for iron-handed leaders in times of economic uncertainty and political instability. Foreign scholars echo the domestic press, considering the phenomenon of "Ceauşescu nostalgia" an essentially antidemocratic expression of "strong paternalist leanings throughout Romanian history" enhanced by post-Socialist economic decline, political corruption, and an intense identity crisis in a rapidly globalizing world (Kideckel 2004: 123–47). Less concerned with Romanians' nostalgic reminiscences and self-perceptions, a series of televised talk shows about Romania's expected integration into the European Union reframed the discussion in terms of "country branding."[1] Lamenting the unfortunate popular associations of Romania with its Communist dictator or Bram Stoker's Dracula in the foreign press, these debates focused on the impact that the international media, in its thirst for sensationalism, had on the negative branding of the country.[2]

It is fair to say that, complicated by concerns with Romania's image in the world and the challenges to its European identity, public debates about memory practices deemed nostalgic of communism are conducted in a register of national humiliation. That explains why various social actors invoking Ceaușescu's name and image feel the need to justify their acts in order to avoid being disqualified as "Ceaușescu nostalgics."[3] While the failure to outwardly reject the embarrassing Communist past constitutes serious grounds for criticism, some of these practices of remembrance are also treated with uneasiness and ambivalence in the press because they are perceived to be inappropriately cast in comic and ironic registers. Since they tend to acquire a disturbingly entertaining quality in print and broadcast media and encourage a consumerist attitude to the past, some journalists argue that they are morally questionable. Especially when consumed by young audiences, these comic representations of the traumatic Communist past threaten to trivialize a tragic subject in Romanian history and obstruct the process of coming to terms with the Communist past (Chivu 2006).

By contrast to sweeping accusations that seek to delegitimize ironic representations of the past as trivializing, nostalgic, and antidemocratic, this essay argues that scholars of post-Socialist societies would be better served by an analysis of the critical potential of irony to challenge mainstream memory discourses. The term "countermemory" in the title indicates those residual strains of social memory that, having not congealed into a master narrative, work to disrupt widely accepted discourses about the past. My analysis is intended as an excursion into alternative memory practices that are often cast in ironic and comic modes, relying on potent symbols of the Communist regime and on the ability to conjure up memories of the Communist period in widely reaching contexts such as commercials, concerts, theatrical performances, or street demonstrations. Drawing on recent theories of irony that distinguish it from humor, emphasizing instead its polemical and social character as a discursive strategy (Chambers 1990; Gutwirth 1993; Hutcheon 1995; Kundera 2000), I hope to prove that ironic practices of remembrance can be deadly serious. Prominent among these works is Linda Hutcheon's *Irony's Edge*, whose convincing arguments about the *edgy* nature of irony—i.e., its sharp, biting, and provocative character—have inspired my analysis in the second section of this essay. This section explores the political and social consequences of irony in relation to its semantic complexity and instability, its affective charge, and its actualization by discursive communities who can choose to "make" or "not make" irony happen (Hutcheon 1993: 6). For the sake of brevity, it will focus on the interactive and critical potential of verbal, visual, and aural irony in a series of popular commercials and the parodic performance of the song "Ceaușescu Hasn't Died" by Ada Milea, a Romanian Hungarian artist.

The processes of ironic resignification should be read in the context of an important perspectival shift among those experiencing the post-Socialist transition, from early responses perceiving it as "temporary" to an increasing awareness of the transition as "permanent discomfort" so that, by the mid-1990s, "the unfolding of the transition itself became the central consideration" (Creed 1999: 224). Inspired by Gerald Creed's suggestion that we have to attend to "the dynamics of transition" in order to understand the meaning of appeals to socialism, I would argue that these performances should be seen as active and strategic responses to present-day challenges rather than as "survivals" of communism. In an attempt to account for their potentially subversive function as social and political critiques of the post-1989 context, I will explore the reasons why the figure of the former Communist leader is felt to be a more compelling symbol of the past than others and how it has been resignified in the post-Communist context.

The essays in Borneman's 2004 collection, *The Death of the Father*, articulate a useful framework for discussion with their varied anthropological analyses of the crisis of political authority engendered by the death of paternalist leaders and the end of twentieth-century totalizing regimes. In his chapter, "The Undead: Nicolae Ceaușescu and Paternalist Politics in Romanian Society and Culture," David Kideckel argues convincingly that Ceaușescu's strategic self-presentation as a father figure inspired intense, even if ambivalent, emotions of devotion and revulsion in his subjects, a strategy that can account both for the enduring power of the leader's Communist regime and for his grip on post-Communist political imagination (2004: 123–47). However, Kideckel goes on to claim that the national propensity to seek comfort in ambivalently benevolent and stern father figures is a running thread throughout Romanian history: not only was it reflected in Romanians' ambiguous love-hate relationship with their Communist leader, but it survived the execution of the presidential couple in the attempts to rehabilitate Ceaușescu, the growing popularity of similar father figures, such as Romania's first post-Communist president, Ion Iliescu, and even the desired entry into NATO and the EU (2004: 125–41).[4] Insisting that the political culture of paternalism is "grafted on to Romanian cultural perceptions and relationships," Kideckel presupposes the existence of a perfect consonance between political symbolism (the stern leader) and the actual sentiments and values of his subjects (2004: 124).[5] By comparison, I argue that the symbolic afterlife of Romania's Communist dictator has less to do with Romanians' paternalist leanings and more with the fact that, in both life and death, Nicolae Ceaușescu came to effectively embody the Communist regime and its violent collapse. Whether they desire an iron-handed leader or not, Romanians seeking to make sense of the transition are likely to find a compelling and virtually uncontested symbol of totalitarian power in the figure of the former Communist dictator.

As Hansen and Stepputat's reconceptualization of sovereignty reminds us, "The body is always the site of performance of sovereign power" and ritual performances of sovereignty are as central to modern political regimes as they are to traditional ones (2006: 297). The authors also point out that, much like royal power, modern sovereignty is informed by the tension between "the ideal form" of the body politic (the nation, the state) and its "always transient and imperfect embodiment in a specific leader" (Hansen and Stepputat 2006: 299–302). Throughout his rule, Ceaușescu emerged as the epitome of the seemingly omnipotent party-state, becoming the site of a whole range of popular emotions that ranged from loyalty to humiliation, helplessness, fear, and revulsion. In a mirror image of the Great Leader's ritual performances of political authority before 1989, his trial and execution exposed his old age, mortality, and vulnerability at the hands of his accusers (symbolically representing "the people"). However, as images of Ceaușescu's execution only reached Romanians four months after December 1989, rumors of the leader's death were received with distrust at the time, intensifying the state of anxiety over political authority.[6] The temporary disappearance of the leader's body, the rumors about the circumstances of his trial and execution, and the timing of the events during Christmas enhanced the ritual character of the execution, likened by many to the destruction of an evil spirit in a struggle with larger occult forces. It is because Nicolae Ceaușescu embodied both totalitarian power and the impossibility of its absolute sovereignty with an aura of mystery that he returned to capture the public eye and popular imagination in the uncertain times of transition.

Less common in the early 1990s, memory practices that exploit the critical potential of irony only emerged in more recent years, when the symbolic rigidity of the 1990s could be overcome. Whether engaged in forms of covert resistance to the Communist regime or complicity with it through collaboration or duplicitous behavior, the majority of Romanians experienced the last decade of communism as a time of economic deprivation, frustration, humiliation, and a diffuse sense of fear of state repression (Verdery 1991, 1996; Kligman 1998). Subsequently, for a long time after the collapse of the regime, it seemed impossible to dissociate the traumatic effects of Romanian communism from the figure of its prominent leader, which functioned as a highly constraining mnemonic device. My contention is that, with time, the affective intensity associated with Nicolae Ceaușescu was gradually discharged, releasing the figure's wider symbolic potential. While popular emotions are still strong enough to provoke criticisms of the seemingly trivializing attempts to laugh away national tragedy, they can tolerate parodic representations that open the symbol to resignification through a process of "defamiliarization."

The Emergence of the Dominant Mode of Remembrance

The tendency to disqualify alternative practices of remembrance as revivals of communism can be best understood against the background of a major concern dominating the years immediately following the events of December 1989, i.e., the imperative to come to terms with the Communist past in a morally responsible manner. Starting with the early 1990s, public intellectuals and representatives of the political opposition legitimated by anti-Communist dissidence or active participation in the 1989 events have been prominent in invoking the imperative of assuming responsibility and of facing the Communist past and its legacy. Their injunctions for accurate and appropriate remembrance insisted on the necessity to come to terms with the past by distinguishing between victims and perpetrators even while acknowledging the existence of grey zones of responsibility. In the political arena, for example, this took the form of demands, articulated in documents such as "Proclamația de la Timișoara" (11 March 1990), to bar former Communist Party activists and Secret Service officers from running for political positions for three consecutive electoral sessions (Ștefanescu 1995: 451–57). It is only more recently in 2006 that some of these demands have found an echo in the creation of an Institute for the Study of Communist Crimes and the heated debates around the lustration law.

Drawing on the dominant perception of the December 1989 events as a revolutionary break with the Communist past, public intellectuals and journalists invoked a sense of mission and responsibility in leading a traumatized nation on the way to becoming a healthy society. Needless to say, this self-assigned national duty ensured that intellectual and political elites enjoy the "moral capital" that scholars such as Katherine Verdery consider to be "a type of political capital having special currency in Eastern Europe and the former Soviet Union" (1996: 106). Given the pervasive sense of victimization of the Romanian people under the Communist regime in the early 1990s, the "moral capital" derived from resistance to the party and suffering under communism was an invaluable political asset. The appeals of the political opposition were also meant to counter competing claims to revolutionary legitimacy by the recently created Democratic National Salvation Front, the chief party of former Communist bureaucrats. Capitalizing on the visibility of its leader—Ion Iliescu—during the events, the Front presented itself as the liberator of the people from Communist dictatorship and the only guarantee of future stability, normalization, and national solidarity. The political and intellectual opposition responded by discharging that the Front "stole" the revolution and betrayed the revolutionary spirit of 1989. Both before and after the parliamentary and presidential elections in May 1990 that sanctioned the victory of the National Salvation Front, its political legitimacy was seriously challenged by street protests whose most famous slogans suggested an undesirable continuity with the Communist past. Slogans such as "Yesterday Ceauşescu, today Iliescu" or "Sleep well, you elected a dictator" played on a sense of continuity both in the Communist allegiances of political leaders and in the behavior of the electorate.

Thus, the struggle to secure political and moral legitimacy among contending actors in the political arena contributed to strengthening the sense that the desired break with the past initiated in December 1989 had not been yet accomplished. It was also successful in expanding intellectual concerns with the unhealthy survival of Communist legacies beyond the political sphere to the Romanian society as a whole. The political and intellectual opposition tended to explain electoral behavior and the more general indifference to democratic reforms and liberal values in terms of a survival of the "Communist mentality" characterized by gregarious behavior and conformity. Portrayed as an essentially sick society, suffering from the inertia, passivity, and somnolence induced by the Communist regime, Romanians were called upon to take a more active and self-critical attitude by working through the traumatic Communist past.

Scholars such as Daniel Barbu have pointed out the weakness of these explanations in rationalizing post-1989 manifestations, arguing convincingly that they reproduce the Communist rhetoric of collective destiny and assume that the regime was successful in "re-educating Romanians" and in leveling personal ambitions and desires as well as behaviors and mentalities (1998: 175–97). No matter the weakness of its explanatory power, the imperative to overcome the burden of the Communist past has emerged as a major discourse in post-1989 Romania. It is certainly strong enough to cast suspicion on practices of remembrance whose reliance on comic or ironic registers seems to be at odds with a more suitable mode of remembrance of the Communist past in a tragic register and in an accurate and morally responsible manner.

Alternative Memory Practices

Irony and Defamiliarization

My analysis does not aim at disqualifying attempts to produce more accurate and morally responsible accounts of the Communist past, but at exposing the constraints of a dominant discourse that presents itself as the only appropriate memory practice. This approach makes room for an account of the nature and function of alternative memory practices that are orchestrated neither by prominent politicians nor by public intellectuals. By contrast to accounts of the past claiming historical accuracy and moral legitimacy, memory practices cast in ironic and comic modes by actors, stage directors, singers, or advertising companies subordinate concerns with accuracy and truthfulness to a variety of other goals, amongst them entertainment, advertising, or organized protests. Although they do not articulate an essentially subversive or radically different discourse about the Communist past, they rely heavily on "defamiliarization," reframing potent symbols and experiences associated with Ceaușescu and evocative of life under communism.

The concept of "defamiliarization" (*ostranenie,* "making strange") developed by Victor Shklovsky, a major figure of Russian formalism, in his 1917 essay, "Art as Technique," can throw light on the function of ironic reframing in the Romanian context. For Shklovsky, art employs defamiliarization to challenge received knowledge and the processes of "habitualization" or "over-automatization" of objects and realities (1988: 16–30). The strategy of defamiliarization involves the representation of familiar objects in uncommon ways through the manipulations of forms in order to prolong the process of perception and enhance the audience's experience of "artfulness" in objects:

> Habitualization devours works, clothes, furniture, one's wife, and the fear of war. ... The purpose of art is to impart the sensation of things as they are perceived and not as they are known. The technique of art is to make objects "unfamiliar," to make forms difficult, to increase the difficulty and length of perception because the process of perception is an aesthetic end in itself and must be prolonged. *Art is a way of experiencing the artfulness of an object; the object is not important.* (Shklovsky 1998: 20)

The alternative practices of remembrance that make the object of this study have a similar effect, frustrating Romanians' horizons of expectations in order to make new perspectives possible. In this case, defamiliarization confronts the intensely canonized and ritualized representations of Nicolae Ceaușescu both during and after the collapse of the regime. Whether celebrated as a heroic leader and benevolent father of the Socialist Romanian nation during communism or reviled as a malefic spirit and all-powerful dictator after 1989, Ceaușescu's figure loomed so large in the Romanian imagination that only the registers of the sublime, the heroic, or the tragic could contain him.

By contrast, ironic reframings not only demean but also diminish or cut down to size the figure of the former Communist leader. Playing with and against the registers of the sublime and the tragic, ironic memory practices are both indirect processes of remembrance of the Communist leader in an often demeaning or irreverent manner and processes of resignification. Although my focus in this essay is on aural ironies in musical performance, visual ironies can best illustrate the perspectival shift described above. The series of commercials featuring Ceaușescu to advertise cellular phones, car tires, or social actions such as the adoption of stray dogs use unofficial images of the leader walking his dog in one of his luxurious estates or previously censored images of Ceaușescu losing his cool during a speech. Although they are not intended as history lessons on the recent past, the sharp contrast between these images and the representational patterns canonized by the cult of personality of the 1980s performs an indirect form of memory work. In the two cases mentioned above, the contrast contributes to the dominant historiographical interpretations of Ceaușescu's leadership as an instance of "dynastic socialism" bolstered by state orchestrated propaganda and censorship (Georgescu 1988; Tismăneanu 2003). Alternatively, restructured representational patterns characteristic of the Communist period can illuminate continuities in popular perceptions and political practices that tend to be obscured by the pervasive anti-Communist discourse.

At the same time, the ironic juxtaposition of visual records of communism with verbal messages that redirect attention to current political and social situations can function as critical comments on the realities of the transition period. For example, an ad for the animal protection foundation AnimaPro exploits the tension between the image of Ceaușescu walking his dog and the verbal message "A dog loves you the way you are. Adopt one!" It thus generates an ironic meaning with a critical potential. In contrast to Communist propaganda exclusively focused on the leader, the commercial privileges the dog, resignifying an image likely to express exploitation for a Romanian audience in order to send a message of social responsibility and care.

Since they do not derive legitimacy from claims to truthfulness, these modes of remembrance tolerate the ambiguity characteristic of indirect forms of communication such as irony, thriving on the instability and plurality of meaning. Being essentially a form of indirect communication such as metaphor or allegory, irony belongs to "the mode of the unsaid, the unheard, the unseen," privileging inferred over literal meaning (Hutcheon 1995: 9). Thus, ironic meaning is both multiple, emerging from the relational difference between the said and the unsaid, and highly unstable, depending both on the intended ironist and the audience for its actualization (Hutcheon 1995: 9–29). Despite their alleged indifference to historical accuracy, the efficiency of ironic practices of remembrance depends on their ability to strike a sensitive chord in their audiences by drawing on their memories of the Communist period even as they actively construct and shape these memories. In fact, as devices of indirection, they rely heavily on the "cultural competence"[7] ensured by shared discursive and experiential contexts (Hutcheon 1995: 18). For example, the ironic message of AnimaPro's commercial will more likely be inferred by Romanian audiences who experienced Communist propaganda and are familiar with the post-Socialist attempts to solve the problem of stray dogs in urban areas.

Most importantly, ironic meaning is doubled by a "critical edge" that can account for "the range of emotional response (from anger to delight)" generated by irony (Hutcheon 1995: 15). Irony depends not only on semantic but also on affective inference, the ironist's and the interpreter's abilities to infer the other's emotional position and evaluative/judgmental attitude. The diversity of affective reactions to post-1989 ironic reframings of Ceaușescu indicates how important the process of attributing evaluative intentions and emotional positions to the ironist is to the actualization of ironic messages. Among the historians, political annalists, journalists, and advertising experts invited to give their opinion on the success of the "Ceaușescu brand" in an essay entitled "The Ceaușescu Fashion," some refused to attribute ironic intention to the producers of commercials or shows that advocated the brand. To argue, as they do, that this brand appeals to "Ceaușescu nostalgics" or that "it will sell when the truth about the Communist past is revealed" is to read invocations of Ceaușescu as attempts at rehabilitating his personality or the Communist past (*Ziarul* 2004). Consequently, the interpreters' choice to take the message literally short-circuits the critical potential of the ironic message.

A Case Study

The following section provides a more detailed analysis of aural irony in Ada Milea's performance of the song "Ceaușescu Hasn't Died," offering further insights into the function of irony in alternative memory practices. Although reception is notoriously difficult to document and interpret, I conducted a small-scale inquiry into the reactions generated by the song among a group of ten Romanian graduate students in their late twenties, living in Romania, France, and the United States. The insights provided by these reactions were worked into my interpretation of the discursive, generic, and broader cultural references evoked by the interaction between the song lyrics, its musical line, and interpretation.

I will preface the analysis with a few comments on the artist's personal background, musical record, performative style, and social activism. Born to a mixed family in Târgu-Mureș in 1975 and raised in the interethnic environment of Transylvania, Ada Milea is a Hungarian Romanian artist. She became a popular figure on the Romanian musical scene ten years after the collapse of the Communist regime with the launching of a series of albums, among which *The "Mioritic" Romanian Republic* [Republica Mioritică Română] (1999), *No Mom's Land* (2002), *Absurdistan. The Africa Under Our Nails* [Absurdistan. Africa de sub unghii] (2003), and *Why Does the Baby Boil in Polenta?* [De ce fierbe copilul în mămăligă?] (2003). Her music functions as an ironic commentary on the self-congratulatory perception of the transitioning Romanian society characterized by intense feelings of national pride and the desire to overcome the Communist past. As befits an artist, Ada Milea's politics are not transparent. In virtually all the interviews that inquire into the social and political messages of her songs, Ada Milea assumes an "apolitical" stance or dodges the questions, shifting the burden of interpretation to either the composers of her songs or her audience.[8] However, her critical attitude can be derived from the multi-layered messages of her songs and the context of her shows.

Thus, the album *The "Mioritic" Romanian Republic* plays on the Socialist name of the country (the Socialist Republic of Romania), forcing together in its title references to Romanians' resented relation to the Communist past and major symbols of national culture celebrated in poetic creations like the epic ballad, "Miorița."[9] In fact, the inner tensions and homogenizing ambitions of national identity are recurrent themes in Ada Milea's musical creation. In compositions such as "Song for Ethnic Reconciliation," the singer explores these themes in an autobiographical key, performing the tension between her ethnically mixed background and the dominant narrative of national unity and solidarity.[10]

The singer's performative style enhances the critical message of her compositions. Pursuing both professional training as an actress and an amateurish interest in guitar playing and singing, the young artist emerged on the Romanian scene as an extremely gifted and charismatic artist, combining acting and singing skills. Most of her performances are staged as ironic engagements with Romanian and international musical genres recognizable to Romanian audiences. Spiced up with shifts in voice pitch and tonality, the performances rely on parodic remakes of musical genres as diverse as heroic-epic ballads, lullabies, Romanian round dances (*hore*), heavy metal, jazz, "*manele*," wedding songs, or Christmas carols.

Similarly, Ada Milea's politics can be inferred from the context of her performances, which take place in broadly oppositional loci that are critical not only of the Socialist past but also of the transitional present with its capitalist-style consumerism, environmental indifference, and continuity in the behavior of political elites. The Romanian public was introduced to the singer's idiosyncratic style through her performances in alternative music festivals initiated as social protests—the rock festival Stufstock, a homemade version of Woodstock organized on the Black Sea coast; and the annual music festival in Roşia Montană. Stufstock was initiated in the summer of 2003 as an act of artistic protest against the unauthorized sprawl of commercial buildings and tourist-related activities into an area of the Romanian Black Sea shore previously associated with alternative rock and jazz culture. Much in the same way, the music festival at Roşia Montană was initially a form of social protest—supported by ecological organizations and a group of Romanian artists—against the planned transformation of that mountainous region into an industrial mining area.[11]

The potential social effect of a cultural artifact such as "Ceauşescu Hasn't Died," included on her 2003 album *Absurdistan* depends on its ability to engage actively with a whole range of public discourses and concerns about the Communist past. Even a cursory examination of the lyrics indicates that the song echoes the recurrent public expressions of concern with an essentially "sick" society and with the alleged inability of Romanians to unlearn their Communist mentalities, practices, or ideologically charged language:

> Ceauşescu Hasn't Died
> He watches over us relentlessly
> Ceauşescu is a school
> Ceauşescu is a disease
>
> He is in me, he is in you
> He is in apartment buildings and in factories

Each of us carries him within today
Ceaușescu will never die

Ceaușescu Hasn't Died
History has lied to us
His wooden tongue
Haunts our ancient tongue

Ceaușescu Hasn't Died
History has lied to us
We are those alive and dead
We are all Ceaușescus[12]

Much like the major discourse of the intellectual and political opposition, the refrain "Ceaușescu Hasn't Died/History has lied to us" makes indirect references to the continuity in manipulative strategies characteristic not only of the former Communist regime but also of the current political establishment. In this sense, the lines refer back to anti-Communist demonstrations in the early 1990s, targeting the new political establishment with the already mentioned slogan, "Yesterday Ceaușescu, today Iliescu" or with the equally imaginative "You've lied to the nation/With the TV station."[13]

These indirect criticisms of the post-1989 political establishment acquire a more marked character if the song "Ceaușescu Hasn't Died" is read against the significant background of a series of six songs preceding it on the album *Absurdistan*. All these six songs evoke "roses," the electoral symbol of the political party in power in 2003, when the album was launched, in a series of musical genres suggestive of the new forms of political manipulation of the people. To give just one example, one of the songs plays on the musical line of a lullaby to tell the story of a people put to sleep by the rhetoric of normalization and stability of the Social Democrat Party, none other than the former Democratic National Salvation Front.

However, the song does not merely repeat the familiar discourse of the intellectual and political opposition. It engages with it by excessive and unqualified generalization of the Communist legacy: "Each of us carries him within today," "We are all Ceaușescus." This expansive move of the song might explain the reactions of uneasiness to its evocation of an all-inclusive national "we" among my respondents. One of them criticized the song for implying that "*we* are *all* going to always be 'thieving, duplicitous, lying and depraved' because of a Communist past impossible to eradicate," placing the series of unflattering attributes in quotation marks to signal a discourse that she assumed would be recognizable to me. Expressing a similar uneasiness at undifferentiated inclusion, respondents who read the song as a just criticism of the current state of Romanian society perform a move of critical detachment: "Romanians' problem is not Ceaușescu. Romanians' problem is that now, when the personage does not exist anymore, they behave in the same way, have the same expectations, the same fears."

The effect of this expansive move of the song is to perform an offensive and resented form of national identification, suggesting that, despite the general anti-Communist rhetoric, the only thing that binds together the national community of Romanians is the haunting presence of its former Communist leader. This implication gains significance in light of Ada Milea's performance of the song in the interpretive style of a popular Romanian folk singer, Tudor Gheorghe. The melodic line of the song, the attempts to produce fiddle-sounds on the guitar, thus imitating a musical instrument employed in folk performances, the insertion of shouted couplets characteristic of traditional folk music, and shifts to sentential inflections articulated in a low, male-like voice during the refrains signal Tudor Gheorghe's performative style. His repertoire includes heroic-epic ballads and laments imbued with a strong sense of national pride and solidarity performed in a heroic and tragic register. Here for example is the refrain of one of his most popular songs, "Mother, We Are a People of Stone" ("Muică, suntem neam de piatră"), that Ada Milea seems to echo in her song:

> We are a people of stone
> In defense of the motherland/hearth
> We are the sons of the *Brâncoveanus*,
> Of the *pandours* and of the *Jianus*.[14]

The sense of uneasiness generated by "Ceaușescu Hasn't Died" comes from its superimposition of the register of national dignity and pride characteristic of folk artistic creation on a register of national indignity, embarrassment, and dissatisfaction at the collective association with Ceaușescu as a unifying national symbol. Recent studies of irony as an indirect form of communication argue that "it is the superimposition or the rubbing together of these meanings (the said and the plural unsaid) with a critical edge created by a difference of context that makes irony happen" (Hutcheon 1995: 19). In this case, irony happens in the performative act of rubbing together "the said" (the lyrics: "Ceaușescu Hasn't Died," "We are all Ceaușescus") with "the unsaid" (the familiar register of heroic national descent and national solidarity: "We are the sons of the *Brâncoveanus*/The *pandours* and the *Jianus*") evoked by the interpretive style. The resulting tension is disturbing particularly because it points to the deeper complicity between the Communist and nationalist registers, suggesting that the nationalistic evocations characteristic of folk music lent themselves to appropriation both during communism and after its fall.

Scholars like Katherine Verdery and Gail Kligman have pointed out the efficacious appeal to national values and the employment of traditional folk songs by the Romanian Communist Party in order to achieve nationwide mobilization. Drawing on ethnographic research conducted in the late 1970s in rural areas in Romania, Kligman explores "the symbolic manipulation of folk songs for purposes of pro-Communist commentary" by the Romanian Communist Party, arguing that the latter used familiar poetic forms in order to make its message about Socialist progress persuasive and to claim a legitimacy that was "seen to stem historically from the heroic tradition of the Romanian people themselves" (1983: 83–84). Similarly, Katherine Verdery claims that the party was to some extent "*forced* onto the terrain of national values (although not unwillingly)" (1991: 122) and examines at length the homogenizing policies of the Socialist regime, indicating that they were meant to constitute the nation as "an extended family" (1996: 64).

While Ada Milea signals the complicity between the Socialist and nationalist rhetoric by evoking the style of heroic epic ballads, she further enhances it by having the lyrics of her song reproduce the characteristic phraseology of patriotic Communist poetry with which, needless to say, most generations of Romanians are likely to be familiar. The opening lines of the song, "Ceaușescu Hasn't Died/He watches over us relentlessly" evokes the celebration of the leader's paternal benevolence towards the people in Communist poetry, oscillating ambiguously between implications of paternal protection and the sense of generalized surveillance. Much in the same vein, the line "Ceaușescu will never die" and the references to his survival in common Romanians or in the linguistic heritage of the regime remind one of the rhetoric of eternal youth in poetic celebrations of Ceaușescu and the Communist Party leading the extended family of the Romanian people towards eternal progress.

The Romanian and foreign scholarship on the development of nationalist sentiments and nationalist movements after socialism explains the phenomenon by attending to the continuities between the ways in which the Romanian brand of national communism shaped subjectivities, practices, or institutions and their post-Socialist manifestations. However, the government's anti-Communist rhetoric in the early 1990s and the fact that the Romanian public generally reviles the name of communism serve to obscure these continuities. In fact, the nationalist sensibility, invested as much in traditional folk music as in patriotic poetry, seems to have survived its appropriation under communism, resurfacing after 1989 when the struggle for freedom from the Communist regime was expressed in indisputably nationalist terms.

To stay in the domain of musical creation, I will illustrate this tendency with an ethnographic study first published in 1994 in Bucharest and suggestively entitled "The Romanian Revolution of December 1989 and Its Reflection in Musical Folklore." Presenting itself as a collection of spontaneously created musical material, the essay indicates that, faced with the challenge of expressing their perceptions of the revolution as mediated by live broadcasts, Romanian singers from various rural areas found the language of national struggle and liberation readily available. They relied on the musical line of laments, burial songs, or Christmas carols in order to narrate the struggle against the Communist regime, conflated with Ceaușescu, as a struggle between vaguely defined "wicked enemies" and "Romania/Romanians" (Popa 1996: 156–75).[15] Ada Milea's albums and performances engage actively in exposing the complicity between the Communist, post-Communist, and nationalist registers. In effect, they seem to employ irony as a means to challenge the legitimacy of the nationalist register, generally perceived as anti-Communist, on grounds of its complicity with the Socialist rhetoric.

I would argue that such multilayered performances remain politically and socially risky even when audiences of various political leanings or cultural backgrounds choose not to activate their ironic messages. Inasmuch as ironic meaning is produced at the intersection between intended meaning and audience response, audiences play a central role in inferring and attributing ironic message and intent. Thus, even if Ada Milea's performances are suffused with ironic intent, there is no guarantee that audiences will necessarily interpret her performance as politically subversive. Some of Ada Milea's audiences simply do not have the cultural competence to make interrelated musical and cultural inferences. For example, Romanian teenagers who grew up in a significantly changed context in the 1990s may not pick up the references to Communist poetry or to Tudor Gheorghe's performative style. Among those who are familiar with Ada Milea's parodic musical style and have the cultural competence to infer ironic intent, there are audiences with opposing ideological leanings who might resist reading the song in an ironic key. Alternatively, some of the graduate students I interviewed for reactions to Ada Milea's "Ceaușescu Hasn't Died" refused to accept irony as an appropriate register: "Ada Milea is right, but I wouldn't listen to the song and I wouldn't be amused by it." Another remarked that her initial reaction to the title of the song was one of *disgust* and *oversaturation* with discussions about Ceaușescu and the Communist regime reflected by her decision not to name Ceaușescu, using instead the appellatives "him" or "the personage:" "Haven't we forgotten him?" Their criticism recalls the sense of personal indignity and national humiliation at this association, challenging the efficiency of this strategy on grounds of its moral impropriety.

Whether audiences differentiated along political, ethnic, and even generational lines choose to activate or short-circuit ironic meaning, it is fair to say that their reactions acknowledge the socially and politically provocative character of memory practices that evoke the figure of Romania's Communist dictator in an ironic key.

Conclusion

Much like other historical phenomena dominated by major dictatorial figures, the relation between Romanians and their former Communist leader seems to force scholars on the murky terrain of psychohistory. Debates over the phenomenon labeled "Ceaușescu nostalgia" fall in the same category, conflating a variety of public invocations of Ceaușescu's name and image and discrediting them as attempts at rehabilitating Communist practices and personalities, survivals of Communist mentalities, or undemocratic tendencies in the psychological/cultural profile of the Romanian nation. While attention to the psychological effects of powerful symbols and personalities is justified, the insistence on enduring beliefs and mentalities at the expense of changing social interests and actors, economic conjunctures, and political arrangements does more to obscure than explain the phenomenon.

Acknowledging the affective nature of potent and controversial symbols of communism like Ceaușescu, this essay addresses the social and political function of ironic practices of remembrance in the context of competing memory discourses. It suggests that if we attend to the register, genre, and agents of remembrance, we can better understand why certain social actors choose to invoke Ceaușescu's name and image and what they mean by it. In my analysis, the pervasive invocations of the former leader can be at least partially attributed to a shift in the public nature of the symbol. Being the exclusive domain of state propaganda before 1989, this potent symbol has since become readily available to agents from diverse social categories, with individual social actors and institutions employing it not only as an important object of historiographical research, but also as an efficient advertising strategy or as a form of protest. According to publicity designers, it is the unexpected advertising opportunity created by a thirty-year investment in Ceaușescu's image by the Communist regime that makes him into a "brand." This is why, as I showed in this essay, the effectiveness of ironic reframing rests on their defamiliarizing effect, on their ability to create a striking contrast with the more familiar registers of the heroic and the sublime previously employed in portrayals of the leader.

Dwelling on the semantic plurality and affective charge of irony as a discursive strategy employed in genres as diverse as commercials, musical creations, or theatrical performances, the essay unravels a diverse range of messages with relevance both to the Communist past and the transitional present. It implies that ironic messages are characterized by a certain richness that allows them to perform memory work and sociopolitical critiques simultaneously. They might, for example, reenact the ideological atmosphere of late communism as a means to criticize unacknowledged complicities between national pride and Socialist propaganda (Ada Milea), expose continuities in political culture from Communist to post-Communist regimes (Ada Milea), or encourage social responsibility and civic virtues in their audiences (AnimaPro).

Given their focus on Nicolae Ceaușescu as the embodiment of sovereign power, these public performances follow in the tradition of the "ubiquitous jokes of the Socialist period" that Katherine Verdery defined as "little oppositional moments enacted repeatedly in daily rituals of sociality whose humor lay precisely in the expressed opposition to the system" (1996: 96). Viewing such instances of totalitarian laughter as both covert resistance to the Communist regime and complicity with its dichotomous logic, Verdery argued that Socialist jokes reinforced the dichotomy between "us" and "them" (society and state, public and private, etc.) even as they turned it on its head in comic situations. With Ceaușescu's death enacting the collapse of the regime in the eyes of many, Socialist jokes lost both their target and their function of releasing potentially subversive political tension, eventually disappearing in the early 1990s. Reclaiming Nicolae Ceaușescu as a symbolic vehicle rather than the target of their irony, current public references seized on the very embodiment of sovereign power at a time when political authority is admittedly more difficult to locate. In the context of current political fragmentation, social tensions, and interethnic conflicts, it is the consecrated figure of the Communist dictator that emerges to mediate debates about the past or castigate the present. The public performances discussed in this essay laugh at the former Communist leader only incidentally, targeting different political establishments and social arrangements in order to make sense of the past. One can safely argue that, two decades after the death of Romania's Communist dictator, irony is still a risky business. No longer a criminal offence bordering on national treason, irony fulfills an analogous function in the post-Communist period, circumventing the hegemony of state narratives about the recent Communist past and the transitional present.

Notes

For stimulating conversations and suggestions at various stages in the conception of this essay, I am grateful to Bruce Grant; the editors of this volume, Maria Todorova and Zsuzsa Gille; and Tim Pilbrow.

1. See for example, the talk show *My Name* hosted by the news channel Realitatea TV in July 2006. The moderator, Dragoş Olteanu, debated the significance of Nicolae Ceauşescu as a country brand with the psychologist Aurora Liiceanu, the fashion designer Venera Arapu, the director Ducu Darie, and the political annalist Cristian Pîrvulescu.
2. As some have noted, international journalists capitalized on two of Romania's most famous symbols, Ceauşescu and Dracula, in reportages based on distastefully assorted historical inaccuracies. See Siani-Davies (2005: 282f): "The *Guardian* correspondent Michael Simmons wrote of Tepes having a personal security force, the *sluji*, which bore an uncanny resemblance to the Securitate while in *Le Monde* Claude Fischler coined the term "draculization" when he spoke of Ceauşescu as a "paranoic Dracula," "tyrant of the Balkans," and "proletarian despot."

   Similarly reflecting on the tension between Romania's official tourist promotions that gloss over the Communist past and the commodification of its recent past in Western publications, Duncan Light argues that English-language travel guides advertise the capital city, Bucharest, as a significant site of the country's Communist legacy and the 1989 revolution in response to Western travelers' interest in "dark tourism" (or "travel to witness individual or mass deaths") and "Communist heritage" tourism.
3. During a student demonstration in Jassy in 2003, interviewed participants who carried Ceauşescu's portraits countered the suspicion of nostalgia that would have disqualified their protest: "This [Ceauşescu's portrait] is the most efficient criticism of the government. It is not nostalgia for the past. We really don't want communism. It was students who fought against communism in 1989." Quoted in "To Humiliate the Government," *Adevarul/The Truth*, no. 4150 (31 October 2003).
4. Although Kideckel points occasionally to distinct social and economic structures (such as Socialist command economies or the post-Socialist economic decline) in order to explain paternalist beliefs and relations, he attributes them to national culture and psychology. Consequently, the author fails to explain how paternalist beliefs and political structures endured throughout Romanian history from the fifteenth-century medieval ruler, Vlad Ţepes, to the Socialist president, Nicolae Ceauşescu, or how Romanians' preference for father-leaders differs from the instances of European populism mentioned by the author: LePen in France, Bossi in Italy, and Haider in Austria (2004: 125).

5. Anthropologists concerned with the theorization of sovereignty such as Hansen and Stepputat warned that functionalist views, which assume that leaders embody the actual values of their people, have often been employed to conceptualize political authority in "primitive" and non-Western contexts (2006: 298–99).
6. The presidential couple was tried and executed on Christmas (25 December 1989). The Romanian Television broke the news of the trial and execution at 8:30 PM that night, but it only showed censored scenes of the trial (so that the faces of those in the jury panel remain anonymous) that did not include the execution at 1:30 AM that night.
7. The concept of "cultural competence" is central to this discussion. Rejecting the widely accepted view that irony can only be activated by intellectually sophisticated audiences, Linda Hutcheon argues that it is cultural competence that ensures the success of irony as a discursive strategy (1995: 89–95). Within a shared discursive community, insiders conversant with the political events, symbols, and narratives of their respective community can choose to attribute ironic intent or not.
8. See for example the following exchange in Peter Sragher, "'I sing when I feel like it': Interview with Ada Milea," *Observatorul cultural,* 9–15 September 2003:

    Interviewer: Are your songs, like the original American folk music, meant to criticize our social and political flaws?
    Ada Milea: I've never theorized. The more I try to rationalize, the less inspired I am.
    Interviewer: How about this song, where you say, "let's skin Rodica alive and make her into a flag"? Do you hate the army?
    Ada Milea: It's not necessarily about the army. The message is what the audience gets out of each song. I don't criticize anything, I'm just playing. Some understand this playfulness, others run away from it.

9. The adjective *mioritic* is derived from the common noun *miorița* (ewe, lamb) and its usage is associated with the title of the most famous Romanian folk ballad, "Miorița," presented by textbooks of Romanian literature as the masterpiece of folk art and a proof of the poetic genius of the Romanian people.
10. Essentially, Ada Milea's "Song for Ethnic Reconciliation" problematizes the collective "we" whose heroic experience is the preferred subject of folk music. Employing traditional musical lines, the Transylvanian dialect, as well as Hungarian phrases that open up references to the Hungarian folk tradition, Milea starts in a subversive confessional mood: "My mother is Hungarian, az szép/ My Romanian father, dear God, is valiant as a mythical dragon." The "child narrator" recounts a story of domestic infidelity (the mother's attraction for another man who, as suggested by the song, belongs to "an ethnic minority") that takes the proportions of a nationwide conflict, thus recasting the heroic register of heroic-epic ballads into a comic one. For one who straddles the border between "the people" and its "minorities," autobiographical narratives can best be told in an ironic mode, using the deceiving idiom of the nation-state in the title "Song for *Ethnic Reconciliation*," yet telling a narrative of domestic and national strife. [*Az a szép* [The Beautiful One] is the title of a famous Hungarian folk song.]

11. Ada Milea joined the social protest for the protection of the mountainous region of Roșia Montană that was to be turned into an industrial mining area, an event that received the support of the Romanian Association for the Conservation of Bio-Culturally Protected Areas and the international organization Greenpeace.
12. Original Romanian version:
    Ceaușescu n-a murit
    Ne veghează îndârjit
    Ceaușescu e o școală
    Ceaușescu e o boală

    E în mine, e în tine
    E în blocuri și uzine
    Azi îl poartă fiecare
    Ceaușescu-n veci nu moare

    Ceaușescu n-a murit
    Istoria ne-a păcălit
    Limba lui de lemn se plimbă încet
    Prin vechea noastra limbă

    Ceaușescu n-a murit
    Istoria ne-a păcălit
    Noi suntem viii si morții
    Ceaușești suntem cu toții.
13. Romanian: "Ieri Ceaușescu, astăzi Iliescu" and "Ați mințit poporul/Cu televizorul."
14. Constantin Brâncoveanu was a Wallachian prince, famous for his cultural patronage and attempts to negotiate anti-Ottoman alliances with the Habsburg Monarchy and Russia in the early eighteenth century. The Ottomans deposed, tortured, and eventually beheaded the prince and his sons. In national mythology, Brâncoveanu grew to legendary proportions, becoming a symbol of sacrifice at the hands of the infidels as well as a symbol of national courage and dignity. Arguing that the reason for his and his sons' execution was their refusal to give up their Christian faith and convert to Islam, the Romanian Orthodox Church declared them saints and martyrs in 1992. Iancu Jianu was a legendary nineteenth-century *haiduk* leader from Oltenia. In national mythology, he represents both the struggle for social justice against local landowners (*boyars*) and for national freedom against the *phanariots*, the Habsburgs, and the Ottomans. *Panduri*, here synonymous with *haiduks*, refer to Iancu Jianu's followers.
15. Street protesters were referred to as "the soldiers of our homeland" while the outcome of the popular rebellion was portrayed in terms of national liberation: "Romania, Romania/Be proud, Romania/ You have broken free from bondage." Moreover, both the songs and the interviews with the performers portray the actions of the Communist regime, personified by the presidential couple, as antinational: "Why didn't death take that woman [Elena Ceaușescu], who tortured and oppressed this people, this house of ours in which we live?"

References

Barbu, Daniel. 1998. "Destinul colectiv, servitutea involuntara, nefericirea totalitara: trei mituri ale comunismului romanesc" ["Collective Destiny, Involuntary Servitude, and Totalitarian Unhappiness: Three Myths of Romanian Communism"]. In *Miturile comunismului romanesc* [The Myths of Romanian Communism], ed. Lucian Boia. Bucharest: Nemira.

Borneman, John, ed. 2004. *Death of the Father: An Anthropology of the End in Political Authority.* New York: Berghahn Books.

Chambers, Ross. 1990. "Irony and the Canon." *Profession* 90 (MLA): 18–24.

Creed, Gerald W. 1999. "Deconstructing Socialism in Bulgaria," In *Uncertain Transition: Ethnographies of Change in the Postsocialist World,* ed. Michael Burawoy and Katherine Verdey. Boston: Rowman & Littlefield.

Georgescu, Vlad. 1988. "Romania in the 1980s: The Legacy of Dynastic Socialism." *Eastern European Politics and Societies* 2: 69–93.

Gutwirth, Marcel. 1993. *Laughing Matter: An Essay on the Comic.* Ithaca, NY: Cornell University Press.

Hansen, Thomas Blom, and Finn Stepputat. 2006. "Sovereignty Revisited." *Annual Review of Anthropology* 35: 295–315.

Hutcheon, Linda. 1995. *Irony's Edge: The Theory and Politics of Irony.* London and New York: Routledge.

Kideckel, David A. 2004. "The Undead: Nicolae Ceauşescu and Paternalist Politics in Romanian Society and Culture," In *Death of the Father: An Anthropology of the End in Political Authority,* ed. John Borneman. New York: Berghahn Books.

Kligman, Gail. 1983. "Poetry and Politics in a Transylvanian Village." *Anthropological Quarterly* 56 (2): 83–89.

Kligman, Gail. 1998. *The Politics of Duplicity: Controlling Reproduction in Ceauşescu's Romania.* Berkeley: University of California Press.

Kundera, Milan. 2000. *The Art of the Novel,* trans. Linda Asher. New York: HarperPerennial.

Light, Duncan. 2000. "An Unwanted Past: Contemporary Tourism and the Heritage of Communism in Romania." *International Journal of Heritage Studies* 6 (2): 145–60.

Popa, Steluţa. 1996. "The Romanian Revolution of December 1989 and Its Reflection in Musical Folklore." In *Retuning Culture: Musical Changes in Central and Eastern Europe,* ed. Mark Slobin. Durham, NC: Duke University Press.

Shklovsky, Victor. 1988. "Art as Technique." In *Modern Criticism and Theory. A Reader,* ed. David Lodge. London: Longman.

Siani-Davies, Peter. 2005. *The Romanian Revolution of December 1989.* Ithaca, NY: Cornell University Press.

Ştefănescu, Domniţa. 1995. "Proclamaţia de la Timişoara, 11 martie 1990," In *Cinci ani din istoria Romaniei* [Five Years in Romanian History: A Chronology of Events December 1989–December 1994]. Bucharest: Editura Maşina de scris.

Tismăneanu, Vladimir. 2003. *Stalinism for All Seasons: A Political History of Romanian Communism.* Berkeley: University of California Press.

Verdery, Katherine. 1991. *National Ideology Under Socialism, Identity and Cultural Politics in Ceaușescu's Romania*. Berkeley: University of California Press.
Verdery, Katherine. 1996. *What Was Socialism and What Comes Next?* Princeton, NJ: Princeton University Press.

Romanian Media

Cercelescu, Monica. "Nostalgia terorii în publicitate" ["Nostalgia for Terror in Advertising"]. *Săptămâna financiară* 11, 16 May 2005.
Chivu, Marius. "'Comunismul e ca un suc de portocale.' Interviu cu Alexandru Dumitrescu, director de creație adjunct, McCannErickson" ["'Communism as Orange Juice.' Interview with Alexandru Dumitrescu, Assistant Director of Design for McCannErickson"]. *Dilema veche*, 13 October 2006.
My Name, talk show hosted by the news channel Realitatea TV, July 2006. The moderator, Dragos Olteanu, debated the significance of Nicolae Ceaușescu as a country brand with the psychologist Aurora Liiceanu, the fashion designer Venera Arapu, the director Ducu Darie, and the political annalist Cristian Pîrvulescu.
Pârvulescu, Cristian (political annalist); Aurora Liiceanu (psychologist); Dan Moraru and Bogdan Enoiu (directors of advertising agencies); Emil Hurezeanu, Ion Cristoiu, and Roșca Stănescu (writers and journalists); Andrei Gheorghe and Șerban Huidu (radio/TV personalities); and Sergiu Nicolaescu (director) quoted in "Moda Ceaușescu," ["The Ceaușescu Fashion"]. *Ziarul*, 20 aprilie 2004.
"Pentru a umili guvernanții, studenții din Iași au scos portretele lui Ceaușescu" ["To Humiliate the Government,"]. *Adevărul*, no. 4150, 31 Octombrie 2003.
Sragher, Peter. "'Cânt atât cât mă simt bine să cânt.' Interviu cu Ada Milea," ["'I sing when I feel like it': Interview with Ada Milea"]. *Observatorul cultural*, 9–15 September 2003.
Stanciu, Alina. "Ceaușescu lucrează pentru capitaliști." ["Ceaușescu Works for Capitalists"] *Cotidianul*, 6 August 2005.

10

GOOD BYE, LENIN! AUFWIEDERSEHEN GDR
On the Social Life of Socialism
Daphne Berdahl[1]

In the seventeen years since its collapse, socialism has become the object of significant historical curiosity, memory making, and contestation. In addition to more public sites like the Museum of Communism in Prague (next to a McDonald's) or the Budapest Statue Park and House of Terror (to name just a few examples), the cultural landscape of post-Socialist memory also includes private exhibitions of Socialist material culture or Communist kitsch (depending on the context and the eye of the beholder) (Ten Dyke 2001; Berdahl 2005), published personal memoirs (Hensel 2002), mass-mediated images in film or television, commemorations, silences, and an ongoing dynamic between individual biographies and collective histories—between personal narratives and public re-presentations. Of course socialism was being remade into memory from the very beginnings of its end, as new histories were created out of unsanctioned memories of the past (Watson 1994), in emergent nationalizing projects (Wanner 1998), and in symbolic acts of legitimizing new states (Verdery 1999). In the realm of memory, then, socialism has had a complex and often unpredictable social life.

My aim in this chapter is to reflect upon the social life of socialism by focusing on memory and the present in a context with which I am most familiar: post-Wall Germany. In his work on commodities in cultural perspective, Appadurai has shown that the social life of things is subject to longer-term shifts in value and demand (Appadurai 1986). I am arguing that the same processual approach is relevant for understanding the production and circulation of historical memory: the social life of socialism has been, and continues to be, a process informed by large-scale political shifts, economic developments, and cultural dynamics.

My use of the concept of memory refers to practices, performances, representations, and other modes of shaping images of the past. Memory, although it may be a "reservoir" of history (Watson 1994), is not the same as history. Instead, history may be viewed as a particular configuration of historical representation—usually in written or narrative form, including "official histories" of the Socialist states—that itself is open to questions of interpretation and interpretive authority (Cohen 1994: 130). Memory, on the other hand, is a more infinitely malleable, contestable, interactive, and social phenomenon. Produced and constructed on a variety of fronts, memory can be personal as well as public, individual as well as collective. Museums, commemorations, and monuments give an important physicality to memory, but they are not necessarily separate from history; indeed such representations may also entail in a dynamic relationship between both memory and history, between public and private. (See also Cohen 1994; Connerton 1989; Davis and Starn 1989; Huyssen 1995; Watson 1994.) Whether deployed strategically in everyday practices or constructed through mass-mediated narratives and images, memory puts the past into dialogue with the present. To what ends, we should then ask, and with what effects?

I attempt to address these and other questions through a reading of the wildly successful German film, *Good Bye, Lenin!*, released in 2003. I am an anthropologist with admittedly no training in film theory, so I ask for readers' patience as I make my way through this analysis. But, I should add, as an anthropologist, this film is a kind of "in your face" ethnographic object that cannot be ignored. Its production and reception in a post-Wall Germany still fraught with East-West tensions both reflect and constitute historically specific negotiations, discourses, and debates about the meanings of memory, nostalgia, and the politics of the present. The film also represents the apex of the post-Socialist cultural phenomenon known in Germany as *Ostalgie*, to which I shall return later.

Virtually Existing Socialism

Good Bye, Lenin! is the story of an East German family during the tumultuous year of the *Wende* ("turning point," the term used in referring to the events surrounding the fall of the Berlin Wall). The mother, Christiane, is a devout and active party loyalist who has been deeply committed to the Socialist state since the departure of her husband for West Germany in 1978. Eleven years later, in October 1989, she is on her way to celebrate the fortieth anniversary of the GDR with party dignitaries and observes her young adult son, Alex, clash with police during a prodemocracy protest march. The trauma of seeing her son among the demonstrators, combined with the shock of witnessing the brutality of the regime, causes her to have a heart attack and sends her into a coma for the next eight months. While she is sleeping, the Berlin Wall falls, Eastern Germans embrace Western capitalism and consumerism, and Germany is catapulted toward reunification. Alex loses his job in the state-owned television repair service and begins selling satellite dishes, while his sister starts sleeping with a *Wessi* (West German) and abandons her studies in order to work at Burger King. When Christiane emerges from her coma, doctors warn her children that any unexpected shock could complicate her recovery and potentially prove fatal. Her son Alex thus resolves to recreate the GDR in her bedroom, concealing from his mother all the changes of the past eight months. Western-style Ikea furniture is hastily replaced with East German particleboard, Venetian blinds are pulled down and polyester curtains are put up, and the Socialist iconographic hero Che Guevara goes back up on the mustard-colored floral wallpaper. Within this seventy-nine-square-meter apartment, then, the GDR lives on.

Alex's efforts to make time stand still grow increasingly complicated as his bed-ridden mother's health improves. With East German products gone from the store shelves following the currency union in July of 1990 when West German companies took over distribution networks, he frantically searches for familiar goods, repackaging foodstuffs and refilling pickle jars from the recycling bin with Dutch imports to satisfy his mother's craving for Spreewald gherkins. He enlists friends and family members to participate in the lie: demanding that visitors wear Eastern German clothing, paying former pupils to perform pioneer songs for her birthday, and encouraging a neighbor to take dictations of *Eingaben* (legally sanctioned complaints) to state authorities, for which she had been well known before her illness. With the help of an aspiring West German filmmaker friend from his new job, Alex fabricates GDR newscasts for his mother to view on a TV that is linked to a VCR machine in an adjacent room .

The dizzying pace of change and a few puzzling encounters make it progressively challenging to continue his fantasy, but whenever his mother comes close to figuring out the truth, Alex invents a plausible explanation. The unfurling of a Coca-Cola banner on a nearby building that had been draped in a Communist Party red banner just months before—a powerful visual metaphor embodying the cultural and political upheaval—is explained in the next day's fake news bulletin as being a result of a recent discovery that the formula for Coke was actually an East German invention. The presence of Westerners in East Berlin is attributed to a decision by President Erich Honecker to grant asylum to those disillusioned with capitalism. With his filmmaker friend posing as the news anchor, the fictitious *Aktuelle Kamera* report explains:

Unemployment, dire prospects for the future, and the increasing electoral success of the neo-Nazi *Republikaner* have moved the clearly unsettled West German citizens to turn their backs on capitalism and attempt a new beginning in the worker and peasant state.

Several months into his charade Alex realizes that the fantasy is as much for himself as for his mother, admitting that "the GDR I created for my mother was increasingly becoming the GDR that I might have wished for myself."

Indeed, Alex ultimately rewrites the end of the Cold War, casting communism as the victor. In his final fake newscast, intended to put an end to his deception by informing his ailing mother that the border between East and West Germany is gone, Alex creates a narrative in which Erich Honecker resigns and his childhood hero, the cosmonaut Sigmund Jähn, assumes leadership of the party and the GDR. Alex solicits Jähn's help after a chance encounter with him (or a convincing doppelgänger) as a taxi driver one evening. While the GDR national anthem plays in the background, Jähn delivers his scripted speech in Sachsen dialect (which had become identified with Eastern Germans and mocked in the West) to the nation:

> Dear citizens of the GDR: Once you have experienced the miracle of seeing our planet from the cosmos, you see things differently. ... When viewed from outer space, this is a very small country, and yet thousands of people have come to us in the past year. People whom we used to see as the enemy and who want to live with us today. ... Socialism means not to be fenced in. Socialism means approaching others, living with other people. Not only to dream of a better world, but to make it come true. I have thus decided to open the borders of the GDR.

The anchor's commentary is juxtaposed with well-known footage of 9 November, with Germans dancing on the Berlin Wall and climbing up the Western side:

> In the first hours since the borders opened, thousands of citizens from the Federal Republic of Germany have already taken the opportunity to visit the German Democratic Republic. Many want to stay. They are searching for an alternative to the brutal struggle for survival in the capitalist system. Not everyone wants to participate in the addiction to career and the terror of consumerism. Not everyone is made for the elbow society. These people want a different life. They realize that cars, videorecorders, and televisions are not everything. They are prepared to build a different life with nothing but goodwill, determination, and hope.

Christiane dies three days after Germany is reunified, blissfully unaware, Alex believes, of the truth. In a small ceremony of family and friends, her ashes are scattered over Berlin by the kind of rocket ship that Alex used to play with as a child, a fitting and proper sendoff for his mother, his childhood, and his country.

The Long Goodbye

After its premiere in February 2003, *Good Bye, Lenin!* quickly became one of the most successful films in German movie history, breaking box-office records and garnering multiple national and international awards. Crowds flocked to see it in East and West (unlike the 1999 GDR retro film *Sonnenallee,* which was popular in Eastern Germany but criticized in the West for glorifying the Socialist regime); theaters were packed and shows regularly sold out. Critics talked about its "cathartic release" and attempted to find meaning in its unprecedented success: for some, the passage of time had allowed for enough critical distance to produce a "requiem for the failed Honecker state" or a "dirge for the century of communism" (Von Vestenberg 2003). For others, the film's success could be explained by an enduring nostalgia for the Socialist past, or *Ostalgie,* a term that plays with the German words for East, *Ost,* and nostalgia, *Nostalgie.* While these are important observations (and I shall return to them momentarily), they fail to capture the multiplicity of meanings underlying this film as a cultural document and cultural event.

To begin with, there are several recurring themes in the film that make it particularly effective and resonant across generational and East-West divides. A major motif involves the tensions and gaps between appearance and reality, between fact and fiction. This theme invokes a dominant discourse about socialism and its demise: socialism collapsed, goes this argument, because of this ever-widening gap. The film's central premise of the fabricated GDR that Alex creates for his mother is echoed in parallel stories of family secrets and lies: toward the end of her life, Christiane confesses to her children that their father had not fled to the West for another woman, as they had been led to believe, but that his departure had been planned with the intention of having the family follow him as soon as possible. After he was gone, she tells them, she lacked the courage to go through with the plan; his unopened letters to the children are hidden behind a cupboard in the kitchen. Another layer of the confusion between appearance and reality comes at the end of the film when it is revealed that, unbeknownst to Alex, his mother is aware and deeply appreciative of his charade.

It is the film's central premise, however, that begins to explain its resonance by allowing for different readings and receptions. On the one hand, the GDR is nothing but a façade or a childhood fantasy—an interpretation that would arguably confirm many perceptions and stereotypes among Eastern but mostly Western Germans. On the other hand, the sense of promise and possibility contained in Alex's phantasmagorical recreation of a GDR that never existed accesses for many Eastern Germans shared sentiments of loss and longing in the context of the broken promises and disillusionments of reunification. With very few exceptions, this nostalgia did not reflect a longing to return to the GDR, but a sense of lost possibilities and critiques of the present.

Dominant discourses of East-West relations are most effectively addressed in the film, however, by not addressing them explicitly. Indeed, reunification is celebrated as a joyful moment, with a newly reconfigured family from East and West (including the father from West Berlin with whom Alex has made contact, and the West German boyfriend who is the father of Alex's sister's baby). In Alex's new workplace, sales teams consist of one Eastern and one Western German, and his filmmaker friend and *Aktuelle Kamera* accomplice is a coworker from the West.

More effectively, however, it is the narrative device of a subplot focusing on Alex's childhood idol, the cosmonaut Sigmund Jähn, and the metaphor of space travel that is subtly suggestive of East-West dynamics. Jähn had been the first German to travel in space, a battleground of the Cold War, aboard Soyuz 31. It is a moment that Alex characterizes as the "GDR attaining a world standard"; it is also a moment that Alex connects to his father's flight to the West, for he learns of his father's departure while watching television coverage of Jähn's historic flight in space. The analogy between the West and outer space would be recognizable to many Eastern Germans, for whom West Germany before 1989 seemed to be, in a common phrase, "as far away as the moon." It is no coincidence, then, that Jähn is the apparent taxi driver who takes Alex to his father's home in West Berlin. Similarly, Jähn answers Alex's question about what it was like "up there" by simply replying "really nice, only a long way from home," a description that would echo a widespread and frequently articulated sentiment among Eastern Germans about having "emigrated without leaving home."

A leitmotif connected to this subplot concerns the children's television bedtime character, the *Sandmann*. Jähn brings the *Sandmann* with him on his voyage and Alex sends him off into space in a homemade rocketship. The figure also makes an appearance when Alex shows up at his father's house unannounced and finds himself watching the show with his father's young children. For many Eastern Germans, the *Sandmann* is a potent symbol and cultural icon. Under socialism, East German school children were frequently subjected to the *"Sandmann* Test" until it became legal to watch Western television in 1971. An artefact of the Cold War waged on the front of mass media, both East and West German television aired their own brief children's show, *Der Sandmann,* before the evening news. Following the show, a clock would appear on the screen until the beginning of the news broadcast. The West German clock had small lines in place of numbers, the East German clock small dots. In school, teachers would ask children if the clock after their "Sandman" had dots or lines, thus forcing children to reveal unwittingly whether parents were watching Western television. After 1989 the East German Sandman was one of the few cultural and political institutions that didn't lose out to Western forms, and there are few Eastern Germans who will not mention with pride that "our" Sandman prevailed if the subject arises.

This kind of shared, insider knowledge works effectively to produce feelings of solidarity and belonging among Eastern German audiences. The film's attention to detail, ranging from East German products and repeated references to GDR consumer culture to party rhetoric and Socialist icons excludes any viewer—real or imagined—who has not experienced socialism. In a context where, almost overnight, the value of Eastern Germans' cultural capital plummeted—or, as a GDR trivia game explained, around 50 percent of the knowledge East Germans acquired during the course of a lifetime was rendered useless through sudden and unforeseen events—the portrayal of everyday Socialist objects and practices produced a privileged knowledge for those in the know. Although critics may have hailed the film for uniting Easterners and Westerners in laughter, *Ossis* and *Wessis* were frequently laughing at very different things. When describing their reactions to the film, for example, Eastern Germans I talked to often spoke with pride about moments when *Wessis* were unable to appreciate the humor in particular cultural references. Laughter—who laughed and at what—emerged as an important gauge of a newly recognized cultural competence, and quickly became a key topic of postfilm discussions and discourses.

In order to understand the film's resonance with Eastern German audiences, however, it is most critical to point out how *Good Bye, Lenin!* gives expression to the largely unacknowledged and forgotten experiences and memories of Eastern Germans during a period of dizzying change. The complicated and often contradictory feelings of euphoria, bewilderment, possibility, and loss are captured in the film's careful attention to detail, ranging from the disappearance of *Spreewaldgurken* to billboards in which Trabants morph into Western cars. As one audience member remarked, "Hopefully our fellow citizens from the old federal states [Western Germany] will also see this film in order to understand how it really was." Similarly, another commented: "A film for every *Ossi* and those who want to learn more about us." When asked about the fact that the director was a *Wessi*, Eastern Germans often replied that he had clearly done his "homework" and deserved to be an "honorary *Ossi*."

The re-presentation of GDR culture at the moment of its vanishing relates to another dominant theme and cultural meaning of the movie as a ritual of farewell (cf. Ivy 1995). There are many goodbyes in this film: to childhood, family secrets, fantasies, a mother, a state. All of these converge in the mother as symbol, whose ashes are rocketed into space during a rooftop ceremony at the end of the film. An earlier symbolic gesture of letting go occurs in a scene where Alex tosses 30,000 marks of his mother's Eastern German currency, now valueless and unexchangable because of a missed deadline, from the roof, like confetti in the wind.

The film's most memorable farewell is, to borrow a phrasing from Katherine Verdery, a "corpse on the move" (Verdery 1999). In this key scene, Christiane ventures out of her reconstructed GDR (while Alex is sleeping) into an entirely new world, full of Western neighbors, consumer goods, automobiles, and advertisements. The influx of Western capitalism and consumer culture is set against a backdrop of Socialist waste, signified by heaps of discarded GDR furniture. A bewildered Christiane wanders through this unfamiliar landscape and observes the torso of a Lenin statue, an icon familiar to most inhabitants of the former Eastern bloc, being transported by helicopter across the East Berlin skyline. Lenin floats by, hand extended in a gesture of both ephemeral greeting and long goodbye. As her frantic children rush to rescue their mother from possible injury as well as from the shattering of an illusion, Lenin vanishes into the sunset.

Katherine Verdery has written eloquently about the political symbolism of dead bodies in the post-Socialist period, arguing that reburials of particular human remains and the dismantling of iconic statues have been widespread and important "foundational acts of new states" (Verdery 1999: 21). The image of Lenin in the film partakes of and comments on this larger iconoclasm, invoking not only earlier foundational acts of the new state, but providing a powerful visual metaphor for saying goodbye to an old, and, in some cases virtually lingering one.

Indeed, as I mentioned earlier, one explanation for the film's unprecedented success is its cultural meaning as a sendoff—for an imagined GDR, I would add, in whatever form. The film's director, Wolfgang Becker, acknowledged in an interview that there had been no time for a proper funeral for the East German state. Other critics have expressed the hope that the film will put an end to East-West divisions, finally bringing together what belongs together. The actress Katrin Saß, a former GDR film star who plays Christiane, similarly said: "One should see in *Good Bye, Lenin!* how actors from East and West tell a story about our history. Perhaps we will finally succeed in putting this era [of division] behind us" (Saß 2008). Indeed, this might have been part of the intention behind a collective viewing of the film by 180 members of the German parliament, a "work outing" (*Betriebsausflug*) characterized by a headline in *Der Spiegel* as "The Bundestag Bids Farewell to Lenin" (Der Spiegel 2003).

Actually Existing Postsocialism

The cultural practices surrounding the film have not just been about saying goodbye, but are also about an *Aufwiedersehen* in the literal sense of the word (see you again). The premiere and success of *Good Bye, Lenin!* unleashed a new wave of *Ostalgie* throughout post-Wall Germany. Keeping with its tagline, "The GDR lives on," theaters across Eastern Germany were decorated with GDR paraphernalia. National and multinational movie theater chains featured displays of GDR memorabilia — old East German newspapers, party medallions and certificates, consumer goods — and often included a small living area (10 square meters) of "GDR." Theater employees and audience members donned young pioneer scarves, Free German Youth shirts, or NVA uniforms and were encouraged to bring in East German souvenirs; during the first week of the film's showing a theater in Berlin accepted admission in now defunct Eastern marks. A theater entrance in Leipzig was adorned with a Lenin bust from a building at the old trade fair (Messe), on loan from the collection of a *Wessi* who normally has it sitting in his garden alongside other objects of the vanished state.

In the aftermath of *Good Bye, Lenin!*'s success, *Ostalgie* has become an even more widespread merchandizing industry. *Ostalikers,* as practitioners of *Ostalgie* are called, can now rent out the film set and throw an *Ostalgie* Party. Local, national, and international retail businesses as well as Internet sites feature a seemingly endless supply of books, games, music, and other mementos, including a "GDR in a box" kit to "help you discover the *Ossi* in yourself," complete with Mocca-fix, plastic chicken egg-cups, and a *Neues Deutschland* newspaper. In the summer of 2004, *Ostshows* premiered on six major television networks featuring ice-skating princess Katarina Witt wearing a Free German

Youth shirt, a parade of Trabant cars, Communist Party songs and slogans, and other cultural references. For a brief period, there was serious discussion of building a GDR theme park in Eastern Berlin, complete with grumpy guards, Socialist songs piped throughout the park, and of course spluttering Trabant cars. *Ostalgie,* then, in its many manifestations, meanings, and practices, has become a highly visible cultural phenomenon in the actually existing post-Socialist landscape.

To dismiss this as history returned as farce, however, would ignore the historically specific cultural contexts and asymmetrical relations of power in which many such practices have emerged. As I have argued elsewhere, earlier forms of *Ostalgie* that emerged in the mid-1990's—including a reinvention, reproduction, and mass merchandising of East German products, and the collecting, cataloging, and "museumification" of GDR everyday life—captured feelings of profound loss, longing, and displacement in a period of intense social discord. *Ostalgie* in this sense echoed Kathleen Stewart's definition of nostalgia: "a cultural practice, not a given content. ... In positing a 'once was' in relation to a 'now,' it creates a frame for meaning, a means of dramatizing aspects of an increasingly fluid and unnamed social life" (Stewart 1988: 227).

While earlier sentiments and practices that transformed Socialist rhetoric and symbols into nostalgic icons endure, *Ostalgie* in its current incarnation is frequently dominated by a certain cynicism, irony, and parody. There is widespread awareness reflected in discourses about *Ostalgie,* for example, of the ironic fact that the bust of Lenin is now an "advertising gag" for the film, that many of these East German products are now often produced by Western German firms, sold by Western German Internet businesses, or stocked by Wal-Mart. In its hypercommercial and self-parodying form, then, current practices of *Ostalgie* celebrate and naturalize capitalism as the inevitable outcome of socialism's demise.

Quite predictably, the film *Good Bye, Lenin!* and the subsequent *Ostalgie* boom have reignited familiar debates about the meanings, memories, and representations of the Socialist past. One of the principal criticisms of *Ostalgie* is that it provides a means of eliding questions of complicity, responsibility, and accountability in relation to a burdened GDR past—in other words, that it glorifies what had been a brutal regime. While these observations raise legitimate concerns about representations of the past and thereby contribute to ongoing debates about historical memory, dismissals and attempts to belittle *Ostalgie* may also be viewed as part of a larger hegemonic project to devalue Eastern German critiques of the politics of reunification. More generally, the allegations of "mereness" and accusations of neglect, as well as the culturally specific practices of *Ostalgie,* both reflect and constitute struggles over the control and appropriation of historical knowledge, shared memories, and personal recollections—all of which interact in highly complicated ways (cf. Lass 1994).

The anthropologist Caroline Humphrey has recently asked whether the category "postsocialism" still makes sense given the diverse range of post-Socialist contexts and trajectories (Humphrey 2001). It's a reasonable question, and something people like us should probably think about. Like Humphrey, though, I would argue that the category retains its usefulness for a number of reasons, particularly as long as the Socialist past remains a prime reference point for many people in their own personal histories and memories as they struggle to make sense of the present. The category will remain compelling, it seems to me, as long as socialism continues to have an active social life that people engage and make meaningful in cultural practices and productions.

But it remains important for another, perhaps more pressing, reason; postsocialism, with its implicit temporal positioning of relating to the present in terms of the past, offers the possibility of positing socialism in relation to its world-historical Other: capitalism. Katherine Verdery has argued that "the context in which we should assess postsocialism's emerging forms is—far more than before—the international one of global capital flows" (Verdery 1999: 25). I would expand on this insight to suggest that it also works the other way around: postsocialism's "emerging forms" provide a means of assessing and critiquing global capitalism.

This brings us, in a rather roundabout way, back to the topic of memory, nostalgia, and the present. For it is in the realm of memory—whether through routine cultural practices like the consumption or display of East German things or mass-mediated representations—that capitalism's world-historical Other (socialism) is given meaning and significance, even if a parodied one. The various domains in which memory is produced, negotiated, and deployed can be where capitalist forms and practices are both contested *and* affirmed.

In a rich essay on millennial capitalism, John and Jean Comaroff aim to interrogate "the experiential contradictions at the core of neoliberal capitalism," suggesting that that many of these contradictions are most visible in "so-called postrevolutionary societies" (Comaroff and Comaroff 2000: 298). They continue by noting that "a good deal is to be learned about the historical implications of the current moment by eavesdropping on the popular anxieties to be heard in such places" (299). Following their lead, in addition to the fieldwork I have conducted in different regions of the former GDR, I also attempted a form of "eavesdropping" in its postmodern version: by "lurking" on Internet bulletin boards and discussion groups focusing on themes of *Ostalgie* and German-German relations. In a lengthy Internet forum devoted to the film, located on the *Good Bye, Lenin!* website (www.good-bye-lenin.de), I "overheard" mostly enthusiastic reviews of the film as well as predictable debates about the phenomenon of *Ostalgie*. There were also voices like "Eike," articulating a minority but not uncommon sentiment:

> The fall of the Wall that was staged for the mother's benefit at the end of the film is exactly what I might have wished for myself. ... Whoever criticizes the GDR for being oppressive and undemocratic has NOT TRULY lived and worked in capitalism.

Other postings expressed similar reactions: "I could have cried during Sigmund Jähn's speech," one contributor wrote, "it really spoke to me"; or, "The perspective of a society with no 'terror of consumerism'" or "Elbow society broadens one's horizons, especially now when capitalism isn't functioning very well any more."

Such are the contexts, large and small, for the production and circulation of historical memory. My suggestion for thinking about the role of memory in the post-Socialist present calls for us to think out of what Bruce Grant has called the "Socialist–post-Socialist box" and engage with larger theoretical debates about the meanings of the market, the contradictions of millennial capitalism, the cultures of neoliberalism, among other topics (Grant 2006). Following the social life of socialism through its various forms, uses, and trajectories has the potential of illuminating these and other phenomena. As one instantiation of socialism's social life, *Good Bye, Lenin!* as a mass-mediated history of the present has contributed to the construction of cultural realities that themselves are a function of the political landscape they inhabit and reproduce.

Notes

1. We are grateful to Matti Bunzl for polishing and editing this posthumous chapter.

References

Appadurai, Arjun, ed. 1986 *The Social Life of Things: Commodities in Cultural Perspective.* Cambridge: Cambridge University Press.

Berdahl, Daphne. 2005. "Expressions of Experience and Experiences of Expressions: Museum Representations of GDR History." *Anthropology and Humanism* 30 (2): 156–70.
Cohen, David William. 1994. *The Combing of History.* Chicago: University of Chicago Press.
Comaroff, Jean, and John Comaroff. 2000. "Millenial Capitalism: First Thoughts on a Second Coming." *Public Culture* 12 (2): 291–343.
Connerton, Paul. 1989. *How Societies Remember.* Cambridge: Cambridge University Press.
Davis, Natialie Zemon, and Randolph Starn, eds. 1989. *Memory and Counter-Memory.* Theme Issue of *Representations* 26 (1).
Grant, Bruce. 2006. "Cosmopolitan Baku." Paper presented at the conference "Post-Communist Nostalgia." University of Illinois at Urbana-Champaign, 7–8 April.
Hensel, Jana. 2002. *Zonenkinder.* Reinbek bei Hamburg: Rowohlt.
Humphrey, Caroline. 2001. "Does the Category 'Postsocialist' Still Make Sense?" In *Postsocialism: Ideals, Ideologies, and Practices in Eurasia,* ed. C. N. Hann, 12–15. London: Routledge.
Huyssen, Andreas. 1995. *Twilight Memories: Marking Time in a Culture of Amnesia.* New York: Routledge.
Ivy, Marilyn. 1995. *Discourses of the Vanishing: Modernity, Phantasm, Japan.* Chicago: University of Chicago Press.
Lass, Andrew. 1994. "From Memory to History: The Events of November 17 Dis/membered." In *Memory, History, and Opposition under State Socialism,* ed. Rubie Watson, 87–104. Santa Fe, NM: School of American Research.
Saß, Katrin. 2008. *Interview mit Katrin Saß.* Electronic document, http://www.good-bye-lenin.de/int-sass.php, accessed 21 February.
Der Spiegel. 2003. "Der Bundestag nimmt Abschied von Lenin." *Spiegel Online,* 3 April. Electronic document, http://www.spiegel.de/kultur/gesellschaft/0,1518,243206,00.html, accessed 21 February 2008.
Stewart, Kathleen. 1988. "Nostalgia: A Polemic." *Cultural Anthropology* 3 (3): 227–41.
Ten-Dyke, Elizabeth. 2001. *Dresden: Paradoxes of Memory in History.* London: Routledge.
Verdery, Katherine. 1999. *The Political Lives of Dead Bodies.* New York: Columbia University Press.
Von Vestenberg, Nikolaus. 2003. "Kinder haften für ihre Eltern." *Der Spiegel,* 24 March: 114–16.
Wanner, Catherine. 1998. *Burden of Dreams: History and Identity in Post-Soviet Ukraine.* College Park: Pennsylvania State Press.
Watson, Rubie, ed. 1994. *Memory, History, and Opposition under State Socialism.* Santa Fe, NM: School of American Research.

11

"BUT IT'S OURS"
Nostalgia and the Politics of Authenticity in Post-Socialist Hungary

Maya Nadkarni

One of Hungary's most popular Socialist-era films, Péter Bacsó's 1969 comedy *The Witness* (A Tanú), tells the story of József Pelikán, a dike keeper who becomes trapped within the regime's absurd machinations in the years before 1956. Caught for illegally slaughtering a pig, Pelikán expects years of hard labor and jail time, but he is instead befriended by the mysterious party functionary Comrade Virág. Virág rewards Pelikán with a series of increasingly prestigious positions, promoting him after each failure until he is high in the party echelon. The hapless Pelikán has no understanding of the reasons for his preferential treatment—until, in the final sequences of the film, Virág orders him to provide false testimony against a friend in a show trial.

Banned for over a decade by Communist authorities, *The Witness* met with an enthusiastic reception when it was finally permitted for general release in the early 1980s. Its jokes and portrayal of the well-intentioned yet bumbling Pelikán (whose literal-minded attempts to fulfill the requirements of each position inevitably expose the absurdity of the system that gave him these assignments)[1] soon gained a wide and enduring cultural currency. One of its most famous scenes depicts Pelikán's job of running an agricultural institute tasked with creating a "Hungarian orange." Despite the difficulty of growing such southern fruit in Hungary's continental climate (Pelikán himself says that he has not eaten one in twenty years), the institute finally succeeds in producing a single orange, which is then celebrated with a visit from a leading party official. Moments before the ceremony is to begin, however, Pelikán discovers that his son has stolen the orange and eaten it. In desperation, he turns to Virág for help, who orders him to use a lemon instead. The party official tastes it and screws up his face in dismay, but—with a glance at Virág—Pelikán hurriedly explains, "It's the new Hungarian orange. It's a little bit yellow, a little bit sour. But it's ours!"

With this appeal to national pride and Socialist advancement, Pelikán is saved, and the official's grimace relaxes into a smile.

The ironies of the "Hungarian orange" (*magyar narancs*) caught hold of Hungary's cultural imagination in the last years of the Soviet regime. As a symbol of the irrationality of the Communist system, the Hungarian orange could be interpreted a number of ways: as a demonstration of the power of the regime to determine reality; as another example of the "shared lie" of communism (summed up in the well-known joke, "You pretend to work and we pretend to pay you"); and as a critique of the unnaturalness of any attempt to plant Soviet communism in Hungary's presumably inhospitable cultural soil. In other words, the Hungarian orange became the epitome of the inauthenticity of Hungarian communism itself—so often qualified as "goulash communism," "real existing socialism," and other such terms to distinguish Soviet principles from the "new" Hungary actually produced by its ideology.

After the demise of socialism, however, the primary appeal of the Hungarian orange no longer derived from its critique of the former regime's irrationality. Instead, the emphasis shifted to a nostalgic appreciation of how the orange exemplified the resilience, imagination, and humor of Hungary's response to the imposition of communism.[2] Most important of all, I would argue, was the claim to the national specificity of this response. That is, if during the socialist era the stress was implicitly upon the humorous understatement of Pelikán's "It's a little bit yellow, a little bit sour," and how this fierce denial of reality exemplified the blindness of the regime, what resonated in the post-Socialist context was the claim to national possession and uniqueness that nonetheless endowed this sour lemon with value. Pelikán's "But it's ours" thus stood in stark contrast to the nationalist discourses usually invoked to describe Hungarian identity. It highlighted the inauthenticity of its construct, but nonetheless found a specific national value within it—and, indeed, within the act of artifice ("the *new* Hungarian orange") itself.

As such, the "Hungarian orange" provides insight into the post-Socialist debates concerning national pride and authenticity that dominated political and public discourse after the end of socialism. Many such disputes tended to be figured in terms of competing claims to historical legitimacy or as attempts to revive the pre-Socialist past as the source of authentic national tradition. In this essay, however, I shall examine the productivity of putative *inauthenticities* (epitomized in the Hungarian orange), and how the nostalgia for such artifacts of the Socialist era inspired novel ways to envision cultural value and identity.

For, as elsewhere in the former Soviet bloc, nostalgia for the Socialist past became a popular memory practice, narrative mode, and marketing tool during Hungary's first decade of postsocialism. Entrepreneurs furnished new coffeehouses and restaurants with carefully salvaged furniture and objects from the former era; beverage manufacturers reintroduced soft drinks from the 1960s; and advertisers revived television spots from the 1970s or created new ones that attempted to target similar memories. A number of films, invariably narrated from the limited perspective of a child or teenager, managed to win local audiences back to Hungarian cinemas with their sympathetic narration of the conflicts and everyday pleasures of life under late socialism. And, just as several popular books and museum exhibitions catalogued the material culture of the recent past, collections of official Socialist-era songs also topped the charts. Even the word *nostalgia* itself became fashionable, giving its name to parties, raves, bars, and even new business ventures without explicit reference to what, if anything, was intended to be the target of this emotion.

Such an efflorescence of cultural memory might easily be interpreted as reflecting the wistful desire to return to the Socialist past. Following Kathleen Stewart's argument that nostalgia is a "cultural practice, not a given content" (1988: 227), however, I shall demonstrate that the popularity of nostalgia in the Hungarian context was less concerned with reviving the Socialist past than with making sense of the post-Socialist present. Indeed, nostalgia functioned as a way to break from previous era: first, by displaying a properly ironic distance from the kitsch of official state culture, and then later by commodifying and assigning new value to the outdated artifacts of everyday life in Hungary under socialism. In so doing, it challenged current regimes of value in post-socialism by finding worth in the cultural detritus of a past once reviled as inauthentic. At the same time, the marketing of this nostalgia also reinforced current values by commodifying these relics and subjecting them to a contemporary market logic—thus legitimizing the often-disappointing experience of transition itself.

Nostalgia thus complicated not only historical politics in Hungary, where polarized political discourse discouraged any positive reevaluation of the past, but also the desire to catch up with Western standards of consumption that had structured Socialist-era fantasies of a better life. Ironically, however, this politics of the everyday—the determinedly apolitical quotidian world conjured up by nostalgia's objects and practices—was itself an artifact of the previous regime, where the sharp divide between the private domestic sphere and the public world of political action was the very condition of political subjectivity under late socialism. As such, nostalgia's refusal of politics, and the incommensurability of its cozy recollections of innocence and security with memories of the oppression also suffered under the past regime, functioned as a metacommentary on the construction of politics in both eras.

Most importantly, like the Hungarian orange, nostalgia provided a discourse about cultural value and authenticity through which to debate the Hungarian national subject itself: what is "ours," what could be kept from a now discredited past, what must be disavowed in order to constitute national selves as new post-Socialist subjects. That is, nostalgia became a technology of cultural identification: a claim to national pride that recovered a presumably inassimilable past under the benign marker of cultural inheritance. If the Hungarian orange was once a symbol of retaining a specifically Hungarian humor and inventiveness in the face of *Soviet* occupation, it and other nostalgically recuperated symbols from the past era thus later enabled Hungarians to argue for an identity that was distinct from the *West* — and, in some ways, superior to it.

Homesickness and the Irretrievability of the Past

Nostalgia's etymological meaning is "homesickness": *nostos* and *algia,* a longing for home. Despite its seemingly antique origins, however, the term is a recent invention, introduced in the seventeenth century to describe a physical illness: the pain experienced by sailors and the military sent far from home (Boym 2001: 3). The meaning of the term soon shifted, however, from spatial displacement to the more pervasive sense of temporal discontinuity and loss endemic to modernity, "with its alienation, its much lamented loss of tradition and community" (Hutcheon 1998). This transformation from an individual medical condition into a cultural response also entailed a transformation in the object of nostalgia's longings. Once cured by a trip home, nostalgia now mourns for origins perceived as always already lost and irretrievable. That is, nostalgia responds to the subject's perception of being exiled from the present by imagining the past as the site of a lost and utopian "immediacy, presence, and authenticity" (Hutcheon 1998). In this formulation, home becomes an ideal state that can only appear in its retrojection through repetition (Ivy 1995: 22).

Nostalgia, as Svetlana Boym reminds us, is thus a historical emotion (2001: 7): the product of a modern temporality that views individuals and societies as caught up in a destructive and irreversible flow of time. Such homesickness can take the form of a recuperative, virulent nationalism — a nostalgia that does not know itself as such (2001: 49). But it can also be "reflective," focused upon the breach between past and present rather than a desired return (2001: 49). For, while nostalgia is often interpreted as the insistence that the past may be made present again, it is in fact the irrevocability of the past that makes such longing possible: nostalgia is defined by "its inability to approach its subject" (Fritzsche 2004: 65).

As such, nostalgia can paradoxically function as the very means by which the present is disarticulated from recent history. This explains why, in Hungary, nostalgic consumption of the detritus of official state culture began even before its first democratic elections took place. Newspapers chronicled how Western investors were buying up busts of Lenin, red stars, Soviet medals, and even now-obsolete statues in order to profit from the sudden age value of these objects. Meanwhile, Socialist-themed parties, happenings, and even a pizzeria ("Marxim") appeared, cleansing Soviet symbols of their ideological content by reframing them as historical kitsch. The very speed with which such kitsch became fashionable, however, demonstrated that it had little to do with a desire for restoration or return. Rather, it helped to produce the difference between the "Soviet" past and the "Western" present by rewriting the Socialist era solely in terms of Soviet occupation. Making the soft dictatorship of yesterday equivalent to that of the repressive Stalinist 1950s—a period that for decades had already been experienced as past—helped to distance an everyday suddenly consigned to the dustbin of history. (Indeed, the poster for the winning party during Hungary's first democratic elections in 1990 featured a garbage can surrounded by busts of Lenin and other party memorabilia with the slogan "National Spring Cleaning!" (*Országos tavaszi nagytakarítás!*)) Moreover, in decisively announcing the failure of the previous regime, such acts of distancing gave a sense of completion to an ideological project that had long been stalled by the practical concerns of "real existing socialism."[3]

This commodification of the official culture of late socialism was part of a larger cultural process of ascribing new visibility to objects and symbols that for most had been relatively unnoticed facets of everyday life under the soft dictatorship. For example, when in 1993 Budapest removed its Socialist-era statues to a Statue Park Museum (*Szoborpark Múzeum*) on the outskirts of the city, city authorities justified the creation of the park in order to protect the statues from defacement—as well as to protect Hungary's new Western democratic values that prized preservation and education over political iconoclasm. What this rhetoric sought to conceal, however, was the fact that little such vandalism or public outcry against the statues had actually occurred. Instead, most Hungarians regarded the statues—which mostly commemorated local Hungarians and bore few of the excesses of Socialist realism—as uncomplicated landmarks in their own personal and cultural geographies of the city. For example, the Osztyapenkó statue was a memorial to a Soviet captain that stood on one of Budapest's main highways. A familiar sight on the way to and from Hungary's popular vacation spot, Lake Balaton, Osztyapenkó was popular with hitchhikers and regarded by many with great affection.

Removing Osztyapenkó and other such statues erased their cultural significance from the landscape of the city, reducing them to their ideological content. By redefining late socialism in terms of a Soviet occupation that could be isolated from the lived flow of post-Socialist experience, such efforts thus enabled city authorities to produce the sense of break necessary to concretize the experience of transition. And, by commodifying these historical relics as humorous kitsch to appeal to the nostalgia of both local and international visitors, the Statue Park Museum was now able to demonstrate not only its emotional distance from the recent Socialist era—but also the success of Western capitalism in Hungary (Nadkarni 2003).

Authenticity and the Fantasy of the West

The marketing of such nostalgia was indeed particularly suited to Hungary's entrance into the temporality of the market economy, with its accelerated obsolescence and the commodification of age value (Jameson 1991). Capitalism makes a fetish of authenticity: that auratic perception of singularity which, as Benjamin (1968) reminds us, only arises at the time of its passing. In contrast, Soviet ideology was emphatically antinostalgic, locating its utopian yearnings in the future rather than in a largely discredited national past.

Yet Soviet citizens were not immune from nostalgia. It emerged, however, as a spatial rather than temporal longing: the imagined dream of the West and the fantasies of mobility and abundance it represented.[4] For Hungarians, this fantasy of escape was explicitly articulated in terms of material consumption and a Western standard of living broadly perceived as superior to what socialism offered. Western material culture thus became the standard of the "normal" (*normális*) through which Hungarians developed their own consumer consciousness and articulated their critique of the Socialist regime (Fehérváry 2002). Indeed, the lower quality of the Hungary's mass-produced goods, perceived as cheap imitations of Western ones (such as Trapper, Socialist Hungary's brand of "designer" jeans), was perceived to be emblematic of the lower quality of life within the Soviet bloc more generally. Utopia appeared to be located just outside Hungary's borders, in a Western European/North

American culture characterized by unlimited Toblerone, bananas, and consumer choice.[5]

With the demise of socialism, many Hungarians initially expected that they would quickly regain authenticity and attain (or return to) normality by matching not only the political freedoms but also the consumption patterns and living standards of the West (Fehérváry 2002). It is thus no surprise that a fetish for all that was perceived as Western and new characterized the advertising and consumption during the first years of postsocialism, as Hungarians sought to counter the image of being backward, dowdy Socialist neighbors and to repudiate a perceived past identity as consumers of both Socialist ideology and inferior material culture. The economic challenges of postsocialism, however, soon disenchanted this dream of consumer plentitude—as well as the ideal that had undergirded this fantasy. For while the Soviet system may have been considered to be a perversion of the normal life experienced elsewhere, its citizens had nonetheless preserved the notion of an external standard: what Salecl describes as the fantasy structure of a "something else" that reveals the innocence that underlay many Socialist-era cynicisms (1999: 92). The demise of socialism (and the crime, corruption, and economic uncertainty the introduction of capitalism was perceived to unleash) paradoxically meant the "loss of the normal"—or, at least, the rhetoric that it was in crisis, destabilized, or under threat from named or nebulous conspirators.

One of the first commercial successes of Hungary's post-Socialist film industry was thus a nostalgic revival of these fantasies of Western normality: the low-budget musical *Dolly Birds* (Csinibaba, 1997). Set in the early 1960s in order to evoke both the privation and optimism of the first years of post-1956 normalization, the film's loose narrative chronicles the activities of the members of a Socialist housing block under the bumbling supervision of block warden Uncle Simon. Inspired by the chance to win a trip to Helsinki in a talent contest, a group of teenagers form a rock band, dreaming of an escape to a West imagined as a fantastic surplus of commodities: Coca-Cola, Chesterfield cigarettes, and the spectacular form of Anita Ekberg (whose projected image sparks a riot in a theater showing *La Dolce Vita*).

While *Dolly Birds* is thus a film about the losses experienced under state socialism (and the fantasies these absences inspired), its nostalgic reception reflected distinctly post-Socialist realities. By mythologizing the now lost pleasures of everyday life in early 1960s Hungary—outdated fashions, teased hair, "Bambi" (an artificial orange soft drink), and the popular hits of the day—it revived the dreams of that era: a time when both the Socialist utopia predicted by Communist ideology and the fantasy of self-fulfillment promised by Western consumerism had not yet failed to come to pass. *Dolly Birds* thus mourned a specific configuration of the West itself, as an object of longing around which Socialist-era subjectivities were constituted.

Dolly Birds' local success (unusual in the context of a film industry that then specialized in art films that found their primary audience at international festivals) paved the way for a plethora of nostalgic phenomena that began to emerge during this time. This included not only a number of films that similarly conjured up the fantasies and imaginative constructs of the past era,[6] but the commodification of the consumer and material culture that structured everyday life under socialism. From the revival of the soft drink Bambi[7] to the museum exhibitions and books that cataloged Socialist-era mass and material culture (Gerő 2001; Poós 2002), this second wave of nostalgia differed from the earlier marketing of Soviet kitsch, which invoked the past in order to break with it. Here, nostalgia took the form of gentler, more affectionate attempts to recapture the atmosphere, objects, and gestures of the past era, in order to mourn of a way of life now indeed experienced as irretrievable.

Like the earlier form of nostalgia, however, this nostalgia did not seek to recreate or recover the Socialist past, and nor was it explicitly concerned with the accuracy of its representations. Rather, it reflected the fundamental logic of nostalgia as the "desire to desire" itself (as Susan Stewart explains via Lacan [1993: 23]). It paradoxically attempted to recapture the structure of fantasy under the previous regime by projecting it onto a new target: Socialist-era styles and objects now assigned the same emotional value once invested in foreign goods. Once reviled as cheap and inauthentic imitations of the West, they now appeared auratic and desirable compared to now familiar Western brands and products.

For example, a nostalgia festival in autumn 2000 to promote the film *Little Journey* (Kis Utazás, 2000) included a promotional publication that asked local celebrities and business leaders what they considered to be the most memorable objects from the era. Many fondly remembered the Western goods (Adidas, Levi 501s) that by then had become available to those who could afford them[8] or purchase them abroad, as well as those objects (such as the "American" diplomat bag (*amcsi dipo*), used as a school satchel) that conjured up the glamour of Western consumption. Greater emphasis, however, was placed upon the emphatically local fashions of the time, such as the gas mask bag (*szimatszatyor*) also used as a school satchel, and the Hungarian-made closed-toe sandal called the *alföldi papucs* (Octogon 2000). These responses thus commemorated not only the memories, fantasies, and associations these objects once inspired, but also the context of their creation: what Berdahl (1999) analyzes as a nostalgia for the era of production itself, in contrast to Hungarians' post-Socialist identities as consumers of primarily Western goods.[9] As such, the publication functioned as an inventory of the cultural mythologies and emotions of a lost age: attempts to evoke or capture the "fugitive sensibilities" of the late Socialist era (Sontag 1966: 276).

Such nostalgic practices mourned not only a disappearing material culture, but a lost sociality as well. Production and distribution of Socialist mass culture did not function according to market rules of fashion and planned obsolescence. Starting in the early 1960s, several generations of Hungarian Socialist consumers played with similar toys and consumed the same brands, and each generation had more-or-less similar access to Western goods. This enabled a collective sense of identity that only now became visible at the moment of its disappearance, when both age and increasingly disparate financial circumstances were resulting in very different capacities to consume both local and Western products. At the same time, of course, remembering these products also served to justify and make more glamorous the present-day possibilities of consumption by reminding Hungarians of the previous era of relative scarcity.

Like the practices outlined in the previous section, this second wave of nostalgia thus did not concern the past itself, but rather the subjects' memory of their own past investments and fantasies, as well as the imagined futures these fantasies projected. As Benjamin recognized several generations previously, this is what gives the outdated detritus of consumer culture in particular such poignancy: too recent to possess age value as relics, these objects in their obsolescence nonetheless revealed the diverse hopes once embedded within them, by making palpable the disjuncture between these former dreams of the future and the present reality (Buck-Morss 1989, 2000). Thus, the seemingly trivial and impersonal consumer products of Socialist mass production ironically offered a powerful idiom through which to mourn the "loss of the normal" and the disenchanted dream of the West, via the personal and societal naiveté these objects were perceived to represent. Imbricated in discourses of authenticity and utopianism, such nostalgia enabled its subjects to reawaken the utopian impulses in the Socialist project itself—as well as its now obsolete sites of fantasy and resistance.

Childhood and the Politics of Nostalgia

Giving shape and form to a more pervasive sense of cultural loss, the appeal of such nostalgia lay in its potential to illuminate the forgotten possibilities, unrealized futures, and long-dormant fantasies hidden in the objects and discourses it awakened. Many Hungarian and international commentators, however, nonetheless deplored nostalgia as an uncritical attempt to resurrect past presence and imagined origins that sought to forget everything that was painful and difficult about the Socialist era. Treating the status of memory in post-Socialist societies as a cultural diagnostic, such criticism assumed nostalgia to possess an intrinsic political content that threatened Hungary's cultural "health."

As a result, each new film or fad was accompanied by articles and reviews that made a point of arguing that the objects and practices themselves had little to do with politics, and even when they did, they were not actually perceived as such at the time. For example, a collection of Socialist songs called *The Best of Communism* was number one in Hungary for several weeks in 1998. While the foreign media interpreted this popularity in terms of political kitsch or reactionary politics, my informants argued that they valued these songs neither despite nor because of their political content. Instead, their nostalgia was based upon the personal and communal experiences associated with these songs (singing around the campfire, stealing one's first kiss), rather than the ideology they represented.

For many people, nostalgia was thus nothing more than the universal longing for childhood itself as an easier, more innocent time. (This perspective is canonized in the title of a popular ballad from the 1960s that was frequently invoked in this context: "I Only Remember the Beautiful" [*Csak a szépre emlékezem.*]) The political transition was thus often narrated as a collective coming-of-age, in which the demise of paternal authority brought about a painful but necessary loss of innocence. While such narratives spoke most directly to people then in their thirties, whose personal biographies best corresponded to Hungary's recent history, they comprised a common cultural vocabulary relevant to older and (to a lesser extent) younger generations as well.[10] In other words, shared cultural dreams and fantasies—rather than personal experiential memory—were the precondition for nostalgia.

The nostalgia films mentioned in the previous section explicitly thematized this argument, by paralleling the youth of their protagonists to the perceived overall immaturity of Hungarian society under the paternalist Socialist system. As Fehérváry (1998) argues in her discussion of the film *Dolly Birds,* entrance into the harsh economic realities and symbolic upheavals of postsocialism is thus narrated as the passage from childhood into the freedoms and responsibilities of adulthood itself. Crucially, however, these films' youthful protagonists invariably give priority to personal rites of passage over national ones, often with humorous results. For example, the film *Moscow Square* (Moszkva Tér, 2001) is a gentle comedy that follows a group of graduating high school students in the final days of socialism. Concerned with parties, girls, and cars (the film's slogan: *Buli, Csajok, Verda*), these teenagers are insouciantly indifferent to the adult world of politics. For them, the end of communism means the chance to travel to the West, to purchase new exotic foreign goods, and to skip their qualifying exams in contemporary history, which the recent events force the state to cancel. Even the most defining moments of this period of political turmoil fail to attract the students' attention; the 1989 televised reburial of Imre Nagy, martyr of Hungary's failed 1956 uprising, is met with apathy: "Who the fuck is Imre Nagy?"

Nostalgia for childhood is for a time of limited perceptions, when one is not even aware of political considerations. Explaining the appeal of films such as *Moscow Square* simply in terms of childhood memory as a transhistorical experience, however, enabled a crucial misrecognition of politics under late state socialism. For it was the state itself that encouraged the very distinction between public political involvement and private material concerns that such films depict: a logic by which the paternalist regime constructed its citizens, regardless of age, as *childlike*. That is, rather than represent the absence of politics, the retreat into a private realm of action seemingly free of political concerns was in fact the very condition of political subjectivity.

This logic was one of the many ironies that emerged in the later decades of socialism. While Socialist rule was consistently paternalistic in character, its ideology initially aimed to break apart the axes of private and public: the bourgeois distinction between the private domestic realm and the public arena of political thought, culture, and action. As Crowley and Reid explain, the everyday was thus a specific site of ideological intervention in early socialism, resulting in such novel forms of spatiality and sociality as communal apartments (2002: 6). Boym (1994) describes this in the Russian context as the war on *byt*—the banality of the everyday that communism attempted to destroy by declaring the bourgeois interior itself suspect, with its rubber tree plants and kitschy bric-a-brac.

In the waves of normalization that followed 1956 in Hungary and 1968 in Czechoslovakia, however, Socialist regimes attempted to reconfigure the basis of their legitimacy by offering in advance some of the material rewards that communism had long been promising. In exchange for a raised standard of living, security, and relative freedom from harassment, however, Socialist citizens were expected to withdraw into private life away from political participation. The ensuing enthusiasm for consumer luxuries and weekend houses (as well as the second jobs necessary to acquire them) thus meant that it was the regime's own policies that produced the modern consumer subjectivity that made possible the fantasies of Western consumption explored in the previous section. Such efforts ultimately came at the cost of producing an atomized population whose overriding concern for the pursuit of private happiness ended up being not all that different from what is found in the West (Bren 2002; Fehérváry 2002; Lampland 1995; Pittaway 2006). Yet regardless of the ideological problems these policies produced, the regimes nonetheless tacitly (and sometimes explicitly) encouraged such reinforcement of the public/private divide (Bren 2002). Political compliance, rather than action, was the goal; as Žižek argues, by the years of late socialism, "the paradox of the regime was that if people were to take their ideology seriously it would effectively destroy the system" (Boynton 1998: 44–45). Belief in ideological norms was dangerous, for it could expose the gap between the inglorious present and the radiant future promised by Communist ideology.

While the forms, practices, and structures of feeling found in contemporary nostalgia were quintessentially post-Socialist, the logic that propelled it was thus inherited from the previous era. Such nostalgia was not apolitical, but instead reflected the specific form of "antipolitics" sought by Hungarian citizens and encouraged under the previous regime: a cultural fantasy about the insularity of private life under socialism that stood in contrast to the political battles that characterized life in post-Socialist democracy.[11] As such, I will now demonstrate, nostalgic memory failed when imported as an ideological program into the political arena, precisely because of the way it was constructed as antipolitical in both the object of its longing and in its contemporary implications.

"When was it better to be young?"

In the summer of 2001, at the height of the annual political news drought that Hungarians call "cucumber season" (*uborkaszezon*), the head of the highly marginalized Workers' Party[12] proposed that the state permit the erection of a statue to Communist leader János Kádár. As General Secretary, Kádár had led Hungary through three decades of relative economic security. Representing the face of normalization and Hungary's "goulash communism," he was known as an avuncular, plain-spoken figure whose policies emphasized a steady increase in living standards, subsidized by foreign loans. Only in 1988, when political reform became inevitable in light of Gorbachev's perestroika and Hungary's own economic crises brought on by foreign debt, did reformers in Kádár's party nudge him out of office; he died a year later.

One of Hungary's recently established commercial television stations, TV2, picked up the story and devoted its weekly news roundup *Focus* (Fókusz) to examining this campaign and to collecting viewer opinions via its weekly phone-in poll. To everyone's apparent surprise, 80 percent of those who phoned in agreed that Kádár deserved a statue of his own, and the question for the following week's poll—"Is it better now to be young?" (*Jobb-e most fiatalnak lenni?*)—also received an emphatic response in favor of the past. Even many of the celebrities interviewed for the program praised the past regime for the opportunities and material security it provided its citizens. "It's true, there was nothing," one rock musician admitted. "But you could build on that nothing, and people still live in the houses that were built on this nothing."

Months later, a revised version of *Focus*'s catchphrase ("When was it better to be young?") found its way back into public currency as the Workers' Party campaign slogan for the national elections in spring 2002. Despite the apparent popularity of its argument, however, the party was unable to the leverage emotional capital of Kádárism into political gain. Instead, in the first round of elections, the Workers' Party once again failed to win the 5 percent necessary to gain parliamentary representation.

What accounted for the Workers' Party's inability to mobilize the emotions summoned by nostalgia for political ends? One answer concerns simple political expediency. Nostalgia in the Hungarian context was concerned with fantasy: both the fantasy of a more innocent past, and the past's own fantasies about what the future might bring. As a specific ideological project of restoration, however, nostalgia had little appeal in a country then already committed to EU integration.[13] Politicizing the homey sentiments summoned by nostalgia would have opened the policies of the past regime to political critique, thus invalidating its usefulness and emotional legitimacy across the political spectrum. It would subject the left to a condemnation of the Kádár regime's lack of democratic values, and at the same time, it would also be read as a rejection of—and hence incompatible with—right-wing ideology. Indeed, during the election campaign, Fidesz (the leading party in the center-right coalition government then in power) made such appeals to nostalgia a target of their anti-Communist rhetoric. By warning that the victory of the government's chief rival, the Hungarian Socialist Party, would mean the return of communism to Hungary, the coalition attempted to represent the Socialist Party in the worst possible light: as not a new European party, but an old and corrupted one that bore all the sins of the past era.[14]

On the other hand, as long as Hungarians could justify their fond memories solely in terms of their "stomachs"—that is, their memories of material comfort and security—the emotions summoned by nostalgia could be effective on both sides of the political divide. The Hungarian Socialist Party, impatient to reinvent itself as a European Socialist party with no links to the past, could make vague reference to protecting the concerns of the "common people" without taking responsibility for the injustices of socialism; while the right wing could explain nostalgic practices as merely the expression of dissatisfaction with postsocialism on the whole, rather than an endorsement of communism and hence a specific rejection of right-wing anti-Communist discourse.

More important than the ideological incompatibility between the fantasized past and present-day ends, however, was that Hungarians viewed the domestic realm evoked by nostalgia as a refusal of politics itself. As explained in the previous section, this distinction between the domestic and the political was not inevitable, but rather reflected the very basis of political subjectivity itself under the previous regime. The "apolitical" nature of the material sphere in Kádár's Hungary rendered present-day nostalgia for it also seemingly apolitical—and in so doing, it thus renarrated the political concerns that animated nostalgia for Kádárism as private and personal issues.

For this reason, as the *Focus* interviews made clear, support for a Kádár statue did not necessarily entail support for him as a historical actor. Rather, as many interviewees argued, Hungarians wanted to commemorate Kádár as a symbol of the desire to remember the past as safe and childlike: a time when the populace felt protected by the hand of the paternalist state, and a basic standard of living seemed assured. Of course, many others criticized erecting such a monument, arguing that it would reverse the work of the Statue Park Museum a decade earlier by reinstating ideological content now long removed from the spaces of the city. But these critiques missed what was truly radical about the Workers' Party proposal and its enthusiastic reception. The Statue Park Museum was created to distance the recent past through a new semiotics of public space in which the meaning and purpose of monuments were reduced to their intended political message. By redefining late socialism in terms of a Soviet ideological presence that could be isolated from the flow of post-Socialist experience, the creators of the park attempted to distance the past and disavow all that continued peacefully to remain from the Socialist era in institutions, behaviors, and structures of feeling, as well as in the landscape and material culture. A monument to Kádár would thus not merely be the equivalent of returning statues such as Osztyapenkó to their former locations. Rather, it would be as if the Osztyapenkó statue were reerected not to commemorate a Soviet soldier who died defending Hungary, but as a memorial to all the Hungarians who had used his monument as a hitchhiking stop, or welcomed his waving flag when returning to Budapest after a trip to Lake Balaton. In this sense, a statue to Kádár would serve as a memorial to the domestication of socialism itself.

What was at stake with the Workers' Party proposal was thus the suitability of bringing a nostalgia based on youthful private memories of Kádár's "childlike" citizenry into the political sphere of urban monumentality. Such arguments were torn between what *Focus*'s reporter summarized as "freedom or material security": values that the Kádár regime had rendered irreconcilable. "It's interesting to see that when we asked famous people, the usual reaction was anger or laughter," he observed. "Kádár's name still divides society." Yet while the historical interpretation of Kádár may have been divisive, it would be a mistake to narrate this conflict as simply reflecting a split between two communities of memory: one with positive memories of the Socialist past, and the other without.[15] Rather, the question was one of the commensurability of memories constructed as apolitical being brought into dialogue with more painful (and hence explicitly politicized) experiences of oppression under the previous regime.[16] The film *Dolly Birds* illustrates the stakes of this dilemma, in its opening scene of block warden Uncle Simon broadcasting the morning lottery numbers over the local public address system. He stutters when he discovers that one of the numbers is "56" (the year of Hungary's failed uprising against the Soviets), and hastily instructs the block residents to check the newspaper for the numbers instead. Within the film's narrative, of course, we are to understand that Uncle Simon refuses to say the words out of fear of political reprisals, but this scene also has an extradiegetic purpose. "Not saying 1956" is the film's condition for all that comes after: a portrayal of the early years of normalization as greatly circumscribed, but joyful nonetheless.

Nostalgia in the Hungarian context thus functioned as the apparent *limit* of politics. It gave voice to broadly perceived social truths that could not be voiced in the political sphere because it would subject these claims to a critique of the past regime's antidemocratic policies. (Indeed, rather than represent the desire to return to the past, nostalgia's inherent irretrievability was what made such discourse possible: Hungarians could "afford" to be nostalgic, as it were, because they saw no actual possibility of return to the Kádár era.) Yet what the elegiac idiom of nostalgia impeded was precisely the recognition of how the cultural logic of Kádárism continued to penetrate the present, since the seeming apolitical nature of nostalgia was itself the artifact of a regime that demanded the political withdrawal of its citizens.

As such, nostalgia's apparent refusal of politics was in itself a political stance; post-Socialist nostalgia for the Socialist past could thus be described as the final cog in the "antipolitics machine" of Kádár's Hungary (to borrow from Ferguson's [1994] analysis of the politics of development in Africa). Nonetheless, I would argue that my informants' repeated insistence upon the apolitical nature of nostalgia did not merely reflect the very condition of political subjectivity under the former regime. It also offered a politics of personal experience that offered a critique of the disappointments and insecurities of the present—and in so doing, it revealed the inadequacy of the highly polarized party discourse that dominated Hungary's post-Socialist public sphere for discussing or debating the past. More than simple Freudian denial, nostalgia for the everyday life of Kádár's Hungary offered one of the few safe discourses available for talking about the previous era. Because it evaded being harnessed for explicitly political ends, it provided a powerful tool for structuring collective and individual identities that was otherwise unavailable within Hungary's sharply divided political and cultural climate.

Indeed, given the perceived incompatibility of nostalgia with such contentious political topics, nostalgia offered perhaps the *only* idiom through which to find common ground in discussions of the Socialist era. Socialist nostalgia enabled Hungarians "to not talk about the past while talking about it." It permitted its consumers to retain their childhood memories while refusing to pass definitive judgment upon the larger political and historical context within which they took place, and it thus functioned as both a counterpoint to and evasion of the highly polarized representations of the past in the public sphere. In this way, nostalgia functioned not merely as a discourse about the past, but as a metacommentary on what it meant to talk about the past in post-Socialist Hungary.

"But it's ours": Nostalgia as Cultural Inheritance

A number of paradoxes thus characterized nostalgia in Hungary's first decade of postsocialism. Nostalgia distanced the past, even as it appeared to draw the past near. It found affective power in a former world of objects and narratives once experienced as inauthentic, yet it did so in response to the disenchantments of a present that the past had once long yearned for. Nostalgia's focus upon the material texture and sociality of the quotidian was interpreted as apolitical, but this distinction was itself inherited from the politics of the past era. As such, the paradoxes of nostalgia in Hungary illuminated some of the paradoxes of the past regime—but, again, the determinedly personal optics of nostalgia obscured such recognition.

While the rosy picture nostalgia painted of the past may have had as much to do with repressing the past as it did with remembering, however, this did not deny its capacity to be critical of present-day circumstances. Instead, I shall now conclude, the power of nostalgia in post-Socialist Hungary lay not merely in how it helped Hungarians to recuperate the past independent of current political considerations, but also how it enabled them to articulate cultural value in the present. Specifically, nostalgia provided an idiom to assert a distinctive national identity vis-à-vis both the Soviet past and the current experience of the West. It did so through the language of cultural inheritance: a global discourse of authenticity and value that simultaneously reinforced and challenged the ways Hungary was represented in the West—and how Hungary in turn represented itself as a new Western subject.

Earlier, I discussed how the marketing of state kitsch at the time of political transition enabled Hungarians to demonstrate their distance from a quickly receding Soviet past. These attempts to disavow the recent era, I now want to argue, were nonetheless forced to confront the Cold War nostalgia of Western visitors themselves, whose mass-mediated fantasies of toppled monuments and headless statues of Lenin had erroneously characterized Hungary's bloodless and peaceful democratic political transformation. As Žižek argues, what made such imagined spectacles so compelling—and necessary—was that they reinvented democracy by reinventing the West as an object of desire: "in a likeable, idealized form, as worthy of love":

> The real object of fascination for the West is thus the gaze, namely the supposedly naive gaze by means of which Eastern Europe stares back at the West, fascinated by its democracy. It is as if the Eastern gaze is still able to perceive in Western societies its *agalma*,[17] the treasure that causes democratic enthusiasm and which the West has long lost the taste of. [1990: 50]

The subsequent efflorescence of nostalgic practices in Hungary and elsewhere in the Soviet bloc was thus similarly read as confirmation of the West's own fantasies about the failures and triumphs of socialism and communism. For some Western observers, as discussed earlier, the commodification of Socialist-era goods proved the victory of market capitalism. For others, however, Socialist nostalgia offered a vision of popular resistance to capitalism that more traditional forms of political mobilization failed to ensure. This interpretation often motivated a politics by which every nostalgic gesture toward the past was read as subversive, even though these same nostalgic gestures might be used with equal effectiveness to maintain the status quo.[18]

For Hungarians, such encounters with the West's own (and often inaccurate) fantasies and assumptions about past and present-day Hungary entailed a double loss of the dream of the West through which Socialist-era Hungarians constructed their own identities. On the one hand, this fantasy represented the dream of utopia and a "normal life": the desire to consume Western products at Western levels and to catch up with its industrial production and consumer culture. On the other hand, it also symbolized the longing to be accepted and recognized as *preexisting*, rather than potential, members of the European cultural and historical community.[19] The frustrations of this were perhaps best exemplified by the Rubik's cube (*bűvös kocka*): a toy that in the early 1980s found its way into nearly every Western household just as it did within Hungary, but was rarely recognized as a specifically Hungarian invention. It thus failed to export the Hungarian self-image as a nation whose scientific skill and creativity was on par with that of more affluent countries, even as it demonstrated that its products could indeed provoke reciprocal consumer desire.

Nostalgia in post-Socialist Hungary responded to this perception of misrecognition, as well as to the more general sense of disenchantment with the extravagant claims of capitalist advertising and Western consumer products and culture. Now, not only was access to products limited by price rather than politics, but also many Hungarians believed that Western firms and advertisers failed to acknowledge them as sophisticated and knowledgeable consuming subjects. Indeed, while many Hungarians may not have necessarily believed that North American and Western European visitors actually looked down upon them, the risk of wholeheartedly accepting what they perceived to be "Western" values, standards, and logic was that at best it constructed Hungarians themselves as inadequate imitations, and at worst it rendered their recent history and cultural experience pathological and inassimilable.

People I spoke with explicitly described this shared experience and now obsolete cultural knowledge in terms of cultural intimacy and intranslatability. As one informant explained, "We know how to consume as Westerners, but we have additional knowledge that Westerners lack." For example, a 2001 television advertisement for the popular Hungarian beer Dreher presented a dazzling selection of teenaged slang, images, and icons from the Socialist 1980s with the slogan "We Speak One Language" (*Egy nyelvet beszélünk*). Several informants praised the historical accuracy of its references, so dense in cultural meaning that despite my own cultural and linguistic knowledge of Hungarian, it took one of them nearly half an hour to help me decipher this thirty-second spot. Similarly, a self-described "yuppie" in his thirties praised *Moscow Square* not merely because it rewrote his personal biography in terms of the collective memory of his generation: as he said several times, the film "was about me—I am that character." The film was also "important," he argued, because it brought back to life the tiny objects and gestures that he himself had been on the verge of forgetting. Its appeal lay in the perceived authenticity of its miniscule, extradiegetic details that conjured up the prosaic textures of a seemingly now distant reality, such as the kind of shopping bag used by the protagonist's grandmother, or the way upon entering her apartment she took a seat, opened a small wooden box of cigarettes, and lit one with a match.

Both the density and the specificity of these cultural references thus stood in stark contrast to the earlier wave of Soviet kitsch, so easily commodified, interpreted, and consumed by foreigners and locals alike. Yet when pushed to explain the significance of such a detail, or to extrapolate a larger narrative of everyday life under state socialism from the memories of such scenes and objects, my informants would insist upon the self-evidence of the memories themselves as a form of explanation. The mere fact of personal significance was its own justification, and attempts to analyze a larger meaning behind these memories and references would thus often lapse into what my informants themselves termed banalities—reminiscent of Pelikán's defense of the Hungarian orange decades earlier. "It was stupid, but it was our life." "It had soul (*lelke volt*)." "It was ours." The importance of these details thus lay in what was perceived to be their indexical rather than iconic quality: their function as marks of past presence that could only invite interpretation, and not provide it (Krauss 1985).

On the one hand, this inability or refusal to extract broader meaning can be read as a protest against abstraction itself, against the very fantasy of pure translatability epitomized by the capitalist logic of exchange value. As such, it reflected a mourning for what was now narrated as a different, more authentic relationship to the material culture of the Socialist era. As Creed notes, under state socialism, commodities were not fully fetishized: the effort exerted and connections necessary to acquire them were part of their perception and meaning. Thus, even the packaging of valued or exotic goods was preserved and displayed in order to make visible "social relations and valuable connections or resources that transcended the time or period of consumption" (2002).

At the same time, however, such an assertion of indefinable uniqueness was at the heart of what Žižek (1990) terms the "National Thing," the unnameable, irreducible core of enjoyment (*jouissance*)—perpetually under outside threat—around which modern national identities are constituted. The emphasis that consumers and audiences placed upon the authenticity of the atmospheres, gestures, and memories conjured up by these objects and films—rather than their practical or narrative value—thus functioned to signify the uniqueness and incommunicability (which, crucially, did not prohibit the commodifiability) of the shared experience of growing up under state socialism. As Boym observes, such a logic was perhaps best epitomized by the fact that many nations insist that their word for a culturally specific kind of nostalgic longing (for example, the Czech *litost*, the Russian *toska*, the Portuguese *saudade*) is itself untranslatable: "While each term preserves the specific rhythms of the language, one is struck by the fact that all these untranslatable words are in fact synonyms; and all share ... the longing for uniqueness" (2001: 13). From this perspective, nostalgia in Hungary was thus not so much a discourse of cultural intimacy as it was a discourse *about* cultural intimacy.[20] It offered a way to assert one's distinctiveness from the Western products that had flooded the Hungarian market, but it did so in an idiom of cultural inheritance that was itself part of what Herzfeld calls a "globalized system of cultural value" (2004: 322).

The self-proclaimed otherness and intranslatability of Hungarians' enjoyment thus both contested and affirmed the construction of Socialist and post-Socialist Hungarian identities through a reconfigured Western gaze. In other words, Socialist nostalgia responded to the dilemma of identity politics in an era of globalization more generally: the longing to be accepted as equal partners and the simultaneous desire to be seen as unique (and not a secondhand imitation). The Dreher beer advertisement, which attempted to unify its Hungarian audience under the slogan "We Speak One Language" thus represented the fantasy of resolving this tension, by framing its scenes of the Socialist 1980s through the memories of a group of successful, yuppie Hungarian thirty-somethings, enjoying their Dreher beers at a fashionable bar. It used Socialist nostalgia not to mourn the past, but to suggest that one could "have it all": be culturally distinctive and, at the same time, produce oneself as European by consuming and achieving at Western levels. (Indeed, not only the advertisement itself but the very fact of its existence suggested this, by targeting the people who had such memories as a desirable market demographic.) In so doing, this nostalgia functioned as a narrative fetish, which Santner in his work on Holocaust memory defines as a mode of representing the past that seeks to eliminate from recognition the very loss that called that narrative into being (1992: 144). The nostalgic pleasures of the Dreher beer ad thus offered "a strategy of undoing, in fantasy, the need for mourning by simulating a condition of intactness" (144): a dream of personal and cultural transformation in which everything changes, but nothing is lost.

Notes

This chapter is based on fieldwork and archival research conducted in Budapest and a village in northeastern Hungary from 1999 to 2002. It was funded by a National Science Foundation Graduate Fellowship, a fellowship from the International Dissertation Field Research Fellowship Program of the Social Science Research Council with funds provided by the Andrew W. Mellon Foundation, and an East European Studies Dissertation Fellowship from the American Council of Learned Societies. An earlier version of this essay was delivered at the Soyuz Symposium of Postsocialist Cultural Studies, February 2002, and portions of the section on the political ramifications of nostalgia were previously discussed in a 2004 article in *Ab Imperio* (coauthored with Olga Shevchenko). I am grateful to Zsuzsa Gille, Bruce Grant, Martha Lampland, József Litkei, Rosalind C. Morris, and Olga Shevchenko for their comments on this and earlier versions.

1. For example, Pelikán is put in charge of creating a haunted house ride in an amusement park. Instructed to give the ride a Socialist flavor, he produces tableaux that include a sheeted specter "haunting Europe" and manacled stick figures of the proletariat rattling their chains.
2. Indeed, it was proof of the broad appeal of the Hungarian orange across political lines that in the late 1990s, the then-governing center-right political party Fidesz, which used the image of an orange as its logo, temporarily prevented the left-wing weekly magazine *Magyar Narancs* from using the name.
3. Historians András Gerő and Iván Pető term this perception of abeyance "unfinished socialism": "Time seemed to have stopped: socialism was being built, but the construction process appeared to be uncompletable, never ending" (1999: 7).
4. For the ordinary citizen, such aspirations were as unattainable as the space travel produced by communism's own imperialist ambitions. Indeed, possibilities of movement—that is, emigration and exile—were so circumscribed that they retained the sense of irreversibility and finality that characterizes modern nostalgia (Nadkarni and Shevchenko 2004: 492). The German nostalgia film *Good Bye Lenin!* (2003) wittily illustrates these yearnings in its opening scenes, which chronicle the grief of the young boy Alex when his father abandons his family to emigrate West to his mistress in the late 1970s. *Good Bye Lenin!* parallels this loss to Alex's hero-worship of the East German cosmonaut Sigmund Jähn, who launches into space that same night.

In Alex's youthful perception, both paternal figures are equally out of reach and inaccessible, even as the content of these imaginative constructs (his father lost to the decadence of the West; Sigmund Jähn representing the national pride of the East) stand in stark contrast.

5. At the same time, Hungarians also defined themselves as superior vis-à-vis the standards of production and consumption found elsewhere in Eastern Europe. While the material benefits of "goulash communism" allowed many Hungarians to consume higher-quality goods than their Socialist neighbors, however, this mythology was rarely actualized on the level of production, given the division of industrial production across the Soviet bloc. Nonetheless, one of my informants, who briefly worked in a canning factory during the 1980s, told me that he was instructed to take far better care of the products intended for internal consumption than of those scheduled to be exported east to the USSR. At stake here was not only the obvious resistance to Soviet occupation, but also the perception that unlike Hungarians, people in the former Soviet Union would "consume anything."

6. *6:3, avagy játszd újra Tutti* (6:3, or Play It Again, Tutti, 1999), also made by *Csinibaba*'s director, Péter Timár); *Kis Utazás* (Little Journey, 2000); *Moszkva tér* (Moscow Square, 2001); *Csocsó, avagy éljen május elseje* (Csocsó, or Long Live May 1, 2002); and *Előre* (Forward, 2002). The German films *Sonnenallee* (Sunshine Alley, 1999) and *Good Bye Lenin!* (2003), both of which were enthusiastically received in Hungary, also fall into this category.

7. Other examples include the grape soda Traubi, Trapper jeans, and Tisza sneakers, which had been worn during the 1980s as a substitute for the Western Adidas.

8. Both Adidas and McDonalds had opened up shops in Budapest by the mid-1980s.

9. Ironically, many local products were also bought up by multinationals after the end of socialism; thus, some of my informants would introduce me to "classic" Hungarian products such as the Sport candy bar (*Sport szelet*) without realizing that these brands were now foreign owned.

10. While older consumers enjoyed the way nostalgic sites and practices evoked almost-forgotten personal and communal memories, what appeared to attract younger consumers, however, was the way nostalgic sites and cultural practices masterfully reiterated popular clichés about the past. Ivy (1995) provides an important rubric to distinguish among such different communities of nostalgia (and the patterns of consumption and desire that impel them). The first—*modernist nostalgia*—consists of those practices and objects with direct (metonymic, indexical) links to the past, and is part of discourses of authenticity and origin. Such nostalgia draws its affective force from relics and icons, whether busts of Lenin, the monuments in the Statue Park Museum, or a pair of Tisza sneakers. The second—*postmodern nostalgia*—encompasses those practices more concerned with producing the effect of a more generalized past. Here, nostalgia takes form as style, evidenced in the creation of "authentically" Socialist-era atmospheres and settings that seek not to evoke a specific past, but rather to render pastness itself. From this perspective, apart from this younger generation's curiosity about their parents' history, there was little to distinguish their craze for

consuming Socialist relics from the similar interest expressed toward anything distant in time and space (such as theme nightclubs and restaurants devoted to "Alcatraz," "Wall Street," and medieval Hungary).
11. This stated indifference to political culture was of course distinct from the antipolitics celebrated by Hungarian dissident intellectual George Konrad (1984), for whom antipolitics represented civil society's challenge to government institutions and ideology.
12. *Munkáspárt*, one of two successor parties to the Hungarian Socialist Workers' Party (*Magyar Szocialista Munkáspárt* [MSZMP]). Despite its attempts to reinvent itself as a modern alternative to capitalism, in each election cycle it failed to win the 5% electoral vote necessary for representation in parliament.
13. Indeed, leaders of the Workers' Party themselves were insistent that a return to the past was neither possible nor desirable (interviews with Gyula Thürmer and Attila Vajnai, 2 October 2000). However, given the party's lack of popularity as a contemporary Socialist movement, its appeal to memories of the Kádár era was nonetheless intended to give voters the impression that the party would return to following Kádár's path.
14. Fidesz ultimately lost this bid for reelection. However, its defeat was narrow and highly contested, which indicates the success of their attempt to mobilize public sentiment and transform the emotional tenor of the elections from a political battle to a "holy war."
15. After all, many of my informants who enthusiastically consumed Socialist nostalgia were also the same ones who, in other contexts, decried the past regime and called attention to what they perceived to be troubling social and economic continuities between the Socialist past and post-Socialist present. One young professional who supported the anti-Communist rhetoric of the center-right party Fidesz, for example, nonetheless gleefully told me about the mix tapes of state-approved Socialist-era rock bands he was making as Christmas gifts for his friends.
16. Another example of such incommensurability is the fact that while most Hungarians rejected any notion of returning to the Socialist era, a majority nonetheless selected Kádár as the most positive politician in twentieth-century Hungarian history (Medián 1999).
17. The mysterious object in the Other that triggers the subject's love (used by Lacan, sometimes interchangeably with *objet petit a*).
18. Elsewhere, Olga Shevchenko and I analyze how similar nostalgic practices in Russia and Hungary were mobilized to support very different political agendas (2004).
19. For the productivities of this opposition between East and West in Hungarian discourse, see Gal 1992. Boym also discusses the Eastern European nostalgia for a fantasy of Europe—a desire represented not in terms of "euros, but Eros"—but she focuses upon the ideals of democracy, humanistic liberalism, and highbrow cultural production that characterized this dream for the region's intellectuals (Boym 2001: 222).
20. As Herzfeld points out, "Cultural intimacy is not the public representation of domesticity ... but the often raucous and disorderly experience of life in the concealed spaces of public culture" (2004: 320).

References

Benjamin, Walter. 1968. "The Work of Art in the Age of Mechanical Reproduction." In *Illuminations*, trans. Harry Zohn, ed. Hannah Arendt. New York: Harcourt Brace Jovanovich.
Berdahl, Daphne. 1999. "'(N)Ostalgie' for the Present: Memory, Longing, and East German Things." *Ethnos* 64 (2): 192–212.
Boym, Svetlana. 1994. *Common Places: Mythologies of Everyday Life in Russia.* Cambridge: Harvard University Press.
———. 2001. *The Future of Nostalgia.* New York: Perseus Books.
Boynton, Robert. 1998. "Enjoy Your Žižek!: An Excitable Slovenian Philosopher Examines the Obscene Practices of Everyday Life—Including His Own." *Lingua Franca* October (7): 41–50.
Bren, Paulina. 2002. "Weekend Getaways: The *Chata*, the *Tramp* and the Politics of Private Life in Post-1968 Czechoslovakia." In *Socialist Spaces: Sites of Everyday Life in the Eastern Bloc,* ed. David Crowley and Susan E. Reid. Oxford: Berg.
Buck-Morss, Susan. 1989. *The Dialectics of Seeing: Walter Benjamin and the Arcades Project.* Cambridge, MA: MIT.
———. 2000. *Dreamworld and Catastrophe: The Passing of Mass Utopia in East and West.* Cambridge, MA: MIT.
Creed, Gerald W. 2002. "(Consumer) Paradise Lost: Capitalist Dynamics and Disenchantment in Rural Bulgaria." *Anthropology of East Europe Review* 20 (2). Electronic document, http://condor.depaul.edu/%7Errotenbe/aeer/v20n2/Creed.pdf, accessed 10 October 2008.
Crowley, David, and Susan E. Reid. 2002. "Sites of Everyday Life in the Eastern Bloc." In *Socialist Spaces: Sites of Everyday Life in the Eastern Bloc,* ed. David Crowley and Susan E. Reid. Oxford: Berg.
Fehérváry, Krisztina. 1998. "Innocence Lost: Cinematic Representations of 1960s Consumption for 1990s Hungary." Paper presented at the Annual Meeting of the American Anthropological Association, Philadelphia, November 1998.
———. 2002. "American Kitchens, Luxury Bathrooms, and the Search for a 'Normal' Life in Postsocialist Hungary." *Ethnos* 67 (3): 369–400.
Ferguson, James. 1994. *The Anti-Politics Machine: "Development," Depoliticization, and Bureaucratic Power in Lesotho.* Minneapolis: University of Minnesota Press.
Fritzsche, Peter. 2004. *Stranded in the Present: Modern Time and the Melancholy of History.* Cambridge, MA: Harvard University Press.
Gal, Susan. 1991. "Bartók's Funeral: Representations of Europe in Hungarian Political Rhetoric." *American Ethnologist* 18 (3): 440–58.
Gerő, András, ed. 2001. *A XX. század ujjlenyomata* [Fingerprint of the Twentieth Century]. Budapest: Városháza.
Gerő, András, and Iván Pető. 1999. *Unfinished Socialism: Pictures from the Kádár Era.* Budapest: Central European University Press.
Herzfeld, Michael. 2004. "Intimating Culture: Local Contexts and International Power." In *Off Stage/On Display: Intimacy and Ethnography in the Age of Public Culture,* ed. Andrew Shyrock. Stanford, CA: Stanford University Press.

Hutcheon, Linda. 1998. "Irony, Nostalgia, and the Postmodern." Electronic document, http://www.library.utoronto.ca/utel/criticism/hutchinp.html, accessed 1 February 2007.
Ivy, Marilyn. 1995. *Discourses of the Vanishing: Modernity, Phantasm, Japan.* Chicago: University of Chicago Press.
Jameson, Frederic. 1991. *Postmodernism, or, The Cultural Logic of Late Capitalism.* Durham, NC: Duke University Press.
Konrad, George. 1984. *Antipolitics: An Essay,* trans. Richard E. Allen. New York: Harcourt Brace Jovanovich.
Krauss, Rosalind E. 1985. "Notes on the Index, Part 1 and Notes on the Index, Part 2." In *The Originality of the Avant-Garde and Other Modernist Myths.* Cambridge, MA: MIT Press.
Lampland, Martha. 1995. *The Object of Labor: Commodification in Socialist Hungary.* Chicago: University of Chicago Press.
Medián Közvélemény és Piackutató. 1999. A 20. század értékelése [Evaluation of the Twentieth Century]. Electronic document, http://www.median.hu/object.75f7c814-dc6e-4309-b2d5-43c0a8ab2da0.ivy, accessed 20 March 2008.
Nadkarni, Maya. 2003. "The Death of Socialism and the Afterlife of its Monuments: Making and Marketing the Past in Budapest's Statue Park Museum." In *Contested Pasts (Memory and Narrative),* ed. Kate Hodgkin, Steve Sturdy, and Susannah Radstone. London: Routledge.
Nadkarni, Maya, and Olga Shevchenko. 2004. "The Politics of Nostalgia: A Case for Comparative Analysis of Post-Socialist Practices." *Ab Imperio* (2): 487–519.
Octogon. 2000. "Tárgyas Ragozás [Objective Conjugation]." Special issue, "Kis Utazás: A 70–80-as évek fesztiválja [Little Journey: The 70s and 80s Festival]." *Octogon Architecture and Design:* 3–10.
Pittaway, Mark. 2006. "A Home Front in the Cold War: Hungary, 1948–1989." *History in Focus* 10 (Spring). Electronic document, http://www.history.ac.uk/ihr/Focus/cold/articles/pittaway.html, accessed 1 February 2007.
Poós, Zoltán. 2002. *Szivárvány Áruház: Egy korszak kultikus tárgyai* [Rainbow Department Store: The Cultic Objects of an Era]. Budapest: Papirusz.
Salecl, Renata. 1999. "The State as a Work of Art: The Trauma of Ceausescu's Disneyland." In *Architecture and Revolution; Contemporary Perspectives on Central and Eastern Europe,* ed. Neil Leach. London: Routledge.
Santner, Eric. 1992. "History Beyond the Pleasure Principle: Thoughts on the Representation of Trauma." In *Probing the Limits of Representation: Nazism and the "Final Solution,"* ed. Saul Friedlander. Cambridge, MA: Harvard University Press.
Sontag, Susan. 1966. "Notes on Camp." In *Against Interpretation.* New York: Dell Publishing.
Stewart, Kathleen. 1988. "Nostalgia—A Polemic." *Cultural Anthropology* 3 (3): 227–41.
Stewart, Susan. 1993. *On Longing: Narratives of the Miniature, the Gigantic, the Souvenir, the Collection.* Durham, NC: Duke University Press.
Žižek, Slavoj. 1990. "Eastern Europe's Republics of Gilead. *New Left Review* 183 (September/October): 50–62.

12

Looking Back to the Bright Future
Aleksandr Melikhov's *Red Zion*
Harriet Murav

Svetlana Boym's distinction between ironic and restorative nostalgia serves as the point of departure for my analysis of two post-Soviet works by the Russian-Jewish author Aleksandr Melikhov. Ironic nostalgia, according to Boym, is "fragmentary and singular" and "accepts (if it does not enjoy) the paradoxes of exile and displacement." In contrast, restorative nostalgia, which is "reconstructive and collective ... stresses the return to that mythical place somewhere on the island of Utopia ... where the greater patria has to be rebuilt" (2001: 48–51). Melikhov's provocative novella *Izgnanie iz Edema: ispoved' evreia* (Exile from Eden: The Confession of a Jew) (1994) expresses an ironic and melancholic longing for the Soviet Union, the homeland that never accepted him as a Jew; in contrast, his work *Krasnyi sion* (Red Zion), published ten years later in 2004, while not free of ironic displacements, creates nonetheless a sense of national belonging that the earlier work rejects. In the first novel, Leningrad is the site of the narrator's longing for the Soviet Union; in the second, that fulfills his wish for national belonging by returning to the Soviet Jewish homeland, Birobidzhan.

One of the most important Soviet Jewish experiments, the Jewish Autonomous Region of Birobidzhan was established in 1934, having been designated in 1928 as a region of Jewish settlement. While political and military concerns in part motivated the Soviet decision to create a Jewish settlement in the Far East, near the Chinese border, as Zvi Gitelman writes, Birobidzhan offered the greatly impoverished Jews of the former Pale of Settlement "economic rehabilitation and social respectability through agricultural work; the preservation and promotion of language, culture—and implicitly—of the Jewish people itself—through compact settlement" (1998: 8).

The promotion of the Jewish people was, however, an enterprise fraught with ambivalence, since it was part of a larger policy aimed at the withering away of all forms of nationalism. The Birobidzhan project both competed with Zionism and shared in the emotive stew of Zionism's restorative nostalgia. As the Soviet Yiddish author Itsik Fefer remarked in his speech at the first congress of the Soviet Writer's Union in 1934, "at the same time that Hitler's Germany is showing its brutal face, when a dark wave of anti-Semitism has the capitalist countries in its grip, Soviet power has organized the autonomous Jewish region—Birobidzhan" (1934: 167). Fefer emphasized the age-old problem of the homeland for the Jews, and stressed that Soviet Jewish writers, like Jewish workers everywhere had one true native land, the Soviet Union. Palestine, Fefer asserted, was never the home of the Jewish masses, but only of Jewish exploiters, and, furthermore, Palestine was "now a colony of British imperialism" (1934: 167).

Birobidzhan never achieved the goal of turning Jews into agricultural workers, not only because of its harsh physical conditions, but also because of previous occupations, training, and preferences of the settlers, many of whom found work in the cities of Khabarovsk and Vladivostok. Major Yiddish authors, including Fefer, Itsi Kharik, Perets Markish, Dovid Bergelson, Der Nister, and others, wrote novels, plays, and poems about the Jewish Autonomous Region. They and other leading Jewish cultural figures were murdered in 1952, but the next generation of Yiddish writers, including Khaim Beider and Boris Miller, had important ties to Birobidzhan. Emmanuel Kazakevich, who won the Stalin prize for his 1948 war novella *Zvezda* (*The Star*), started his career as a Birobidzhan writer. Although the region was a significant site of Jewish settlement following World War II, the purges of the 1930s and the anti-Jewish campaign of the postwar years decimated the local leadership and severely undermined the Yiddish-language cultural institutions that had been introduced at the beginning of Birobidzhan's existence. The 1990s saw a revival of Yiddish and Jewish activity in Birobidzhan (Weinberg 1998).

The turn of the twenty-first century continues to evidence interest in Birobidzhan. The noted ethnographer Valerii Dymshits, in an essay accompanying the 2003 exhibit of photographs of Birobidzhan at the St. Petersburg Center for Judaica, writes that the Jewish Autonomous Region ought to be considered as part of the "mainstream" of Jewish history, as an experiment that "touched the fate of hundreds of thousands of people"—who "deserve a place in our memory" (Dymshits 2003).

Memory is crucially important not only to Dymshits, but also to Melikhov. His novel *Red Zion* both looks back to the past and attempts to intervene actively in the present, in the construction of Jewish memory today. It is Melikhov's contention, repeated in his fiction, essays, and interviews that memory, myth, dream, and illusion—"rendering the past poetic"—lie at the core of national identity (Rebel 2006). Not blood and soil, and not a commonly held economic system (as Stalin argued) make a nation (*narod, natsiia*), but their common stories. Using this definition, a more precise reading of the two novels emerges: the first novel's ironic nostalgia is the dominant trait of its chronicle of Jewish destruction and self-destruction, whereas the second novel marshals restorative nostalgia for its project of Jewish self reconstruction.

Melikhov, born in 1947, holds a PhD in math and physics. He is a journalist, serving on the editorial board of the St. Petersburg literary journal *Neva* (Neva), a critic, and fiction writer. *Exile from Eden,* which received the Nabokov prize from the St. Petersburg Union of Writers, is the fictitious autobiography of a Jewish writer with the resonant name of Katzenelenbogen. The hero, the son of a Jewish father and a Russian mother, spends his childhood years in the late Stalin period in Kazakhstan, the border area between Russia and Central Asia. The critic Andrei Nemzer disparagingly sums up the work's disparate contents as including: "the Jewish question, and also the problems of the nation, creativity, the individual and society, childrearing, democracy, the younger generations, the market, Soviet history (*sovka*), the floors, the ceiling, and the toilet" (Nemzer 1998).

The work opens with a challenge: "Tell me," the narrator asks, "is it possible to live with the name Katzenelenbogen?" (Melikhov 1994: 3). This name, uttered out loud in the "portals of the Soviet leviathan" has the same effect as the word *syphilis,* because Katzenelenbogen is synonymous with—and here the text gives only the first two letters of the Russian word—*Jew* ("ev" for *evrei*). The narrator comments, "It is easier even physically to spit at myself in the face" than to read this word. Of course, Melikhov has just forced us to do just that—read the word *Jew* (*evrei*) in the subtitle, "Confession of a Jew." Indeed, a review of Melikhov's work published in 2000 notes that the subtitle "Confession of a Jew" "still grated on the nerves" when the work was published in 1994. Readers of this text are implicated in the scandal caused by the very word *Jew,* contaminated in the disease, partners in the crime being confessed to.

Nemzer's review also points to a complicity between Melikhov's text and its post-Soviet audience, which ceased believing in political authority and in the authority of culture. The work and its audience are well suited to one another, because the "malicious," "melancholic," and "resentful" reading public requires precisely the "ironic, irresponsible, formless, tired, and anemic writing" that Melikhov offers them. Irony and melancholy circle around the question of nostalgia. Both the work and its audience suffer from the same the post-Soviet malaise of love, hate, and longing, now turned against the external world, now turned in on the self. This is a form of nostalgia laden with the ambivalence of melancholy, nostalgia that carries a wound.

In *Exile from Eden* the cause of the hero's melancholia is anti-Semitism, which he compares to a panoptical all-penetrating glare of an x-ray. The x-ray reveals the truth underneath the assimilated Jew's professed loyalty: the Jew's interiority is always suspect. The x-ray tells the truth that the Jew finally comes to accept: "Is it possible to live with the name Katzenelenbogen?" Under the pressure to assimilate and the gaze of the "x-ray," the hero destroys his own heritage. This memoir about remembering is also about the deliberate destruction of memory. The hero describes how his Jewish father would dive lower and lower into the river of forgetfulness until the blood ran from his ears in order to "wave before his offspring" a scrap of the *peyes* (sidelocks) of some "unknown" Ruvim. The son's all-consuming need to become "one of us" drives him to destroy the scraps of memory that the father rescues. Stung by his schoolmates' mockery of the stories he tells about his uncle Moishe and his uncle Ziamia, he describes himself drowning their memories and admits that an old, chipped chamber pot had more of a chance to rise to the surface of memory than the members of his father's family. The narrator describes the process as a struggle to the death: "If I permitted him to emerge on the surface only once, I would have to sink to the depths." In a domestic enactment of the official Soviet campaign of "dejudacization" the son kills off his father's memories, transforming him into "a person without childhood games and friends, without brothers and sisters, without first precious games and memories" (Melikhov 1994: 21). To put it another way, the son destroys the father's nostalgia.

The child's violence has consequences for the adult, whose grownup image of his ancestors' past is nothing more than an absurd and fragmented mosaic:

> And now I carefully grope with my hands in the underwater gloom, where I drowned everything that my father wanted to share with me, (now when he doesn't compromise me, I love him a thousand times more, perhaps when all the Jews disappear they can find forgiveness?), but I only stumble on the senseless broken pieces, which I don't know where to put—the *tsimmeses*, [cooked dish of carrots] *lekakhs* [honey-cakes], Purims. ... I try to assemble a panel a thousand kilometers wide, matching together tens of fragments the size of a handspan, but the pictures that result are all different. ... Now a dead world appears—a shtetl ... a half-darkened *heder*, where children are brought either from the age of five, or from the age of two, to be taught exclusively the rules of Talmud (a seven-year-old boy memorizes the judgments of seventy-three wise

men about the nuances of the divorce process), and a rebbe with a goat-like beard, whom I guess at only through the Paris dreams of Chagall beats the guilty ones on the palms of their hands. (Melikhov 1994: 21)

The picture becomes increasingly unclear as the narrator describes the rebbe's wife kneading dough, which, he says, she will have to bury in a sacred place, spitting to the left and the right if she omits even one of the "666 ritual intricacies"—mistaking the number of the Beast in the Apocalypse of John for the 613 *mitzvot*.

The passage above is important for what it reveals about Melikhov and late twentieth-century nostalgia. The context in which the rituals, images, and bits of knowledge would be meaningful is gone, and the unifying social codes and institutions that held them together, long destroyed. The only feature that the objects share in common is their fragmentariness. Classical nostalgia, in contrast, shows a different face. In the eighteenth-century medical literature that developed the model of nostalgia as a disease, involuntary, associative memory plays a crucial role. The victim is overcome by a single, overriding desire, triggered by a taste, or, especially, a sound that reminds him of home. For the victim, everything connects in the pain of homesickness and the memory of home (Starobinski 1966). Melikhov's hero lacks the integrity and wholeness present even in the pathological symptoms of the classical nostalgia patient. His memory is not involuntary, but the product of hard labor; not integral, but fragmented; and finally, it is not his own, but borrowed from others, including Chagall. His is a nostalgia that is the result of bricolage, which, as we know from Lévi-Strauss, is an assemblage of contingent, heterogeneous, and recycled materials "that come from other constructions and destructions" (Lévi-Strauss 1966: 19). It is not, of course, just the eighteenth-century patient that provides the countermodel to Melikhov's hero, but in addition, the late twentieth-century nostalgic, whether in Russia or the West, for whom the past, embodied in artifacts, speaks in unified, homogeneous messages about a simpler, better time.

In Melikhov's self-writing, the past is filtered through a triple lens of loss: the exclusion from the "unity" of the nation, membership in which required the destruction of the father's memory, and subsequently, the loss of Soviet Russia:

> My Homeland is not Russia, but the USSR, that is, Soviet Russia, the typical picture of my childhood, which makes my heart contract ... is not a weeping willow and not the curving bank along a pond, but a rusty motor in an oily steam, faded malachite green foliage, shifting heaps of crushed stone, the deafeningly loud dance space of the city park. (Melikhov 1994: 104)

The author goes on to say that when the "longing for his Homeland" (*toska po Rodine*) becomes completely unbearable, he makes his way to a garbage heap outside St. Petersburg. There he feels at home:

> Among broken pieces of brick, smashed concrete, old logs, rusted caterpillar tires, carburetors, among the twisted pipes, the worn out accordions of steam heating, ruined toilet tanks, flattened tin cans, canisters, jars from imported Vietnamese fish, varnish, insecticide, there along whole miles of garbage along the sea gates of Petersburg, once again I feel calm. That is, indifferent. That is, happy. (Melikhov 1994: 104)

The past is fragmentary, discarded, and outmoded; it is found in the trash heap, the incoherent list of objects that no longer have any use in the material culture of daily life but function only as signs of a civilization that is destroyed.

Boym mentions but does not elaborate on Roman Jakobson's "Two Aspects of Language and Two Types of Aphasic Disturbance" as the catalyst for her own model of the two types of nostalgia, restorative and ironic. In his essay Jakobson distinguishes between "contiguity disorder," in which speakers fail to make connections between verbal units, and "similarity disorder," in which speakers fail to substitute one word for another but only provide links between units. The lack of context and link in contiguity disorder leads to what Jakobson calls the "degeneration of the sentence into a mere word-heap" (1987: 106). The "word-heap" of contiguity disorder (the inability to tell a story) and the image of the garbage heap are linked. I will show later how similarity disorder (the inability to use words outside of stories) is linked to restorative nostalgia.

In the last days of the Soviet Union, Russian writers declared that the myths in which Soviet civilization had been grounded had come to an end. Natal'ia Ivanova, a prominent literary critic and journalist, wrote that the utopian myth of building a "bright future" was over (1990). Whether she would take the same position today is an open question. The collapse of the grand narrative of Soviet culture meant that everyone began to suffer from contiguity disorder, so to speak, because the story they had been hearing for seventy years no longer made sense. Its artistic realization is the "word-heap" found in the final passage of Melikhov's *Exile from Eden: The Confession of a Jew*. Lev Katzenelenbogen, who has no grand narrative to hang on to, but enjoys his symptoms, lists one article of garbage after another in a seemingly endless list.

The contrast between *Ispoved' evreia* and *Krasnyi sion*, published ten years later in 2004, is striking. The dominant motif of the work is return: the implied author, Melikhov, returns to Jewishness. Language, having degenerated to the word-heap, returns to contexture, to story, to myth and fairy tale; indeed, the term "fairy tale," *skazka*, is a significant repeating element of the text. On the front cover of *Red Zion*, the author's original and more Jewish surname "Meilakhs" replaces the Russified pseudonym "Melikhov." In a personal communication, the author states that this replacement was made without his knowledge, and further explains that he took on the Russified surname to begin with because an editor told him he had little chance of getting his work published otherwise.[1] Commercial considerations clearly play a role in the assumption and removal of Jewish identity. In *Confession* the term *Jew* is a source of shame, denoting "the social role of an outsider" and "a nation that practically does not exist." In *Red Zion*, in contrast, *Jew* means something more than a term of abuse, and this positive meaning has emotional resonance for the hero and the implied author. *Red Zion* overcomes the pain of nostalgia by textually and fictively creating a return to the past, and it indulges the fictive and textual pleasure of national belonging. The hero returns to Birobidzhan, the Soviet and Jewish national homeland. The return is not complete, but the emphasis, nonetheless, is on the value of restoration, the importance of myth, and the meaning of memory.

The hero of *Red Zion*, Bentsion Shamir, is a generation older than Lev Katzenelenbogen. He is a well-established Israeli writer, and *Red Zion* is both his autobiography and the story of how he wrote it. As a young boy living in a town on the border of Poland and Russia in the 1930s, he had an ideally happy childhood with his brother and sisters, mother, and father, a doctor: "Everything that surrounded him was not simply unique in its own way, but was the only possible way it could be" (*ne prosto edinstvennym v svoem rode, no dazhe edinstvenno vozmozhnym*) (Meilakhs 2005: 25). The symptom of substitutability disorder is the dominant artistic device of the work as a whole. The experience of a happy childhood is the belief that there could be no other childhood. Contrast what Melikhov had said ten years earlier in *Confession of a Jew*: "Reminiscences of one's barefoot childhood are one of the most intolerable genres of Soviet official nationality" (Melikhov 1994: 15). In *Red Zion*, however, the idyllic childhood does not last long. The Germans invade Poland, and Bentsion and his family flee east to the country of the Soviets. One sister is shot by the Germans, one dies from conditions on the transport train; the Soviet-imposed forced labor leads to the father's suicide; the brother is arrested for thieving; and Bentsion survives because his mother hits on the idea of abandoning him in an orphanage soon after their arrival in Central Asia.

As a boy, Bentsion befriends a hunchbacked Jewish shoemaker, Berl, an ardent Stalinist, whose only desire is to go to Birobidzhan. Berl, who cannot quite pronounce the word "Birobidzhan" recites from Kalinin's speeches by rote and declares "in ten years Bori ... Beri ... Birobidzhan will be the most important, if not the only custodian of Jewish socialist national culture" (*let cherez desiat' 'Bori ... Beri ... Birobidzhan budet vazhneishim, esli ne edinstvennym khranitelem evreiskoi sotsialisticheskoi national'noi kul'tury*) (Meilakhs 2005: 11). Berl's use of language, both here and in other instances (he calls himself "*rabotnik tyla*" (a rearguard worker) and describes camels as "*vazhnoe transportnoe sredstvo*" (an important means of transport) typifies Jakobson's substitution disorder. To use Jakobson's terms, but in a different sense, words only function in "pre-fixed, bound blocks"—and what they are bound to is the Soviet ideology of the idealized workers' state, the bright socialist and, in the case of Birobidzhan, the bright national tomorrow for Soviet Jews. These words cannot be substituted for or removed from their Soviet ideological context, the *skazka* or fairy tale of socialism, or else they lose their meaning. Substitution disorder captures the restorative variant of post-Soviet nostalgia.

In the text of Meilakh's novel, Birobidzhan exercises its allure not as a beacon from the future, but as a remnant of the past, whose reality is never realized except as a museum to what has been destroyed: "Jews in Birobidzhan played the same role as Indians in America: the exoticism of those who have perished" (Meilakhs 2005: 146).

The destruction of Birobidzhan as a living community—and the destruction brought by WWII—makes the hero's nostalgic return to Birobidzhan possible. After the war, Bentsion makes his way to Israel, where, the narrator says, he "composes if not a heroic, then a completely respectable biography for himself": he serves as a young officer in the Israeli war of independence, earns his PhD, marries, becomes a well-respected author of fiction, and finally a cultural representative to post-Soviet Russia. Along the way to his success, however, he loses his sense of purpose; there is no one around him with whom he could share his "myth." Only in Moscow, after suffering a heart attack, does he experience a turning point. Berl had bequeathed to him a silver cigarette case containing his portrait, and Bentsion decides to take Berl's gift to Birobidzhan. The decision transforms his routinized life into a meaningful "drama," and everyone around him becomes, knowingly or not, a participant in the "mass spectacle" (*massovka*).

In Biroidzhan Bentsion accomplishes his goal. He discovers a tiny museum to a fictitious Soviet Yiddish writer, Meilekh Terletskii, whose first name, of course, calls to mind the author's own original name of Meilakhs. The last name "Terletskii" is in homage to Aleksandr Melikhov's real-life father, who came from the shtetl of Terlits. The famous Yiddish author in the novella is a fictionalized version of the real-life Yiddish author Boris Izrailovich (Buzi) Miller (1913–1988) who lived in Birobidzhan and served as the main editor of the *Birobidzhaner shtern* (Birobidzhan Star). Convicted on the charge of nationalism in 1949, during the outbreak of the anti-Jewish campaign of the postwar years, he spent seven years in the gulag. In the novel, the so-called museum to the Yiddish writer is located in his apartment, lovingly maintained by his widow. Her poverty and her thickly accented speech ("*Zdkhkhavstvyite, chto vam intekhkh'esuet*"; she cannot pronounce "r") touch the hero to the quick, taking him back to his childhood in Poland. The writer's widow gives the hero her late husband's stories to read, and the last twenty-five pages of Meilakh's novella are given over to lengthy excerpts from Buzi Miller's Birobidzhan stories, translated from Yiddish into Russian (Russian-language translations appeared, for example, in 1974). These are stories about the last holdout in a shtetl, who hides gold from the communists, and dies a disgraceful death ("Zoloto"); about a heroic son who goes off to be a builder in Birobidzhan and then a frontline soldier in World War II ("Synov'ia"). Miller's works typify the socialist realism of the time.

The scene of reading accomplishes several things at once. Birobidzhan is an object of representation in the work, but of a very particular kind. Meilakhs gives us descriptions of Birobidzhan as it is today, for example, a restaurant that provides its customers with Soviet kitsch — another form of nostalgia. The scene of reading, however, suspends the forward motion of time in the novel at the same time that it allows the past and the present to merge. The lengthy excerpts from Buzi Miller's stories render Birobidzhan a "pre-fixed bound block of language," the kind of language symptomatic of substitution disorder. We cannot read a summary of Buzi Miller's works; we have to read his words in the order in which he wrote them to get the full effect. The words cannot be substituted for; they can only appear as a bound block of language. This model of the "bound block of language" is not limited to Jakobson. Meilakhs explicitly describes the Yiddish's writers style as "consisting of ready-made blocks" (*sostoiashchii iz gotovykh blokov*, 222). The artistic representation of substitution disorder corresponds to the emotion of nostalgia.

The insertion of bound blocks of language does not necessarily mean that all meaningful engagement with the quoted text is impossible. The quoted text is not simply an inert monolith. The use of the bound blocks of language requires a more nuanced reading, especially in light of Melikhov's own statements about the role of myth and poetry in the construction of national identity. Alexei Yurchak's work suggests the ways that the also create a more dynamic and dialogic possibility. In his study of late Soviet culture, *Everything Was Forever, Until It Was No More: The Last Soviet Generation,* Yurchak convincingly argues that the formation of prefabricated, bound blocks of official discourse was both a stabilizing and a destabilizing force in Soviet culture. Their meaning (constative dimension) became less important as their performative function increased, leading to the possibility of new meanings. The same text could have multiple meanings, depending on the contexts in which it was introduced and the uses to which it was put (Yurchak 2006: 53). In the novel *Red Zion,* the quoted texts perform the function of creating a renewed sense of Jewish belonging today. There is no content or foundation for this belonging: it does not depend on a return to either the Zion of the Middle East (to which there is markedly little emotional connection in the novel) or to the Red Zion of the Far East; it does not require the observance of ritual or the possession of special knowledge; it needs only the circulation of narrative, of myths.

If in *Confession of a Jew* readers were made complicit in the shame of Jewishness, here they are made complicit in the sentiment of nostalgia. At first Bentsion finds the famous Yiddish writer's prose unbearable in its ordinariness and its colorlessness, but he gradually finds it more and more appealing: "The more schematic, colorless and sickly-sweet the story, the more cozily Bentsi fit into it. He took pleasure in its ordinariness, as if he were in a warm bath." (Meilakhs 2005: 223)

Bentsion decides finally to imitate the Yiddish writer—to write something simple and noble, just as he did, and to call it *Red Zion.* The hero "would be reembodied as Meilekh Terletskii" and he "would create a piercingly sad and noble tale (*skazka*) of an unrealized Jewish homeland, similar to a *matreshka,* placed inside another, mighty and universal fatherland" (Meilakhs 2005: 225). Whereas the hero of the 1994 *Confession* by Aleksandr Melikhov "gropes in the underwater gloom" only to emerge with an incoherent bricolage of recycled Jewish memory, the hero of the 2004 *Red Zion* by Aleksandr Meilakhs slips comfortably into a warm bath of Birobidzhan prose. The imagined pleasure of nostalgic return resonates with childhood, with motherhood (the *matreshka*), and with the Soviet fairy tale of the bright Socialist and Jewish national belonging. There is much that is tongue-in-cheek in *Red Zion,* but the homage to the past, to a past that was Soviet and Jewish, is unmistakable.

The shift from Melikhov to Meilakhs and from Lev Katsenelenbogen to Bentsion Shamir may be more properly described as both post-Jewish and post-Communist nostalgia. "Post-Jewish" signals here the knowledge that there is no return to a 1930s childhood, to Red Zion, or to the Zion of Israel, for which the implied author has little emotional connection. The only return for the implied author and his readers is the imagined return made possible by the act of reading. The distance between us and that world is underscored as we read the character reading the embedded text. The world of the 1930s was one in which Soviet Jews could and did believe in Red Zion. The term *post-Communist* is important, however, in another respect. The works of such Yiddish writers as Dovid Bergelson, Itsik Fefer, and Buzi Miller were available in the Soviet Union both in Yiddish and in Russian translations that began appearing in the 1970s. The act of reading them, however, is, if not new, then at least newly revived, and has new value in the post-Communist world.

Notes

1. Interview conducted 7 September 2006, in St. Petersburg. The twists and turns of Judeophobia and Judeophilia in the Russian publishing world are a separate story.

References

Boym, Svetlana. 2001. *The Future of Nostalgia.* New York: Basic Books.
Dymshits, Valerii. 2003. "Krasnyi sion: Proekt evreiskoi avtonomii v Krymu i na Dal'nem Vostoke." Retrieved 21 September 2006, from http://judaica.spb.ru/exbsh/ex10/ozet_r.shtml.
Fefer, Itsik. 1934. *Pervyi vsesoiuznyi s'ezd sovetskikh pisatelei stenograficheskii otchet.* Moscow: Sovetskii pisatel'.
Gitelman, Zvi. 1998. "Introduction." *Stalin's Forgotten Zion: Birobidzhan and the Making of a Soviet Jewish Homeland.* Berkeley: University of California Press, 1–11.
Ivanova, Natal'ia. 1990. "Farewell to Utopia, Or, a Subject for an Unwritten Novel." *Literaturnaia gazeta* 4.
Jakobson, Roman. 1987. *Language in Literature.* Cambridge, MA: Harvard University Press.
Lévi-Strauss, Claude. 1962. *The Savage Mind.* Chicago: University of Chicago Press.
Meilakhs, Aleksandr. 2005. *Krasnyi sion.* St. Petersburg: Limbus Press.
Melikhov, Aleksandr. 1994. "Izgnanie iz Edema: Ispoved' evreia." *Novyi mir* 1: 3–104.
Nemzer, Andrei. 1998. *Literaturnoe segodnia.* Moscow: Novoe literaturnoe obozrenie.
Rebel, G. 2006. "Birobidzhanskaia skazka." *Novoe vremia* 32 (13 August).

Starobinski, J. 1966. "On the Idea of Nostalgia." *Diagones* 54: 81–103.
Weinberg, R. 1998. *Stalin's Forgotten Zion: Birobidzhan and the Making of a Soviet Jewish Homeland.* Berkeley: University of California Press.
Yurchak, Alexei. 2006. *Everything Was Forever, Until It Was No More: The Last Soviet Generation.* Princeton, NJ: Princeton University Press.

Dwelling on the Ruins of Socialist Yugoslavia
Being Bosnian by Remembering Tito
Fedja Burić

Bosnia-Herzegovina as a Metonymy for Socialist Yugoslavia

In the decades following the bloody collapse of Socialist Yugoslavia, many former Yugoslavs continue to resurrect images of the Socialist Federative Republic of Yugoslavia (SFRJ) in lamenting the loss of their country. Refusing to join the nationalist euphoria of the post-Yugoslav age, they choose to dwell on the ruins of their old identity, congregating around the memory of Tito, carefully policing and protecting it from the continuous assaults launched by the post-Yugoslav nation-states that see their Yugoslav past as an aberration, a dark age comparable only to the Ottoman occupation. This collective pilgrimage to the memory of Tito has been evident in numerous commemorative acts that seem to be motivated by nostalgia: the continued visits to his birthplace in Kumrovec and his grave in Belgrade; the appearance of Tito's homepage on the Internet,[1] which has generated thousands of emails addressed to the deceased Marshal; the writings of several Yugoslav exiles, including the recently compiled encyclopedia of life in Socialist Yugoslavia titled *Lexicon of Yu-Mythology* (Adrić et al. 2004).

Although the so-called Yugo-nostalgia is evident in almost every corner of the former Yugoslavia, the echoes of the Socialist past are perhaps loudest in Bosnia-Herzegovina. As a republic that was often described as a metonymy for Yugoslavia, Bosnia-Herzegovina was also the terrain where the destruction of Yugoslavia proved to be most brutal. In the era of nation-states, the multiethnic Bosnia seems stranded in the perpetual transition between its Yugoslav past and the frequently promised (but always delayed) European future. Its identity and territorial sovereignty inextricably tied to the Yugoslav project, Bosnia-Herzegovina often clings onto the memory of this project in defining its current identity. Tone Bringa points out that even as Yugoslavia was being dismembered and nationalist leaders of Serbia tried to symbolically bury the Tito legacy by moving his body from Serbia to Croatia, Bosnian politicians offered the Bosnian city of Tuzla as the final resting place for the late president. During the increasing nationalist euphoria of the late 1980s when Tito became a taboo word, Bosnians extended the memorial at Sutjeska where Tito had been saved from a German bomb by his dog during World War II (Bringa 2004). Following the brutal war—which transformed the multiethnic Bosnia-Herzegovina into a barely functioning entity of three mini-nation-states—Tito nostalgia inhabits the streets of Bosnia and the minds of many Bosnians: the graffiti "Tito Come Back, We Have Forgiven You Everything" that decorate the walls of many Bosnian cities; the opening of Café Tito in Sarajevo where waiters wear t-shirts with his signature; the hundreds of emails sent to the Tito Homepage on the Internet by thousands of Bosnians throughout the world; and the weekly transmissions of old Partisan movies on the central Bosnian television station all reveal the continuing relevance of the Socialist past in Bosnia's post-Socialist present.

The continuing echoes of the Yugoslav past in Bosnia's present stem from the special place Bosnia occupied in the forty-six-year-long effort to create a viable, multiethnic and Socialist Yugoslavia. The prominence of the Bosnian Muslims in the imagining of Socialist Yugoslavia has been well documented. As a result of regime's modernization policies and a fairly liberal nationality policy, Socialist Yugoslavia witnessed an emergence of an increasingly powerful Bosnian Muslim elite. According to Robert Donia and John V. A. Fine, the regime perceived the Bosnian Muslims as a core around which a Yugoslav identity might emerge (1994: 178). The prominence of this political elite became especially evident in 1971 when a powerful Muslim from Mostar, Džemal Bijedić, became the president of the Federal Executive Council of Yugoslavia (*Savezno Izvršno Vijeće*), a position second only to Tito's. Ivo Banac argues that the ascendance of Bijedić, a proponent of Bosnian Muslim nationhood, into the highest echelons of power was due to Tito's increasing reliance on the Bosnian Muslims in navigating between Croatian and Serbian demands for greater control (Banac 1993). Tone Bringa claims that the high number of mixed marriages in Bosnia-Herzegovina, especially in major cities, as well as a high number of Bosnians declaring Yugoslav as their official nationality reflected Bosnia's role as the kernel of Yugoslav identity (Bringa 2004: 173). Although some demographers have convincingly shown that the number of mixed marriages in the federation has been exaggerated (Botev 1994), the number of those declaring themselves Yugoslav reached 12 percent in Mostar, 16 percent in Sarajevo, and 21 percent in Tuzla in the last census in 1991 (*Etnička Karta Bosne i Hercegovine* 1991).² Finally, even the flag of the Socialist Republic of Bosnia-Herzegovina, a plain red background with a small Yugoslav flag in the upper left corner (Figure 13.1), marked the republic as a metonymy for Yugoslavia.

Figure 13.1 The flag of the Socialist Republic of Bosnia-Herzegovina.
Source: http://en.wikipedia.org/wiki/File:Flag_of_SR_Bosnia_and_Herzegovina.svg

The Setting

Bosnia-Herzegovina's centrality in both the construction and the dismemberment of Yugoslavia makes the memories of today's Bosnians a particularly rich source in studying the ways in which remembering serves as an occasion to dust off and reassemble an identity that has supposedly been relegated to the garbage heap of history. With this in mind, this chapter examines the Yugo-nostalgia of a group of Bosnian Muslim men who have been uprooted by the breakup of Yugoslavia and currently reside in Chicago, Illinois. It is based on my visit to their weekly workshop at a cultural center in Chicago where they gather to share their impressions of the life in the United States, talk politics (American and Bosnian), occasionally discuss readings, or simply tell jokes in their daily struggle against boredom. At the meeting I attended, all of the men were seniors, in their sixties or early seventies, except for one who was in his late fifties.

The meetings are always presided over by Muharem, who serves as the official moderator of the discussion and often introduces their weekly topics. His long career as a prominent journalist seems to have placed him in the role of the group's leader to whom the others look to for guidance in explaining certain historical concepts or arbitrating a contentious debate. The meeting reminded me of an upper-division college seminar where there is often a lively discussion in which everyone participates, but where there is a clear deference to the professor.

On the day I visited, Muharem asked the men to give their "honest and unbiased opinions of Tito," emphasizing that all opinions would be given the floor as long as everyone was respectful of each other. At the mention of Tito as the topic of that day's discussion, most of the men immediately raised their hands, asking for their turn to speak. Instead of lasting one hour, as it normally does, the meeting lasted for three hours. Several days later, Muharem emailed me to let me know that "that was one of the most productive meetings we have ever had."

It is clear that any conclusion drawn from a fieldwork based on a single visit can be nothing but tentative. Many of the themes outlined in this chapter correlate to many conversations I have had with displaced Bosnians not only in Chicago, but also in Louisville and St. Louis in the months following the post-Socialist nostalgia conference for which this chapter was originally written. While these additional explorations into the memories of Bosnians living in America have confirmed the central theme of this chapter—the inextricability of contemporary Bosnian Muslim identity from the memories of Socialist Yugoslavia—integrating these more recent findings into a more coherent analysis would take up much more space and will hopefully result in a new project of in the near future. During my dissertation research trip to Bosnia-Herzegovina in 2007–2008, on the topic of mixed marriage that is not necessarily related to the topic at hand, I discovered that the Yugo-nostalgia of Bosnians living in Bosnia has a distinct flavor from the one articulated by their fellow countrymen and women in diaspora. In other words, while many Bosnians in Bosnia still nostalgically remember socialism and continue to hold Tito in high regard, their memories are often filtered through the prism of intense ethnic segregation that continues to characterize postwar Bosnia. On the other hand, the Yugo-nostalgia of my informants in this chapter aims at creating an identity that does not necessarily fit into the rigid Dayton-mandated ethnic lexicon of Bosnia. Thus, there are many aspects of Bosnians' Yugo-nostalgia that should be further investigated, and this chapter hopes to illustrate some elements of this nostalgia rather than offer definitive answers.

I would like to express my deepest gratitude to my informants, who were so generous as to let me impose on their treasured weekly meeting and so gracious to let me rummage through their memories in coming up with my own arguments. Any misinterpretations, gaffes, or potential controversies are entirely of my own making. Finally, in protecting their anonymity, I use first-name pseudonyms for all of my informants.

The Fissures of Bosnian (Muslim) Identity

In this chapter I argue that remembering Socialist Yugoslavia offers my informants an opportunity to articulate different Bosnian identities, and it is precisely the arguments over the central symbols of these identities that become constitutive parts of the contemporary Bosnian (Muslim) national identity. The men at the workshop resurrect two distinct conceptions of Bosnian identity, both of which are echoes of specific historical periods in Bosnia's history. Men of different generations seem to adhere to mutually exclusive ideas of what it means to be Bosnian, revealing the generational fissures that have characterized the evolution of Bosnian (Muslim) identity. However, the image of Tito as the father of the nation (whatever the exact meaning of this "nation" might be) straddles the generational divide by making it easier for the men to relate to each other. The lone woman in the workshop ruptures the gender-based consensus by passionately challenging the masculine image of Tito, which the men had narrated into existence. Furthermore, her social background challenges the men's secular understanding of Bosnianness, adding yet another fissure to Bosnian identity. But it is precisely the collapse of consensus along generational, gender, and social lines that congregates these individuals into a conversation about what it means to be Bosnian.

Seeing the fissures of identity—whether they be generational, gender-based, or social—as constitutive parts of a national ideology echoes the insightful work of anthropologist Tim Pilbrow, who is also a contributor to this volume. In his research on Bulgaria's national identity, as articulated in the country's education system and public discourse, Pilbrow argues that there is a never-resolved tension between Bulgaria's insistence on the country's organic connection to Europe and its ironic acknowledgment of being excluded from the very same Europe. Pilbrow sees the lack of consensus regarding this central element of Bulgarian national ideology not as a sign of lack of such ideology but rather as its constitutive element. What is particularly attractive about Pilbrow's argument is his call for "a reconceptualization of national identity away from a consensus model toward a model in which identity can be seen to coalesce around ambivalence and conflict regarding central symbols" (Pilbrow 2005: 123). Similarly, my informants expose a deep ambivalence over two central symbols of Bosnian identity today: the relationship between Islam and Bosnianness, and the role of Tito in the development of such identity. Rather than seeing these disagreements as somehow indicative of a lack of Bosnian (Muslim) identity, I see my informants' nostalgic sighs, shouts, anecdotes, and debates as ways in which they reveal that very identity.

Halid: "I wanted to be a Bosanac"[3]

At the meeting, I was particularly struck by a man who, through his memories of socialism, articulates a coherent ideology of Bosnian identity. In remembering Tito, Halid—a man in his early seventies from the small Bosnian town of Čajniče—references three separate strands of thought on the nature of Bosnianness: the interwar-era debates on the relationship between Islam and Bosnianness, the multireligious conception of Bosnianness, and finally, the criticism of the nationally divided post-Yugoslav Bosnia-Herzegovina. Despite the multiplicity of voices echoing from his stories, Halid unequivocally commits to multireligious Bosnianness, which was popular during the early years of Tito's regime, specifically in the early 1950s when Halid came of age. The generational specificity of Halid's understanding of Bosnian identity was also evident in the stories of other informants who belonged to different generations. The lack of generational consensus regarding Bosnianness has accompanied all historical attempts to define this as an unambiguous national category. In teasing out the different strands of thought that permeate Halid's understanding of Bosnianness I quote his monologue at length:

> My name is Halid from Čajniče. In Čajniče I was an *omladinac*, a *SKOJEVAC*. [The terms *omladinac* and *SKOJEVAC* refer to the membership in the Communist Youth Organization]. That was forty-eight or -nine, I am not sure, maybe even fifty. ... I loved Tito so much that I think I would have done anything for him.
>
> However, later I had some troubles regarding the question of nationality. In the military, I had to write down my nationality and I had the option of putting down undecided but I didn't want to, I wanted to be *Bosanac* [his emphasis]. They said, you can't be *Bosanac*, you can be either Serb or Croat, and I didn't want to be undecided. Out of spite, I said I would be a Montenegrin. The commander of my *četa* was a Croat, and the commander of my brigade was a Serb: they both laughed at me and I was reported. ... When I came out of the army it said in the book that I was a Serb and I crossed that and I wrote that I was a Montenegrin. I told them to look at my original form on which I had written that I was a Montenegrin. ... However, afterwards I kept thinking: what are we, what are we? ...
>
> And I had another problem when it came that you can write down that you were a Muslim. Again, I didn't want to be a Muslim, because I considered that to be a religion and not a nation. Because for a nation, you have to have a territory and a language, and a Muslim didn't have anything at that time, did he? So, again, I got into trouble when they wanted to elect me as the president of the Worker's Council and I think this was 1969, 1970, or 1971 and they chose me as a Muslim. I rebelled again and told them to look at my ID card where it said that I wasn't a Muslim, but a Montenegrin. Then they took me off the ballot and they chose someone else, because they needed a Muslim for the ethnic balance on the council.

Halid's portrayal of his former self as a rebellious man who had always struggled against a system, which in its arbitrariness refused to recognize his true Bosnian identity, references the interwar discourse on the Bosnian Muslim identity. As the historiography dealing with national identity in the Balkans has often pointed out, the Bosnian Muslims were one of the last groups in the region to organize themselves along the national lines. Robert Donia has argued that the movement for Bosnian Muslim cultural specificity gained momentum only after the Austro-Hungarian annexation of Bosnia-Herzegovina in 1878 (Donia 1981). But, the Muslim elites continuously emphasized their religious and nonnational character and expressed loyalty to the occupation regime. The religious nature of the movement left open the possibility of the Muslims being co-opted by either the Croatian or Serbian national ideology. The campaign to nationalize the Muslims of Bosnia-Herzegovina became especially intense in the interwar period when many Muslim intellectuals did declare themselves as either Croat or Serb. Nevertheless, Ivo Banac has argued that at least one-third of the intelligentsia and "the overwhelming majority of ordinary Muslim masses shunned any process of 'nationalization,'" knowing that this would have divided the population and might have even jeopardized the territorial integrity of the province (Banac 1984: 366). Squeezed between the two increasingly aggressive and assimilationist nationalist ideologies, some Bosnian Muslims of the interwar period reacted in the manner similar to Halid. To quote Banac: "Caught in the agonizing web of demands to nationalize themselves, the Muslims rebelled in still more absurd ways. Some declared themselves neither Serbs nor Croats, but Slovenes" (1984: 374). Thus, Halid's memory of declaring himself a Montenegrin is a thread in the larger quilt of the historical polemic on the nature of the Bosnian Muslim identity. His memory of the disparaging attitudes of the Croat and Serb officers to his newly adopted Montenegrin identity and his memory of crossing out "Serb" in his identity card rearticulate the portrayal of the Bosnian Muslim identity as being under siege from the two aggressive nationalisms.

However, unlike the religiously based identity of many Bosnian Muslims during the interwar period, Halid's understanding of Bosnianness is secular: he becomes visibly emotional in talking about his refusal to declare himself a Muslim in the first census when this became possible in the early 1970s. His commitment to multireligious Bosnianness is rooted in the early 1950s emphasis of Tito's regime on an overarching Yugoslav identity that would eventually supersede ethnic allegiances and remove the main reason for future conflicts. Dejan Jović has argued that in the early 1950s, Tito supported the statist solution of the national question, which argued that a strong Socialist state would eventually cause the withering away of national animosities (Jović 2003).

This meant deemphasizing differences between individual nations, and for Bosnia—which the postwar constitution defined as a republic of three constituent nations—this translated into a promotion of an overarching Bosnian identity. However, as Jović and other scholars of Yugoslavia have argued, by the 1960s, the regime abandoned these attempts and emphasized the inviolability and uniqueness of each nation within Yugoslavia. John V. A. Fine has argued that, constrained by the unpopularity of Yugoslavism due to its associations with the interwar Yugoslavia and the entrenchment of ethnic identities, "Tito avoided working toward a Yugoslav super-ethnicity and supported existing nationalities, promising each in areas of its concentration its own ethnic republic."(Fine 2007: 277) For Bosnia-Herzegovina, this resulted in the recognition of the Bosnian Muslims as a distinct nationality, a recognition formalized by the 1974 Constitution (Bougarel 2003). Halid explicitly rejects this conception of Bosnia by remembering his refusal to declare himself Muslim in the early 1970s despite losing his seat on a workers' council. His exasperation with the Socialist nationality policy is in not having an adequate category under which he could comfortably identify himself as a *Bosanac*.

Halid's commitment to multireligious *Bosanstvo* is also a rejection of Bosnia as imagined by the Dayton Peace Accords, which, while ending the war, turned the country into a dysfunctional, ethnically segregated state in which religion-based ethnicity dominates every aspect of life. He resists the logic of what Robert Hayden has called constitutional nationalism, which defined every republic as a homeland of the majority nation, relegating other groups to minority status. This was the logical culmination of the Socialist regime's approach to nationalities adopted in the 1960s and enshrined in the 1974 constitution. When applied to the ethnically mixed Bosnia-Herzegovina, in which no nation can claim the titular status, this logic inevitably led to war. The advocates of constitutional nationalism pointed to Bosnia's Socialist constitution, which had defined the republic as a state of three constituent nations, in arguing for the division of the republic into three nation-states. Thus, frequent denials of the existence of a multireligious Bosnian nationhood eventually undermined Bosnian state's raison d'être and engulfed the country into a series of localized civil wars that eventually destroyed the multiethnic fabric of the society and erected three homogenous nation-states (Hayden 1999).

Seeing Bosnia-Herzegovina as a region with many different religions, but one nation, Halid refuses to recognize the existence of any other nation but the Bosnian within its borders. He denies the Serbianness of a Serbian neighbor who moved into his apartment after having pillaged it, destroying Halid's beloved library: "A former *SKOJEVAC,* who had been very progressive before the war, moved into my apartment. He was a Christian Orthodox. I don't call them Serbs, but Christian Orthodox [*pravoslavci*] … but during the war, he became a notorious *četnik.*" Thus, while his concept of multireligious Bosnianness is tolerant in that it allows for the coexistence of numerous religions within the borders of Bosnia-Herzegovina, it also denies the self-determination to those who might not see themselves as Bosnian. Halid's assertion of the multireligious Bosnianness that has been delegitimized by the Dayton Constitution—which defined Bosnia-Herzegovina as an entity of three constituent nations: Bošnjaks (Bosnian Muslims), Serbs, and Croats— might also be read as his attempt to gain some control over his self-definition, something that had been denied to him during the war.

Alija: A Bosnian Muslim Nation

While Halid's remembrances articulate a multireligious concept of Bosnianness, the remembrances of the university-educated Alija, who was the youngest informant in the group (in his late fifties), delineated a more exclusively Muslim Bosnianness. Remembering the late 1960s when the regime recognized the Bosnian Muslims as a distinct nationality, Alija notes that this was an act of Tito's generosity: "A nation cannot be given as a gift, but it has to be earned through struggle. Because when someone gets something as a gift, he doesn't know how to appreciate it. The Muslims got their nation as a gift because they had never been united and they had never fought for their nation. … During the First World War and the Second World War, the Muslims dispersed to all sides: some went to the *ustaše,* some to the Partisans, some even to the *četniks*. But look at the Albanians in Kosovo. They are 100 percent united in their opinion on their nation and their state." Alija's statement powerfully captures the self-consciousness of many Bosnian Muslims regarding the genealogy of their current national identity. Highlighting the historical lack of consensus among the Muslims of Bosnia on their religious and national identity, he shows a highly developed awareness of the ambiguity that has accompanied the development of this national category. But rather than questioning the very notion of a Bosnian Muslim nation, which would have echoed Halid's multireligious Bosnianness, Alija invokes the memory of Tito in asserting the existence of the Bosnian Muslim nation: "The Muslims got their nation in 1968 because Tito and his colleagues passed the judgment that the Muslims are a distinctive nation that is different from the others, that has its own tradition." Thus, Tito becomes the ultimate arbitrator of the deeply contentious debate regarding the national status of the Bosnian Muslims.

In teasing out the roots of Alija's Bosnianness, it is important to briefly outline the political conditions under which he was educated. The late 1960s and early 1970s represented the culmination of liberalizing reforms accompanied by lively political discussions on national identity and the future course of the country. The liberalizing reforms of 1966, coupled with the removal of the main centralizer and Tito's interior minister, Aleksandar Ranković, empowered those within the ranks of the Yugoslav League of Communists who were pushing for greater decentralization as republican leaderships became increasingly powerful at the expense of the federation (Rusinow 1977). The Croatian Spring movement, which culminated in 1971, openly called for greater autonomy for Croatia and the recognition of Croatian as a separate language (Ramet 1984). While Tito eventually sacked the leadership of the Croatian League of Communists, the mood among the intellectuals was increasingly nationalist as the idea of Yugoslav identity was branded as chauvinistic and reactionary. Writing in 1968, one of the leading Bosnian Muslim Communist intellectuals, Salim Ćerić, called for the recognition of Bosnian Muslim specificity and warned against supporting the "illusion" of a Yugoslav identity, which he saw as harmful to the Bosnian Muslims (Ćerić 1968: 24). The increasing prominence of the Bosnian Muslims within the Yugoslav League of Communists and Tito's reliance on the Bosnian Communists in counterbalancing Croatian and Serbian nationalisms eventually led Tito to recognize Bosnian Muslims as a distinct nationality in 1968 (Banac 1993).

The tension between Halid's multireligious Bosnian nationhood and Alija's Bosnian Muslim nationhood lies at the very core of the ambiguity that is concomitant to the attempts to neatly fit the Muslims of Bosnia-Herzegovina into a national category. Alija's understanding of Bosnianness as defined by religion echoes the debates on the nature of Bosnian Muslim identity from the late 1960s and early 1970s, the time during which he was attending a university. Halid, on the other hand, grew up during the immediate postwar years and was socialized during the early 1950s, at a time when integral *Bosanstvo* was particularly popular.

Masculinity of Nostalgia

The maleness of the workshop becomes pronounced if one considers the masculine characteristics of Tito that the men emphasize: his protective embrace of the Bosnian Muslims, his fatherly qualities, and even his physical attractiveness. The masculinity of their nostalgia thus relates to Tanja Petrović's chapter in this volume in which she illustrates how her male informants use their memories of their army days as "a means of social construction of masculinity" (p. 69). Keeping in mind Petrović's argument, it is interesting to note that out of seven men who spoke at length at the workshop, four of them started their monologues with stories from the army. Whether they use these stories to highlight the arbitrariness of the official nationality categories (as Halid from the beginning of the chapter did) or the purported Serbian hegemony in the military, it is through their army experiences that these men relate to each other and by extension to Tito, the archetypal soldier and the founder of the Yugoslav Army (JNA). After a young woman enters the workshop and contests the men's interpretation of Tito's legacy, the masculinity of their nostalgia becomes explicit as the workshop turns into a shouting match between the men and the lone woman.

The Tito that emerges out of the men's memories is a protective and loving father who meticulously cared for his entire household—Yugoslavia—but who was repaid in kind only by the Bosnian Muslims, his most loyal children. Muharem claims that Socialist Yugoslavia offered a true haven for the Muslims: "During Tito's times, we blossomed. We got our citizenship under the name of 'Muslim,' which was much better than undeclared Yugoslav. ... It was him who gave the order to Kardelj [Tito's chief theoretician] ... and ordered them to insert the Muslim nationality into the constitution. For the first time in history. The Serbs growled, the Croats growled. It was only thanks to Tito." He contrasts the safety the Muslims enjoyed in Tito's Yugoslavia with the fear with which they now live in postwar Bosnia: "Now we have a democracy. Ten years after the war and you can't sleep peacefully as a Muslim in Srebrenica, and you can't sleep peacefully in Čapljina or Stolac [in Herzegovina]." Ahmet adores Tito because he provided for him: "Without a good head of the household there is no good home. ... That was the period during which I got educated, worked, and lived out my best years. ... Even had he been the worst dictator imaginable, for me Tito is a saint." For their part, the Bosnian Muslims emerge as the only genuine Yugoslavs, unwaveringly loyal to Tito. The seventy-year-old Ahmet claims that he witnessed the animosity other nations felt towards Tito: "I traveled up and down Yugoslavia. I know the mentality of all the peoples. I know that they did not like Tito in Croatia. I know they did not like Tito in Serbia." Halid echoes this description: "Tito created a very comfortable life, *especially to us Muslims* [he emphasizes, raising his voice], but I know that the rest of them did not have a good opinion of him. Neither the Slovenes, or the Croats, or the Serbs—I am not sure about the Montenegrins and the Macedonians—liked him very much. Serbs did not like him because of his attitude towards the Albanians. Others did not like him for other reasons. But the point is, that he had a lot of enemies, even at the top levels of the government." Thus, the well-providing father had in the Bosnian Muslims obedient citizens who knew how to repay his generosity.

Besides his fatherly qualities, the Tito that these men rescue from the wreckage of Yugoslavia is also a handsome man whose physical characteristics endowed him with almost supernatural powers. Muharem tells the story of a Croat from the Western Herzegovina region who tried to assassinate Tito during a rally. Upon approaching him, however, the would-be terrorist shook his hand and lost his nerve. When asked why he did not fire his gun, the man reportedly said: "When I saw those blue eyes and the beautiful smile, I just could not take out my gun. I felt as if my hand would have become paralyzed if I had." Tito's striking physical features could thus mesmerize even his most determined enemies.

My informants' portrayal of Tito as a handsome father echoes the cult of Tito that was meticulously created during his regime. As Tone Bringa argues, the image of Tito as the father was at the center of the heroic cult of self-sacrifice that emerged out of World War II. The narratives of the Partisan war and the widely popular Torch of Youth (*Štafeta Mladosti*)—during which the youth and children from all across Yugoslavia engaged in a symbolic marathon to Belgrade where they would present Tito with the torch on his birthday—all articulated the image of Tito as the father of the nation. The cult of Tito as the father became especially important in Bosnia-Herzegovina, the epicenter of major Partisan battles during World War II (Bringa 2004). As Bringa argues, the preservation of the cult of Tito became integral to the preservation of Yugoslavia in general and Bosnia in particular. While the newly elected nationalist leaders of Croatia and Serbia in 1990 attempted to distance themselves from Tito's legacy, many Bosnians continued to cling on this image as the only way to preserve the republic. In the words of Bringa:

> Tellingly, Bosnians wanted to be the keepers of Tito's true legacy, as reflected for example, in their welcoming Tito's remains when other republics wanted to discard them, but Bosnia was also the place where legacies of Tito were most brutally dismembered, while the Bosnians were forced into the role of executioner. (2004: 187)

The strands of Bosnian identity that the men weave into a unifying masculine image of Tito unravel when a woman in her early twenties enters the room and contests the men's interpretation of Tito's legacy. In the process she not only articulates a distinctly different strand of Bosnian identity but also reveals the gendered and generational exclusiveness of the men's nostalgia. She interjects her memory of Tito during one of Ahmet's many wistful sighs that sporadically interrupt his story of his days when he worked as a volunteer in one of Tito's youth brigades (*omladinske brigade*) during the country's massive postwar reconstruction effort. Visibly agitated by Ahmet's praise of Tito's ability to inspire the country's youth to volunteer, she scolds his entire generation: "My dear Ahmet, I belong to the young generation. And when you talk about those youth brigades and criticize my generation for not organizing them, you should consider that this might not be because there is no more Tito, but because our generation is much smarter than yours. You forgave them the twelfth massacre, but this time, my generation said, this is it." Her words shatter the image of Tito as the generous father who cared for his Muslim citizens even recognizing their nationality. Admitting that she was never forbidden from going to *medresa* [religious school], she remembers being punished by her high school teacher for claiming she believed in God: "The professor of my Marxism class failed me only because I said I believed in God." The Tito the men resurrect is a man who strove to create a just society in which the Muslims were protected. The Tito of Melisa's past is a man who cynically repressed the memory of the wrongs committed upon the Muslims and restricted the freedom of religion.

Melisa's interjection causes a murmur among the men and leads to a passionate discussion on the role of Islam in contemporary Bosnian identity. Agitated by the woman's blunt criticism of Tito and his generation, Ahmet wags his finger at her, accusing her generation of becoming too radicalized: "Melisa my sunshine, you know why your generation doesn't want to work [for free]? Because you have transgressed from Islam into Wahhabism and the Wahhabis are now spreading evil throughout Bosnia. They are spreading immorality; they are making the whole world hate Islam. They are the reason why we as Muslims are under the attack from the whole world." For Ahmet, many Muslims of Melisa's generation have abandoned the Bosnian strand of Islam by adopting the puritan Saudi ideology of Wahhabism, which has been associated with the September 11 terrorist attacks. According to Ahmet, this identity is foreign to Bosnians: "But we are European Muslims. We are the most unique, the purest Muslims and as such we have nothing to do with Arab Muslims." Melisa seems to take great offense at Ahmet's accusations and what she seems to perceive as his patronizing tone. She not only rejects being branded a Wahhabi, but denies him the authority to comment on Islamic practices due to his secularism: "Don't you tell me what Wahhabism means. It is people who do not live in complete accordance with Islam—people who do not pray five times per day, the people who never go to mosque—it is these people who brand us the Wahhabis. Today whoever practices true Islam and keeps a long beard is a Wahhabi for these people." Melisa's attempt to exclude the man from Islam is met with defensive shouts from the crowd: "Well, you can't judge like that who is a Muslim and who isn't," Ahmet insists; another man adds: "You can't go to any extreme. Moderation is always the best." Realizing that passions may have become too inflamed, Mehmet abruptly ends the meeting promising that the next time they would discuss the ideology of Wahhabism.

Melisa's intervention reveals the generational, gender, and social fissures that run through the core of Bosnian Muslim identity today. The generational lack of consensus among the men such as Halid and Alija on the nature of Bosnian identity are easier to reconcile because they are both based on the masculine image of Tito as the protector of the Muslims. Despite the fact that Halid's multireligious *Bosanstvo* conflicts with Alija's exclusively Bosnian Muslim nationhood, the two are unified—however temporarily—in the memory of Tito as the father of the nation (whether this is a Bosnian or Bosnian Muslim nation). Melisa's interruption of the men's nostalgic reminiscing exposes the gendered nature of the identities articulated by both men. Furthermore, her youth (she is in her early twenties) and her social background (she comes from a family of imams[4]), which was visually symbolized by her *hijab*,[5] add two additional barriers to consensus and explain the inflamed passions at the end of the meeting. It is precisely these fissures that congregate my informants into a conversation that reveals the constitutive elements of contemporary Bosnian Muslim identity.

Conclusion

In her latest book dealing with Yugoslav nostalgia among the former Yugoslavs in Amsterdam, Dubravka Ugrešić beautifully captures their attempts to deal with the degradation of their lifelong commitment to Yugoslavia: "What had till recently meant everything to them—their faith, their nationality—was suddenly worthless currency. Survival took over. And once survival was assured, once they had landed on a safe shore, heaved a sigh and pinched themselves to make certain they were alive, many of them again hung out their flags, put up their icons and escutcheons, and lit their candles" (Ugrešić 2006: 16). Similarly, the Bosnian men at the workshop in Chicago dwell on the still-smoldering ruins of Yugoslavia in order to pick up and dust off their Tito icons which become central symbols of their contemporary national identity. Their nostalgia is not some painful homesickness as the root of the word suggests—from the Greek *nostos*, "to return home," and *algos*, meaning "painful condition" (Wood 1999: 145)—but an ongoing negotiation over what it means to be Bosnian in a world without Yugoslavia. The lone woman joins the men in rummaging through the ruins, but refuses to pick up Tito icons, exposing the gendered and generational nature of men's nostalgia. Thus, rather than achieving a consensus, the conversation reveals the ambiguities that have latched onto the historical trajectory of Bosnian (Muslim) identity. As Tim Pilbrow has pointed out in the case of Bulgaria, it is the very ambivalences regarding national identity's central symbols (Tito and Islam in our case) that congregate individuals into a collective identity (Pilbrow 2005).

Following my gracious informants to the ruins of Yugoslavia has opened up a series of questions regarding the role of nostalgia in the construction of contemporary national identity: How does gender relate to our perceptions of the past? Does belonging to the same generation override or at least assuage the gendered prism through which men and women view their common past? How does social background fit into this fissured landscape? And finally and more specifically, is there a potential for Yugo-nostalgia to congregate individuals from the opposite sides of the newly rigidified national boundaries into a new (postnational?) consensus? While my brief investigation suggests a negative answer to the last question, the impending integration of the region into the European Union might lead to even more creative uses of the constantly changing past.

Notes

1. Created in 1994 by two Slovenian students, Martin Sretbotnjak and Matija Marolt, the website known as Tito's Homepage (http://www.titoville.com) is a space that allows for the coexistence of contested interpretations of Tito's legacy. The site enables the visitor to view hundreds of Tito's pictures, listen to his speeches, and to the Yugoslav songs celebrating Tito's role in the liberation of the country from the Nazis. However, far from being engaged in an unambiguous worship of Tito, Srebotnjak's site includes numerous jokes, disparaging Tito's weakness for kitsch, a reference to the Goli Otok prison camp, and a listing of all the women that Tito supposedly charmed.
2. This category also included "others," meaning any other identity that was not officially recognized. However, in my conversations with the cartog-

rapher who was one of the authors of this map, he emphasized that the number of "others" in this category was very low and that it represented mostly Yugoslavs.
3. The term *Bosanac* is literally translated as "Bosnian," but in the local language the term also carries regional connotations. Thus, many people living in Herzegovina would not use this term to define themselves, often preferring the regional identity of *Hercegovac* (Herzegovnian). But most *Bosanci* and *Hercegovci* refer to themselves as "Bosnians" when in the United States.
4. Muslim clerics.
5. Based on its Arabic origin meaning "cover," the term denotes the traditional Muslim woman's head veil.

References

Adrić, Iris, Vladimir Arsenijević, and Djordje Matić, eds. 2004. *Leksikon Yu-Mitologije*. Zagreb: Postscriptum.
Banac, Ivo. 1984. *The National Question in Yugoslavia: Origins, History, Politics*. Ithaca, NY: Cornell University Press.
———. 1993. "Bosnian Muslims: From Religious Community to Socialist Nationhood and Postcommunist Statehood." In *The Muslims of Bosnia-Herzegovina: Their Historic Development from the Middle Ages to the Dissolution of Yugoslavia*, ed. Mark Pinson. Cambridge, MA: Harvard University Press.
Botev, Nikolai. 1994. "Where East Meets West: Ethnic Intermarriage in the Former Yugoslavia, 1962–1989." *American Sociological Review* 59 (3): 461–80.
Bougarel, Xavier. 2003. "Bosnian Muslims and the Yugoslav Idea." In *Yugoslavism: Histories of a Failed Idea, 1918–1992*, ed. Dejan Djokić. Madison: University of Wisconsin Press.
Bringa, Tone. 2004. "The Peaceful Death of Tito and the Violent End of Yugoslavia." In *Death of the Father: An Anthropology of the End in Political Authority*, ed. Jon Borneman. New York: Berghahn Books.
Ćerić, Salim. 1968. *O jugoslovenstvu i bosanstvu: Prilog pitanju jugoslovenska nacionalnost ili jugoslovenski socijalistički patriotizam*. Sarajevo: NIP Oslobodjenje.
Donia, Robert. 1981. *Islam Under the Double Eagle: The Muslims of Bosnia-Herzegovina, 1878–1914*. New York: Columbia University Press.
Donia, Robert, and John V. A. Fine. 1994. *Bosnia and Herzegovina: A Tradition Betrayed*. New York: Columbia University Press.
Fine, John V. A. 2007. "Strongmen Can Be Beneficial: The Exceptional Case of Josip Broz Tito." In *Balkan Strongmen: Dictators and Authoritarian Leaders of Southeast Europe*, ed. Bernd J. Fisher. West Lafayette IN: Purdue University Press.
Hayden, Robert M. 1999. *Blueprints for a House Divided: The Constitutional Logic of the Yugoslav Conflicts*. Ann Arbor: University of Michigan Press.
Jović, Dejan. 2003. "Yugoslavism and Yugoslav Communism: From Tito to Kardelj." In *Yugoslavism: Histories of a Failed Idea, 1918–1992*, ed. Dejan Djokić. Madison: University of Wisconsin.

Markotić, Ante, Ejub Sijerčić, and Asim Abdurahmanović. 1991. *Etnička karta Bosne i Hercegovine*. Sarajevo: Altermedia d.o.o. i NUB BiH.
Pilbrow, Tim. 2005. "'Europe' in Bulgarian Conceptions of Nationhood." In *The Nation, Europe, the World: Textbooks and Curricula in Transition*, ed. Hanna Schissler and Yasemin Soysal. New York: Berghahn Books.
Ramet, Pedro. 1984. *Nationalism and Federalism in Yugoslavia, 1963–1983*. Bloomington: University of Indiana Press.
Rusinow, Dennison. 1977. *The Yugoslav Experiment: 1948–1974*. Berkeley: University of California Press.
Ugrešić, Dubravka. 2006. *The Ministry of Pain*. Trans. Michael Henry Heim. New York: Harper Collins Books.
Wood, Nancy. 1999. *Vectors of Memory: Legacies of Trauma in Postwar Europe*. New York: Berg Publishing.

14

THE VELVET PRISON IN HINDSIGHT
Artistic Discourse in Hungary in the 1990s
Anna Szemere

In his book coining the metaphor "the velvet prison" to describe the artists' predicament in state socialism, Miklós Haraszti (1987) writes:

> We are tied to a society of progress and necessity by bonds that are stronger than fear. I am one of those who is privileged to articulate my thoughts publicly. Other than the Party politician, I am the only individual who can freely remark upon life's complexities and freely use the accepted principles of discourse. What is more, I can be subjective; after all, I am a member of an artistic community that is supposed to express permitted subjective preoccupations. Naturally I come up against restraints. But I am too deeply involved for my position to be explained simply in terms of the barbed wire that surrounds me. I am not a silent inmate of the Gulag. (71)

Small wonder that the book challenging the dominant paradigm of state oppression vs. the arts' resistance—yet suggesting a more subtle and insidious operation of power—first came out in France in 1983 to be followed three years later by a samizdat edition in Communist Hungary. The image proved powerful enough to catch on in the social sciences and cultural studies to refer to a specific stage in the trajectory of state socialism. More recently, Jeroen de Kloet (2000) borrowed it to characterize the ambiguities of rebellion and conformity in China's fast-changing popular musical scenes. When do state Socialist societies appear as "velvet prisons" to artists and intellectuals? Such a perception, I will argue, arises from a conjuncture of various socioeconomic and political developments. First, in the expanding marketplace of late socialism, cultural production is regulated more and more by popular demand rather than ideological dictum. The party-state gradually loses its grip on people's minds, their fantasies, beliefs, fears, and dreams. Second, an unpredictable but increasingly permissive government allows for a limited yet vigorous public sphere for alternative movements and ideas to thrive. Next to the more outspoken dissident fringe culture, an informal contract is made between state officialdom and professional artists. The late Socialist party-state, according to Haraszti, is a "live network of lobbies. ... We [the intellectuals] play with it, we know how to use it, and we have allies and enemies at the controls." (1987: 78–79)

The velvet prison as a metaphor evokes comfort and softness, even elegance, mitigating the inmates' claustrophobia. A twin image comes to mind, the "Hotel Abyss" (*Grand Hotel Abgrund*) introduced by the philosopher György Lukács (1982) as a sarcastic reference to the Austro-Hungarian writer Robert Musil's self-enclosed, inward-looking intellectual world at the turn of the twentieth century. Given its precarious foundations, the Hotel Abyss provided its residents a space in which protection and angst were thoroughly enmeshed. Compare this to the even more acerbic metaphor devised in an underground rock song of the 1980s where Hungary is portrayed as a "five-star mental ward" [*osztályonfelüli elmeosztály*]. Thus one can stretch a virtual thread between distant temporalities and remote spaces: the underground rock world resonating with the literary community of early twentieth-century Central Europe as well as with the rock 'n' roll dissenters of China's globalizing popular culture.

Evidently, the most privileged inmates of the velvet prison were not the young avant-garde artists in Hungary. Older and more respectable representatives of high culture, predominantly in film and literature, enjoyed that status. For rockers, nonetheless, it proved to be a stimulating space of creativity grounded in close-knit community life (in more detail, see Szemere 2001: 29–73). The questions I am addressing in this chapter are as follows: What was the nature and object of nostalgia before 1989? How did the velvet prison become remembered and reimagined in the musicians' post-1989 narratives? What was being longed and mourned for in the early 1990s?

The Double Articulation of Nostalgia in Underground Rock

Through studying the cultural experiences of post-Socialist Russia and Eastern Europe, Svetlana Boym (2001) has classified the multiple shapes and colors of nostalgia. Originally viewed as an individual mental disturbance, nostalgia, in Boym's compelling analysis, is a historical emotion produced by modernity. It paralleled as well as eroded the optimistic belief in progress (xvi); it is "a longing for a home that no longer exists or has never existed" (xiii).

Nostalgia is an alluring yet elusive phenomenon of postrevolutionary mental landscapes. Looking at the Hungarian rock underground's musical and verbal discourses, I will argue that it did not merely follow but preceded major social turmoil. Its nature and content was obviously quite different before and after the regime change, respectively. In the 1980s, it was the artistic texts in and through which nostalgia surfaced. In the 1990s, however, the diffuse sense of emptiness and displacement conveyed through the songs gave way to a very concrete sense of disorientation. If the songs of the 1980s were mementos of yearning for an imagined home, post-Socialist melancholia—detectable less in the songs than in the musicians' reflections and daily struggles—hinged on remembering a way of life that enabled them to become the spokespersons, if not heroes, of a generation. In the 1990s the aging underground rockers engaged in a curious romance with the past as well as struggled for defining its meaning.

Nostalgia, Alienation, and the Arts

Nostalgia, Boym states, "charts space on time and time on space" (2001: xviii). It connotes sentimentalism, weepy-eyed lamentation over something distant and vague. "Nostalgia is to memory as kitsch is to art," stated Charles Maier (cited by Boym: xiv). It may follow a single plot based on the belief that the lost home can actually be reconstructed. What Boym calls *restorative* nostalgia is the fuel of fundamentalist nationalist and religious movements (xviii). Such longing is transparent, earnest, and, regarding its obsession with a single trajectory to salvation, it is akin to *totalitarian kitsch*, a phrase coined by the novelist Milan Kundera (1987) in reference to collectivist, future-oriented utopias. In Kundera's description, totalitarian kitsch banishes "every display of individualism (because a deviation from the collective is a spit in the eye of the smiling brotherhood); every doubt (because anyone who starts doubting details will end by doubting life itself); all irony (because in the realm of kitsch everything must be taken quite seriously" (251–52).

Reflective nostalgia, in contrast, is skeptical, ironic, elusive, and more artistically productive. It reveals the impossibility of simple paths, "dwell(ing) on the ambivalences of human longing and belonging" and of the virtual nature of modern consciousness (2001: xviii). As Boym wittily put, one may feel homesick yet be sick of home (xix). Her concept of reflective nostalgia is dislodged from any distinct point or place in the past or in a utopian future. It is an opaque and subjectively defined "elsewhere" that nostalgics attempt to inhabit. Like Walter Benjamin's flâneur, they seek a melancholic pleasure in traces and fragments, the meanings of which are indeterminate and unfixed.[1]

But can we talk about nostalgia without a clearly shared reference point in time and space, imaginary or historical? How far can the concept be broadened without losing its analytical value? Isn't Boym's reflective nostalgia merely another name for alienation? While not addressing the difference between the two concepts head-on, she compellingly claims that alienation is intricately tied up with nostalgia of the reflective kind, that is, with longing (*algia*) but with no return (*nostos*). In her case study on the Russian exile writer, Joseph Brodsky, she makes two points. First, the psychological state of estrangement may be transformed into art practice. Drawing on structuralist and avant-garde theories, Boym demonstrates that the language of art, by definition, is "strange" and unusual: "Poetic language is always a foreign language" (290). Estrangement moreover connotes not only distance but dislocation as well. The artist, metaphorically, is the inhabitant of another country, an idea evidenced by tracing the words *ostranenie* (alienation) and *strana* (country) to their common root, *stran*. (One might confirm this etymological link by looking at other languages—English or Hungarian, for example—where the words "alien" and "foreign[er]" are synonyms.)

Second, beyond recognizing the aesthetic potential inherent in estrangement, Boym contends that art may serve as a cure for it. By writing poems, making a film, or composing a song, one's life is enriched and made livable: "Everyday life can be redeemed only if it imitates art, not the other way around. ... [Artistic estrangement] embraces the romantic and avant-garde dream of a reverse mimesis that would encourage people to live artistically" (290–291). In this way, she strings lived experience, artistic text, and a way of life on a common thread such that art's separation from life—its autonomy—is simultaneously sustained and eroded: "Art is only meaningful when it's not put entirely in the service of real life or realpolitik, and when its strangeness and distinctiveness can both define and defy the autonomy of art" (291).

It is tempting to view nostalgic or alienated art as politically regressive, implying passivity and pessimism. Such art, some would say, has its practitioners extricate themselves from the present or the future, by losing themselves in the past. But Boym rehabilitates nostalgia through her emphasis on the imaginative and active uses of this experience in various art forms. Even the most apparently alienated piece of music, film, or fiction has the power to make one's life inhabitable—a point where she, implicitly, deviates from T. W. Adorno's celebration of the musical articulation of alienation as the hallmark of autonomous (modern) art and its separation from everyday life (Adorno 2002). Art, in Boym's view, is a potent, life-shaping force. In and of itself, this is not a new proposition, lying as it does at the foundation of the fledgling field of art therapy. The poet Ted Hughes highlights art's roots in human pain: "Every work of art stems from a wound in the soul of the artist. ... Art is a psychological component of the auto-immune system that gives expression to the healing process. That is why great works of art make us feel good" (cited by Rosslyn 2001: 91).

Art's ability to shape experience and a community's life is central to theories of popular culture, whether the effects are deemed detrimental or, on the contrary, empowering. In either case, popular culture's effects tend to be discussed in political terms. When discussing a rap song or a television show, what concerns most critics and media scholars is how the artwork participates in reproducing or, alternately, challenging the sociopolitical system. The individual existential roots and effects of art——be it fine or popular—are often overlooked. This is where Boym's analysis of nostalgia and alienation deepens our understanding of how art is embedded in culture and individual lives. Not only does she address the existential problems involved in creating and consuming aesthetic works, she proposes links between alienation, the "alien" language of art, and, finally, the manner in which art-as-text is incorporated into life as reverse mimesis, a therapeutic tool.

Music as the Carrier of Nostalgic Sentiments

To the extent that nostalgia charts time on space and space on time, of all aesthetic materials, music as a nonreferential medium is arguably the most powerful to convey, play on, and arouse nostalgic sentiments (Crafts et al. 1993; DeNora 2000). Music has the capacity to transport us in time and space, whether our "trip down memory lane" is intentional or not. Everyone is familiar with the sudden and often stirring experience of being, momentarily, jolted back into a younger self upon hearing a long-forgotten or half-forgotten melody from one's past. Individually and collectively, however, we tend to cultivate our ability to reconnect with our history through music as a mnemonic device. Relying on empirical research on music's role in people's personal lives, DeNora (2000: 57–58) suggests that we turn music into symbols to remember key people, places, and moments of our lives. A song, an album, or even a specific style of music can stand for an attachment to one's father, for a time spent with a lover, or a place fondly remembered from one's childhood. Evidently, music can also retrieve negative memories such as fear, hatred, or humiliation. Music that we heard and danced to, enjoyed or repudiated, collected or disowned is woven into our emotional biography and is integral to our self. More viscerally than visual images, musical pieces prod reflexivity for many people, and, in this capacity, are bound up with identity-work, a creative and ongoing project (De-Nora 2000: 46–75).

The entertainment industry is not merely aware of music's influence on memory. It vehemently cashes in on music's tie-up with remembering or reliving the past, especially one's youth. This is evident in the formatting of radio stations ("oldies" stations), in releases of compilation albums (e.g., "Hits of the 80s"), re-releases of famous stars' back catalogs, or in launching of nostalgia tours for ad hoc reunited veteran rock bands.

More broadly, it is arguable that "imagined communities" (Anderson 1983) such as generations, nations, religions, and other ideologically or value-based communities depend for their existence on musical symbols, being as they are integral elements of rituals whose purpose is to build on shared memory, or to construct it as part of strengthening the community's collective identity. Visual symbols such as flags, stars, crosses, crowns, uniforms, and folk costumes tend to be vastly more effective when paired up with musical symbols such as anthems, hymns, marches, or choreographed dances (Cerulo 1995: 3–4). Music, image, and movement thus mutually reinforce and solidify established associations attached to collective identities. The project of restorative nostalgia involves a preference for a set of symbols with fixed meanings. The Hungarian rock opera *István, a király* (Istvan, the King)—and especially its film adaptation—offers a preeminent example of identity-work as its makers deployed a rich arsenal of visual and musical symbols to titillate the nationalist imaginary (Milun 1992). Reflective nostalgia, on the contrary, creates new, unexpected, or unusual associations between symbols (e.g., visual and musical) or destabilizes, in semiotic terms, the relationship between signifier and signified. In the remaining part of this chapter I will explore how various forms and styles of nostalgia manifested themselves in the musical and discursive output of Hungarian underground rockers.

Reading Nostalgia in the Musical Texts

Many would bristle at the association of the 1980s underground music scene with nostalgia. It comprised, after all, a diverse set of attitudes, styles, and art practices influenced by such irreverent, in-your-face icons of punk and avant-garde rock as the Velvet Underground, Patti Smith, David Bowie, the Sex Pistols, the Clash, Frank Zappa, Captain Beefheart or the Talking Heads, to name just a few. Yet if nostalgia hinges on a sense of being ill-at-ease with the spatial and temporal coordinates of existence, if it is, as Boym put it, a double exposure of the here-and-now and the "elsewhere," the underground expressed and fostered a wide array of nostalgic sentiments. A paradox of longing for an imagined home among underground rockers was that it marked a prelude to the system's fall. This music represented the first political voice to announce, in those crowded, run-down clubs of Budapest's outskirts, that the "East Side Story"—Eastern Europe's state Socialist experiment—failed. As the group Európa Kiadó (a pun translatable either as Europe Publishing House or Europe for Rent) put it: "We'll disappear like the last metro / This is an endless journey ... / Everything's for sale / But we ran out of everything." Or, in the group Sziámi's (Siamese) phrasing: We kicked the habit / We're using nothing / This is the last hour / We'll remain sober now.[2]

Harbingers of social change, the movement's contribution to the breakdown of the system—an important theme regarding rock music in postsocialist transition studies (Wicke 1992; Mitchell 1996; Ramet 1994)—is complicated and tenuous. Rather than furthering a particular vision of sociopolitical change, this subculture voiced an almost cosmic sense of "homelessness" in time and space: "This city is a distant planet / It's not good to live here, though not bad either / A five-star mental ward" (Európa Kiadó). A similar sentiment is captured in the lines: "You're an alien who somehow got stranded here / You don't quite comprehend the news' (Kontroll Csoport [Control Group]). The group Balaton (named after Hungary's largest lake and popular resort place) offers the most personal expression to the mundane daily experience of hopelessness: "This house may crumble for all I care / It stole my time / The corner of my eye quivers / It makes no difference." Another song by the A. E. Bizottság (Albert Einstein Committee) forebodes a dangerous and unknown future: "I could also be a kamikaze / It's August 13, 1993,[3] it may not be Friday / I'm alone, I may not be alive / I'm completely alone, all alone / Flying alone, all alone."

For the most arcane form of nostalgia we must turn to the art and performance practice of Vágtázó Halottkémek (Galloping Coroners), abbreviated as VHK, whose stage name already announced their intent to shake and shatter. The band started out with an unusually radical imagery of "elsewhere," and the method of reaching it—ecstasy—was inextricably tied up with that image. Fusing hard-core punk with tribal rhythms and postmodern gloom, the band intended to conjure up a vision of ancient shamanistic rituals and infused it with antimodernist philosophy. (For a detailed discussion of this unique amalgam, see

Szemere 2001: 66–69; Milun 1992: 16–24). The later albums of the band moved increasingly from reflective toward restorative nostalgia. While the vast sweep of historical time remained essential to their project, the previously unstructured stream of intense rhythms, atonal, melodyless shouts, and overamplified and distorted instrumental sounds gave way to metric poetry, simple and repetitive tonal folk-musical motifs, and danceable rhythms, all within the broader rock idiom. The once-shocking and ecstatic cacophony of the stage sets and costumes, which signified shamanism in its most stylized form, became replaced with rituals attributed to "my [Hungarian] predecessors."[4] Costumes that included fish and feathers covering the musicians' bodies were disposed of in favor of shiny satin tunics. The iconography, visual and poetic, is yet another representation of old Hungarian history steeped in mythology. The VHK's creative work cannot be divorced from the broader political forces and currents of which it formed a part. While their early music placed them among the most subversive of underground art, the later creative output, with its unmistakable antiliberal ideological connotations, allied the band with the nationalists who reinvented an ethnically pure version of Hungarian history and identity.

Európa Kiadó, my second example to discuss at some depth, represented a more familiar and transparent form of nostalgia. Most notably, EK instigated nostalgia by announcing a number of their shows as the last one, a farewell. Through these acts they became an object of remembrance and longing. Whether Európa Kiadó intentionally manipulated the audience's moods and feelings by such tactics or, they were indeed recurrently on the verge of breakup is not easy to tell and may not even be important. The effect, in either case, was to stir emotions by performing departures and reunions and thus dramatizing the emotional tension between present and past, presence and absence, or, in psychoanalytic terms, life and death (and rebirth). Such an interpretation is supported by the prevalence of live events over recordings, which characterized the pre-1989 era (Szemere 2001: 4–47). From a textual point of view, the EK's songs evoke the here-and-now as an intensely ambiguous, anachronistic space, which should have been relegated to the past: "My watch says it's been tomorrow for long / My head is about to explode." Yet, this present-as-past in the quoted song speaks the new popular musical language of Western cities of the early 1980s: a minimalist, repetitive, angst-ridden tune supported with sparse instrumentation. In many other songs, too, the present time appears as a vestige of the past; and the "city," used metaphorically to refer to the broader framework of existence, "will never fully build up." A favored poetic strategy is to double the lyrical subject's perspective, who is thus simultaneously inside and outside of it: "This city is a remote planet / Living here is not good but not half bad / A five-star mental ward / That's the salary of fear / One wants the most of the best / But even this is better than nothing.⁵

This double vision allows for an escape from the mundane realities and from the anguish of being stranded in a place/time that is doomed to disappear. The witty futuristic song "Jó lesz nekünk" (It's Gonna Be Good for Us), for instance, shoots its hero and heroine out to the rarefied privacy of alien stars to "make love in weightlessness."⁶ On the other hand, the insider, the city-dweller lives the conflicted nature of everyday life by finding pleasure in pain, a sense of belonging amidst estrangement, and love (or lust) along disdain and self-loathing:

> Arouse me! Pamper me!
> Let's allow to come what is to come
> The present is long gone
> Destroy its memory softly. ....
> The city's buzzing under us
> It's small and insignificant
> I don't know what I'm waiting for
> But will recognize it when it appears.
> Be bad! Throw me off my feet!
> Gently, nicely and quietly. ...
> Be bad! Throw me off my feet!
> Very rudely and quite slowly.⁷

Another mode of charting the vacuous space of the present place/time onto a desired or significant one is via employing the figure of "Europe," a heavily charged concept, emotionally and politically, in Central and East European discourse during the transition (Todorova 1997; Neumann 1999). Europe was constructed as the desired destination to "return to" after the Berlin Wall's fall, even though ideologues and intellectuals in Poland, Czechoslovakia (or, after 1992, the Czech Republic), Slovenia, and Hungary—inhabitants of the newly reinvented "Central Europe"—had never ceased to consider themselves members of the European (read: Western) community excluded, temporarily, by the Yalta agreement and the resultant four decades of Soviet occupation. The stage name "Európa Kiadó" itself, in a tongue-in-cheek manner, taps into this explosive amalgam of desire, fantasy, resentment, and hope in the region. In this most disquieting song by the same title, the phrase "Europe to Rent" as a refrain repeats more than a dozen times over the heady, alarming, siren-like melodic motif and an asymmetric rhythm pattern simulating an irregular heartbeat. Neither the harmonic nor the melodic pattern offers any closure. The singing voice articulates a curious mix of resignation and passion. The words evoke the bleak black-and-white reality of Eastern European artists, in this time captured by the image of a "refugee camp":

> Wind of Athens and rain of Sparta
> We're sitting by the fire, me and Time
> The years of singing are slowly passing by
> The oversized souls are hiding in cellars.
>
> *Refrain:* Europe to rent, Europe to rent
> Europe to rent, Europe to rent
>
> I get frightened of my voice
> Will disappear from rock 'n' roll
> It's like a refugee camp
> Everyone's here who's not brave enough
>
> *Refrain:* Europe to rent, Europe to rent
> Europe to rent, Europe to rent

"Europe" as a figure appears here as an "elsewhere," but it is not the shiny, glamorous "other" of Eastern Europe. Rather this morose, rainy, and windy place is merely a refugee camp writ large:

> The messenger is coming and waving
> There are no news for long
> The electric chair of desire[8] is sparking up.[9]

But if Europe is to be rented, who should be her new tenants? And who would be her proprietors? Maybe Westerners, who would offer opportunities for some of those "oversized souls" who broke out of the refugee camp? Or, perhaps a new order is about to take shape? The words are too cryptic to allow for a solid answer to these questions. Rain and wind, after all, may signify the storm that soon will fling open the doors of the velvet prisons.

Longing After the Velvet Prison

These songs and performances came across to their audience as compelling and authentic expressions of their own historical and generational experience. The following song, also by Európa Kiadó, tempering desperation with a tint of irony, was especially popular across generations of Hungarian youths:

> I can't restrain myself
> I wanna be a hero

I can't restrain myself
Nothing else would suffice
A real hero, a real hero, a real hero, a real hero.[10]

Peculiarly enough, the autobiographic subject of the song *was*, in fact, a hero, even though he was not fully aware of it until the politics of history made rock music obsolete and relatively insignificant during the latter part of the 1980s. Jenő Menyhárt, Európa Kiadó's principal songwriter, and his fellow musicians were all heroes and heroines precisely because of their power to forge a collective identity through the intensity, relevance, and growing popularity of their art. The 1980s offered a liminal space for politically charged artistic initiatives. This was a time of effervescence in cinema and theater, as well as contemporary experimental music (Szemere 2001: 29–31, 109–11; Havasréti and K. Horváth 2003; for several other Soviet Bloc societies, see Kenney 2002: 157–91). The velvet prison represented a measure of freedom that, paradoxically, the new regime dried up. Thomas Cushman, in his ethnography of Russian underground bohemia, calls it *existential* freedom in contradistinction to *political* freedom brought about by post-Soviet transformations (1995: 320–22). Earning one's livelihood in state socialism had scarcely any relation to the art one produced. Yet in whatever kind of day jobs the underground musicians were hired for, they did not limit or deter them from making music. Through their contacts with the professional and semiprofessional art world, especially in film and theater, the underground had easy access to unskilled or artistic freelance jobs. The amateurism they engaged in had no professional Other. More accurately speaking, Hungarian rock professionals were sell-outs in their underground counterpart's eyes. The former did not set a standard to which the latter measured its value, performance, and credibility. In this relatively sheltered space, the underground was able to experiment with the kind of music and performance art that they thought was most genuinely innovative and authentic. The money they earned from live events was inconsequential. By and large, they didn't have to deal with the gatekeepers of the music business (record companies and the broadcast media) because that music business did not want to deal with them either. The audience, especially in the early days, consisted of friends and peers. The musicians were not competing for a specific market niche since their fans were drawn to all of the bands. The bands' membership was fluid and performance oriented. In order to appear in public, the musicians did not need any credentials from juries or professional guilds, unlike their professional counterparts. The only pressure to engage in this endeavor came from their creative impulse as individuals and members of a close-knit community. Underground rock lived on the stage and often poorly prepared cassette recordings, although on occasion each of the major bands had access to professional studios to at least make, if not release, an album. Kept at a bay from the media and often prevented by police or party officials from staging their events even when scheduled, they could clearly sense the state's ever-present surveillance. Yet while the oppression was palpable enough to titillate both the artists and their audience with a sense of risk, courage, and credibility, it was relatively feeble and inconsistent to squash the movement or thwart the thrill of exploring an uncharted territory.[11]

The unique nature of this artistic freedom producing the celebrities of the underground did not become evident for the community until after that freedom had evaporated. Only its very loss called attention to it as a thing of the past. Yet, as I have pointed out, this kind of freedom was the material and existential context, or even precondition, of creativity. During my research, I encountered few explicit references to the generosity of the state Socialist welfare state. However, retrospectively, some angry filmmakers compared it favorably to the Antall government[12] rejecting the latter, rather shockingly, as "money fascism" for their neglect of the arts and artists. State Socialist bureaucracy, they argued, used its power to censor or ban certain songs, films, concerts, or theatrical productions, whereas they bemoaned the new system for denying them a chance to produce art that did not have a mass appeal. The fate of numerous clubs and projects launched and gone out of business in a few years proved this prophecy true. No less importantly, a mere subsistence level of existence became more difficult to sustain after 1989. Musicians lost their most valuable asset, their free time.

But there was more to post-Socialist nostalgia than the material and existential conditions of creativity. And certainly the longing was never unqualified. Musicians welcomed their new passports that allowed them unrestricted travels and participation, even if limited, in the global music scene. Some of them felt relieved by breaking out of the straightjacket of politicized music and began to cultivate new directions in their artistic career. Others enjoyed finally speaking the language of left liberal or radical politics (multiculturalism, feminism, gay rights, environmentalism, etc.), which tore down the wall between Eastern and Western alternative artists. Many such efforts became manifested in innovative forms of cultural entrepreneurship. Musicians, producers, and journalists growing out of the 1980s music scene delightedly took advantage of the post-Socialist civic rights, which enabled them to run or sign up with independent record labels, radio stations, subcultural venues, or even launch festivals with marked alternative and multiculturalist appeal.[13]

In hindsight, however, the velvet prison appeared as a known or knowable world. Allies and enemies could rarely be mistaken. As Haraszti conjectured, everyone was familiar with the rules of the game inside of the prison and even had some solid assumptions as to what lay beyond it. The emergent tumultuous, fluid, and swiftly altering realities of the early 1990s undermined the musicians' ability to get a handle on their social world and understand the nature of new power relations, both in society and in one's face-to-face community. The late literary critic Péter Balassa expressed this predicament most succinctly:

> In the old regime, in the last stages of its existence, it was not the political system *per se* that abused the artist, the scholar or the intellectual. Things worked more complicatedly, and problems couldn't always be attributed directly to the mechanics of the system as such. But now it seems the very intelligibility of the system is plucking on our nerves—as if we were confronted with a wrestler who spread too much oil on his body to prevent us from getting a grip on him. (1994: 48)

Nostalgia Displaced

The new developments of the 1990s fragmented the former underground community. What had existed independently of market relations became subject to competition and commoditization. The previous underground not only had to reinvent its identity—it had to do so in a fashion that sold well in the vicinity of the international and domestic pop and rock stars for an increasingly fragmented audience. This audience set new and high standards for its local entertainers. Longing for the stardom achieved in the 1980s was an understandable but profoundly problematic response to this plight. However, unlike nostalgia after secure employment or subsidized groceries, which was explicitly voiced in post-Socialist public discourse, nostalgia for underground art in late socialism, including rock, surfaced in quite subtle and indirect ways. Before discussing it, let me take a short digression.

The genre conventions inherent in pop music allow its practitioners and listeners to be overtly sentimental and nostalgic. Good pop artists and entrepreneurs can creatively respond to and manipulate their audience's need for repetition and remembrance. Pop music can afford to display its commercial roots and affiliation. Far less can rock 'n' roll do so. The discourse of rock, especially on the alternative fringes, is elitist and self-conscious. Unlike pop, rock constructs its own history and maps of lineage. The avant-garde sensibility revolts against repetition, sameness, or imitation. Dynamism and originality are highly regarded aesthetic values just as in autonomous art. Nostalgia, in rockers' vocabulary, equals stagnation, a fixation on the past.

But how could the rock community avoid even the appearance of being sentimental and yearning for bygone glory? The new era deprived many of them of their previous status, prestige, and a social network cemented by solidarity. Therefore any musical event or act that smacked of longing for the past was frowned upon and attributed to the Other—and now the Other was inside rather than outside of the community. Musicians faced nostalgia in a fellow musician or close friend's act and dismissed it as a fundamentally flawed and inadequate way of coping with new challenges. I will illustrate how such sentiments arose as a form of projection in the community's social life and critical discourse.

To cover a song composed and performed by another artist may have a variety of different motives. The musician may want to pay tribute to the composer/performer, he or she may find the music artistically rich and timely to lend itself to reinterpretation, or he or she would like to engage in a dialog with an artist and the era in which the song was made (Lipsitz 1990: 99–132). In the early 1990s, Ágnes Kamondy, a talented veteran of the folk and alternative music movement, staged and performed a program entitled *Dalok Közép-Nirvániából* (Songs from Central Nirvania), which was comprised of the most popular and widely known songs of the underground repertoire. Her cover versions reflected her unique feminine sensibility as well as her complex emotions toward the era evoked, the early 1980s, when the songs were premiered. Did her act indicate her nostalgia after the velvet prison or, as she called it, the ghetto? She would certainly deny it. In my interview with her (November 1993), she stated: "For me, [*Nirvania*] was an act of concluding something. I'd like to forget the ghetto." Then she talked about giving due respect to these songs by treating them as precious artworks born of pain. Let me delve a little more into our conversation:

A.S.: Does [this music] become art as it gets released from the ghetto?

Á.K.: Yes. At least, I guess I succeeded in experiencing and conveying it as art. ... What's so fantastic about art is that it gives absolution even as the grim realities surface in it.

Kamondy thought that, through reinterpreting the songs, she helped negotiate the traumatic transition from the 1980s, a world of tight-knit friendships and intense, albeit often grim, experiences to that of the 1990s, a new era marked by individualism and competition. Although the concept of nostalgia was not explicit in the critical reception of *Nirvania*, Kamondy's fellow musicians, precisely the ones whose songs she took liberty to rearrange, viewed and condemned her practice as such. They opined that Kamondy, by the mere act of transporting the songs from the rock stage to a more conventional theatrical stage, had erected a "costly marble monument" to the "surviving composers and performers," which "one might just call apotheosis." But that was a serious mistake, since "it's not usual to celebrate the urban folk style called rock 'n' rot (*rock 'n' rohadj meg*)."[14] These rockers claimed that Kamondy had reworked the songs into museum exhibits. And the era of art as museum, they contended, was over just as the era of "grand universal statements" made about serious and commercial art forms (Menyhárt, personal interview, November 1993). The underground music was in a sense serious art and addressed profound existential questions (Cushman 1995: 98–102). The new, post-Socialist and postmodernist era, on the other hand, "[became] dominated by microworlds and the personal" as Menyhárt aptly stated, and by a new, postmodern sensibility. Kamondy was accused of sustaining obsolete modernist cultural attitudes and expressive styles. Overall, musician-critics all agreed that Kamondy's artistic project had been motivated and discredited by nostalgia. Rather than paying tribute to the past, "Nirvania" became stranded in it.

Kamondy turned the accusation against the accusers. Deeply offended by her friends' response, she retorted that their negativism disguised an act of self-aggrandizing. By challenging the songs' legitimacy in her rendition, they were the ones to engage in building their own monuments and weaving myths from their past success. Art, Kamondy believed, begs reinterpretation; myths, in contrast, thrive on immutability. Trying, as her fellow musicians did, to seal the musical texts as documents inseparable from their original performing context, she thought, was a way of freezing them dead.

Boym's conceptual pair of restorative versus reflective nostalgia throws new light on this conflict, which in a gendered controversy set the men against a woman, past against present, art against myths (see also Szemere 2000). Each party attributed to the other a flawed construction of the past discredited as sentimental, rigid, and ill-suited to cope with the present. Both parties implied that such an act destroyed the very essence of these texts, whether it was their "aesthetic value" (Kamondy) or their street credibility. In different ways, they both circumscribed the notion of restorative nostalgia and projected onto the other. Their own mode of remembering, in contrast, was deemed free of sentimentality in recognizing the true significance of cultural and personal change. Sensitive, sophisticated, and articulate, both Kamondy and her friends would agree to call themselves reflective nostalgiacs, thus demonstrating that acts of remembrance can as much reveal and foster divides as sustain, under different circumstances, a sense of unity and solidarity.

Conclusion

In the wake of the "velvety" transition to post-Socialism, the 1990s brought along new antagonisms in Hungary's politics, social life, and popular culture. Looking back to the recent past enabled social actors to have a better grip of their shifting realities and to assess new possibilities and constraints in repositioning themselves. In this chapter I explored how a particular conceptualization of intellectuals' relationship with the state, the velvet prison became a focal point for confronting the past with present. In this confrontation diffuse sentiments and longings could be expressed and examined. Maurice Halbwachs, famously, claimed that the past is a different country (Schudson 1992). More than that, the past may be viewed as a kind of fun-house mirror that refracts and reflects, reveals and conceals the motivations of those who seek to understand their present. Reflections often become tinted with a peculiar and complex sentiment called nostalgia. Nostalgia erupted at diverse sites and types in Socialist popular culture, but, in its most reflexive, creative, and politically contentious form, it inhabited the underground art world of 1980s, which then became the very object, along with its broader sociopolitical context, of post-Socialist interrogation of the past.

Late Socialist nostalgia helped musicians and their audiences make sense of their disaffection with a decadent society. Giving aesthetic form to it congealed a community ready for social change. As the carnivalesque years of transition passed, however, nostalgia became bound up with a new kind of anxiety about how to handle the underground legacy in the context of market competition, commoditization, and fragmentation. Clinging to the past and its glory, incompatible with the underground sensibility, hit dangerously close to home. This led some prominent members of the community to externalize, displace, and dismiss this sentiment as the perceived nostalgia of "someone else." In doing so, they engaged in a discussion about the politics of rock and art, proposing intriguing distinctions between rigid and pliable, mythical and creative, stagnant and dynamic uses of the past.

Notes

This chapter is a significantly revised and enlarged version of my presentation by the same title at the conference "Postsocialist Nostalgia" held by CEEP of the University of Illinois, Urbana-Champaign, April 2006.
1. Benjamin's flâneur (walker) is a complex social type emerging with the modern anonymous city, the quintessential embodiment of which was nineteenth-century Paris. The flaneur studies, reads, savors, and enjoys the city as a compendium of historical knowledge as well as a site of diversity and intoxicating sensory stimuli (Benjamin 2002 [1999]: 416–56).
2. See an excellent video clip for this song on YouTube: "Sziámi—Mi már leszoktunk róla" (taken from the film *Moziklip*, dir. Péter Tímár, 1987) http://www.youtube.com/watch?v=_xlQfgiUUmc. For a 2004 performance, see http://www.youtube.com/watch?v=_ozyeoHtn5Q.
3. The song was first performed in 1981.
4. To illustrate the transformation of style and attitude, see two video clips, the first one taken from the film *A kutya éji dala* (The Dog's Night Song, dir. Gábor Bódy: http://www.youtube.com/watch?v=r9KU8AnV4rM); the second entitled *Őseimmel* (With My Ancestors): http://www.youtube.com/watch?v=S0gkMrpvQi0.
5. "EK Ez a város Live Bp 2004." http://www.youtube.com/watch?v=_ozyeoHtn5Q.
6. "EK Jó lesz Live Bp 2004." http://www.youtube.com/watch?v=R8WtA9SwAjo.
7. "EK Romolj meg Live Bp 2004." http://www.youtube.com/watch?v=K_RapdP6ItY.
8. Like rappers, the songwriter Jenő Menyhárt also fills his lyrics with local cultural references via puns. In this case, the phrase "the electric chair of desire" (*"a vágy villamosszéke"*) is a pun on the Hungarian translation of the popular play by Tennessee Williams, *A Streetcar Named Desire* (A vágy villamosa).
9. "EK Európa Kiadó Live Bp 2004." http://www.youtube.com/watch?v=5FP25Tu722s.
10. "EK Igazi hős Live Bp 2004." http://www.youtube.com/watch?v=crTSavys5kQ.
11. A whole hidden world of an unbelievably close and inept police surveillance of rock music, underground and official alike, was disclosed by Tamás Szőnyei in his 2005 book *Nyilvántartottak. Titkos szolgák a magyar rock körül, 1960–1990.*
12. József Antall's center-right coalition government (1990–1994) was the first democratically elected one in post-Socialist Hungary.
13. The most ambitious and hugely popular enterprise of the post-Socialist music scene is the *Sziget Festival*, a week-long series of musical and cultural events taking place annually on one of the Danube islands (Pepsi Sziget), Budapest, since 1993. It has been attracting hundreds of thousands visitors from all over Europe since about half of the performers are international artists representing a wide array of musical styles and performing arts. The

initiative came from a key figure of the former underground scene, Péter "Sziámi" Müller, who is also the festival's director.

14. See Péter "Sziámi" Müller, "Kamondy Ági lovag, Nirvánia megmentője," in the booklet accompanying the CD of Kamondy Ágnes, *Dalok Közép-Nirvániából* (Bahia, Budapest, 1995).

References

Adorno, Theodor W. 2002. "Why Is the New Art So Hard to Understand?" In *Essays on Music*. Ed. R. Leppert, trans. Susan H. Gillespie. Berkeley: University of California Press.
Anderson, Benedict. 2006. *Imagined Communities: Reflections on the Origins and Spread of Nationalism*. New York: Verso.
Balassa, Péter. 1994. "Ahogy esik, időszerűtlenül." *Kritika*, no.12 (December).
Benjamin, Walter. 2002. *The Arcades Project*. Trans. Howard Eiland and Kevin McLaughlin. Cambridge, MA: Harvard University Press.
Boym, Svetlana. 2001. *The Future of Nostalgia*. New York: Basic Books.
Cerulo, Karen A. 1995. *Identity Designs. The Sights and Sounds of a Nation*. New Brunswick, NJ: Rutgers University Press.
Crafts, Susan D., Daniel Cavicchi, and Charles Keil (with the Music in Daily Life Project). 1993. *My Music: Explorations of Music in Daily Life*. Middletown, CT: Wesleyan University Press.
Cushman, Thomas. 1995. *Notes from Underground: Rock Music Counterculture in Russia*. Albany: State University of New York Press.
DeNora, Tia. 2000. *Music in Everyday Life*. New York: Cambridge University Press.
Haraszti, Miklós. 1987. *The Velvet Prison: Artists Under State Socialism*. Trans. K. Landesmann and S. Landesmann, with S. Wasserman. New York: Basic Books.
Havasréti, József, and Zsolt K. Horváth, eds. 2003. *Avantgárd: underground: alternatív. Popzene, művészet és szubkulturális nyilvánosság Magyarországon*. Budapest-Pécs: Kijárat-Artpool, Department of Communication, University of Pécs.
Kenney, Padraic. 2002. *A Carnival of Revolution: Central Europe 1989*. Princeton, NJ: Princeton University Press.
Kloet, Jeroen de. 2000. "Audiences in Wonderland: The Reception of Rock Music in China." In *Changing Sounds: New Directions and Configurations in Popular Music, IASPM 1999 International Conference Proceedings*, ed. Tony Mitchell and Peter Doyle, with Bruce Johnson. Sydney: Faculty of Humanities and Social Sciences, University of Technology.
Kundera, Milan. 1987. *The Unbearable Lightness of Being*. Trans. Michael Henry Heim. New York: Harper and Row.
Lipsitz, George. 1990. *Time Passages: Collective Memory and American Popular Culture*. Minneapolis: University of Minesota Press.
Lukács, György. 1982. "Szakadék Nagyszálló." In *Esztétikai írások, 1930–45*, ed. László Sziklai, trans. Ottó Beöthy. Budapest: Kossuth Könyvkiadó.

Milun, Kathryn. 1992. "Rock Music and National Identity in Hungary." *Surface.* http://www.pum.umontreal.ca/revues/surfaces/vol1/milun/html.
Mitchell, Tony. 1996. "Mixing Pop and Politics? Rock Music in the Czech Republic." In *Popular Music and Local Identity: Rock, Pop and Rap in Europe and Oceania.* New York: Leicester University Press.
Mukerji, Chandra, and Anna Szemere, 2002. "Compliance and Resistance in Cultural Reproduction." Paper delivered at the Meeting of the American Sociological Association, Chicago.
Neumann, Iver B. 1999. *Uses of the Other: "The East" in European Identity Formation.* Minneapolis: University of Minnesota Press.
Ramet, Sabrina P., ed. 1994. *Rocking the State: Rock Music and Politics in Eastern Europe and Russia.* Boulder, CO: Westview.
Rosslyn, Felicity. 2001. "That Fox Again Review: The Laughter of Foxes: A Study of Ted Hughes." *Cambridge Quarterly* 30: 91–96.
Schudson, Michael. 1992. *Watergate in American Memory: How We Remember, Forget, and Reconstruct the Past.* New York: Basic Books.
Szemere, Anna. 2000. "'It's Yesterday's Train That's Late': Gendered Theories of Art in Postsocialist Hungary." *ArtMargins: Contemporary Central and Eastern European Visual Culture,* 6 April. http://www.artmargins.com/index.html.
———. 2001. *Up from the Underground: The Culture of Rock Music in Postsocialist Hungary.* University Park, PA: Penn State Press.
Szőnyei, Tamás. 2005. *Nyilvántartottak. Titkos szolgák a magyar rock körül, 1960–1990.* Budapest: Magyar Narancs – Tihany Rév Kiadó.
Todorova, Maria. 1997. *Imagining the Balkans.* New York: Oxford University Press.
Wicke, Peter. 1992. "The Times They Are A-changing: Rock Music and Political Change in East Germany." In *Rockin' the Boat: Mass Music and Mass Movements,* ed. R. Garofalo. Boston: South End Press.

 15

VACANT HISTORY, EMPTY SCREENS
Post-Communist German Films of the 1990s
Anke Pinkert

> Hooray, history is back from the dead!
> —Jean Beaudrillard, *The Illusion of the End*

When the Berlin Wall opened in 1989 and the GDR state collapsed, the demise of the East German film company DEFA was soon to follow. Despite the unique opportunity to realign the most critical efforts of disparate and previously divided German cinemas within new constellations, films produced after reunification tended to settle for popular appeal and mainstream fare. Responding to historical rupture by reclaiming the stabilizing effects of classical narrative and generic conventions, filmmakers supplied the domestic audience throughout the 1990s with a new wave of romantic comedies, road movies, action films, and literary adaptations (Hake 2002: 179–92). Critics have responded very differently to this popular new German cinema. Some see it as a refreshing departure from the angst-ridden agendas and romantic genius cult of the formally ambitious and politically engaged films of Fassbinder, Herzog, and Wenders and as a continuation of popular trends that started in West Germany in the mid-1980s. As Sabine Hake has pointed out, these critics are quite happy to see that recent German films, in contrast to the earlier auteur cinema, accommodate the audience and its desire for less complicated narratives of Germanness and more optimistic visions of Germany as a multicultural society (2002: 180). The hope is here that films that take up more profitable commercial interests and rely on the promotion and self-representation of new domestic film stars will finally allow German productions to compete with mainstream Hollywood movies on the domestic market. On the other hand, interlocutors, adhering to the Frankfurt School's critique of the Cultural Industry, have deemed post-Wall film as a "New German Cinema of Consensus," to use Eric Rentschler's term, a historically revisionist and affirmative cinema that, similar to the films during the restorative era of the "economic miracle" in the West in the 1950s, lacks oppositional energies and critical voices and that avoids any serious political reflection or sustained historical inquiry (2000: 263).[1]

Notably, the existence of an East(ern) German cinema before and after the opening of the Wall does not play any role in these debates, polarized around the relationship between popular and reflective cinema in a postunification culture of diversion (*Spassgesellschaft*). In that way cultural critics themselves have contributed to the erasure of an important, if not alternative, strand of postwar film history in the East, whose comparative standing in relation to West German cinema still needs to be explored (Byg 1995: 150–68; Elsaesser and Wedel 2001: 3–24; Trumpener forthcoming). The absence of East German traditions as a reference point in these critical contestations after 1989 was warranted by the dissolution of the GDR film company DEFA, whose studios for feature film, animation, and documentary production had released around eighteen fully subsidized films every year. In a twist of history, since 1990 these films have enjoyed considerable success in retrospectives abroad, including screenings of the Berlin films, the forbidden films, or director-centered series organized by the Goethe-Institut. An extensive show of DEFA films at the Museum of Modern Art in New York in 2005 sold out for each screening and reached a wide public audience.

Sociologists have argued that the dismantling of the DEFA exemplifies the worst side of the takeover of East Germany's industry and institutions by the West. In 1990, the Treuhand head, Detlef Rohweder, in charge of the reprivatization of East German industry, recognized what was actually at stake for East German film culture when he claimed, "Now that we are taking away everything from those in the East, at least we should leave them DEFA, because it is there that the consciousness of East Germany finds its artistic expression" (quoted in Naughton 2002: 60). What Rohweder might have recognized here, to paraphrase Stuart Hall, is that there is no way in which people can act, speak, create, come out from the margins and talk, or begin to reflect on their own experience unless they come from somewhere, come from some history, unless they inherit certain cultural traditions. Although East Germans never moved geographically, they migrated into a new economic, political, and cultural space, which displaced previous sets of identifications and required their reformulation and translation. Here cultural memory is crucial. But, as Andreas Huyssen reminds us, it is also "a very tenuous and fragile thing, and it needs to be buttressed with the help of institutions of documentation, preservation, and participatory debate" (1995: 84). The process by which cultural, artistic, and intellectual traditions were redistributed after 1989 was not devoid of very real desires for power and their social and discursive effects. The DEFA, like almost all cultural institutions of the GDR, appeared too dubious and inefficient to legitimately carve out a public space in which new modes of belonging in a transitional period could have been worked out. Instead, after a series of prolonged negotiations and very underpriced, the East German film company, which had been founded in the Soviet occupation zone in 1946, was sold in 1993 to a French investment firm. This sale marked the end of the career of many people involved with the DEFA; of the 2,400 staff members, only 350 were still engaged at the studios by 1997 (Naughton 2002: 54). Volker Schlöndorf, ironically, a director associated with the West's critical New German cinema, became the new head of the DEFA's successor. He envisioned Babelsberg, the town near Berlin where the DEFA studios were located, as an innovative center of European filmmaking. Responding to East German colleagues who had criticized the disbanding of the DEFA, he stated, "The name DEFA is colorless and without smell. It belongs, just like the name UFA [the German film company during the Weimar Republic and the Third Reich], to history" (quoted in Feinstein 2002: 235).

This implicit equation between the GDR and the Third Reich resonated with the overall public efforts after 1989 to create a seamless national narrative of democratic victory, spanning postwar West German society and postunification Germany. According to this trajectory, the collapse of socialism itself confirmed that the West alone had come to terms with Nazism and the Holocaust, whereas the GDR, and the anti-Fascist and Socialist films it had produced, were ideological manifestations of power and repression. I have shown elsewhere that the DEFA created complex historical imaginaries that provide insights into elegiac and critical engagements with war violence, death, and perpetration (Pinkert 2008). Recognizing these films as an alternative cultural archive that is part of, rather than excluded from, Germany's postwar transformations will require the undoing and reconfiguring of the normative constellations of the dominant national narrative of the past. But, in turn, these efforts will enable new reparative modes and relational links within a memory discourse that shuttles between two positions: on the one hand, a reconciliatory desire to account for German suffering, often at the price of eclipsing or mitigating the suffering the Germans inflicted on others (i.e., Oliver Hirschbiegel's *The Downfall,* Der Untergang, 2004; Sönke Wortmann's *The Miracle of Bern,* Das Wunder von Bern, 2003) and, on the other, a public embrace of collective shame and guilt that is not seldom characterized by a numbing detachment from rather than a postconventional engagement with the past.

Whether films produced by the DEFA after 1990 would have participated in these complex shifts of cultural memory or whether they would have devolved into localized, even provincial sites of identity productions remains mere speculation. What did emerge throughout the 1990s were the so-called post-*Wende* films—films that, in one way or another, engage with the social, political, and psychological effects of the collapse of the GDR and the end of socialism in Eastern Europe. Often these productions traverse conventional boundaries between artisan and popular sensibilities; they are produced by directors from the former East as well as the West, by filmmakers belonging to different generations, and with mixed independent and state television funding. In many ways, the thematic concerns and stylistic reorientations of post-*Wende* films resemble the situation after 1945. In line with the overall orientations of post-Wall film, some of the post-*Wende* productions, including the so-called unification films, drew on the stabilizing effects of classical narrative and genre conventions. Taking this route, Margarete von Trotta's *The Promise* (Das Versprechen, 1995), Volker Schlöndorff's *The Legend of Rita* (Die Stille nach dem Schuss, 1999), Peter Timm's *Go Trabi Go* (1991), Leander Hausmann's *On the Short End of the Sonnenallee* (Am kürzeren Ende der Sonnenallee, 1999), Wolfgang Becker's *Good Bye, Lenin!* (2003), and Frank Beyer's two-part television production *Nikolai Church* (Nikolaikirche, 1995) became modest commercial successes on the domestic and, in some cases, the international market, despite their varying cinematic styles. Hake rightly suggests that these cinematic attempts to come to terms with the Socialist past leading up to the collapse of the GDR state seem "at once more conventional in their reliance on the identificatory effects of classical narrative and more conservative in their validation of the personal in opposition to the political" (2002: 186). Melodramatic inquiries into postwar divisions, such as in Trotta's *The Promise*, where two young lovers divided by ideology are meant to be united, provide a happy ending for the nation that comes with a "post-ideological identity of a unified Germany" (2002: 189). These postideological tendencies were all too well supported by reunification comedies, such as *Go Trabi Go*, which confirmed an ahistorical sense of Western prosperity and stability through the eyes of stereotypically backward East Germans traveling through Europe.

Other post-*Wende*, or more aptly post-Communist films, already announce in their melancholy-inflected titles that they are situated in the margins of the post-Wall cinema of consensus. I am thinking here of Andreas Dresen's *Silent Country* (Stilles Land, 1992) and *Night Shapes* (Nachtgestalten, 1999); Andreas Kleinert's *Lost Landscapes* (Verlorene

Landschaften, 1992); *Outside Time* (1995); *Paths in the Night* (Wege in die Nacht, 1999); Jörg Foth's *Latest from the DaDaeR* (Letztes aus der DaDaeR, 1990); and Oskar Roehler's *No Place to Go* (Die Unberührbare, 2000). Incidentally, Roehler's film (the only director from the West in this group) had quite successful runs in Germany and at festivals abroad. Already at a first glance these films indicate a proliferation of an elegiac visual language that is underscored by stories of suicide, depression, displacement, and social decline. These affective modes, styles, and themes resonate with various cinematic projects in the two decades after the end of the war. Not unlike German postwar rubble films, if for different historically contingent reasons, these post-Communist films constituted a substitute public discourse after 1989 where the effects of a historical break, if not trauma, were played out.[2] In other words, while in most cases the East German or Socialist past never transpires in the narratives, the films nevertheless address the more complicated effects of historical loss and liberation related to the end of the GDR, which did not enter the dominant cultural discussions centered around national victory. Ironically, the phenomenon of *Ostalgie*, a nostalgic sentiment for the East, supported notions of Western success quite well and therefore the media had great interest in manufacturing such feelings of loss. Even potentially parodist renditions of nostalgia such as *Sonnenallee* and *Good Bye, Lenin!* ultimately reinforced a tendency since the 1990s to dispose of an inquiry into everyday practices in the East by transforming them into *Heimat*-folklore and post-Socialist kitsch (Boyer 2006).[3]

If German postwar film in the 1940s and 1950s had replaced the past with visions of a Socialist future or commodity culture, post-Communist and post-*Wende* films after 1989 are part and parcel of a larger postmodern moment where past and future have blended into a seemingly perpetual present. From this postideological vantage point, these films engage with and display a paralysis of the utopian imagination, "a desiring to desire," as Jameson put it succinctly (1994: 90). Within this historical vacuum, the object of historical "loss"—socialism, the GDR, anti-Fascist memory, utopian discourse—is often no longer discernible and history itself increasingly disappears into spectacle and simulation. While the more conventional narrative films align with efforts of other East European cinemas after 1989 to recover stories of individual decency in a past of oppression, the often more formally ambitious post-Communist films have focused on the vacancies created by the social and symbolic implications of the breakdown of socialism in 1989. Searching for a visual language that is more suitable to a reflective mode of filmmaking centered on crisis, post-Communist films have reworked various earlier cinematic styles, including expressionism, film noir, postwar rubble film, the DEFA's social realism, and New German Cinema's auteurism. Most notably, however, at a time when film has become mimetic and mainstream, directors such as Kleinert, Foth, Böttcher, and Roehler explore whether film can deploy a specific language that captures the vanished, empty, and absent, without simply imitating earlier postwar avant-gardist traditions and appearing to be anachronistic or even nostalgic outposts in a radically changed public sphere.[4]

In contrast to the more conventional post-*Wende* films in which fiction tends to be passed off as reality, the projects that I call "post-Communist" are more attuned to what is markedly left out from the postunification national imaginary. The degree to which they aim at a workable compromise between commercial and art cinema differs, yet they all register the vanishing of an often amorphous past, the movement of something passing away, something that is still felt but can no longer be comprehended in the present. Jörg Foth's *Latest from the DaDaeR* (1990), one of the last films produced by the DEFA, deploys an episodic style to capture the traces of the GDR's decay and eventual dissolution. Drawing on musical cabaret-revue, Foth charts the journey of two clown-like characters (both former GDR cabaret performers) through the ruins of the GDR. The various sites they traverse stand in "for the utter bankruptcy of the social project and the emptiness of its utopian promise" (Feinstein 2002: 239). The film echoes the proliferation of disconnected and unused urban locations in early postwar European cinemas. The camera, over and again, pans defunct industrial sites, garbage dumps, waste grounds, interiors of slaughter houses, abandoned railways, and desolate graveyards. The result is a phantasmic landscape that comments not only on the decrepit state of the GDR apparatus but also on the rejection of Socialist histories from Western teleologies after 1989. The film ends with a shot of a gravestone bearing the inscription "Farewell" (*Auf Wiedersehen*), a poignant closure that marks the vanishing point of the GDR.

Although a sense of loss is palpable in many of these post-Communist films of the early 1990s, none goes so far as to regret the demise of the GDR or to nostalgically reinvest in its recuperation. Rather they dramatize the modes of disappearance themselves as a source of historical knowledge and aesthetic pleasure. This is particularly poignant in Jürgen Böttcher's *The Wall* (Die Mauer, 1990), produced by the DEFA studio for Documentary Film in 1990. Devoid of any voice-over commentary, the film captures the actual dismantling of the Wall and the public spectacles surrounding unification. Critics have praised the documentary for its detachment from the euphoric displays of the changes in 1989. The camera is positioned outside of the celebrating crowd near the Brandenburg Gate, and for most of the film's ninety minutes, it simply records people from all over the world chiseling away the Wall. By the end all that is left in the powerful final shot are fragments of the wall "to be stored like sculptures or gravestones in bizarre museum-like yards." Helen Hughes and Martin Brady suggest that the film comments in this way on how a symbol of world separation has metamorphosed into a target for collectors of objects, memories, and experiences of the past (1995: 281). At the same time that the film renders visible how the present passes into history, it also reveals how film participates in the process of creating gaps, phantoms, and slippages in collective memory. Projecting documentary footage of the erection of the Berlin Wall in 1961 onto the remains of the actual Wall, the film brings home this point most palpably. While we hear the clicking off-screen sounds of an old-fashioned film projector, compilations of archive footage show men and woman desperately attempting to get through the newly set up wired fences and other people watching them on both sides of the border. As these images move in and out of focus on the unevenly textured surface of the Wall, they morph into specters that shift across different temporalities. In this way, it becomes possible for us to feel that Germany's division and the global Cold War history is indeed over. But as these images hover over the scarred surface of the Wall covered with red graffiti blotches, they also suggest that their "original" historical meaning, especially with respect to stories of individual suffering, will soon be replaced by new, more triumphant national narratives in which postwar divisions and the historical reasons that led to it might slip away.

Other less stylized post-Communist films, including Michael Klier's *Ostkreuz* (1991), *Heidi M.* (2001), and Andreas Dresen's *Night Shapes* (Nachtgestalten, 1999) and *Policewoman* (Die Polizistin, 2000), take a more socially critical approach to the transformations in the nineties. While they differ in the degree to which they attempt to combine commercial, realist, and art cinema, they all draw attention to the underclass of urban outsiders and their perilous existence on the fringes of society. The displaced characters, homeless, foreigners, immigrants, unemployed, and prostitutes pass through rough and constantly changing urban places. Among them are former East Germans pushed to the margins of prosperity, but their specific pasts or the historical changes in 1989 are rarely elaborated, so that these protagonists appear in a larger postindustrial landscape of dislocation, economic disparity, and ethnic exclusion. The transience of the past is vividly staged in Klier's *Ost-*

kreuz, where the long-shots of abandoned industrial sites and container homes reflect the desolation and hopelessness of the main characters, including a middle-aged woman who left the GDR via Hungary shortly before the fall of the Wall. Drifting through the city of Berlin whose borders have been opened after all, her life continues to be equally depressing when she is unable to find a job and a permanent home for herself and her teenage daughter. The melancholic long-shots of barren wastelands, the slow-paced rhythm, and close observation of social detail are indebted to Klier's own work on Rossellini, Wenders, and Truffaut that goes back to the beginning of his film career in West Germany in the 1970s. The recurring urban scenes of young people, stranded and roaming around in deserted buildings, echo postwar rubble films such as *Somewhere in Berlin* (Irgendwo in Berlin, 1946) or *Corona 1–2-3* (1948), which, in turn, were influenced by Weimar street films. Drawing on these different traditions, *Ostkreuz* visually postulates another Zero Hour, commonly ascribed to the imaginary tabula rasa following the Second World War, but in contrast to the earlier projects, the historical referents of loss or change have almost completely disappeared. The various pasts, including the Cold War, Germany's division, modernity, or the Socialist project, let alone WWII and Nazism seem gone once and for all in these postmodern imaginaries. Neither intentionally forgotten, nor unconsciously repressed, the signs of the past simply do not have enough gravity to take hold in the present. Hughes and Brady put it nicely: retrospection is dependent on prospection (1995: 281). A view toward the future could enable an understanding of the past as past and thus as something having really taken place; yet this is foreclosed at a moment of historical stasis, where the utopian imagination is paralyzed.

Some of the most radical elegiac allegories of loss and displacement after 1989 are provided by Andreas Kleinert's *Paths in the Night* (1999) and Roehler's *No Place to Go* (2000). Kleinert was born in 1962 in East Germany, where he also worked as assistant director for DEFA; Roehler, born in 1959, grew up in the West. Recalling, most radically, the austere black-and-white cinematography and lyrical minimalism of modernist European cinema, they both spiral back in time through simulations of earlier cinematic traditions responding to the postwar situation after 1945. Both films revolve around a character who suffers from a crisis of identification that is related to the loss of a certain social status no longer enjoyed after the collapse of the Wall. In *No Place to Go,* Hanna Flanders, a West German writer and strong believer in Lenin, whose books were only printed in the GDR, loses her only publisher; the protagonist of Kleinert's film, Walter, has lost his job as a manager when the factory where he worked in East Berlin closed down. The films track the psychic disorientation of their heroes through a political and social landscape they no longer understand. Similar to other post-Communist films, the time before 1989 remains highly elusive here; all the while a self-reflexive perspective on modes of historical amnesia prevails. In early postwar DEFA films, the "crisis of symbolic investiture" (Bourdieu), whereby an individual is filled with a symbolic mandate that informs his or her identity in the community, was played out with respect to war returnees who could not be integrated into narratives of anti-Fascist and postwar renewal. In the post-1989 films, the tear in the symbolic structure creates in the protagonists feelings of anomie and anxieties associated with a more diffuse sense of absence rather than a specifiable, historically marked loss. Both films show that the collapse of symbolic power and authority can be experienced within the most intimate core of one's being, involving states of paranoia, depression, and suicide (see Santner 1996: xii).

Paths in the Night opens with slowly paced shots over derelict furnaces at a deserted industrial plant. The industrial rubble and decrepit factories are remnants of the GDR, which give expression to a depressive state of emotion. The only thing that has remained since Walter became unemployed is his commanding tone and his former claim to authority. The only people who accept this authority are the two youths with whom he hangs out to restore order in the underground every night. The film's settings are desolate and ghostly, and when the plant site recurs at night in dimly lit on-location shots, it closely resembles the stylized ruins in the rubble films immediately after the war. Walter refers to these abandoned places as the "realm of death," and nevertheless it is here that he returns when he is overcome by hopelessness. Similar to earlier cinematic representations of the war returnee, this protagonist who was associated with the previous regime roams the debris left behind by history, but no new identificatory models are available to fill the palpable vacuum. This is brought home through long-shots of wastelands in which Walter witnesses the detonation of housing complexes and is minimized by the vastness of distant vision.

These scenes attain spectral qualities that echo the melancholic dramaturgies in East and West German postwar films of the sixties, such as Wolf's *I Was Nineteen* (Ich war Neunzehn, 1968), Carow's *The Russians Are Coming* (Die Russen kommen, 1968/87), or Kluge's *Yesterday's Girl* (Abschied von Gestern, 1968), which, in turn, were indebted to the various European New Waves related to the shattering of the action image after 1945. Even as the rich histories of postwar political and cinematic division between East and West Germany, East and West Europe, never enter the diegetic or discursive realm of *Paths in the Night*, they are embodied and reanimated by the actor Hilmar Thate, who plays Walter. Thate, born in 1931 and originally from the East, appeared in a number of anti-Fascist DEFA productions, such as Kurt Mätzig and Günther Reisch's film about the November revolution, *The Song of the Seamen* (Das Lied der Matrosen, 1958), and Gerhard Klein's *The Gleiwitz Case* (Der Fall Gleiwitz, 1961). The latter dramatizes the 1939 surprise attack by a Nazi unit on a radio station in Poland, which started the Second World War, and in which Thate played a concentration camp inmate. Most notably, Thate also acted in Konrad Wolf's *Professor Mamlock* (1961) as the Communist son of a German-Jewish physician who refuses to join the anti-Fascist resistance and in the end commits suicide. After protesting the expulsion of the Marxist dissident Wolfgang Biermann from the GDR in 1976, Thate left for the West where, not without difficulty, he began to start a new career as theater and film actor. In 1982, Fassbinder chose the actor for the part of the sports journalist Robert Krohn in his film *Veronica Voss* (Die Sehnsucht der Veronika Voss, 1982), which belonged to his postwar trilogy and attempted to address the Nazi past that had as yet not been worked through by the West German public. These are the crucial, highly mediated historical and cinematic reference points of Kleinert's "lost landscapes," which is also the title of another post-*Wende* film by him. But the distance the viewer needs to travel to recapture these traces of the postwar past speaks to a general shift where historical losses are replaced by the disappearance of history itself. In this postmodern context the film shows how historical suffering slides into structural suffering, rendering specific mourning tasks related to historical losses and agencies ineffectual or obsolete.[5] In the final scene of the film, Walter returns to the plant, and echoing gun shots imply that he has taken his life.

At a time when the domestic film market privileged lighter fare and Kleinert's pensive films were limited in circulation, Oskar Roehler's *No Place to Go* (1999) was hailed as the best German film since Rainer Werner Fassbinder. This renaissance of the New German Cinema was described by the media as strangely out of step: "an irritating, strangely alien movie experience that seems to be out of time. Nothing about this film is in keeping with the time: not its subject matter, the journey toward death of a failed writer who is addicted to pills and nicotine; not its aesthetic, which conjures memories of the halcyon days of German films without becoming completely imitative; not the black and white shots with their calm angles devoted entirely to the actors" (Spiegel 2000). It is in this twilight zone of cinematic memory that Roehler's film is transformed from a personal, autobiographical account of his mother's life into a complex reflection on the various postmodern "endings" reinforced in 1989, including the end of history, ideology, and possibly art cinema itself. Oskar Roehler's mother, the writer Gisela Elsner, became famous in the 1960s for her radical leftist critiques and stylistically dense novels. Her popularity declined in the 1970s to the point that Rowohlt canceled her book contract, and Elsner, meanwhile a chain smoker, tablet addict, and washed-out bohemian, was able to publish only in the GDR. In 1992 Elsner killed herself, jumping out of a window from a Munich hospital where she had lived in total isolation. Roehler condenses this story into a minimalist station drama of deferred death that chronicles the last week of the protagonist Hanna Flanders (played by Hannelore Elsner), including the fall of the Wall; her spontaneous visit to East Berlin, where she encounters various strangers; and her restless travels through Germany that end in suicide.

In contrast to the celebrations in the media, the fall of the Wall appears as a historical end point in the opening of Roehler's film: like an *Abspann*, the credits run over an original soundtrack of muffled voices that applaud the toppling of the border. Next we see Hanna in her living room near a television broadcasting the end of Germany's postwar division. From the outset Hanna is overwhelmed by anxieties related to the loss of ideological certainties that have shaped her political identity and sense of self. Instead of chiming into the joy of the East Germans depicted on TV, we see her on the phone with a friend whom she tells that she finds the desire of the East Germans for Western consumer goods repulsive and that she intends to kill herself now (this is delayed though until the end of the film). In the opening scene, the camera captures the end of a collective project and potentially Hanna's life in an abstract image of symbolic loss. An extreme close-up of the arsenic bottle she holds in her hand creates an empty circle, hole, or gap that resembles the barrel of a gun or a camera lens but also the vacant symbol of power left behind on East German buildings and GDR flags.

A self-reflexive interest in the mediality of the cinematic apparatus is a convention of art cinema in general and the New German Cinema in particular. In the context of post-1989, however, the film's fascination with "imaging"—with carefully structured frames, camera distances, lighting, stark black-and-white photography, and calculated minimalist acting—addresses the issues of belief, ideality, and ideology that had been expelled from the post-utopian world of the 1990s. Here, *No Place to Go* engages with both the mode of loss, which is situated on the historical level and is the consequence of particular events, *and* the mode of lack, the void central to the subject's foundational psychic structure (LaCapra 2001: 64). Following the explicit, if perhaps imperceptible, visual reference to historical suffering and structural absences in the opening frame, we later see pictures on Hanna's walls that capture Lenin and Russian revolutionaries in front of the Kremlin. Interviews with a young journalist reveal her political convictions and involvement in the leftist movements of the sixties. This positioning of Hanna's subjectivity within grand ideological narratives of twentieth-century history and their various failures is undercut by the film's and Hanna's own obsession with her image. In many scenes the protagonist appears with an iconic black Cleopatra wig and with dramatic makeup that makes her look pale and accentuates her eyes with dark shadows. This masquerade and the exchange of mirror images through which it emerges dramatize her crisis of identification through issues of excess and spectacle related to lack. In other words, historical loss related to the failures of ideology and political identifications are repositioned within the psychic workings of lack that organize desire. The lesson seems to be that people might seek strong identifications with collective causes, yet in the end these investments are incapable of recapturing the real fullness whose loss is the price of being a subject in the world.

That Hanna's masquerade should indeed be read not only as a literal armoring of an unprotected self but indeed as the covering of a gap within the psychic structure is revealed in her fear of bodily decomposition. How this notion haunts her idealization becomes particularly clear in an exchange with her former husband. Explaining to him why she cannot bear to take off her wig or be touched, she says: "I am afraid that it will go 'Pop!' when you lie down on top of me. That I will burst like a potato puff. And all the fluffiness will come out in a cloud." On one level, this metaphor refers to Hanna's self-destructive addiction to cigarettes and foreshadows her literal death. However, in the larger context of the film's concern with transpositions between historical and structural suffering or trauma, Hanna's comment needs to be situated on the level of fantasy. The fear of internal decomposing, of being made up of dust or ashes—of being dead and wasting away—plays out the psychic trajectory of idealization, a momentary exposure of the morbidity that leads from self-idealization to self-disgust (see Silverman 1996: 68). Attesting to the unavoidable imbrications of the imaginary and the symbolic, Hanna's fantasy of decomposition also dramatizes the breakdown of the performative magic when an attributed social role fails to produce identification (see Santner 1996: 12).

Such a crisis, the experience of historical loss as the foundational logic of psychic lack (and the duplicity of cinema within it), is of course also at the heart of Fassbinder's film *Veronica Voss*, based on the story of the former UFA star Sibylle Schmitz. After the collapse of Nazi Germany,

Voss can no longer gain a foothold in postwar West German society; she turns into a drug addict and ends up killing herself. Roehler's film abounds with visual references to Fassbinder's movie. Rehearsing some of Fassbinder's earlier concerns, it revolves around a longer historical axis that leads back to UFA film, National Socialism, and postwar West German society. Both, *Veronica Voss* and *No Place to Go*, reveal what the melancholy of their characters obfuscates, the fact that the historical object that appears to be lost is lacking from the very beginning. From Roehler's vantage point of the late 1990s, however, this particular take on ideology formation also means that the historically specific aspects of the Socialist project and the Western left have been rendered inaccessible and moved out of view.[6]

When by the end of the film all of Hanna's plans to reconnect with people have fallen through, she gets drunk and collapses in the streets of Munich. The final scenes at a hospital appear highly surreal as if we have finally entered into a "no man's land" where historical time and space have been abolished. Hanna is diagnosed with a *Raucherbein* (smoker's leg) and told that one of her legs will have to be amputated if she does not stop her addiction. In this moment the protagonist's failure to affirm the unity of her self—through an image, through the Cleopatra masquerade—comes full circle. Threatened by the amputation of her leg, her fantasy or fear of corporeal disintegration is literalized through the evocation of a fragmented body, incidentally also recalling meanings of war injury.[7] The last sequence repeats the film's preoccupation with operations of imaging and idealization through carefully composed shots and double framings. Hanna hides out in a restroom stall on the upper floor of the hospital to smoke her last cigarette. Captured in a last extreme close-up, the claustrophobic closeness by which the camera zooms in on her face marks a deficiency in relation to what can be seen. When she gets up to approach the wide-open window, she is enveloped in overexposed light that is most reminiscent of Fassbinder's *Veronica Voss* (see Elsaesser 1996: 114). Fassbinder's shadowless, white mis-en-scène allegorized a drowning out of past memories related to the Nazi past through various compensatory addictions; that is, it was invested in a critical project of examining, if not recuperating those memories and agencies. The closing scene of Roehler's *No Place to Go* two decades later points into a very different direction. Hanna rests for a moment on the edge of the windowsill and then throws herself sideward like a *Kippfigur* beyond the threshold of the visible world.[8] Hannah's body is sucked into the rays of light toward a void. The disconnected melancholy spaces lived by the heroine are reunited by the empty space of nonbeing. For a second we are left with a white, overexposed frame of flickering light. This vacancy on the screen renders the end point of the grand narratives, historical fractures, and postwar cinematic divisions of the twentieth century. But the wavering whiteness continuing fluidly out of frame also creates an opening toward the reemergence of new universal visions.

Notes

Pinkert, Anke. 2008. *Film and Memory in East Germany*. Bloomington: Indiana University Press. Reprinted with permission of Indiana University Press.

1. The polarization between commercial and artisan production, popular culture and high art underlying these discussions has been challenged by Bergfelder, Carter, and Goektuerk (2003).
2. For the *Wende* as trauma see Lewis 1995.
3. For the nostalgic co-optation of loss by Western artists before 1989 see Scribner 2003: 13–27.
4. For these earlier trends related to the postwar situation see Deleuze 1986: 120.
5. For these tendencies in West German film of the seventies see Santner (1990).
6. Paul Cooke, in contrast, reads the film rather differently as a partial rehabilitation of the 1960s movements and ideals (2004).
7. See Silverman's discussion of addiction in Ulrike Ottinger's *Bildnis einer Trinkerin* (Ticket of No Return), which can here also serve as a reference point of previous strands in West German cinema (1996: 42–44).
8. The term *Kippfigur*, a figure whose appearance changes depending on the perspective of the viewer, was used by a reviewer.

References

Bergfelder, Tim, Erica Carter, and Deniz Goektuerk. Eds. 2003. *The German Film Book*. Berkeley: BFI/University of California Press.
Boyer, Dominic. 2006. "Ostalgie and the Politics of the Future in Eastern Germany." *Public Culture* 18: 361–81.
Byg, Barton. 1995. "German Unification and the Cinema of the Former German Democratic Republic." *Michigan Germanic Studies* 21 (1.2): 150–68.
Cooke, Paul. 2004. "Whatever Happened to Veronica Voss? Rehabilitating the "68ers" and the Problem of *Westalgie*." *German Studies Review* 27 (1): 33–45.
Deleuze, Gilles. 1986. *Cinema 1: The Movement-Image*. Minneapolis: University of Minnesota Press.
Elsaesser, Thomas. 1996. *Fassbinder's Germany: History, Identity, Subject*. Amsterdam: Amsterdam University Press.
Elsaesser, Thomas, and Michael Wedel. 2001. "Defining DEFA's Historical Imaginary: The Films of Konrad Wolf." *New German Critique* 82: 3–24.

Feinstein, Joshua. 2002. *The Triumph of the Ordinary: Depictions of Daily Life in the East German Cinema, 1949–1989*. Chapel Hill: University of North Carolina Press.

Hake, Sabine. 2002. *German National Cinema*. London: Routledge.

Hughes, Helen, and Martin Brady. 1995. "German Film after the Wende." In *The New Germany: Social, Political, and Cultural Challenges of Unification*, ed. D. Lewis and J. R. P. McKenzie. Exeter, UK: University of Exeter Press.

Huyssen, Andreas. 1995. "Nation, Race, and Immigration: German Identities after Unification." In *Twilight Memories: Marking Time in a Culture of Amnesia*. London: Routledge.

Jameson, Fredric. 1994. *The Seeds of Time*. New York: Columbia University Press.

LaCapra, Dominic. 2001. *Writing History, Writing Trauma*. Baltimore: Johns Hopkins University Press.

Lewis, Alison. 1995. "Unity Begins Together: Analyzing the Trauma of German Unification." *New German Critique* 64: 135–59.

Naughton, Leonie. 2002. *That Was the Wild East: Film Culture, Unification, and the "New" Germany*. Ann Arbor: University of Michigan Press.

Pinkert, Anke. 2008. *Film and Memory in East Germany*. Bloomington: Indiana University Press.

Rentschler, Eric. 2000. "From New German Cinema to Post-Wall Cinema of Consensus." In *Cinema & Nation*, ed. Mette Hjort and Scott Mackenzie. London: Routledge.

Santner, Eric. 1990. *Stranded Objects: Mourning, Memory, and Film in Postwar Germany*. Ithaca, NY: Cornell University Press.

———. 1996. *My Own Private Germany: Daniel Paul Schreber's Secret History of Modernity*. Princeton, NJ: Princeton University Press.

Scribner, Charity. 2003. *Requiem for Communism*. Cambridge, MA: MIT Press.

Silverman, Kaja. 1996. *The Threshold of the Visible World*. London: Routledge.

Spiegel, Hubert. 2000. "Königin Lear auf der Heide," *Frankfurter Allgemeine* 20/21 (April).

Trumpener, Katie. Forthcoming. *Divided Screens: Postwar Cinema in the East and West*. Princeton, NJ: Princeton University Press.

# Postscript

Zsuzsa Gille

Our volume has opened a wide panorama of memory genres in half a dozen post-Socialist countries—a scene that is equally structured and fluid, equally overdetermined and constructed, equally local and global, that we may therefore refer to as a memoryscape.[1] We have watched East German, Romanian, Bulgarian, and Hungarian movies; we have listened to Bulgarian popfolk and Hungarian and Romanian underground rock; we have conversed with Russian and Hungarian artists, Bosnian émigrés, Bulgarian teachers, and veterans of the former Yugoslav army (JNA); we visited museums and monuments, and read novels and mainstream evaluations of all these memory practices. We have heard from people who wanted to forget, who wanted to remember, who thought the past is not really past, and those who wanted to "come to terms with the past," whatever that means. Even within the same spatial and temporal contexts we have identified different emotional and political attitudes to the past and to its relationship to the present. In terms of emotions we have identified a wide array of feelings ranging from self-irony and mockery to melancholy, grief, alienation, depression, anxiety, and trauma. And of course, there are those who feel no nostalgia whatsoever, though they may still engage in other memory work.

It is, however, not this empirical diversity that exposes what Dominic Boyer in this volume calls the heteroglossia of nostalgia, but rather the fact that the object of longing also varies widely. What the JNA veterans expressed through talks of brotherhood in Petrovic's essay is missing the collective unity of the past, and in other essays, too, such as Scarboro's, Berdahl's and Buric's, we overhear a sense of loss of a certain social proximity, even uniformity. In Scarboro's essay, late Communist memoirs mourn the enthusiasm of the early Communist youth brigades, the equalized and equally shared poverty, and the sense of total absorption of the individual into the collective. In Buric's interviews with Bosnian émigrés, a loss talked about is the "peaceful coexistence" of different ethnicities in Tito's Yugoslavia, while in Berdahl's interpretation of *Good Bye, Lenin!* one sees a grief over one's country and shared way of life that disappeared overnight.

Closely related to such issues of subjectivity and collectivity is the search for a lost authenticity or a clearer, more homogenous sense of identity, as expressed in Szemere's and Nadkarni's Hungarian cases. In both cases, the Socialist past provides the test of collective authenticity that the present cannot live up to. There is a striking contrast between these two Hungarian narratives and the two Romanian ones by Popescu-Sandu and Georgescu. It seems that the civil society that developed in Hungary, however constrained, actually made certain opposition and independence possible in the arts, thus allowing a sense of authenticity under state socialism—one that is now threatened by commodification and Westernization. In contrast, we see no such longing by the same generation of artists for Ceauşescu's Romania, where the choices one had to make were more limited and thus now invalidated. As Popescu-Sandu forcefully argues, the Communist past here is doubly negated: first, it was a life that produced no credible and shared knowledge of itself independent of the official self-narratives, and second, it is now silenced and forced to oblivion to create a "clean break." However, a past that is not accessible cannot be properly worked through, and in such circumstances, and in the absence of a legitimate and authentic author(ity), inventing the past is a very difficult, if not impossible, task—an example of mythical blockage. While in Hungary it was under socialism that rock musicians invoked the image of the living dead and called on Hungarians to wake up (see Szemere), in Romania, it is their post-Socialist counterparts that employ such metaphors (see Popescu-Sandu). While in Hungary it was in the 1980s that artists pointed to the "bald censor sitting in one's head" (see Szemere), in Romania, it is in the 1990s that rock musicians assert that "Ceauşescu is in me, he is in you" and that "each of us carries him within today" (see Georgescu).

This brief comparison allows us to assert that while nostalgia is heteroglossic, it is not omnivalent; that is, it cannot mean everything for everybody. The "objective" features of the Socialist past (in this case, the reach or severity of totalitarianism) do limit individuals' memory work however subjective the experience that memory is based on may be. Furthermore, the realities of the past and of the present also influence where the fault lines of memory work fall. Several authors call attention to conflicts in recollections of the last half-century, some using the binary "official" and "unofficial" memory, others presenting a more fragmented memoryscape. Among the latter, Buric finds that the present post-Socialist, postwar, and perhaps even post-9/11 reality significantly colors the way in which Tito is evaluated by young Bosnian Muslims. For the older generation, as mentioned above, Socialist ethnic federalism was peaceful and progressive. However, young Bosnians, who see that era through the lens of ethnic cleansing and violence, argue that socialism's primary feature was that it was oppressive to those practicing Islam. This single aspect of Tito's regime is sufficient to prevent Yugo-nostalgia.

Many contributors to this volume have called attention to other types of conflict, all of whom argued that the various memory practices that are often conflated and labeled as post-Communist nostalgia are in fact oppositional and even antisystemic in nature. Bulgarian high school teachers assert that while the content of the history books they teach may have changed, they themselves have maintained their critical pedagogical methods they developed originally under state socialism in order to foment open-mindedness and critical thinking skills in students. While this may be seen as an ideologically neutral position, Pilbrow convincingly argues, it expresses the teachers' conviction that the post-Socialist and "European" present needs no less questioning than did the Socialist past—an attitude that current self-congratulatory liberalism and new exclusivist nationalism surely would not endorse. Berdahl, too, presents two contradictory attitudes to the GDR: one that wants to "put it to rest," the other arguing that some aspects of the East German regime are worthy of preservation or at least remembering in a positive light. According to Boyer, those who are the most critical of this latter position, commonly and deridingly labeled as *Ostalgie*, are not West Germans but rather the liberal *Ossie* elite, who see in it a dangerous inertia preventing former East Germans from making the adjustments necessary for a successful capitalist future.

But what does this "putting the past to rest" entail? Not mentioning the past at all or talking it over exactly in order to be able to put it to rest, to provide a so-called closure? And do people who propose putting the past to rest tend to fall on a specific—as some of our authors imply, the right-wing—spectrum of post-Socialist politics? As we have seen in Georgescu's and Popescu-Sandu's treatment of Romanian popular music, talk of Ceaușescu is meant to work through or invent the past and to call attention to continuities between that oppressive regime and the present one. Here opponents of such references to the former dictator are recruited not only from the ruling elite that tries to mask its ties to the Communist regime but also from young people on the opposite end of the political spectrum who are simply disgusted by "C" and feel a nauseating oversaturation with talks of "C."

If indeed people from different walks of life and of opposing political viewpoints would rather just silence the past, can we argue that what may be seen as the regurgitation of a past can still be therapeutic even if that past is "shameful"? Does dwelling on past disgraces provide a healthy closure or does it rub salt in raw wounds? Does it thereby prevent the consolidation of a positive self-image of a post-Socialist nation—a collective that is desperate to ground itself after the damage Communist ideology or ethnic cleansing did to it? Schwandner-Sievers demonstrates that in Kosovo, the Albanian nationalist elite opted for the latter when it decided to memorialize not the victims but the victors of the war, not the reprehensible or humiliating but the proud and patriotic acts of armed combat. The thorniest problem with choosing the second route—that is, memorializing in the interest of national strength—is that it might lead to further conflict. We must remember that, after all, just like present Albanian efforts "to control the commemorative discourse and populate it with one's own fraction's 'war heroes' and 'martyrs,' rather than others," as Schwandner-Sievers puts it, the Yugoslav wars of the 1990s also started with laying claim to territories symbolizing national history and identity. Perhaps it is for this reason that through their projects, artists questioned both the new Albanian nationalist memory discourse and the UN peacekeeping administration that for them bore ominous similarities with Tito's oppression of Albanians. The postwar and preindependence Kosovar memoryscape, however, is further complicated by the existence of a privately lurking and still shunned Yugo-nostalgia that has much to do with gender and patriarchy—an issue I will return to below.

Murav, as if pointing to a temporal aspect of the heteroglossia of memory work, analyzes memory conflicts not between different actors but between two perspectives of the same Jewish Russian author, Melikhov, as expressed in his 1994 *Exile from Eden* and 2004 *Red Zion*. She demonstrates that the first novel focuses on critical self-dissociation from Jewish identity exemplifying what Boym calls ironic nostalgia. The later work in contrast presents Jewish self-reconstruction as possible and desirable, a form of memory that is akin to Boym's restorative nostalgia. The first novel, appearing under the author's Russified name, expresses shame, disorientation, and the discrediting of stable identities or, if you will, metanarratives, accompanying the collapse of the Soviet Union. The novel published ten years later under the author's Jewish name, Meilakhs, however, gives voice to a hope in the possibility and meaningfulness of Jewish identity, as at the end of *Red Zion* the protagonist fulfills his lifelong dream by returning to the Soviet Jewish homeland, Birobidzhan. In Murav's distinction, irony, rhyming with postmodernism, is contrasted with restorative nostalgia, which reaffirms the previously dethroned Truth, the rightness of the Soviet past, and thus modernism.

Melikhov's case poses another fascinating question for students of memory. What difference does time, the days, months, and years passed since the collapse of the old regime, make for remembering the past? Petrovic, Murav, and Creed argue that in order for restorative nostalgia to take hold of one's memories, the longed-for past must be irrevocably over. It is not until the impossibility of the revival of the Soviet Union and the Socialist bloc becomes clear that a sense of loss and longing for the Communist past is publicly shared. Creed, based on his fieldwork in Bulgaria, adds another condition. It is not enough for the return to socialism to become impossible, but there also has to be some tangible improvement in everyday life for post-Communist nostalgia to emerge. This might explain, as Creed astutely observes, why nostalgia emerged so much earlier in the former GDR than in other post-Socialist countries. There, the impossibility of remaking the GDR became obvious within weeks of the opening of the Berlin Wall, and though East Germans are still much worse off economically than their Western counterparts almost twenty years after German unification, at least the possibility for higher living standards became obvious sooner than in countries further east. In contrast, the continuity in the Communist and post-Communist elites in Romania—that is, the lack of a clear break with the past—explains the mentioned absence of restorative nostalgia in that country.

The necessity of this time lag points to another aspect of post-Communist nostalgia that several of this volume's essays emphasize, namely, its commodification. With time, nostalgia objects such as medals, clothes, emblematic toys, and home décor items lose their ideological connotations, and in return, as Creed argues, their production for sale increasingly associates them with capitalism. The commodification of nostalgia makes a return to socialism even more unlikely. As Nadkarni also argues, "At the same time, the marketing of this nostalgia also reinforced current values by commodifying these relics and subjecting them to a contemporary market logic—thus legitimizing the often-disappointing experience of transition itself." A further evidence for this connection between capitalism and post-Communist nostalgia is provided by Berdahl's and Petrovic's stories; it was the marketers of the films they analyze that mobilized Communist symbols and icons, and not the artistic creators of the movies. By overexposing, commodifying, and thus co-opting Socialist-era symbols, "nostalgia becomes a resource for the expansion of capitalism," as Creed succinctly puts it.

With this thesis we have arrived at the key question of post-Communist nostalgia, namely, its political content. Does nostalgia express or mask a certain politics? If so, what ideology or what political agenda constitutes nostalgia? There is much disagreement over this question among the authors of this volume—one that cannot be explained with differences in empirical contexts. Buric, Berdahl, and Petrovic argue that the positive recollections of socialism give voice to the negative experiences of postsocialism otherwise silenced in public discourse and provide a critique of retraditionalization and fragmentation. In a similar vein, Buchanan, in her study of Bulgarian popfolk, argues that borrowing from Socialist-era cultural genres, even if ironically, expresses disorientation, dispossession, and disempowerment. The shared object of longing in all of these cases is modernity in its various guises—secularism (Buric); universalism and cosmopolitanism (Buric, Schwandner-Sievers, Petrovic, Murav); the promise of well-being, progress, equality, and a strong, sovereign nation-state (Berdahl, Murav, Creed, Boyer, Scarboro). It is because of this political content that Creed and Berdahl argue that post-Communist nostalgia is not "mere" nostalgia, but neither is it false consciousness—rather, it is social critique, however confused, hidden, subtle, or cautious.

Nadkarni, however, based on her rich case study of Hungary, parts company with these authors and argues that nostalgia can never be political because it remains limited to the private realm (I would add, "private" in two senses: the subjective and highly particular realm of personal memories, and the realm of nostalgic commodities, produced by private producers for private economic benefit). Furthermore, she argues that this aspect of nostalgia expresses a harmful legacy of state socialism: the distrust of the public sphere, and thus politics, and a personal ethics whose imperative was to avoid that realm. Another feature of post-Communist nostalgia, here mostly analyzed through Hungarian movies, makes this proposition even more convincing. Nadkarni, drawing on Fehérváry, proposes that there are both a simultaneity and a structural isomorphism in post-1989 nostalgic narratives and filmic narratives of coming of age. This theme has emerged in the volume's other contributions as the loss of utopia and as a sense of losing one's innocence. The problem of analogizing the private and the public coming of age for Nadkarni is the underlying assumption that this passage from communism to capitalism, while painful, is natural, necessary, and thus inevitable. Furthermore, this analogy testifies to the persistence of characterizing Socialist citizens as childlike, a- or prepolitical. Indeed, in Nadkarni's fascinating example, the post-Communist Kádárist Worker's Party failed in translating popular nostalgia for communism into a feasible and appealing political agenda. Popescu-Sandu documents a similar paralysis in politicizing memory in Romania both by those in government and those outside it. Petrovic too finds that nostalgic recollections of the Yugoslav National Army avoid mentioning the war, thus valorizing interethnic male bonding and suppressing the political meaning of the army. In sum, rather than interpreting nostalgia as political and trying to decipher the political content of nostalgia, as many of our contributors do, we may be better off pitching our analysis at a higher level of signification by arguing that the very existence of nostalgia symbolizes the evasion of talking about the past in the public sphere and in political terms.

Is it possible indeed that what others have described as the conflict between official, sanctioned talk of communism on the one hand and the oppositional or alternative memory practice of those outside power is nothing more than the generic and universally applicable difference between state history and private memory or between a from-above and from-below view with no inherent political valence? Have we conflated the scalar with the political? I do not think so. In fact by the end of her chapter, Nadkarni herself points to a possible politicization of nostalgia. What nostalgia achieves, she says, is that it creates a register of cultural inheritance that provides the building blocks of a distinctive, authentic, and honorable national identity capable of standing up to both the Soviets and the West. Pilbrow makes visible a similar connection between the individual and the national, expressing a hope that private memory practices may "add up to" or may aggregate into a collective sense of authenticity and self-esteem. He beautifully elaborates how in times of a nation's collective humiliation (through the discrediting and discounting of its past among others) individuals' renarrate their pasts and reassert the dignity and autonomy they carved out for themselves with great effort during socialism; such private and particular memory practices may be the only way in which the national collective can itself survive and eventually rejuvenate itself. Pinkert, evoking Stuart Hall, and Petrovic, quoting Belgrade journalist, Teofil Pancic, make this point more generally, but so eloquently, when they argue that "there is no way in which people can act, speak, create, come out of the margins and talk, or begin to reflect on their own experience unless they come from somewhere, come from some history, unless they inherit certain cultural traditions" (Pinkert). That is, talk of the past, though some may dismiss it as nostalgia, provides evidence that "we were and remained somewhere and someone" (Pančić 2004, quoted by Petrovic).

But who is this someone? Is it a straw man, an ideal type, an average? Can everyone equally participate in crafting this identity that might just save the collective or the nation? Some of our authors suggest a negative answer. Of course, already the assumption that the private may be scaled up to the public suggests a liberal and largely male perspective. Indeed not only did Petrovic's veterans have a unique access to a past that women lacked, but the interethnic conflict these veterans suppress in the interest of asserting interethnic male brotherhood had the opposite meaning for women—symbolic ethnic cleansing through wartime rape. Schwandner-Sievers similarly problematizes the silencing of shameful past experiences and the new Albanian elite's choice of male heroic acts for public memorializing. Furthermore, women may feel nostalgia for a different past or a different promise of communism. Schwandner-Sievers attributes still marginal and marginalized Yugo-nostalgia among older Kosovar women to the opportunities Tito's regime created for women in education, work, and politics. Recalling the gender equality promise of state socialism gains special political salience in light of retraditionalization and the demise of secularism in the present, both of which tend to spell doom for women's rights. It is this reversal of the usual Western trajectory, in which women's rights are still generally expanding, that accounts for the inapplicability of Hutcheon's (1998) axiom that women are rarely burdened with nostalgia.

Post-Communist nostalgia, however, is gendered in other ways as well. In Szemere's analysis of post-Communist reinterpretation of Socialist-era underground music, male rock artists collectively condemn a female singer's adaptation of their proudly amateur and alternative music to the theater stage and subsequently to hi-fi and commodified recordings not just as fossilizing their art and thus the Socialist past, but also, I may add, as taking their agency away. From Buchanan's analysis of post-Socialist Bulgarian popfolk, we may indeed see a similar trend of reducing female performers to accessories of male-centered cultural products and to pretty objects of an all-pervasive male gaze. Women's sovereign agency in these musical representations is further eroded by ethnicizing and exoticizing them, thus identifying them with the past.

Petrovic, going to a higher level of abstraction, argues that Yugo-nostalgia is deridingly equated with such "feminine" characteristics as weakness, lack of flexibility, and inability to adapt, and, one may add, the "soft" value of forgiveness. In Berdahl's analysis the mother's character in *Good Bye, Lenin!* also symbolizes the Socialist past, since the protagonist brother and his sister were raised by their mother alone after the father left for West Germany. Indeed, as it has been observed, state socialism effectively emasculated men, among other ways, by ending their role as sole breadwinners, and instead distributed manhood equally across the social and gender spectrum—most obviously in its propaganda images where masculine bodies represented women and men, peasants and workers alike. In other readings, state socialism not only effeminated but also infantilized its citizens. Either way, we find ourselves with a Lacanian reading of state socialism as a profoundly castrating experience, which, in turn, might explain the emotional readiness to dress up Communist (male) leaders everywhere with paternal qualities. Following this logic, nostalgia for communism, whether for Stalin's, Tito's, Kádár's, or Hoxha's, may be construed as the continued relinquishing of masculinity, rather than simply longing for being taken care of by a strong paternal figure. Through the lens of gender one can start seeing how nostalgia for communism can indeed stand in the way not just of the new patricentric cults in post-Yugoslav memoryscapes but also of the new capitalist economy that requires unattached strong bodies.

In closing we must move beyond analyzing the political content of post-Communist nostalgia and reflect on the politics of talking about post-Communist nostalgia. I will take this topic in two directions: the politics of using the concept of post-Communist nostalgia and the attitudes of scholars writing about post-Communist nostalgia to the past and the present.

As I think it has become clear to the reader, post-Communist nostalgia is not simply a shorthand; it is a misnomer. First, lamenting the losses that came with the collapse of state socialism does not imply wishing it back. Certainly our cases proved that not all aspects of state socialism are missed or longed for. Mainstream ideological treatment of this phenomenon, however, would like us to believe that it was all one package—that one cannot have full employment without shortages, interethnic peace without forced homogenization, or free healthcare without totalitarianism. And since allegedly you cannot wish for a part without wishing for the whole, any positive mention of the Socialist past is seen as ideologically suspect or unwholesome. Based on the chapters in our volume, however, we insist that such favorable, because selective, recollections of the old regime can come from the entire length of the traditional political spectrum stretching from left to right, from cosmopolitan to nationalist, from internationalist to imperialist.

Second, not all post-Communist nostalgia references communism. We have witnessed plenty of positive pre-Communist references, whether to the Ottoman or to the Habsburg Empires, and it is plausible that the collapse of state socialism, a regime that was strongly antinostalgic, unleashed long-buried fantasies and desires for all kinds of eras and civilizations. Yet only the Communist reference is marked. After all, we quickly label a video clip sporting Socialist-era commodities as Communist nostalgia, when we obviously would not apply the term *Ottoman nostalgia* to a video clip featuring belly dancers gyrating to Turkic tunes. With this volume we caution against the knee-jerk and sloppy application of the term *post-Communist nostalgia* and have proposed a variety of distinctions amongst memory practices to sharpen the analytical focus. Such an analysis will also point towards similarities with memory practices in the West, and this in turn will prevent the Orientalist identification of Eastern Europe as obsessed with its past—a position Boyer rightly criticizes. Creed pointedly asks if we would ever call nostalgia the longing former autoworkers of Detroit feel for their days of employment. His question, however, does not just call for analytical clarity but also suggests that dismissing something as "mere" nostalgia effectively depoliticizes the social concerns fueling nostalgia-like expressions.

Third, not all talk about communism is nostalgic. As we have seen, in the former Yugoslav republics there can be a very strong dislike expressed towards Tito, since to many Bosnian Muslims or Albanians he represents all that went wrong and ended in two bloody wars. In Romania too, there is talk but no nostalgia. Artists would argue that Ceaușescu needs to be talked about not because they miss him but because his regime forged so much of their own identities.

Fourth, some want no talk at all. But that too is a form of memory work. We even have several names for it: forgetting, amnesia, silencing the past, burying the past, getting on with one's life, not being stuck in the past, to name just a few. Such an attitude, just like longing for the past and talking about it, can move or be moved by different political beliefs (for a brilliant analysis of the power and variable political valence of silence see Gal 1991). In this volume they were represented by the critiques of Yugo- or Tito-nostalgia and East German *Ostalgie*, as well as young liberal Romanians disgusted by Ceaușescu and Kosovar Albanians silencing women's memories of the war. In Murav's analysis, Melikhov's mid-1990s novel is also closer to the rejection and hushing up of the Soviet Jewish past.

Fifth, most of our contributors called attention to the relatively rapid changes in attitudes to the past. The analysis of such transformations in both the content and the form of post-Communist nostalgia must therefore continue rather than end with research such as that of this volume.

Finally, I would like to reflect on the suggestion of two contributors to this volume (personal communication with Nadkarni, conference presentation by Buchanan) that we scholars studying various forms of post-Communist memory work might feel a certain longing for the Socialist past ourselves. If there is indeed such a longing, there may be various ways to read it. The simplest and I think an incorrect interpretation would be to explain it with our alleged leftist beliefs; at least, I cannot imagine this to mean that we would wish the old Communists back into power in Eastern Europe. Another interpretation would be more pragmatic or even cynically instrumental: perhaps scholars lament the loss of the certainty of the Cold War conceptual models and research questions, the relatively unchanging East European landscape in comparison with the present, in which it is a struggle to keep up with the news from the region. Our research findings certainly get outmoded more quickly, and let's face it, the people we research can now access what we write about them, they can come here, and they can speak back to us. While all this does complicate our work, I would be hard pressed to find any East Europeanist who has not been energized by the new theoretical models and research approaches that have flooded our area studies since 1989 and that have proved to be so fertile. I think, instead, that if there is indeed a longing in us, it betrays a more universal state of affairs. Historians and social scientists in all areas tend to overvalorize the past in general, not because they think it was innocent or less oppressive or easier to study than the present, but because they tend to empathize with people whose experience of a monumental political change, such as the collapse of communism, is primarily one of loss, fragmentation, uncertainty, and anxiety, and whose voices tend to be marginalized by whatever new triumphalist rhetoric. Here too, however, we must qualify this empathy: it does not accrue to war criminals, dictators, or other figures complicit with oppression and violence. We only feel compassion towards the "little people" or at most towards disempowered intellectuals, perhaps because academics know from experience what it is like to be ignored if not silenced.

Do we ever get out of this cycle? Can we avoid our own empathies affecting how we research and write about East Europeans' attitude to the past, in turn strengthening our own sense of loss? I would argue that some of our authors already point to that possibility. Buchanan and Murav both close their chapters on the theme of return not as regression but as reorientation. Perhaps we can now start looking for more signs of future-orientedness in the post-Communist region and thereby stop ceding that terrain to the West, which, as Boyer reminds us, claims it as its own prerogative. As I see it, there is much happening there already.

Notes

1. Many scholars have been using this concept for at least twenty years primarily to refer to physical landscapes of memorial objects and monuments, though the most influential user of the term is Lisa Yoneyama (1994). I am using *memoryscape* here to signal a less physical and more figurative panorama of memory practices intersecting and interacting at different scales.

References

Gal, Susan. 1991. "Between Speech and Silence: The Problematics of Research on Language and Gender." In *Gender at the Crossroads of Knowledge: Feminist Anthropology in the Postmodern Era,* ED. M. di Leonardo, 175–203. Berkeley: University of California Press.

Hutcheon, Linda. 1998. "Irony, Nostalgia and the Postmodern." http://www.library.utoronto.ca/utel/criticism/hutchinp.html.

Yoneyama, Lisa. 1994. "Taming the Memoryscape: Hiroshima's Urban Renewal." In *Remapping Memory: The Politics of TimeSpace,* ed. Jonathan Boyarin, 99–134. Minneapolis: University of Minnesota Press.

Notes on Contributors

Daphne Berdahl was Associate Professor of Anthropology and Global Studies at the University of Minnesota. She was the author of *Where the World Ended: Re-Unification and Identity in the German Borderland* (1999) and coeditor (with Matti Bunzl and Martha Lampland) of *Altering States: Ethnographies of Transition in East Central Europe and the Former Soviet Union* (2000). Widely recognized as a key theorist of the transition from state socialism to capitalism as well as one of the finest ethnographers in her discipline, she made important contributions to the anthropology of borderlands, memory, and consumption. At the time of her untimely death in 2007, she was working on two book projects, one on the politics of memory in the former GDR and another on the relationship between mass consumption, globalization, and changing understandings, visions, meanings, and practices of citizenship in post-Wall Germany. Articles from these projects along with other essays were collected in a volume *On the Social Life of Postsocialism: Memory, Consumption, Germany* (2010), edited by Matti Bunzl.

Dominic Boyer is Associate Professor of Anthropology at Rice University. He has published many articles on media, knowledge, and post-Socialist transitions in Europe and is currently researching the transformational effects of digital media in news journalism and social theory. He is the author of two books: *Spirit and System: Media, Intellectuals and the Dialectic in Modern German Culture* (University of Chicago Press, 2005) and *Understanding Media: A Popular Philosophy* (Prickly Paradigm, 2007).

Donna A. Buchanan is Associate Professor of Music and Director of the music ensemble "Balkanalia" at the University of Illinois, Urbana-Champaign, where she teaches courses in ethnomusicology and the musical cultures of the Balkans, Russia, and Eurasia. She is the author of *Performing Democracy: Bulgarian Music and Musicians in Transition* (University of Chicago Press, 2006; with CD-ROM) and an edited collection, *Balkan Popular Music and the Ottoman Ecumene: Music, Image, and Regional Political Discourse* (Scarecrow Press, 2007; with VCD).

Fedja Burić is a PhD candidate in history at the University of Illinois, Urbana-Champaign specializing in the modern history of the former

Yugoslavia. He is currently working on his dissertation, which studies mixed marriages in Bosnia-Herzegovina and how the concept of mixedness has been used in the establishment of neat national categories at the expense of more ambiguous identities.

Gerald W. Creed is Professor of Anthropology at Hunter College and the CUNY Graduate Center, where he is also Executive Officer [Chair] of the Anthropology Program. He has been conducting research in Bulgaria since 1987 on issues of agrarian political economy, ritual, and identity. His book, *Domesticating Revolution: From Socialist Reform to Ambivalent Transition in a Bulgarian Village* (Penn State Press, 1998), won the 1998 Book Award from the Bulgarian Studies Association. A more recent book, *Masquerade and Postsocialism: Ritual and Cultural Dispossession in Bulgaria* (Indiana University Press, 2010), uses spectacular Bulgarian mumming rites to challenge scholarly models of postsocialism.

Diana Georgescu is a doctoral student in History at the University of Illinois, Urbana-Champaign, where she specializes in the history of Eastern and Southeastern Europe. She is currently completing her dissertation on the generational memories and ideological construction of childhood in socialist Romania. Her academic interests include social memory, the cultural and social history of communism, and gender and nationalism. She is the author of several articles on post-communist nostalgia, interwar intellectuals and nationalism, and gendered narratives of European identity in post-communist media.

Zsuzsa Gille is Associate Professor of Sociology at the University of Illinois, Urbana-Champaign. She is the author of *From the Cult of Waste to the Trash Heap of History: The Politics of Waste in Socialist and Postsocialist Hungary* (Indiana University Press, 2007), coauthor of *Global Ethnography: Forces, Connections and Imaginations in a Postmodern World* (University of California Press, 2000). She is also guest editor of *Slavic Review*'s thematic cluster on Nature, Culture, and Power in Eastern Europe, Russia, and Eurasia (Spring 2009). She is presently working on the manuscript *Paprika, Pigs, and Predestination in Hungary: The Cultural Politics of the Eastern Enlargement of the European Union.*

Harriet Murav is Professor, Department of Slavic Languages and Literatures, and Professor, Comparative and World Literature, at the University of Illinois. She is the author of three books, *Holy Foolishness: Dostoevsky's Novels and the Poetics of Cultural Critique, Russia's Legal Fictions,* and *Identity Theft: The Jew in Imperial Russia and the Case of Avraam Uri Kovner,* co-editor of *Photographing the Jewish Nation,* as well as articles on law and literature, and twentieth-century Russian literature and culture. She is currently working on a book of photography from the 1912–1914 S. An-sky Ethnographic Expeditions (with Eugene M. Avrutin) and a study of Soviet Yiddish and Russian-Jewish literature of the twentieth century.

Maya Nadkarni is a Postdoctoral Fellow at Columbia University's Harriman Institute for Russian, Eurasian, and East European Studies. She received her Ph.D. in cultural anthropology in 2009 from Columbia University. Her research focuses upon questions of memory, nation, and the challenge of historical subjectivity in postsocialist Hungary. Her previous publications include articles on socialist nostalgia, Budapest's Statue Park Museum of communist monuments, and spectacles of criminality and celebrity in Hungarian public culture, and she is currently completing a book on Hungary's remains of socialism.

Tanja Petrović is Research Fellow at the Scientific Research Center in Ljubljana and Assistant Professor at the University of Nova Gorica. She is interested in intersection of linguistic, social, and cultural phenomena in the Balkans and Central Europe, with an emphasis on ideologies and remembering. She is the author of *The Ritual Toast of Balkan Slavs* (2006), *The Serbs of Bela Krajna and Their Language Ideology in the Process of Language Shift* (2006, 2009) and *A Long Way Home: Representations of the Western Balkans in Political and Media Discourses* (2009), as well as numerous articles and chapters in edited volumes on linguistic and cultural identities and processes in the former Yugoslavia.

Tim Pilbrow received his PhD (2001) in Sociocultural Anthropology from New York University with a dissertation on changing conceptualizations of national identity in post-1989 Bulgaria as seen from the vantage point of the secondary-school history classroom. He has published several articles on the topic. Currently he is undertaking ethnographic research in relation to Aboriginal land claims, as a Senior Anthropologist at Native Title Services Victoria, in Melbourne, Australia. His ongoing research interests include formal education and social reproduction, history as a means to objectifying identity, and irony as a discursive and narrative strategy.

Anke Pinkert is Associate Professor of German and Cinema Studies at the University of Illinois, Urbana-Champaign. She received her PhD from the University of Chicago in 2000. She is the author of *Memory and Film in East Germany* (Indiana University Press, 2008). The essay in this volume is drawn from this book. She has published on German literature, film, and cultural history in journals, including *German Quarterly*, *Seminar*, and *Germanic Review*. Her current book project addresses the intersection of travel, displacement, and memory in post-Communist literature and film.

Oana Popescu-Sandu is Assistant Professor of World Literature at the University of Southern Indiana. Her dissertation entitled "A Vanishing Act: Gulag Narratives and their Afterlife" is a comparative study of gulag narratives in Russia, Romania, and Bulgaria. Her previous degrees are from Central European University, Budapest, Hungary; and University of Bucharest, Romania.

Cristofer Scarboro is Assistant Professor of History at King's College, in Wilkes-Barre, Pennsylvania. He received his PhD at the University of Illinois at Urbana-Champaign. He is currently completing his first monograph on the question of Socialist humanism in Bulgaria during the 1960s and 1970s.

Stephanie Schwandner-Sievers is Honorary Research Associate at the School of Slavonic and East European Studies, University College London, where she served as the first Alex Nash Fellow for Albanian Studies from 1997 to 2003. She directs a consultancy firm, Anthropology Applied Limited, which has produced numerous studies and reports for national and international courts and agencies. She has conducted ethnographic fieldwork in Albania since 1992 and Kosovo since 2000, and has published extensively on Albanian politics of representation and identity, the construction of tradition, gender, security, myth, memory, nationalism, and transnationalism.

Anna Szemere holds a PhD in Sociology and teaches at Portland State University. Her research interest lies at the interface of popular culture, youth, gender, and politics with a focus on post-Communist societies. She has published numerous articles and book chapters on this topic and has authored the book *Up from the Underground* (2001).

Maria Todorova is Gutgsell Professor of History at the University of Illinois, Urbana-Champaign. Her publications include *Bones of Contention: The Living Archive of Vasil Levski and the Making of Bulgaria's National Hero* (2009), *Balkan Identities: Nation and Memory* (2004), *Imagining the Balkans* (1997, 2009), *Balkan Family Structure and the European Pattern: Demographic Developments in Ottoman Bulgaria* (1993, 2006), *English Trav-*

elers' Accounts on the Balkans (1987), *England, Russia, and the Tanzimat* (1980, 1983), several edited volumes, as well as numerous articles on social and cultural history, historical demography, and historiography of the modern Balkans.

Index

Adem Jashari, as the Legendary Commander, 98–101, 107, 108
Adorno, Theodor, 247
Albanians nationalism, 96–98, 108–9, 281, 285. *See also* Kosovo
alienation, 247–8. *See also* estrangement
antipolitics, 205, 212, 214n11
anti-semitism, 216, 218
Appadurai, Arjun, 139, 144, 177
army story, 65–67
art (the arts)
  and estrangement, 247–48
  and nostalgia, 257
  under socialism, 244–246, 250–251, 254
authenticity, 191–193, 279, 285
  discourses of, 129, 135, 198, 206, 211n10
  personal, 193, 196
  under capitalism, 195
  under socialism, 253–254

Babelsberg GmbH, 265
Badiou, Alain, 10–11
Băsescu, Traian, 121, 124
Becker, Wolfgang, 184, 266. *See also Good-bye, Lenin!*
Benjamin, Walter, 11–12, 195, 198, 246, 260n1
Bergelson, Dovid, 216, 225
Berlin Wall, 180, 269
  fall of, 178–180, 263
Birobidzhan, 215–16, 221–224
Boia, Lucian, 119, 123n12
Borneman, John, 96, 107, 157
Bosnia-Herzegovina, 227–238

Boym, Svetlana, 8–9, 22, 31, 38, 42, 46–7, 69, 87, 96, 115, 118, 129–130, 138–140, 193, 200, 209, 212n19, 215, 220, 245–248, 250, 258, 281. *See also* nostalgia
Brigadier Movement, 47–59
"brotherhood and unity" doctrine 100–01, 106–108. *See also* Tito, Josip Broz
building socialism, 47, 51
Bulgaria, 6–10, 29–44, 82–95, 129–153, 231, 241
Bulgarian Communist Party, 39, 41, 49–50, 130
Bulgarian Socialist Party, 94n8, 133

Café Tito, 228
capitalism, 3, 6, 7, 30, 39, 195, 282
  transition to, 92, 115, 184
Ceaușescu, Nicolae, 6, 10, 123n12, 155–176, 279–280, 287
Chagall, Marc, 219
Chalga. *See* popfolk
childhood, 198–200, 205
Clinton, Bill, 101, 108
Cold War, 1, 182–3
  end of, 180
  as history, 269–270
  nostalgia for, 206, 288
collectivization, 29, 34, 38
Comaroff, John and Jean, 187
commercialization, 39–42. *See also* commodification
commodification, 43, 194–7, 206, 209, 279, 282, 285. *See also* nostalgia
commoditization, 256, 259. *See also* commodification

communism, 3–4
  compared to Nazism, 3–4
  end of, 6, 10–11
  as ideology, 3, 7, 115
  memories of, 7,
  nostalgia for, 224–5, 282–3, 286–7
  nostalgia within, 38, 46–60
  representation of, 38–42
  as utopia, 10
Constantinescu, Emil, 113
consumption, 144, 194–8, 201, 211n10
  nostalgic, 30, 39, 187, 194–198, 211n10
cosmopolitanism, 33–34, 283
countermemory, 156, 284. *See also* memory practices
Croatia, 233, 236–8
cryogeny, 113–6
cultural intimacy, 207, 209, 212n20
cultural memory, 192, 264, 266. *See also* memory
cultural reproduction, 93

Dayton Peace Accords, 230, 234–5
DEFA (Deutsche Film AG), 263–6, 268, 271, 272
Defamiliarization, 159, 161–2
DeNora, Tia, 248
diasporic intimacy, 140
dignifying practices, 84, 93
dignity, 7, 82–93, 284
Dimitrovgrad, 49–60
Dolly Birds, 196–7, 199, 204, 211n6
Draginovo, 135
Dresen, Andreas, 266, 269. *See also* *Night Shapes*
Dymshits, Valerii, 216

East Germany. *See* German Democratic Republic
Eastern Europe, 17–27
education, 82–95
embourgeoisement, 56
Enver Hoxha, 107
estrangement, 247, 252
Europe as a discursive trope, 253
European Union (EU), 37, 113, 120

Europeanness, 22. *See also* Western Europe

Federal German Republic (FRG), 182, 183, 263, 270–1
Fefer, Itsik, 216, 225
FIDESZ, 201, 210, 212nn14–15
folk ensembles, 133–4, 141

Gal, Susan, 287, 212n19
gender, 62, 77n2, 142, 145, 258, 281, 285–6. *See also* masculinity; women
German Democratic Republic (GDR), 18–21, 24, 263–273, 282
Germany, 3–4, 21. *See also* German Democratic Republic; Federal German Republic
Ghodsee, Kristen, 7, 30, 144, 147
Gitelman, Zvi, 215
Gloriya, 139, 150n12, 151n21
Goethe Institute, 264
Good Bye, Lenin!, 24, 210n4, 211n6, 266–7, 278, 285
Grant, Bruce, 188
Grlić, Rajko, 72–3, 75

Hainboaz, 49–50, 53, 56
Halbwachs, Maurice, 118
Haraszti, Miklós, 244–245. *See also* velvet prison
Herzfeld, Michael, 138, 209, 212n20. *See also* cultural intimacy
homesickness, 18, 31–34, 193–5
Hughes, Ted, 248
Humphrey, Caroline, 139, 187
Hungarian orange, 190–3, 208, 210n2
Hungarian Socialist Workers' Party, 201–4, 212nn12–13
Hungary, 10, 190–212, 243–259, 270, 279, 283
Hutcheon, Linda, 2, 156–7, 173n7, 285

Ibrahim Rugova, 99, 108
identification, 20–21, 84–94
imagined communities, 249
Ioanid, Ioan, 116

Iron Guard, 118, 120
Irony, 7–10, 26, 82–3, 92, 100, 149, 155–174, 186, 191–2, 215, 217, 220, 246, 253, 278, 281, 283
   missing, 96
Islam, 231–2, 239–240. See also Muslims

Jakobson, Roman, 220
Jergović, Miljenko, 62, 70
Jews, 215–225

Kádár, János, 201–5, 212n13, 212n16
Kalinka, 140–1
Kelmendi, Migjen, 96, 101–2, 104–7
kitsch, 30, 99, 177, 192, 194–5, 197, 199, 200, 206, 208, 246, 267
Kleinert, Andreas, 266, 268, 270, 272
Klima, Ivan, 6–7
Kosovo, 68, 96–110, 235
Kosovo Liberation Army (KLA), 97–100, 105, 107–8
Kundera, Milan, 46, 156, 246

Laughter, 183
legitimation, 85, 88
Levin, Ted (Theodore), 148
liquidation (of collective farms), 36
Little Journey, 197, 211n6
Lukács, György, 245

Macedonia, 96, 105, 134–8
Mafia, 144, 146–7, 151
Magapasa, 143
male friendship, 66, 76
Malkite Panteri, 140–2
masculinity, 62, 65–7, 69, 75–7, 79n24, 236–7, 286
   socialist, 50
Melikhov, Alexandr, 215, 217–219
memory, 2, 5, 8, 11, 18–9, 37, 43, 46, 63, 67, 72, 75, 96, 98, 100–4, 106–108, 109n7, 117, 121, 129–30, 149, 156, 177–8, 187–8, 198–201, 204, 216, 218, 221, 246, 249
   collective memory, 52, 118–9, 208

hurt memory, 106. See also Ricoeur, Paul
   memory practices, 161–163, 170–1, 191, 278, 280, 284, 286–7, 288n1
   memory work. See memory practices
   public and private memories. See private-public binary
   school memories, 103–7
   See also remembrance
memoryscape, 278–9, 281, 286, 288n1
migration/out-migration, 30, 34, 38
Milea, Ada, 157, 164–5, 167–9, 171, 173n8, 173n10
Miller, Buzi, 223
Milosević, Slobodan, 97, 100, 102–3, 109n10
mimesis, 130, 148, 247–8
mobster baroque, 142, 144, 146
modernity, 5, 9, 17, 23, 31–33, 193, 245–6, 270, 283
Morometzii, 121
Moscow Square, 200, 208, 211n6
music, 162, 164, 166–9, 244–259. See also popfolk
   folk, 134–6
   as trigger for nostalgia, 130, 143, 248–9
   underground, 245, 249–51, 254–9, 260n11, 261n13
Musil, Robert, 245
Muslims, 103, 134, 228, 233–40. See also Islam
mythography, 139
mythology, 135–6, 138–149

narrative appropriation, 86–7
narrative construction of self, 83
narrative fetish, 93
narrative of continuity, 84, 86–7, 89, 91, 93
national ideology, 85, 231
nationalism, 3, 71, 76, 79n24, 90, 96–8, 106, 108, 110, 118, 168–9, 191, 215, 223, 227–8, 233–4, 236, 238

nationalist discourse. *See* nationalism
NATO, 97–8, 122n9, 157
Nemzer, Andrei, 217
neoliberalism, 3, 9, 42–3, 188
New German Cinema of Consensus, 263, 265, 272–3
Night Shapes, 266, 269
Niki and Flo, 117
No Place to Go, 267, 270, 272–3, 275
normality, 195–6, 198, 207
nostalgia
    commodification of, 39–43, 192, 195, 197, 206–7, 282–3, 285–6. *See also* ostalgie
    and exile, 130, 148
    music as trigger for. *See* music
    post-Communist nostalgia, 1–3, 8–9, 11, 129, 138, 280, 282–3, 285–7
    reflective nostalgia. *See* Boym, Svetlana
    restorative nostalgia, 129, 134. *See also* Boym, Sevtlana
    sonic nostalgia, 137
    structural nostalgia, 138. *See also* Herzfeld, Michael
Nostalgiya, 139–40, 150n12
Nostomania, 18–9

Orientalism, 145, 287
Orpheus, 135–6
Ostalgie, 9, 21, 178, 181, 185–8, 267, 280, 287

Pančić, Teofil, 70, 284
Parody, 26, 139, 142, 157, 159, 165, 169, 186–7, 267
Paternalism, 157–8, 172
Paths in the Night, 267, 270–2
patricentric regime, 96, 107
Payner, 139, 141, 144, 147, 150nn12–15, 151nn19–21, 151n23
performance, 139, 157–8, 169
    as artistic genre 250, 253–4
Pintilie, Lucia, 117. *See also Niki and Flo*
pioneers, 104, 142, 179, 185

Pirin songs, 136–8
Poduene Blues Band, 131–2, 149n3
Poland, 5
politics of culture, 16–18, 21
politics of the future, 25–7
Popfolk, 138–149, 150n17
popular nostalgia, 69. *See also* Boym, Svetlana
post-communism, 61, 116, 120, 157, 168, 171
Post-Communist film, 263–276
post-Jewish, 9, 224–5
Post-socialism, 30, 130, 134, 137, 146–8, 172n4, 184, 186–8, 196, 201, 205, 212n15. *See also* post-communism
Postimperialism, 23, 27
Postmelancholic agency, 266, 270–1, 276
Postunification film. *See* Post-Communist film
Postunification loss, 267–8, 270–4, 276n3
practical consciousness, 94n10
private-public binary, 85, 92, 96–8, 101, 106, 108–9, 155, 170–1, 177–8, 192, 200–5, 282–4

Radeva, Mariya, 133, 141, 149n4
Ramush Haradinaj, 108
Ranković, Aleksandar, 101–103
Reihan, 145–6, 150n18, 151nn20–21
remembrance
    modes of, 156, 159, 161–3, 170. *See also* memory
re-patriarchalization, 104
restitution (of property), 29
retraditionalization, 283, 285. *See also* modernity
Ricoeur, Paul, 102, 106
ritual, 34, 47–51, 57–8, 72, 94n3, 98, 158, 162, 171, 219, 224, 249–51
    of farewell, 184
ritualization. *See* ritual
Roehler, Oskar, 267–8, 270, 272–3, 275. *See also No Place to Go*
Romania, 5–6, 9–10, 113–124, 155–174, 279–80, 282–3, 287

rubble films, 267–8, 270–1
Russia, 3, 6, 11, 12, 141–2, 215–225

self-presentation, 83–4, 86, 94n4
Serbia, 6, 61, 66, 69, 72, 74, 97, 228, 233–4, 236–8
Serbs, 64, 67–8, 96–7, 106, 232–8
social reproduction, 93
socialism, 4–6, 9, 29, 35, 37, 40–5, 61, 63, 70, 75–6, 89, 117, 133, 157, 180, 182–3, 187, 191–2, 194, 196, 200–1, 203, 222,
socialist humanism, 47–8
socialist realism, 37
socialization, 83
Soviet Union, 141, 150, 215–6, 220, 225. *See also* Russia
state socialism, 17–8, 20, 89, 91, 94n8, 279, 283–6
  end of, 84, 87, 91–2, 115, 177, 181, 186, 191, 196, 211n9, 244, 254, 256, 265–7
  See also socialism
subversion, 66
symbolic castration, 285

Taxi, 113–4, 117, 120
Tense, 46–8
Tismaneanu, Vladimir, 116–7, 121, 162
Tito, Josip Broz, 71–2, 75, 96–7, 100–9, 228
  homepage, 227–8, 241n1
  memory of, 227, 235, 239–41
  streetnames, 96–7
Tito-nostalgia, 96, 102–3, 105. *See also* Tito, memory of
Todorov, Tzvetan, 3, 10
Tomić, Ante, 71–2
transition, 29, 36–8. *See also* capitalism; communism; socialism; state socialism; neoliberalism
trauma, 5, 9, 19, 34–39, 41–2, 64, 98, 101, 156, 159–60, 257, 267, 274, 276n2, 278
Turkey, Turkish, 134, 137, 139, 142–3, 14–8, 150n16, 151n19

utopia, 1, 3, 10, 12n6, 22, 46–7, 93, 106–8, 193, 195–6, 198, 207, 215, 220, 246, 267–8, 270, 273, 283

Velikonja, Mitja, 1, 6, 12n6
velvet prison, 244–5, 253–4, 256–7, 259. *See also* Haraszti, Miklós
Verdery, Katherine, 108, 177, 184, 187
Vergangenheitsbewältigung, 3–4
Verkovich, Stefan, 136
Vidovdan (St Vitus), 96

Wende films, 266–8, 272. *See also* Postunification film; Post-Communist film
West Germany. *See* Federal Republic of Germany
Western Europe, 22–3, 26–7, 195, 207. *See also* European Union, Europe; NATO
Witness, The, 190–1, 208, 210n1

Yiddish, 216, 22–223, 225
Youth, 35, 41, 48–50, 52–4, 57, 69, 92, 96, 100–1, 105–6, 141–2, 147, 168, 199, 201–2, 217, 238–40, 249, 253, 270
Yugo-nostalgia, 63–4, 70, 73–6, 102, 227, 229–30, 241, 280–1. *See also* Post-Communist nostalgia; Tito-nostalgia
Yugoslav League of Communists, 236
Yugoslav People's Army (JNA), 61–76, 77n1, 77n6, 78n16, 97, 237, 278
Yugoslav Socialism, 63, 71, 96. *See also* Tito, Josip Broz; socialism
Yugoslavia, 1, 8–9, 61–79, 102–8, 227–242, 278. *See also* Tito, Josip Broz
Yugoslavism, 62–3, 77, 234. *See also* Tito, Josip Broz

Zimmermann, Warren, 63
Žižek, Slavoj, 114–5, 118, 201, 206, 209

www.ingramcontent.com/pod-product-compliance
Lightning Source LLC
Chambersburg PA
CBHW071955290426
44109CB00018B/2029